PSYCHOTHERAPY

PROCESSES AND TECHNIQUES

Christiane Brems

University of Alaska Anchorage

Allyn and Bacon

Boston • London • Toronto • Sydney • Tokyo • Singapore

Fuer Bernhard—mit und von ganzem Herzen

Vice-President, Social Sciences and Education: Sean W. Wakely
Series Editorial Assistant: Susan Hutchinson
Editorial-Production Service: Omegatype Typography, Inc.
Manufacturing Buyer: Suzanne Lareau

Library of Congress Cataloging-in-Publication Data

Brems, Christiane.
    Psychotherapy : processes and techniques / Christiane Brems.
       p.   cm.
    Includes bibliographical references and index.
    ISBN 0–205–27532–X
    1. Psychotherapy.   I. Title.
  RC480.B69   1999
  616.89'14—dc21   98–13488
                                                                                CIP

Printed in the United States of America
10   9   8   7   6   5   4   3   2   1   03   02   01   00   99   98

CONTENTS

PART 3   *Endings*

PREFACE

People are always longing for someone to help them realize their best selves, to understand their hidden self, to believe in them and demand their best. When we can do this for people, we ought not to withhold it. We ought not to be just an ear to them.
—*MARY HASKELL,* I CARE ABOUT YOUR HAPPINESS

Over the years of teaching, supervising, and performing clinical work I have had the tremendous opportunity to learn much about psychotherapy from many sources; I have learned from my students, from my supervisees, and from my clients. This book is my way of giving something back to all of them, to thank them for the tremendous growth they have facilitated—directly and indirectly—for so many over the years. My work with all of them has clarified many issues about therapy in my mind and has helped me develop a philosophy about treatment and the human interaction that is psychotherapy. In the following pages I will outline and then describe in depth my understanding of what can and should happen in therapy when the client is open and the therapist is aware.

A PHILOSOPHY OF THERAPY

All therapists need a philosophy or model of psychotherapy that will guide their work so as to be organized, available, and consistent. This model reflects clinicians' basic beliefs about humanity and about the treatment process. A variety of such models have been developed over the years (see Hershenson, Power, & Seligman, 1989, for a summary) and I have borrowed from many of them to come up with my own set of philosophical underpinnings that guides my work with clients and that serves as a basis for the material presented in this book.

- Psychotherapy is a growth, change, and healing process that is helpful to clients who have experienced events in their lives that have somehow interfered with or challenged the healthy development of a cohesive, orderly, and vigorous self (see Kohut, 1984).

- A contextual approach is important to all work with therapy clients because the larger environment of a client is generally important to understanding how the person's phenomenological presentation of self has developed over time and through interpersonal influences. Such an interpersonal matrix approach (see Stern, 1985) will, at a minimum, consider familial influences, community pressures, cultural values, and societal belief systems that have acted on the person.
- Therapy needs to take a holistic approach to the client, investigating (i.e., assessing) and attending to (i.e., intervening with) the person's physical, emotional, cognitive, social, spiritual, behavioral, cultural, and psychological development and well-being (see Brems, 1993).
- Clients are viewed as collaborators in the therapeutic process. They are perceived as having an enormous amount of knowledge about their needs and as having many answers and solutions within themselves that can be activated through the catalytic and interpersonal presence of the therapist (see Rogers, 1961).
- The central growth, change, and healing process is the client–clinician relationship and the client's experiences within that relationship. The experiential component of psychotherapy is attributed more importance than the insight component, and strong emphasis is placed on processing here and now relationships in a holistic, lifetime context (see Kohut, 1984; Teyber, 1997).
- The therapist–client relationship is only one component of a client's journey toward growth, change, or healing and needs to be supplemented with other strategies the client can implement independently of the therapy process (e.g., family strengthening, social support, environmental modification, nutrition and exercise, physical health).
- The therapy process is circular in experience, but is conceptualized or presented in a stage model to facilitate a new therapist's understanding of the processes and skills that are involved.

Overwhelming consensus has emerged that therapy has a beginning, a middle, and an end—three distinct yet overlapping stages of treatment that must be recognized and understood by all clinicians. Within each of these stages, substages have been identified, and here opinions have varied somewhat. However, most commonly there is agreement that the beginning of therapy consists of relationship-building and assessment; the middle is devoted to a working-through process that is designed to facilitate the necessary change, growth, and healing; and the end is devoted to bringing closure to therapy by attending to termination issues and summarizing treatment process and progress. This thumbnail sketch of the stages of psychotherapy can be expanded depending on individual therapists' beliefs about other important interactions between the client and clinician. The stages that underlie the concept of this book are summarized in the following table. They were also used to determine the organization of the book, dictating the sequencing of chapters and contents.

TABLE 1   **The Stages of Psychotherapy**

Stage	Substages	Requisite Skills
Beginning	Forming a Working Alliance	rapport building skills
	Basic Information Gathering	screening and intake skills
	Specialized Information Gathering	ancillary assessment skills
		referral skills
	Understanding the Client	conceptualization skills
	Planning for Treatment	goal setting skills
		treatment planning skills
Middle	Recollection	communication skills
	Reconstruction	affect facilitating skills
	Re-Experience	therapy process skills
	Resolution/Rehabilitation	affect facilitating skills
		communication skills
		therapy process skills
		insight facilitating skills
End	Resolution/Rehabilitation	communication skills
	(continuing)	affect facilitating skills
		therapy process skills
		insight facilitating skills
	Goal Achievement	therapy process skills
		assessment skills
	Temporary Relapse	assessment skills
		crisis skills
	Termination	affect facilitating skills
		closure skills

ORGANIZATION OF THE BOOK

The book is organized into three parts that parallel the therapy process as much as possible, providing a superstructure for work with psychotherapy clients. The three parts provide comprehensive underpinnings for the theory and pragmatics outlined in this text. Further, the book has several outstanding features that make it user-friendly and comprehensive. The book was conceived and written with both the advanced trainee and the private practitioner in mind, and can provide helpful information and guidance for each. It incorporates information and conceptualizations that, while written in an easy to understand manner, are important and conceptually sophisticated, yet often missing from generic psychotherapy texts. Despite its emphasis on conceptualization and the provision of a theoretical super-structure for therapy, the book has a strong pragmatic focus. It provides applied guidelines and detailed structures for therapist behaviors and reactions that can help the less experienced reader feel more comfortable in early therapeutic work. This pragmatism, however, does not translate into simplistic methods or prescriptions. Instead, it challenges the reader to derive concrete interventions from sophisticated conceptualizations and to develop a clear framework of reaction and intervention that is theoretically driven and consistent for all clients, yet sufficiently flexible to accommodate special needs and unusual circumstances.

Parts of the Book

Part 1 provides a detailed conceptual framework for initial client assessment, stressing the importance of this process to accurate conceptualization and treatment planning. It focuses on building rapport, assessment, and referral issues, as these particular topics are most relevant in early interactions with clients. Prior counseling and therapy texts have addressed building rapport and basic assessment but have generally ignored or glossed over detailed information about special assessments, or nonroutine assessments, such as parenting skills assessments, substance use assessments, and similar specialized topic areas.

Part 2 presents the essence of the conceptual underpinnings of psychotherapy and provides the theoretical superstructure that guides case conceptualization, treatment planning, and understanding the therapy process. It focuses on the process issues involved in psychotherapy, ranging from a framework for conceptualization and treatment planning to a discussion of important treatment catalysts to a concise and process-oriented presentation of the interpersonal events and phases in psychotherapy. Most counseling and therapy books that are available today have explored issues of clinician skills and the client–therapist relationship process. Yet few have attempted to provide an organized conceptual model for understanding the overall therapy process; even fewer, if any, have done so from a perspective that accommodates a variety of theoretical orientations on the part of the therapist. This book does both. It provides an overall framework for process that can incorporate a variety of strategies and approaches, it presents treatment catalysts that are generally accepted across schools of thought, and it outlines a process and phase model of therapy that can accommodate (and does, in fact, invite) a blending and selecting of compatible theoretical beliefs and foundations. Nevertheless, it must be acknowledged that although the book presents a relatively theory-free model for assessment and termination (Parts 1 and 3), the theoretical orientation that guides Part 2 is largely interpersonal and dynamic, drawing on a self-psychological model of psychotherapy. It is difficult to view a therapy process completely atheoretically, and no therapy book can be written without some theoretical preferences coming through. However, I generally maintain that eclecticism is appropriate as long as a conceptual thread is visible throughout treatment. The conceptual thread I have chosen for my work is self psychology (Kohut, 1984). This preference will be most obvious in Part 2 of the text but should not hinder readers with other theoretical preferences from benefiting greatly from the relatively theory-free superstructure that is proposed in the book overall.

Part 3 provides a conceptual framework for closure and termination. It shows how to assess whether a client is ready for termination, when to recognize a client's behavior as a signal for impending termination, and how to initiate and successfully negotiate the process of ending therapy. It attends to natural and induced (or premature) terminations, dealing with issues from the therapist's and client's perspective.

Special Features

Throughout each chapter, certain themes are present that are critical to therapy and interwoven in the process on a continual basis. First, *legal and ethical issues* (as well as related issues of professionalism) are incorporated and discussed in detail in all relevant sections of the book (e.g., obtaining informed consent prior to screening in Chapter 1). Second, issues of *record-keeping and proper documentation* are addressed in relevant chapters and sections, with samples provided for the most important documents (e.g., progress notes in Chapter 7; intake reports in Chapter 2; termination reports in Chapter 8). Third, the entire book is written in a *gender and culturally sensitive manner* that is respectful and aware of the uniqueness of individual clients. Specific cultural issues are attended to wherever they can potentially pose particular challenges or problems (e.g., acculturation assessment in Chapter 2; cultural issues in diagnosis in Chapter 4). Fourth, each chapter provides both *pragmatic tips and guidelines* as well as *comprehensive theoretical foundations* on a given topic area (e.g., how to conceptualize a number of difficult therapy situations and, in Chapter 7, how to react to them when they occur; how to conceptualize the substages of therapy and how to translate this knowledge into concrete therapist reactions and behaviors in Chapter 6). Fifth, a *single sample case* is used throughout the entire text to exemplify many important points and conceptualizations (e.g., screening issues in Chapter 1; samples of empathic interventions in Chapter 5). Additional *smaller case examples* are used for further clarification as necessary (e.g., examples of various therapeutic strategies in Chapter 5; interventions in special circumstances in Chapter 7). Sixth, *checklists, figures, and tables* are used for future reference after thorough reading. Similarly, thorough indexes are provided to make quick review of certain materials possible.

A METAPHOR FOR THERAPY

To further clarify the nature and process of psychotherapy subscribed to in these pages, I offer the reader a metaphor for treatment that I routinely share with my students and often relate to clients. This metaphor provides an understanding of the nature and complexity of the process that is psychotherapy, often helping clients gain a clearer recognition of the work which they are about to undertake.

> To me psychotherapy is like traversing the Grand Canyon. Even if you have never done so, I can explain to you what I mean. If you have done this, you will understand even faster what I am talking about. When you traverse the Grand Canyon, you start by first looking at the vastness of this natural wonder and deciding that you want to delve into the difficult hike to get to its other side. You become intrigued with its depth and breadth, its colors and textures,

and you want to get to know it better—from the inside, not just the outside. When you finally embark on your hike, you have done some planning, but there is no way that you can predict everything you will encounter. A good guide can help you down the canyon and back up on the other side, but even this guide can only help you—this person can't do the work for you. The guide has a good idea about what will happen on your journey, having made the journey alone and with others many times. But everyone has a different reaction to the Grand Canyon; therefore, even your guide cannot predict with certainty how long the journey will take, how enjoyable it will be, how many obstacles you will encounter, how much pain you will have to endure at times, and what you will find on the other side. Your guide can guarantee, however, that you will be safe and that you cannot traverse the canyon without being altered in some form. If nothing else, when you emerge on the other side you will still see some of the same terrain you saw from where you started, but you will have a different perspective on it.

Descending into the canyon is enjoyable and easy work at first. You see things that you could see from a distance, but you can now experience them close up; you experience things that you knew were there, but now you can truly feel them. You may realize that some things are not what you expected them to be and that some things are prettier and some uglier than you thought. As you delve deeper and deeper into the canyon, the trails get steeper and rougher; you begin to encounter terrain that you were not able to see from the top and sometimes you have some trepidation because of the unexpected. Sometimes you are surprised by what you see, sometimes frightened, sometimes exhilarated, sometimes angered. Others have traveled here before you, and your guide will point out how they reacted and what they did; your guide will also help interpret some of the new things you encounter and will help you understand the things that surprise you, will help you survive the things that frighten you, and will help you enjoy the things that exhilarate. Your guide can sometimes point out the rocks in your path, the stumbling blocks on the trail, the dangers in your road. But your guide will not always clear your path for you; sometimes your guide will point out the obstacles and dangers and challenge you to deal with them on your own—to confront them head-on despite any fears you may have.

As you descend deeper and deeper, you learn more and more about the canyon and about yourself. You begin to understand what the canyon is about—how it came to be. You see the force of erosion and water and how this interaction with the environment has shaped the canyon. You also begin to understand yourself better. You learn what situations frighten you, which delight you, which anger you, and which soothe you. You may revel in this new understanding and feel yourself growing stronger as a hiker and explorer. When you finally reach the bottom of the canyon and come face to face with the force of the river in its depth, you find yourself swept away with experience. Nothing is more powerful than to look back—to look to the rim of the canyon from which you descended and to allow the reality to sink in that you have mastered something—that you have endured hardship and enjoyed it despite the pain and effort. You know you still have to cross the river and climb the other side—no easy tasks, these. But you realize how much you have learned about the canyon and yourself already and how much you enjoy the process of being here, so you climb on confidently. You cross the river—it's a turning point and a point of no return. You have already been altered through the experience of descending, and this experience will forever be helpful to you and will assist you with your climb back up to the other rim of the canyon. You are looking forward to exploring the other side and can't wait to start.

When you start the ascent, you are full of energy and motivation; you feel strong and ready to complete your hike. As you begin to climb you realize how you are already beginning to apply what you learned on the other side of the river. You begin to recognize the signs of erosion on the path, the signs of the force of the water and the air. These are familiar features to you now, and you climb on. Then suddenly you see something that looks new—totally different—and you become frightened again. Your guide helps you recognize that it is nothing truly new; that it is the same force of the environment interacting with you and the canyon, just in a different shape or form. Your guide challenges you to apply what you have learned already to solve this new problem, and suddenly you recognize that it is true: you can figure this out on your own and keep climbing. The climb is not easy. You have to expend a great deal of energy, moving out of the depths back to the top. But with each step, your view improves and you view things more and more clearly. You begin to feel intense pride as you look back at the path you have already traveled, marveling at how you managed to get to this point. Sometimes you walk along easily; sometimes you stumble. When you stop to think, you realize what a strong and capable hiker you have become without even noticing—how much more confident you feel that you can reach the rim. You are a different hiker now; you need your guide less and less, and sometimes you leave the guide behind to strike out on your own. In your explorations off the beaten path, you meet others; some of these are still descending into the canyon, some are on their way up as well. You share experiences and recognize the pleasure you derive from these interactions. With each step out of the canyon, your horizon broadens. You once again begin to take in life and reality beyond the canyon.

When you finally reach the top, you feel accomplished; you have journeyed far and successfully. Maybe you would have preferred to do some things differently; maybe you would have liked to have more time in the canyon. But the reality is that no matter who you are right now as a hiker, you have changed. You are looking at the same landscape from the other side, but your perspective is different. You perceive nuances you could not see from the other side. You also see things in the canyon that you saw before but could not quite make out—they were fuzzy or strange to you. Now you understand them because you have looked at them directly and spent time trying to figure out why they were there. You see things in the canyon that previously frightened you that have now lost their power over you. As you revel in your experience, you realize you have forgotten your guide. You have pondered your knowledge and experience alone, often remembering words your guide spoke to you. You are startled that you would forget this person who helped guide you through this long hike, and you look around for your guide to share your experience. Your guide is right there, waiting for you to realize that you must say good-bye. Your guide assures you that she or he too is altered from the experience and is sad to have to leave you now. Both of you must move on. You need to attend to your life so you leave your guide behind. Many times in the future you will remember your traverse of the Grand Canyon. You will remember your guide and the experience you shared. You are forever altered; you are forever aware that the Grand Canyon will always be there: majestic, mysterious, waiting to be explored and enjoyed. Someday you may return or maybe you never will, but the voice of the Grand Canyon as you experienced it will forever be with you.

CLOSING COMMENTS

No single book can ever do justice to the complexity of psychotherapy, just as no picture can ever reflect the spectacular beauty of the Grand Canyon with its different colors at different times of day or the life within it. It is my hope that this book will succeed in communicating the fact that therapy is complex, multifaceted, and utterly human and experiential. It is also my hope that the reader will develop a new appreciation for the art that is psychotherapy and the responsibility that comes with it. Therapy is a human interaction that is intense and healing if done respectfully and caringly. It is a great gift to both client and therapist. I hope you will enjoy the journey through this book and through many successful therapies with clients who will emerge from the process happier, healthier, and stronger. I hope you will discover your own Grand Canyon and the joy of the hike. I hope you will become a guide to the many human beings who embark on such journeys and that you will revel in their experience of traversing the Grand Canyon that is the process of self-exploration. No two clients are ever alike, just as no two people can ever hike the Grand Canyon and have identical experiences. But all will experience awe and respect, all will experience happiness and pain. A good guide allows for these experiences and can step back when these need to be felt fully and step forward when these need to be softened. It is my most intense hope that this book can be a guide.

ACKNOWLEDGMENTS

It is impossible for me to acknowledge all those who have contributed in one way or another to this book. This volume is the result of years of learning and experiencing, processes that can never occur in isolation. I owe something to everyone with whom I have interacted in my years as a student, a psychologist, a teacher, and a researcher. I want to thank them all. Foremost, I would like to express my appreciation to

- Mark Johnson, whose love sustains me and often helps guide me; we have hiked the Grand Canyon and many a mountain together and I will always treasure our life together.
- my students, whose desire to learn challenges me and often helps me grow; we have shared moments in the classroom that were intimate and intense, and I will always treasure their honesty and trust in me.
- my supervisees, whose desire to help impresses me and often helps me feel warm and caring; we have explored the lives of clients together and I will always treasure their willingness to place their professional lives in my hands.
- my clients, whose struggle to survive touches me deeply and often helps me learn about myself; we have weathered many sad and joyous moments together and I will always treasure their faith in me.
- to my family, whose caring is forever present and often helps me achieve even more; we have shared many difficult journeys and I will always treasure their unfaltering closeness.

For the reviewers who read this book, I would like to express my appreciation: Pat Alford-Keating, University of California, Los Angeles; David H. Arnold, University of Massachusetts, Amherst; Richard P. Halgin, University of Massachusetts, Amherst; Dana M. Hardy, Middle Tennessee State University; Lynne Kellner, North Central Human Services, Gardner, MA; Wallace A. Kennedy, Florida State University; Christina H. Rasmussen, National University; Linda Webber, University of Alaska. Thank you all.

I especially wish to thank Susan Krusemark and the staff at Omegatype for their thoroughness, patience, and guidance through the final production process.

Happy Trails,
Christiane Brems

1

SETTING THE STAGE

*The clinician's demeanor, behavior, and life outside
the office setting should not be a basic departure from the
qualities he or she exemplifies in the therapy setting. If
therapists lack integrity or act defensively in their
personal lives, they will necessarily be limited in the
amount of assistance they are able to offer their patients.*
—*ROBERT FIRESTONE, SUICIDE AND THE INNER VOICE*

Becoming a therapist carries with it a certain responsibility that cannot and must
not be ignored. Therapists expect their clients to self-disclose with an honesty and
completeness they would not expect from most friends and many intimate partners. Although the therapist's role is often defined as one of a helper or giver (e.g.,
Egan, 1994), it must not be forgotten that the therapist truly only witnesses the
journey of the client to better mental health (see Selzer, 1986). Thus the therapist
must be self-aware and responsive to the client's needs without being self-
aggrandizing and overbearing (Cormier & Cormier, 1991). This is not an easy task,
but it is a process that can be mastered by most persons with some level of insight,
foresight, intelligence, empathy, caring, and personal mental health. This book
seeks to assist therapists in the journey toward becoming more proficient at their
job, toward becoming a guide who traverses the canyon of self-exploration with
every client. However, this book is merely a catalyst for this process and relies on
the therapist's ability to behave responsibly and seek appropriate supervision
whenever necessary. With the assistance of this book, a new therapist can learn to
master the complex tasks of doing psychotherapy in the presence of a supervisor
who will bear witness to the therapist's progress, in the same way the therapist
will bear witness to the client's journey; similarly, a seasoned clinician can gain
valuable insights and perhaps develop a new or changed perspective about the
process that is psychotherapy.

BEFORE THE FIRST CONTACT

A number of procedures and conditions facilitate the therapeutic process for client and therapist. They range from therapist traits to the atmosphere of a clinic or private office to the structure provided by the setting in which therapy is conducted. Therapist traits are best explored from two perspectives—namely, which traits are helpful and which are potential hindrances. The atmosphere of the office must be carefully planned and must be compatible with the structure that is given to the therapeutic relationship that will be established between therapist and client (Brems, 1993, 1994).

Therapist Traits

Therapists, like all people, manifest a number of traits in all life interactions that are either innate, learned, or developed over the years. For therapists to be maximally effective, however, they must develop an armamentarium of traits that reflects a combination of personal and technical competence that is compatible with working with people (Cormier & Cormier, 1991). Personal traits are often more difficult to deal with early on in a therapist's career if they happen to be strong though not conducive to therapeutic work; they are easy to deal with and a great asset, however, if they happen to be important attributes of therapy. Technical skills are the skills that are learned and applied strictly in the context of a therapy relationship. These skills include the ability to use reflection, active listening, reframing, empathy, and similar strategies. Although some of these are clearly related to personal traits, they are generally considered therapeutic catalysts and are covered in a relevant later chapter of this book. What is of importance here are the personal traits therapists bring to their education and the therapy relationship that may either help or hinder the therapeutic process.

Positive Therapist Traits

Self-esteem is an important trait in therapists—they have chosen a profession that would prove extremely difficult for the insecure person. Clients are not always as enamored with our techniques and procedures as we are and may make their displeasure known by verbally attacking the therapist. Insecure therapists who do not have adequate self-esteem may be worn down by the negative client and may come to think of themselves as bad people or poor therapists. A healthy (and realistic) dose of self-esteem makes the therapist less vulnerable to transferential and otherwise undeserved personal attacks by clients (Brems, 1994). A therapist who cannot deal with discomfort in a session is bound for failure or burnout (Kottler & Brown, 1992). Self-respect is also reflected in the therapist's ability to set appropriate boundaries in therapy and with the client. Specifically, the self-respecting clinician is able to adhere to the agreed on time frame for a session without feeling guilty, will request payment as agreed on, and will not accept unnecessary calls or contacts from the client between sessions. Such appropriate setting of boundaries is important not only for the client in that it communicates control and safety of the therapy setting, but also for the therapist as it takes care of the therapist's needs for a predictable schedule and a private life outside of the clinic (see Herlihy & Corey, 1997 for a very complete discussion of boundary issues).

Therapists must have the cognitive skills to conceptualize the client's case and to think on their feet. In other words, a therapist must be knowledgeable, must have the desire and ability to assimilate new information quickly, and must be able to reason abstractly. Only a bright therapist can respond quickly enough to the quick outpouring of data that can occur in therapy and keep up with the client in terms of conceptualizing and revising treatment plans effectively (Cormier & Cormier, 1991; Cormier & Hackney, 1987). Striving for excellence is how Kottler and Brown (1992) refer to the process of constantly learning and increasing the therapist's sense of awareness and therapeutic skill. New clients are viewed as posing new learning opportunities that will stretch therapists' limits and broaden their horizons. Additionally, continuing to learn about therapy and related strategies is essential for a field that changes continually (Egan, 1994). The clinician must also be aware of ethics and fully competent in these. Specifically, most, if not all, mental health professions have a code of ethics that requires that therapists be fully trained, up-to-date, and generally competent at what they do (Swenson, 1997). Therapists must know their professional limits and when to refer to another provider when these limits have been reached by the demands of a case or client.

A therapist needs to possess a high level of self-awareness and maturity, lest all sorts of confounding feelings and attitudes enter into the treatment process (see Knobel, 1990). Self-awareness is a therapist trait that is important in the work with all clients regardless of age (Chrzanowski, 1989; Chung, 1990). It helps prevent countertransference reactions from developing and helps the therapist respond out of a concern for the client, not for the self. The importance of self-awareness is best demonstrated through showing the possible negative consequences for clients created by the lack of self-awareness, which is covered in somewhat more detail later in this chapter (see also Cormier & Cormier, 1991). Self-awareness is also necessary for therapists to recognize when their personal needs may be mobilized in a therapeutic relationship and to keep these needs out of the therapy room. Such needs may need to be addressed by the therapist, but never in the presence of the client (Kottler & Brown, 1992). It is important for the therapist to be willing to seek supervision and consultation to improve and enhance self-awareness—not only when personal needs and limitations obviously rise to the surface (Strupp, 1996), but on a regular basis to prevent inappropriate expression of personal needs in therapy sessions (Basch, 1980; Brems, 1994). Gaining self-awareness and ongoing work on maintaining this also means that therapists practice what they preach, looking at their own feelings, thoughts, and actions regularly and with caring and realistic criticism (Egan, 1994).

Open-mindedness is another critical trait that helps therapists welcome clients whose values may differ from their own (Cormier & Cormier, 1991). Similarly, open-minded therapists will not inadvertently or deliberately force personal values onto the client. This is especially important if the client was raised in an environment that was significantly different from that of the therapist, as is often the case (Castillo, 1997). Unfortunately, the bulk of therapists today have middle-class backgrounds, whereas the bulk of clients tends to come from more disadvantaged socioeconomic backgrounds (Johnson, 1993). These differences in background are likely to have forged different sets of values and priorities for client and therapist. These differences will not threaten treatment procedures as long as the therapist can keep an open mind—in other words, is able to see the client's life from the client's unique perspective. Thus the therapist may need to understand that some behaviors of the client that would have been considered maladaptive or at least questionable in the therapist's own personal background may have great adaptive value in the client's environment. Clearly, neither science nor art (and therapy is generally considered to contain both) can be entirely free of values and value judgments (Lewis & Walsh, 1980). However, therapists are encouraged to be as flexible and open-minded as possible, and to recognize their own values and how these may collide with the values of a client. In other words, although therapists may be unable to refrain from some value judgments, they must learn about their own values that might cloud the work that needs to be done.

Open-mindedness about values and standards is also implied in the therapist's need for sensitivity to ethnic differences (Ponterotto, Casas, Suzuki, & Alexander, 1995). It is important to keep in mind that although there is significant variation across ethnic groups, there is also significant variation within each ethnic group (Johnson, 1993). That is to say that the therapist should never assume that because a client is from a certain ethnic group, the person will display certain attitudes or behaviors. This attitude, which often masquerades as cultural sensitivity, is actually a severe manifestation of prejudice. Sensitivity to and respect for cross-cultural differences are a must; however, such sensitivity should not be used as a way of organizing or categorizing people along certain dimensions (Egan, 1994). There is uniqueness in every person, whether the person is Asian American, African American, or European American. No therapist would ever assume that all White clients have the same traits and concerns. However, it is unfortunately still common to hear therapists talk in such global terms about clients from other ethnic backgrounds (Namyniuk, Brems, & Clarson, 1997).

Cross-cultural awareness depends on sensitivity to the type of language that is chosen, which must never be pejorative (Strupp, 1996). All sexist and racist terminology must be eliminated from a clinician's verbal repertoire (Johnson, 1993). Terms that are openly racist (such as "spic" or "nigger") are easily avoided because great awareness has been raised in society about the complete inappropriateness of such language. However, more subtle racism, sexism, and homophobia continue to prevail and must be avoided by mental health professionals. For example, terms such as "Indian giver" remain commonly used despite their clear racial prejudice. Further, word choices are often sexist without this being the intent of the speaker. For instance, using "he," "his," and "him" as generic pronouns is unacceptable in treatment procedures because of the implicit message that women do not count when one speaks about humanity. Labels such as "mankind," "chairman," "policeman," and so forth are equally unacceptable, especially as less sexist options have been coined (e.g., "humankind" or "humanity," "chair," "police officer"). Sexist assumptions about professions must be monitored as well. The clinician will need to make conscious word and pronoun choices by, for example, eliminating references to physicians, politicians, or construction workers as men, or nurses, secretaries, and teachers as women.

Another way to assure appropriate cross-cultural sensitivity, as well as general therapeutic sensitivity, is through developing empathy. Each therapist must strive to understand how a client feels in a given situation, given that client's specific and unique experiences, history, and background (see Kohut, 1984). Empathy, thus defined, requires the therapist to listen carefully and to hear or see not only the overt content of what is being expressed either verbally or behaviorally, but also to listen to the more latent message that is contained within the client's expression. Such empathy, also termed vicarious introspection (Kohut & Wolf, 1978), is not the warm, fuzzy feeling of caring, but rather is an artful and scientific approach to better understanding. Empathy is also incomplete if it ends with the internal, private understanding of the client by the therapist. Empathy only serves a positive therapeutic purpose if therapists are able to communicate their understanding back to the person. Put differently, once the therapist has listened carefully and believes to have empathically understood the communication of the individual, this understanding must somehow be communicated back to the client. Only when the client receives this message of understanding and feels the therapist's empathic concern is the interpersonal cycle of empathy considered to be complete (see Barrett-Lennard, 1981; Brems, 1989a).

Tolerance and flexibility are two additional traits that are important (Choca, 1988; Cormier & Cormier, 1991; Knobel, 1990). Specifically, in all therapies, new information constantly emerges as work progresses. This results in therapists constantly revising treatment plans and conceptualizations, and requires them to adapt treatment strategies in a meaningful manner (Morrison, 1995a). Not all human beings are capable of functioning in such an environment of ambiguity and tentativeness. Not a few will attempt to make the therapy fit a rigid model, forcing the understanding of the client into a mold. This is a dangerous lack of flexibility that can cause stagnation at best, iatrogenesis at worst. No client, no family, and no therapy fits a specific mold. In fact, the whole therapeutic process relies on change, upheaval, tentativeness, and not uncommonly, ambiguity. Related to the concept of flexibility is the idea that a good therapist must have patience (Strupp, 1996). Therapy cannot be rushed and therapists cannot expect their clients to follow a particular time line.

For a therapist, it is important to be able to deal with unknowns and to be willing to take risks and explore new grounds. Being able to deal with ambiguity is a critical skill of every therapist (Kottler & Brown, 1992). All therapists have to be capable of "epistemological feeling" (Knobel, 1990, p. 61)—that is, they must have the ability to listen empathically and to alter their assessments of a client's situation flexibly and appropriately in response to changing contexts (Cormier & Cormier, 1991). Unwillingness to follow intuitions can result in leaving facets of certain clients undiscovered that may otherwise prove crucial to their growth and change. Although this risk-taking has to be weighed against the possible consequences of making a mistake, it is rare that one failed or inappropriate treatment intervention will derail the entire therapeutic process. Indeed, some clinicians believe that the occasional failure in empathy of the therapist is crucial to successful treatment (Kohut, 1984). Repeated failures are likely to be more impactful than one unfortunate choice of wording or behavior. It is often preferable for the therapist to risk a new intervention than to adhere rigidly to one that is clearly unsuccessful.

In facilitating the therapy process, it is important that therapists allow their own personhood to come through and to be authentic (Knobel, 1990) and genuine (Egan, 1994). It is generally quite impossible for clinicians to deny their real selves outside the therapy room. Personality cannot be hidden, nor should it be camouflaged (Chrzanowski, 1989). Yet authenticity does not imply that the therapist engage in self-disclosure. The therapy is there for the client, not for therapists to self-disclose or deal with their own psychological or emotional issues. As stated previously, to maintain personal boundaries is critical (Morrison, 1995a). However, all therapists have a personality and an interpersonal style. Some are extroverted and active; others are introverted and observing. This general pattern shows through in the type of treatment a clinician chooses (see Keinan, Almagor, & Ben-Porath, 1989; Kolevzon, Sowers-Hoag, & Hoffman, 1989). Finding a way of doing therapy that fits with the therapist's general style and with life values is worth the effort. Only if the style fits the clinician will the person be able to muster the enthusiasm that is so crucial to the treatment of any client. A bored therapist is indeed difficult to picture as successfully instilling a sense of enthusiasm and challenge in the client. Being oneself also implies that common courtesies are extended to clients by the therapist, and that the therapist is friendly and human (i.e., not the blank slate without any type of reaction, often misunderstood as typical of psychoanalytic or psychodynamic thinkers). For example, Wolf (1988) points out that a good therapist will *not* squelch normal common courtesies (e.g., condolences after finding out about the death of a client's family member) under the guise of trying to remain neutral and a target of transference.

Adapting therapeutic style and technique to personal traits is not equivalent to self-disclosure and not equivalent to abandoning the concept of therapeutic neutrality. Being neutral in the sense of being nonjudgmental and not imposing certain opinions or outcomes on a client is still absolutely critical (Kottler & Brown, 1992). However, the neutrality issue can be taken too far if it translates into sterile and impersonal ways of relating to clients. Even psychoanalytic therapists have come to recognize that remaining anonymous does not mean being nonresponsive (see Basch, 1980). It is unavoidable for therapists to be themselves in the way they greet their clients, sit in the room, and interact throughout their sessions. Neutrality is not to be confused with personality restraint. It merely means maintaining clear boundaries and retaining the focus of the session, which is on the client, not the therapist (Brems, 1994; Morrison, 1995a). Chrzanowski (1989, p. 600) describes therapy as a "relational contact with a shared goal," which emphasizes that therapists' personalities play a critical role in how therapy will progress. However, therapists' needs must be kept out of the therapy session. Even when therapists are hungry or upset, they must be able to stifle these needs and feelings while with the client (Kottler & Brown, 1992). This may be one of the greatest challenges for the new therapist, but this becomes second nature as time wears on. It also implies that self-care outside of the therapy room is a critical aspect of therapists' lives so as not to create human beings with limited self-awareness and in denial of their own needs and feelings.

The issue of self-care is also implied in the main trait of successful therapists, which is their personal mental health. Mental health is difficult to define, but self psychologists have succeeded well in providing a rather generic guideline with which to gauge the traits of a mentally healthy person (e.g., Kohut, 1984; Wolf, 1988). The clearest definition has been rendered by Rowe and MacIsaac (1989), summarizing Kohut's conception of personal mental health. These writers suggest that mentally healthy human beings are empathically attuned, have the wish and the ability to understand the needs of others, understand their own needs, are capable of delaying their own needs to meet the needs of others, are realistically self-confident with a clear acceptance of their own flaws and shortcomings, have little fear of rejection or humiliation, possess a certain amount of creativity, have a sense of humor, and are wise. The definitions of the latter three concepts must be provided to understand what they imply. Creativity, in self-psychological terms, refers to the therapist's ability to derive pleasure from problem solving. This pleasure in coming up with solutions to tough situations and circumstances is reinforcing for clinicians and continues to propel them toward finding options and alternatives, both in their own lives and in the lives of clients. A sense of humor is defined as the ability to laugh at oneself. It excludes biting sarcasm or vicious irony and merely refers to the ability to make light of past failures and minor imperfections in oneself. This type of humor is not engaged in at the expense of anyone, but merely reflects the ability not to take life and oneself too seriously. Finally, wisdom is defined as having come to terms with personal limitations and frailties in oneself and others. It means being able to forgive mistakes and lack of ability, accepting self and others fully. Wisdom dictates that parents, teachers, and clinicians can be forgiven and accepted even if they have made mistakes in the past and that the person can maintain a respectful and caring relationship nevertheless. True wisdom is achieved if this capacity is present in relation to others and the self.

Summary of Positive Therapist Traits

- self-respect and self-esteem
- ability to set and enforce limits and boundaries
- self-awareness and willingness for self-exploration
- willingness to seek consultation and supervision
- open-mindedness about values, behaviors, and approaches to life
- restraint from imposing own values, standards, or beliefs
- cultural and gender sensitivity
- awareness of the impact and manifestation of prejudice
- use of non-offensive, non-sexist, non-racist, and non-homophobic language
- respect for clients' needs and wishes
- empathy and willingness to listen
- tolerance for ambiguity and tentativeness
- truthfulness to oneself
- awareness of personal style
- compatibility of personal style with chosen therapeutic style

- neutrality and maintenance of appropriate personal boundaries
- ability to delay gratification of own needs
- ability to put own feelings (arising from personal issues, not therapeutic interactions) on hold
- personal mental health and presence of self-care skills

Hindering Therapist Traits

The primary issue discussed here is lack of self-awareness. Though other therapist traits exist that are not conducive to treatment (e.g., lack of flexibility, inability to tolerate discomfort, inadequate intellectual skills), these were generally dealt with in the previous section through the discussion of their opposites. Lack of self-awareness, however, has so many different faces that it warrants a separate discussion.

Lack of self-awareness allows countertransference to creep into therapy without the therapist recognizing that the therapeutic process is beginning to be influenced by the therapist's personal needs or unresolved feelings (see Holmquist & Armelius, 1996). There are four types of countertransference that commonly develop in the therapist with limited self-awareness: issue-specific, trait-specific, client-specific, and stimulus-specific (Brems, 1994). Issue-specific countertransference represents a therapist's reaction to specific behaviors, feelings, and needs (or transferences) expressed by the client by stimulating unconscious material in the therapist. In other words, a therapist's reaction to a client's issues is flavored by the therapist's own unconscious material. For instance, a therapist who has anxieties about sexuality may be particularly threatened and may respond negatively to the discussion of sexual abuse by a client, especially if that person has learned seductive behaviors and incorporated them in interactions. Another therapist who is free of unconscious sexual conflicts may respond to the same client in an entirely different manner. Therapists themselves may be very capable of treating other clients, who do not stimulate their internal conflicts, without problem and very sensitively. The crux of this countertransference is the coincidental and unfortunate convergence of therapist and client issues (or transferences) that are incompatible, overly similar, or overly threatening.

Stimulus-specific countertransference is independent of the client's needs, feelings, or behaviors, but rather occurs in response to an external, therapy-irrelevant stimulus from the client. For instance, a therapist with issues yet to be explored around sibling rivalry with a younger brother may respond with inappropriate interventions to those male clients who (consciously or unconsciously) remind the therapist of this brother. The reaction is not specific to the client's expressed therapy issues, but rather is specific to the therapist and would occur in the interaction with any such individual, whether a therapy client or not. The crux of this countertransference is the therapist's unconscious and immediate reaction to an external stimulus by a person who is independent of the client's treatment needs or transference expressions.

Trait-specific countertransference is even more global and has previously been labeled the therapist's "habitual modes of relating" (Sandler, 1975, p. 415, as quoted in Bernstein & Glenn, 1988, p. 226) or the therapist's "expression of character traits" (Lilleskov, 1971, p. 404, as quoted in Bernstein & Glenn, 1988, p. 226). Such a countertransference reaction implies that therapists respond to their clients as they would respond to others at any time in their lives. For instance, therapists with rigid morals, who tend to be condescending and judgmental in general, will bring this attitude into the treatment room and it will influence their work with a given client, regardless of the issues presented. Other therapists, who may detest aggression, may be unable to allow people to act out their own angry feelings, however justified they may be. Still other clinicians, who have a high need to please others, may violate therapy limits and boundaries by extending sessions beyond the 50 minutes, waiving fees without therapeutic reason, or engaging in similar behaviors that will make therapy less predictable and appropriate. The crux of this countertransference is therapists' habit-driven manner of relating to people in all contexts, including the therapy setting.

The fourth type of countertransference is called client-specific countertransference. This countertransference is a reaction to the client that is solicited by the client in most, if not all, adults with whom the person interacts. For instance, a very oppositional and demanding client with poor self-esteem and strong attention-seeking behavior may overwhelm and alienate others after prolonged contact. The therapist may experience this same frustration others might encounter with the person. Hence, this reaction is not specific to the therapist, but rather is specific to the client's behavior that solicits a given response in those around her or him. The crux of this countertransference is the client's solicitation of a consistent (e.g., negative, protective, hostile) response from her or his environment.

Client-specific countertransference, unlike the other three, provides the aware clinician with added insight about the client and empathy for the person. Such a countertransference reaction can be used therapeutically with the client as long as the therapist has sufficient self-awareness to tease out which aspect of a reaction to the client is coming from within and which is coming from the client. This countertransference provides information about the client and can provide excellent feedback about the person's impact on the environment, as well as providing information about why the client tends to be rejected in many contexts. It also provides insight regarding target behaviors of the client that need to be modified quickly to help the person become more acceptable to the potentially helpful others in that person's life.

In essence, being self-aware helps therapists prevent and avoid countertransferences that may hinder the therapeutic process (Cormier & Cormier, 1991). It may also help therapists recognize reactions their clients may solicit in others in general and serve as a means of giving quick feedback to their clients about their impact on those around them.

Atmosphere of the Office

Developing an atmosphere conducive to psychotherapy is a critical aspect of setting up a therapy office. This is true regardless of whether a therapist's office is housed in a counseling center, mental health clinic, hospital, or private practice. Certain features apply to all of these settings, though the individual therapist may have to make creative adjustments to implement each feature. An atmosphere that is conducive to treatment will communicate several impressions to clients as soon as they enter the building or lobby of the center. Given the reality that therapy is still somewhat suspect to many people and carries a certain stigma for some, confidentiality is a concern many clients bring with them when they first enter a therapy setting. Thus the office must be set up in manner that communicates confidentiality and privacy immediately upon entry (Hutchins & Vaught, 1997; Wolf, 1988). For example, no client records should be visible in the lobby and waiting area. Unlike in many physician's offices, where patient charts are kept in a shelf or file cabinet behind the receptionist's desk, such a practice is inappropriate for a therapy office. Further, clients should be greeted discreetly by the receptionist without loud announcement of their names. This can be accomplished by greeting clients without using names and following up the greeting with a request for the assigned therapist or intake worker's name. Clinic staff needs to be well-versed in the basics of client confidentiality and in basic interpersonal skills that help put anxiety-prone clients at ease. Staff should be taught that chitchat and social conversation with clients is best kept to a minimum because it is often impossible to predict the mental state of the client (Giordano, 1997). An innocuous social question by a staff person may trigger a flood of emotion in a client that may then embarrass the person. A therapy environment also must be quiet and is therefore incompatible with loud music, noisy staff, or loud equipment (e.g., typewriters).

The waiting room should be large enough that clients can fill out any requested paperwork without fearing that another waiting client may be able to read over their shoulders. Preferably, the waiting area would be located away from the treatment area to maximize privacy (Wolf, 1988) and to prevent clients in the waiting area from overhearing clients who are in the treatment room and who may either be speaking loudly, weeping, or otherwise making noise (e.g., children playing in play therapy). If this is not possible, playing soft, neutral music (e.g., classical music) in the waiting area may be used to cover any sounds coming from the treatment area. The waiting area is best equipped with comfortable seating that includes couches and individual chairs. Although this is not recommended here, some clinics offer coffee or tea. If this is done, therapists need to make decisions before seeing their clients about clients bringing these drinks into the treatment room (see the discussion of structure below). Choice of reading materials in the waiting room can be diverse but should be tasteful and appropriate. For example, copies of magazines that cover controversial or potentially offensive topics that may alienate some clients (e.g., "Guns and Ammo" or "Playboy") or pamphlets by political parties or groups with strong opinions (e.g., anti-abortion or pro-abortion) are out of place in a setting that is designed for therapeutic purposes. In fact, even some women's magazine's that promote highly traditional or stereotypic views of women may be offensive to enough people that their placement in a waiting room may be inappropriate. Because a mental health clinic generally promotes well-being and healthy life-adjustment, choice of magazines that are similarly focused is optimal (e.g., "Natural Health," "Prevention," "Psychology Today," "Backpacker," "Walking").

The waiting room will reflect to a certain degree the level of thoughtfulness of the clinic staff. Magazines that are offensive to any cultural or ethnic groups are out; similarly, wall decorations that are ethnically biased or inappropriate should not be used. Wall decorations need to be neutral and are best devoid of pictures of human beings, either happy or sad. Much beautiful art exists that is free of such content. Relevant pamphlets can be displayed in the waiting area with extra copies provided for clients to take home. Such pamphlets may consist of advertisements/ announcements of mental health or parenting resources in the community, informational brochures about mental health issues (e.g., seasonal affective disorder, anxiety disorders, substance use), or definitional flyers about therapy and the various professionals who provided such services. No pamphlet or magazine should be displayed that a therapist would not want even a single client to see.

The therapy rooms themselves must be appropriately equipped and must be soundproof (Wolf, 1988). Proper equipment includes comfortable seating for therapist and client at a reasonable distance that helps both therapist and client feel comfortable (Basch, 1980). A couch, although once seen as mandatory by traditional psychoanalysts, is now considered optional in a regular psychotherapy practice where the practice of traditional psychoanalytic treatment has all but disappeared. However, a couch may be useful for rooms that are designated for both individual and for relationship therapy. In addition to comfortable seating arrangements, the room should contain a small table that holds appointment cards, clinic brochures, extra forms (e.g., releases of information), tissues (very important), and similar items. A small wicker shelf that holds extras of all of these items can be attractive and functional. A small wastebasket for used tissues should also be provided. Wall and other decorations need to be neutral and tasteful, not reflecting any specific taste or message. Lighting for the room should be adjustable, and table or floor lamps are preferable to overhead lighting. Fluorescent lighting is not conducive to helping create a warm atmosphere and hence is best avoided. Carpeted floors assist with noise absorption and also create a warmer atmosphere than tile or linoleum. Because the focus of this book is on adult therapy, this statement can be made unequivocally. However, if a room were to be used for child treatment, a quite different approach would need to be taken (Brems, 1993).

Structure of the Setting

Many people come to therapy because of chaos and disorder in their lives; all come with various sets of expectations and misperceptions that have to be met and addressed by the therapist. One way to help introduce and model some structure (and thus decrease some of the experienced chaos) is to provide a clearly structured introduction or explicit guidelines about the therapeutic process (Cormier & Hackney, 1987). It is helpful for clients and therapists to know what will be expected of each party and how various situations (e.g., payment and scheduling) will be handled. This prior knowledge protects clients from misunderstandings and assists therapists in maintaining a healthy boundary between their professional and work lives (Kottler & Brown, 1992). Following are some suggested structures and guidelines that would meet these purposes.

It is important for therapists to set clear boundaries about what is and is not done for the client (Kottler & Brown, 1992). Therapy has a fixed structure that generally and traditionally consists of 45- or 50-minute sessions that begin and end on time and generally are scheduled on a weekly basis, usually at the same time each week. This schedule provides predictability and allows the client and therapist to plan schedules around the session for many weeks in advance. How many weeks the client will see the therapist is a therapeutic issue that will be negotiated with the client at the end of the intake process (and will be discussed in a later chapter). It is important for clients to understand the limits of therapy and know that if they choose to be late for sessions, the therapist will still end at the specified time. This is necessary not only to model structure for the client but also to protect the therapist from undue stress. Imagine running over with a late client and then having to run late for all subsequently scheduled sessions, or imagine running late with a client only to have the therapist who is scheduled next for a given therapy room intrude on the session. These situations will not only interfere with the work with the client, but will also increase the stress perceived by both client and therapist. Therapists do vary in opinions about how long to wait for a late client. Some wait 15 minutes; some up to 30 minutes; some wait the entire scheduled time. The important question is how much time is needed to get some therapeutic work done. If that much time is left in the session when the client arrives, the remainder of the session should be used. If the client arrives with less than that amount of time left in the session, she or he should be asked to return for the regularly scheduled appointment during the next week. Once the client returns for the next session, this rescheduling then needs to be processed (more about this in Chapter 7).

Another relatively standard structure is the fact that payment is generally expected at the time services are provided (unless client and therapist have made other arrangements very explicitly and collaboratively). Payment is best accepted before the session starts and should always be acknowledged with a written receipt. If a receptionist takes care of payment, this timing should still be maintained. One reason for taking payment at the beginning, not the end, of the session is that the process of writing a check or finding money in a wallet can then not be used by the client to prolong a session. Further, it protects the client from potential embarrassment should a particularly difficult session leave the client emotionally upset at the end of the session. Having to deal with a receptionist or with payment in front of others at such a time may be difficult for the client.

Social chitchat with clients is to be avoided in most circumstances (including during sessions), but especially in waiting or public areas where others may be present (Basch, 1980). Also, the socially acceptable "How are you?" is not an appropriate greeting with a client in a public area (Brems, 1993; Giordano, 1997). What if the client feels terrible and bursts into tears at the mere inquiry into an emotional state? What if the client begins to self-disclose before the therapy room door has been closed? These violations of the client's confidentiality are easily avoided by greeting the client with a friendly "Hello. Let's go . . . (to the room, on back, etc.)." Once a session is over, it is best to let the client walk out of the room and clinic alone to avoid prolonged confidential conversation in the hall or in another public area. This is best accomplished by a friendly closing of the session that emphasizes the return of the client during the subsequent week before the therapy room door is opened. A simple "I'll see you again next week, same place, same time. . . . Take care" will serve this purpose well. Then the door is opened and the client leaves. The therapist hangs back, perhaps straightening the room for the next person. As an aside, it is good practice to empty wastebaskets between all sessions to avoid the accumulation of visibly used tissues. Also, a check to assure an ample supply of tissues is a good idea at that time. This is particularly true when several therapists share a single office. No therapist should hold another person responsible for stocking the room; all need to take that responsibility for themselves.

Finally, if the client is seen in a clinic where either video- or audiotaping is standard procedure, the equipment should be started before the client is taken to the room. In this manner, the therapist's attention is not distracted once in the presence of the client. Video- and audiotaping of sessions have allowed therapists to avoid taking lengthy notes even during intake sessions when a large amount of information is gathered. Taking notes is a distancing behavior that is not recommended with most clients (Seligman, 1996). Even if a therapist does not work in a setting where taping is common practice, taking notes during sessions is discouraged. In such a setting, therapists are urged to write their case notes as soon after a session as possible, while the memory of the content and process of the session is fresh in the therapist's mind.

Writing case notes is essential and raises the issue of documentation and record-keeping in general. There are specific guidelines that have been provided by the American Psychological Association (1993) that should be followed by all clinicians. These guidelines point out that record-keeping is an ethical and legal obligation of the therapist. Valid records are needed to document and review the services that were provided; to guide treatment planning and implementation; for institutional purposes (e.g., for accreditation review of a clinic), legal proceedings (e.g., a malpractice suit against a therapist), and financial reasons (e.g., a review of services for resource allocation); and to protect the clinician from legal liability in case of lawsuits or ethical charges (American Psychological Association, 1993). Records must include a comprehensive, objective, consistent, retrievable, secure, and current range of information about the client, the therapist, and the services that were provided (Vandecreek & Knapp, 1997). Minimally, they need to include:

- information to document the nature, delivery, progress, and results of services provided
- data about client and therapist, dates when services were rendered, types of services rendered, fees that were charged and collected, assessment plans and reports, and any releases of information collected
- accurate, current, and pertinent records about the client and the treatment so that therapy could theoretically be continued by another care provider in the case of death, retirement, or disability of the current clinician
- documentation of any and all contracts and agreements made with the client

- documentation of all data and considerations regarding risk assessment, diagnosis, or emergency intervention
- information about any concerns the therapist raised with the client regarding case management, about client resistance and lack of cooperation, or concerns the therapist has about the client
- documentation about all consultation and supervision sessions relevant directly to the client's case

Records must be kept in such as way as to protect against unauthorized access and misuse, an issue that must be even more carefully considered if a computer is used for data storage and writing notes (Swenson, 1997; Vandecreek & Knapp, 1997). A complete record must be kept for at least three years after the last contact with the client (unless the clinician practices in a state that has a law that specifies a different time frame); a summary record must be kept for up to an additional 12 years. In the case of a minor client, complete records must be kept for three years after the client reaches age of majority, and then for an additional 12 years a summary record should be maintained (American Psychological Association, 1993). To maintain records they must be guaranteed to be confidential, safe, and kept in such a way as to limit access (e.g., under lock and key; in a restricted area; in a computer with some form of encryption device and password protection). Once the record can be disposed of, this must be accomplished in an equally confidential manner (e.g., the record may be shredded).

In keeping records, the clinician must keep in mind that records can be subpoenaed, and hence they should be kept carefully with some consideration about what should or should not be included. Points that need to be made should be stated succinctly and without speculation or overly subjective interpretation. Notes must be unambiguous and clear; they need to be respectful of the client and need to avoid any type of judgment, prejudice, or hostility against the client; they need to make careful consideration of their implications, not mentioning any symptoms that are questionable or without having attended to them through therapeutic intervention or referral; notes must be honest and true reflections of what is known and what happened; and records must best conform to any clinic-specific rules about records, accreditation organization guidelines, or professional guidelines that are available to the clinician (Gutheil, 1980). During a workshop conducted under the auspices of the American Psychological Association in 1995 in Anchorage, Alaska, Dr. Bruce Bennett of the American Psychological Association highlighted the following quote from Gutheil (1980) that quickly drives home these points: "In writing progress notes [or any other notes contained in a client's record], trainees are urged to hallucinate on their shoulder the image of a hostile prosecuting attorney who might preside at the trial in which their records are subpoenaed" (p. 481). This "hallucination" may help the therapist determine what and how to document.

Although few other guidelines exist with regard to structure for therapy, there are common ways of starting and ending treatment as well as some guidelines for special purpose sessions, such as intakes, crisis interventions, special assessments, and so forth. Specific requirements also exist with regard to documenting services rendered and assessments made, especially in emergency situations.

Legal and Ethical Issues

Every clinician must learn about ethical and professional issues that are relevant to psychotherapy. Ethical treatment of clients begins with obtaining informed consent that outlines the responsibilities of the clinician and the rights of the client, as well as the expectations a client can have about treatment. The "elements of legally adequate informed consent are competence, voluntariness, and knowledge" (Crawford, 1994, p. 56), where competence refers to the fact that the person rendering consent has to be legally competent to do so (i.e., must be over 18 years old and must not be developmentally disabled or otherwise legally "incompetent"). Voluntariness refers to the fact that therapy is entered voluntarily and that informed consent is not rendered under duress. Knowledge refers to the fact that the therapist must ascertain that the client is knowledgeable of and understands the types of rights that would be covered under an informed consent to psychological treatment (Canter, Bennett, Jones, & Nagy, 1994). The following information must be emphasized for each client in person during the first contact with a mental health professional or with a mental health clinic (it is also covered in the written informed consent the client will sign prior to starting the screening session):

- client confidentiality (i.e., the guarantee that the therapist will not disclose information obtained in the therapeutic relationship without proper authorization)
- exceptions to confidentiality (such as the duties to warn, protect, and report)
- limitations of privileged communication (e.g., court orders, diagnostic disclosure to insurance companies to assure payment)
- release of information procedures authorized by the client
- the voluntary nature of therapy
- audio- or videotaping policies
- cancellation policies
- fee and payment schedules
- dual relationship issues
- possible alternatives to therapy for the client's presenting concern
- credentials or educational background of the service provider and this person's supervisors
- supervision or consultation arrangements
- clinic procedures for case staffings and treatment plan meetings

In addition to the information listed above, which must be covered explicitly, directly, and verbally with all clients during the screening session, several other issues are best addressed up front with any new client, either in writing before treatment begins or verbally during the screening session (see Swenson, 1997). For example, clients must be made aware that therapy cannot guarantee positive outcomes and cannot guarantee definite solutions to presenting problems. Further, therapy can have some inherent risks depending on the techniques that may be employed by a given counselor or therapist (e.g., flooding techniques may lead to panic reactions). Information about dual relationships should be provided, pointing out to the client basic ideas about the nature of the therapy relationship. Dual relationship issues are by no means an easy ethical concern, with some lack of clarity remaining in most professional practice standards (Anderson & Kitchener, 1996). The primary area of agreement appears to center on the prohibition of sexual relationships between clients and therapist during treatment and for at least two years thereafter. However, other incidental and intentional dual relationships are less clearly allowed or disallowed, and practitioners must use their own ethical judgments to decide right from wrong, therapeutic from untherapeutic. Practitioners in rural areas face greater dilemmas than their colleagues in urban areas; in the former locations some dual relationships may be unavoidable (Schank & Skovholt, 1997; see also Chapter 7). Stated more globally, however, there is little discussion on this issue; dual relationships are to be avoided lest they confound treatment or continued recovery after termination. Clients also have the right to know where they can turn should they have complaints or grievances about the treatment they receive by a clinic of clinician. Having good informed consent forms, treating clients fairly, discussing client rights and concerns with clients directly, and obeying ethical guidelines of the profession are the best insurance against lawsuits (Swenson, 1997).

According to many clinicians, confidentiality is the cornerstone of therapy: "For therapy to work the client must trust the therapist. For the client to trust, the therapist must keep promises about secrecy" (Swenson, 1997, p. 70). Even Hippocrates, who practiced around 400 years B.C., was convinced of the importance of confidentiality, stating that "Whatever I shall see or hear in the course of my profession . . . I will never divulge, holding such things to be holy secrets." However, much to the chagrin of many mental health care providers, in modern days, important exceptions have been made to confidentiality through laws, legal precedent, and ethical codes. These exceptions must be covered in the informed consent paperwork. Specifically, the informed consent must clarify and explain that all of the following circumstances may limit a client's right to confidentiality and/or the client–therapist privilege (Arthur & Swanson, 1993; Swenson, 1997):

- if the client requests or allows disclosure by signing a release of information
- if disclosure is necessary to prevent certain crimes
- if the client presents a danger to self or others
- if the client discloses or arouses reasonable suspicions about child abuse or neglect
- if the therapist receives a court order or *subpoena duces tecum* for disclosure to serve the cause of justice
- if there is a criminal or civil legal action related to sanity or competence
- if the client has initiated a legal action or ethical charge against the therapist (e.g., a malpractice lawsuit)
- for supervision purposes
- for clerical purposes (i.e., secretary typing reports or filing insurance paperwork)
- for intra-agency sharing that is part of treatment (e.g., case staffings, treatment plan meetings)

Swenson (1997) calls the inclusion of these exceptions in an informed consent the equivalent to a psychological Miranda warning—an apt comparison. He writes, "A psychological Miranda warning lets clients know under what circumstance the therapist will share potentially damaging information so that clients will not be misled into incriminating themselves" (Swenson, 1997, p. 72). He also notes that many clinicians (in fact, more than *half*) fail to give such a warning to their clients, thus shortchanging their clients and putting themselves at risk for lawsuits.

Finally, in this day and age of managed care and health maintenance organizations the issue of confidentiality and privileged communication is becoming somewhat difficult in terms of what type of client information is required of the therapist for third-party payment purposes (Swenson, 1997). Clients need to be informed that, at a minimum, insurance companies require diagnostic information, and, at a maximum, detailed information about symptoms and session progress to continue making payments. Clients need to give informed consent to these procedures if they are required or need to make a decision not to use third-party payment options if they do not agree with the disclosures required by their third-party payor. Most importantly, therapists cannot assume that clients are willing to have this information disclosed merely for the purpose of being financially reimbursed for the cost of treatment (Arthur & Swanson, 1993). Also important to cover in the informed consent is the reality that clients waive their right to privacy vis-à-vis their insurance company when they sign their claims form. Many clients are not aware of this fact, and it should be mentioned in the informed consent. Disclosing excessive information or disclosing any information to the third-party payor without receiving the client's consent to do so may well be considered a breach of confidentiality (Okun, 1997), even if the client signed the insurance claims form. Clients should be encouraged to check with their personal insurance carrier for the type of disclosures that will be required of the clinician before making a final commitment to treatment and reimbursement.

THE FIRST CONTACT

Once familiar with the therapy environment and structure, and being comfortable with having at least some of the positive and few of the negative traits of a therapist, the clinician is ready for the first contact with the client. The nature of this contact will depend on clinic procedures and client circumstances.

Models for a First Contact

There are several possible models (see also Seligman, 1996), the five most common of which are outlined below:

1. The clinic conducts scheduled screening only (i.e., no walk-in appointments) before accepting clients for therapy services and before scheduling an actual intake session.

2. The clinic conducts walk-in screening that requires no prior appointment before accepting clients for therapy services and before scheduling an actual intake session.
3. The clinic accepts walk-in appointments for intake sessions, without requiring a screening for service eligibility.
4. The clinic schedules intake sessions after a phone interview with the client by a staff member (not a therapist) and conducts no screenings for service eligibility first.
5. The clinic also operates emergency services that are available to clients on an as-needed basis.

The most common counseling or mental health center model is the one listed first, followed by the second and third models. The most common private practice model is the one listed fourth (though therapists themselves may also be conducting phone interviews prior to scheduling). The fifth model is almost exclusively used by counseling and mental health centers; private practitioners do not generally deal with walk-in emergencies (though they deal with many in-session emergencies of scheduled clients—more about this later). The difference between models that accept walk-ins versus those that do not is minimal. In fact, the only difference between these two models is an administrative one. A therapy office that accepts walk-in clients must have on-call therapists or intake workers who can see clients on the spur of the moment. This is becoming a rare model given the cost implications of having a staff person not engaged with a client for several hours if no walk-in clients seek services.

The difference between the screening-first versus immediate-intake models is substantial, however. If a screening is conducted first, the first contact between therapist and client is completely different than if such a screening does not take place. If a therapy office moves directly to the intake process, the screening purposes and contents need to be incorporated into the intake and a longer first session may be needed. Both models have advantages and disadvantages. The model that will be presented here is the screening-first model because it allows for more flexibility and often for more differentiated treatment planning for the therapist.

Purpose and Content of Screening Interviews

Generally, clients are asked before the screening to complete and sign a written informed consent form and to fill in various questionnaires about themselves before they actually meet with a therapist or intake worker. The first screening task that must therefore be accomplished with all clients is to ascertain that the client has read and signed the center's or individual therapist's informed consent form and completed the necessary questionnaires (Anderson, 1996; Corey, Corey, & Callanan, 1988). Once this task has been fulfilled, the actual screening can begin. (A sample consent form is shown in Figure 1.1. Text continues on p. 24.)

The initial screening with a potential client has several purposes, covers very specific contents, and follows a process that is distinctly different from the process

Psychological Services Center   Date: _____
3211 Providence Drive
Anchorage, Alaska 99508   Name: _____

Welcome to the Psychological Services Center. This document contains important information about our center's professional services and business policies. Please read it carefully and note any questions you might have so you can discuss them with the clinician conducting your screening appointment. Once you sign this consent form, it will constitute an agreement between you, your therapist(s), and the Psychological Services Center (PSC).

Nature of Psychological Services

Psychotherapy is not easily described because it varies greatly depending on the therapist, the client, and the particular problems a client presents. There are often a variety of approaches that can be used to deal with the problem(s) that brought you to therapy. These services are generally unlike any services you may receive from a physician in that they require your active participation and cooperation.

Psychotherapy has both benefits and risks. Possible risks may include the experience of uncomfortable feelings (such as sadness, guilt, anxiety, anger, frustration, loneliness, or helplessness) or the need to recall unpleasant events in your life. Potential benefits include significantly reduced feelings of distress, better relationships, better problem-solving and coping skills, and the resolution of specific problems. Given the nature of psychotherapy, it is difficult to predict exacly what will happen, but your therapist will do her or his best to make sure that you will be able to handle the risks and experience at least some of the benefits. However, psychotherapy remains an inexact science and no guarantees can be made regarding outcomes.

Procedures

Therapy usually starts with an evaluation. It is our practice at the PSC to conduct an evaluation that lasts from two to four sessions. This evaluation begins with a screening appointment and is followed up with an intake interview (that may last one to three sessions). During the evaluation, several decisions have to be made: the therapist has to decide if the PSC has the services needed to treat the problem(s) you discuss, you as the client have to decide if you are comfortable with the therapist that has been assigned to you, and both you and your assigned therapist have to decide on your goals for therapy and how best to achieve them.

In other words, by the end of the evaluation, your therapist will offer you initial impressions of what therapy will involve, if you decide to continue. Therapy

---

FIGURE 1.1   Sample Informed Consent

Note: This informed consent was developed by this author for use at the Psychological Services Center at the University of Alaska Anchorage based on a sample provided by Drs. Bruce Bennett and Eric Harris of the American Psychological Association during an APA- and AKPA-sponsored workshop on Risk Management in Psychology in Anchorage, Alaska, in November 1995. The original sample (called an Outpatient Service Contract) can be requested from the APA Insurance Trust at 750 First Street NE, Suite 605, Washington, DC 20002-4242.

generally involves a large commitment of time, money, and energy, so it is your right to be careful about the therapist you select. If you have questions about any of the PSC procedures or the therapist who was assigned to you, feel free to discuss these openly with the therapist. If you have doubts about the PSC or your assigned therapist, we will be happy to help you to make an appointment with another mental health professional.

If you decide to seek services at the PSC, your therapist will usually schedule one fifty-minute session per week at a mutually agreed time (under some special circumstances sessions may be longer or more frequent). This appointment will be reserved for you on a regular basis and is considered a standing appointment (i.e., if you miss one week, you will still have the same appointment time next week). The overall length of psychotherapy (in weeks or months) is generally difficult to predict, but this is something your therapist will discuss with you as the initial treatment plan is shared with you after completing the evaluation.

Fee-Related Issues

The PSC works on a sliding fee schedule that will be discussed with you during your screening appointment. Screening appointments always cost $10. Fees for therapy range from $5 to $80, depending on your income and the therapist. In addition to charging for weekly appointments, the PSC also charges special fees for other professional services you may require (such as telephone conversations that last longer than 10 minutes, meetings or consultations you have requested with other professionals, etc.). In unusual circumstances, you may become involved in litigation wherein you request or require your therapist's (and her or his supervisor's) participation. You will be expected to pay for such professional time required even if your therapist is compelled by another party to testify.

You will be expected to pay for each session at the time it is held, unless you and your therapist agreed otherwise. Payment schedules for other professional services will be agreed to at the time these services are requested. In circumstances of unusual financial hardship, you may negotiate a fee adjustment or installment payment plan with your assigned therapist. Once your standing appointment hour is scheduled, you will be expected to pay for it (even if you missed it) unless you provide a 24-hours advance notice of cancellation.

To enable you and your therapist to set realistic treatment goals and priorities, it is important to evaluate what resources are available to pay for your treatment. If you have a health benefits policy, it will usually provide some coverage for mental health treatment if such treatment is provided by a licensed professional. Your therapist will provide you with whatever assistance necessary to ensure that you receive the benefits to which you are entitled, including completing insurance forms as appropriate. However, you (*not* your insurance company) are responsible for full payment of the fee. If your therapist is a trainee, you will not be able to use your insurance benefits.

Carefully read the section in your insurance coverage booklet that describes mental health services, and call your insurer if you have any questions. Your therapist will provide you with all necessary information, based on this person's experience, and will be happy to assist you in understanding the information you

FIGURE 1.1   *Continued*

receive from your carrier. The escalation of the cost of health care has resulted in an increasing level of complexity about insurance benefits that often makes it difficult to determine exactly how much mental heath coverage is available. "Managed Health Care Plans" such as HMOs and PPOs often require advance authorization before they will provide reimbursement for mental health services. These plans are often oriented towards a short-term treatment approach designed to resolve specific problems that are interfering with level of functioning. It may be necessary to seek additional approval after a certain number of sessions.

Although a significant amount of work can be accomplished in short-term therapy, many clients feel that additional services are necessary after the insurance benefits expire. Some managed care plans will not allow your therapist to provide reimbursed services to you once your benefits are no longer available. If this is the case, PSC staff will do their best to find another provider who will help you continue your psychotherapy.

Please be aware that most insurance agreements require you to authorize your therapist to provide a clinical diagnosis and sometimes additional clinical information such as treatment plans or summaries or, in rare cases, a copy of the entire record. This information will become part of the insurance company's files and, in all likelihood, some of it will be computerized. All insurance companies claim to keep such information confidential, but once they receive it, your therapist has no control over what your insurer will do with the information. In some cases, the insurer may share the information with a national medical information data bank.

It is best to discuss all the information about your insurance coverage with your therapist. This will enable you to decide what can be accomplished within the parameters of the benefits available to you and what will happen if the insurance benefits run out before you are ready to end treatment. It is important to remember that you always have the right to pay for psychological services yourself if you prefer to avoid involving your insurer.

Contact Hours

The PSC is open from 9 A.M. to 5 P.M. daily, but some evening and weekend appointments may be available. Your therapist is generally not available for telephone services, but you can cancel and reschedule sessions with the assistance of the receptionist or by leaving confidential messages on the answering machine. If you need to reschedule an appointment, your therapist will make every effort to return your call on the same day, with the exception of calls made after hours or on weekends and holidays. If possible, please leave some times when you will be available. If you have an emergency but are unable to reach your therapist, call your family physician, emergency services at Southcentral Counseling Center, or the emergency room at the Providence or Charter Northstar Hospital. Please note that the PSC itself does not have emergency services or facilities.

Videotaping and Record-Keeping Procedures

Because the PSC is a training facility for therapists, all client sessions are videotaped. These tapes are made for supervision purposes only and are kept locked and in a

FIGURE 1.1   *Continued*

confidential location until the therapist has reviewed them with the supervisor. Once tapes have been reviewed with the supervisor, they are erased. Most tapes are erased in less than a week. In addition to videotapes, therapists also keep case notes. The case notes are reviewed by the therapist's supervisor and then are filed permanently in a client's record. All records, including case notes, are locked and kept strictly confidential. Information in the client records may be used for research and service planning purposes. Such use is entirely anonymous, and no individual client data will ever be used. No client names are ever associated with data extracted from records for research purposes and all data will merely be presented in group data format, a format that preserves anonymity and confidentiality as it never reveals individual client data.

Both law and the standards of the profession of psychology require that therapists keep treatment records. You are entitled to receive a copy of these records, unless your therapist believes that seeing them would be emotionally damaging to you. If this is the case, your therapist will be happy to provide your records to an appropriate mental health professional of your choice. Although you are entitled to receive a copy of your records if you wish to see them, your therapist may prefer to prepare an appropriate summary instead. Because client records are professional documents, they can be misinterpreted and can be upsetting. If you insist on seeing your records, it is best to review them with your therapist so that the two of you can discuss what they contain. Clients will be charged an appropriate fee for any preparation time that is required to comply with an informal request for record review.

If you are under 18 years of age, please be aware that the law may give your parents the right to examine your treatment records. It is PSC policy to request a consent agreement from parents to give up access to your records. If they agree, your therapist will provide your parents only with general information regarding how your treatment is proceeding, unless the risk is high that you will seriously harm yourself or another person. In such instances, your therapist may be required by law to notify your parents of this concern. Parents of minors can also request a summary of their child's treatment when it is complete. Before giving your parents any information, your therapist will discuss this matter with you and will do his or her best to resolve any objections you may have about what will be discussed. Please note that the PSC does not provide treatment to minors without their parents' consent.

Confidentiality

In general, the confidentiality of all communications between a client and a psychologist is protected by law, and your therapist can release information to others about your therapy only with your written permission. However, there are a number of exceptions:

1. In most judicial proceedings, you have the right to prevent your therapist from providing any information about your treatment. However, in some circumstances (such as child custody proceedings and proceedings in which your emotional condition is an important element), a judge may require your

FIGURE 1.1   *Continued*

therapist's testimony if the judge determines that resolution of the issues demands it.

2. There are times when it may be helpful for other professionals to gain access to all or parts of your treatment records. Under such circumstances data can be released from your PSC record if you give your therapist written permission (in the form of a Release of Information) to do so. *Such release cannot take place unless you consent in writing.*

3. There are some situations in which your therapist is legally required to take action to protect others from harm, even if such action requires revealing some information about your treatment:

   • If your therapist believes that a child, an elderly person, or a disabled person is being abused, the therapist is required by law to file a report with the appropriate state agency (in Alaska this is the Department of Family and Youth Services).

   • If your therapist believes that you are threatening serious bodily harm to another person, the therapist is required by law to take protective action, which may include notifying the potential victim, notifying the police, or seeking appropriate hospitalization.

   • If you threaten to harm to yourself (e.g., suicide), your therapist is required to make all necessary arrangements to protect your safety, a process that may include seeking hospitalization for you, or it may mean contacting family members or others who can help provide protection.

   • At the PSC, virtually all therapists are students in a clinical psychology program and therefore are not yet licensed to work independently. As such, all therapists in the PSC are working under the supervision of licensed psychologists who meet with each therapist on a weekly basis to review client cases. Your case will be discussed during these weekly meetings between your therapist and the therapist's supervisor. The supervisor is a part of the PSC staff and is bound by the same confidentiality laws as your therapist. The supervisor and therapist will also review therapy tapes as necessary for the therapist's education.

   • At the PSC, all therapists participate in weekly staff meetings. These meetings are used as opportunities for consultation, and within each session a client case is presented. Your case may be one of those presented during these meetings. The meetings are confidential and only PSC staff participate. Only first names of clients are used, and all members of the PSC staff are bound by the same confidentiality laws as your therapist.

Signatures Verifying Agreement

Your signature below indicates that you have read the information in this document, that you have understood it, and that you agree to abide by its terms as long as you are a PSC client.

_____   _____
Client Signature and Date   Witness Signature and Date

FIGURE 1.1   *Continued*

followed both in an intake and in a therapy session. Such an initial screening has also been referred to as a mental health triage, especially if it occurs under walk-in circumstances. This label has come about because such a screening is similar to a medical triage, which has the purpose of defining the scope and nature of the problem and making quick decisions about the further dispensation of a client. However, this is where the similarity to the medical model ends. The screening session in a mental health setting is more focused and often lengthier than a medical triage. It also does not always occur in the context of an emergency. The primary purposes of a screening session are:

- to familiarize the client with client rights and clinic procedures (e.g., informed consent, fee schedules)
- to define the scope and nature of the presenting problem
- to assess the appropriateness of agency (or therapist) and the service that can be provided for client
- to begin rapport building

Familiarizing Clients with Rights and Procedures (Obtaining Informed Consent)

This section of the screening is best broached immediately on entry into the treatment room. Because it is best introduced by setting it apart from the rest of the screening process, a good way to introduce it is by beginning with, "Before we get started, I want to talk to you about the Informed Consent form you read and signed before we came in here. I just wanted to reiterate that. . . ." Clients are thus familiarized with their consumer protection rights. These consumer rights will not be repeated here because they have been amply covered in this chapter and in other literature (e.g., through ethical guidelines provided by relevant associations such as the American Psychological Association [APA, 1992] and the American Counseling Association [ACA, 1995], as well as through books written on the topic [Anderson, 1996; Corey, Corey, & Callanan, 1988; Herlihy & Corey, 1992, 1996; Swenson, 1997]).

If the ethical information about client rights listed here is dealt with nonverbally through an informed consent form that was signed by clients before they were invited into the session, it is the therapist's responsibility to ask their clients whether they have read the informed consent agreement and understood it. Clients are invited to ask questions about the informed consent, and it is often a good idea to probe with a couple of questions to make sure clients have truly read and understood what they signed (e.g., "Did the information about the fact that we cannot guarantee successful outcomes for therapy make sense to you?", "Did you have any questions about my supervisor/consultant?", "Do you know what information your insurance carrier requires from me to make reimbursements to you?").

Obtaining informed consent from the client is important not only so that the client knows what to expect with regard to therapy, but also to protect the therapist from unnecessary or inappropriate lawsuits. For example, informed consent forms and conversations generally cover the exceptions to confidentiality such as the duty to report, to protect, and to warn. As such, if one of these duties must be invoked during treatment, the mental health professional can be assured that the exception to confidentiality should not come as an utter surprise to the client. In other words, therapists can ask their clients to recall the informed consent they rendered at the beginning of treatment when difficult therapeutic situations arise that may require the breach of confidentiality. Practitioners who fail to collect informed consent leave themselves vulnerable to lawsuits for negligence or malpractice because they have neither established a contract with the client nor informed the client of potential risks, such as the possibility of being reported to child protection services (Arthur & Swanson, 1993; Corey, Corey, & Callanan, 1988).

Finally, toward the latter part of the screening, as the therapist begins to make decisions about treatment plans, she or he may begin to address issues of length of treatment, client and therapist involvement, and type of therapy approaches that may be chosen for the client's treatment. However, it is often the case that these decisions are not made by the person doing the screening. Often the screener is not actually the person who will be working with the client in therapy. If this is the case, then these discussions will be postponed until the end of the intake session. If this information is covered in the preliminary screening, it will be brought up again at the end of the intake, at which time the therapist will have a much clearer idea about what course therapy will take. The issue of involving clients in the treatment plan process will be addressed in the relevant chapter later in this book.

Content, Scope, and Nature of the Presenting Problem

Once the issue of informed consent has been settled with the client, the screener is ready to move on to the most important aspect of the screening interview: the definition of the scope and nature of the problem presented by the client. This discussion is best introduced with a question regarding the client's decision to come to the clinic. The question *"Why did you decide to come for therapy at this time?"* is recommended over all others because it emphasizes the client's choice and decision-making process and does not imply anything that cannot be guaranteed by the therapist (as would the opening question used by some therapists of "How can I help you?"). Further, it generally prevents wisecracks by a client so inclined that are sometimes elicited by the question, "What brought you here?" (e.g., answered with "My car."). Other opening questions may be perceived as rude (e.g., "What is your problem?"), or as challenging or uninviting (e.g., "Why are you here?"), or too vague (e.g., "Tell me about yourself."). Once the opening question has been asked, the screener must be flexible enough to follow the client's lead, yet structured enough to elicit sufficient information to answer the question about the service eligibility of the client at this clinic or with this clinician. The following questions need to be answerable once the screener has completed the inquiry into the scope and nature of the presenting problem:

1. What is the overriding presenting concern?
2. What are the circumstances?
   - When does the problem arise?
   - Where does the problem arise?

- How does the problem arise?
- With whom does the problem arise?
- How often does the problem arise?
- How intense is the problem?

3. What is the history of the presenting concern?
   - How long has the problem been occurring?
   - How has the problem changed over time?
   - When is the first time the problem was noticed?
   - When is the last time the problem was not at all present?
4. Why is the client seeking treatment now (i.e., what was the precipitating event)?

Once these questions are answerable, the screener has met the primary purpose of the screening interview. It is important to note the difference here between a screening and an intake interview. The screening is concerned only about the presenting concern, its scope and nature, and its appropriateness for treatment at the given clinic. Of course, it also has to assess the client's need for crisis services, but this is generally not of primary importance unless the client was a walk-in client who was clearly in crisis. The intake will address itself to a much vaster information-gathering process. It will explore the greater context of the client and will delve into a variety of contents. The screening interview is not the place for such extensive data gathering.

Determining Service Eligibility and Appropriateness

Once clinicians have sufficiently queried their clients with regard to their presenting concerns, they must decide about the client's appropriateness for service at the clinic or with the clinician. This decision is best made on the spot so that it can be shared with the client immediately. However, sometimes this is not possible or allowed. It may not be possible if the clinicians who are screening are still unsure about some aspects of the client that they would like to explore further before making an eligibility decision. Sometimes, it may be impossible because the persons conducting screening are unsure of their own skills with regard to this type of decision-making and prefer to seek supervision or consultation. Sometimes the decision-making process is not allowed, as may be the case in some training clinics, where the persons conducting screening first have to present cases to their supervisors, consultants, or peer consultation groups before being allowed to render clinical judgments.

How the decision is made depends largely on clinic rules and clinician abilities. Some clinics have certain exclusion criteria. For example, some may not work with clients with significant substance use disorders, unless the clients first seek substance treatment on an inpatient basis. Some clinics will not work with clients who are prone to high-risk or emergency behaviors, such as borderline clients with frequent suicidal ideation and acting out behavior. Some clinics may not work with the chronically mentally ill, being unable or unwilling to provide maintenance therapy. With regard to clinician abilities, the limitations for service eligibility are defined by the clinician's scope of practice. Ethical guidelines by the American Psychological

Association and the ACA are clear that therapists or counselors must work within the limits of their training. Thus, some clinicians may have to turn down a client who requires an intervention or requests a type of treatment for which the therapist has not received adequate academic or professional preparation. One example may be a client who presents with symptoms that began in the aftermath of a serious head injury. Such a client may need to be referred for assessment by a neuropsychologist, as well as to care by a physician. Another example may be a client with chronic pain who is seeking a biofeedback intervention.

Sometimes service eligibility is also guided by the severity of the client's presenting concern. For instance, if the client's presenting concern is severe suicidal ideation and the potential for acting this out, a referral for inpatient treatment may need to be made (after the interviewer switches to a crisis assessment mode with the client). Another example may be a client who is clearly psychotic and who may be in need of psychiatric care, either inpatient or outpatient. Another possibility may be a client who, although presenting alone, actually has a presenting concern that involves a spouse, significant other, or family member. If the clinic or clinician is not able to deal with any other type of therapy beyond individual therapy, this client may need to be referred to a couples or family therapist.

If service eligibility is decided on during the screening, the screening interviewer then informs the client of the decision and attempts to facilitate the recommendations as much as possible. In other words, if the interviewer decides the client is eligible for services in the clinic, this person would then explain to the client what happens next (e.g., will someone call the client; will the client see the receptionist immediately to schedule the next appointment). If the client will be referred elsewhere, the interviewer needs to provide the client with several resources and phone numbers and needs to explain the procedure for contacting the referred service provider. If an emergency intervention is necessary, the client will be dealt with as indicated by the particular crisis intervention.

Rapport Building

Throughout the screening interview, interviewers must be aware that they are also potentially giving clients their first experience with a mental health care provider. Thus, even though the screening interviewer may not ultimately be the therapist who will be assigned to the client, that person must still make every effort at building positive rapport with the client. This rapport can be viewed as clinic rapport as opposed to individual rapport. In other words, even though the interviewer may never see this client again, this person will give the client the first impression of the clinic. Thus, the more positive this contact, the more likely that the client will return for services. An interviewer who is rude, hostile, or unable to interact positively with the client may suggest to the client that this is not a place where the client wants to seek services, or may even turn the client away from seeking mental health services at all. Rapport building skills have been addressed in a multitude of counseling and therapy books and hence will not be dealt with in great detail here. The interested reader is referred to Cormier and Cormier (1991), Egan (1994), or Ivey, Ivey, and Simek-Morgan (1997) for more information. A discussion of rapport building with children, which may differ significantly from therapeutic work with adults, is presented by Brems (1993).

Basic rapport building refers to the development of a relationship with the client that will facilitate change for the client in an atmosphere of respect, caring, and realistic appraisal. It implies that the client feels comfortable with the therapist from several vantage points. First, the client must perceive the clinician as trustworthy (Cormier & Cormier, 1991). Such trustworthiness must be earned, and this is generally accomplished through putting into motion the many positive therapist traits that were outlined earlier. In other words, the therapist who deals with the client in a respectful manner, who reflects warmth, genuineness, and concern, and who treats the client as an equal who has important contributions to make to the therapy process will more likely be trusted by the client than the clinician who is confrontational, rude, or self-aggrandizing. Trustworthiness also implies that the client feels comfortable that the clinician will maintain confidentiality and will keep the client safe by setting appropriate therapeutic limits and making an appropriate treatment plan. Second, the client must view the therapist as an expert (Cormier & Cormier, 1991). This person must walk away from the interaction feeling comfortable that the clinician is well-trained, self-aware, open to new learning, skilled in helping clients with problems similar to those presented by the client, and capable of designing a treatment plan that will maximize therapeutic progress. Third, the client must perceive the therapist as someone who is a positive human being, concerned with the client's welfare. This is often referred to as counselor attractiveness. This term may be somewhat misleading, suggesting a strictly physical dimension in therapist evaluation. However, this is not so. Although physical attractiveness appears to be helpful in initial rapport building, with clients being more likely to continue to see a therapist whom they find physically attractive (Cormier & Cormier, 1991), this dimension of the relationship refers more strongly to the interpersonal attractiveness of the clinician. As such, it relates to the therapist's ability to put the client at ease, to reduce the client's initial anxiety, to convey a sense of shared humanity, to create positive expectations in the client about therapy, and to be a genuinely likable human being.

If the client finds the therapist trustworthy, expert, and attractive, treatment is likely off to a good start and more active rapport building can take place. This includes, but may not be limited to, therapist behaviors that engage clients in the therapy process, that encourage clients to share themselves with the therapist, that help clients recognize the value of therapy (counteracting any perceptions of stigma associated with the process), and that challenge clients to stretch themselves to find solutions to the problems that have become the focus of treatment. Behaviors that will facilitate these critical components of therapy success—in other words, those that support relationship building—include active listening, attention to nonverbal behaviors by the client, reassurance about the safety of the therapy process, structuring of the relationship and procedures, empathy, and the expression of understanding. All will reflect acceptance, optimism, support, respect, and caring. Rapport is greatly facilitated by therapists who can be themselves and who do not imply value judgments or create a power differential between client and therapist.

Although therapists are clearly the experts and their clients are clearly the persons seeking help, therapists who want to build good rapport will not make the mistake of feeling superior to the client or of presuming that they know their clients better than the clients know themselves. Instead, relationship building will be much easier if therapists and clients set out together in the attempt to help the clients decide how to improve their lives life or how to reduce their problems and pathology.

Process of Screening Interviews

Implied in the earlier statement that the screening and intake have vastly different purposes as far as data gathering is concerned, is the fact that the screening and intake also differ greatly with regard to the type of process that is anticipated in them. Further, both intake and screening are vastly different from actual therapy sessions. It is the responsibility of the screening interviewer to recognize these differences and to develop a distinct set of skills for the screening process. Specifically, the screening is usually:

- brief
- directive
- problem-focused
- future-oriented

Unlike an intake session, which can take as long as an hour-and-a-half to two hours, a screening session is brief, often lasting no more than twenty to thirty minutes. Unlike a therapy session that has a well-defined beginning and end that reflects either a 45- or 50-minute hour, the screening has a well-defined beginning, but ends whenever the screening interviewer decides that sufficient data have been gathered to answer the questions about the presenting concern and about service eligibility.

To be able to meet the objective of keeping the screening brief, the interviewer has to be directive and to the point. The interviewer will need to be very specific about what questions need to be asked and will not engage in much reflection and other listening strategies that tend to prolong client respnses. Because therapy is not the purpose of the screening, the interviewer remains focused on a single task, which is to collect data. Of course, if a client presents with a crisis, the interviewer may have to switch to crisis management mode. However, even crisis management mode is different from therapy. It tends to be much more compatible with a screening process, also being very directive, focused, and problem–definition oriented. Finally, the screening is future-, rather than past-oriented. In other words, the screening interviewer and the client are engaging in their interaction to define what the client needs from therapy in the future and how the client hopes to change later. This is very unlike the bulk of the intake, which is often past-oriented, exploring where clients have been, how they have developed, and what they have experienced. The process of a screening is often somewhat uncomfortable for new therapists because it is more focused and less client-centered. The therapist must take the lead in the session and is responsible for managing time and structure with the client.

Given the vast differences between screening, intake, and therapy sessions, screening interactions are often either begun or ended with the screening interviewer making the client aware of these differences. It is good practice to let the client know what to expect of therapy and of the intake process and how both are different from the screening meeting. Such a preparation for treatment can often make the difference between successfully initiating the client to therapy and losing the client to treatment altogether. Given the importance of this aspect of the screening process, a sample transcript is provided of an opening of a screening session that reflects this type of preparation of the client for what will happen next.

Therapy Transcript: Screening versus Therapy Introduction

(This is done toward the beginning of a screening interview; some of the extraneous transitional phrases may differ if the interviewer explains the difference toward the end of the screening.)

THERAPIST: All right, now that we have covered the information about your rights as a client and about our clinic procedures, let me tell you a little bit about what we will do today. As our secretary told you on the phone, this is a screening. In a screening what I do is to try to find out from you why you chose to come to our clinic and what you are hoping to get from therapy. We have only a limited amount of time together today, so I am going to be very focused—kind of like your doctor when you go there with a physical problem, I'm going to ask you a lot of questions about your concerns. I'm going to be very straightforward with my questions and will sort of keep us on track. I know that's probably pretty different from what you may have expected. And in fact, what I'm going to do today is not really therapy. In therapy, you'll be in charge of setting the agenda and you and your therapist will take a lot more time talking about any one topic. Your therapist won't have nearly as many questions as I'll have today and you will probably move at a slower pace that's more set by you. Please bear with me today—doing the screening is important because it helps me figure out if we can help you and if we are able to develop a therapy plan here in the clinic that would meet your needs. For you the screening is important too because it helps you get focused on why you're here and what you are hoping to get out of therapy. Do you have any questions?

CLIENT: Yes, what if I'm not sure exactly what I want to get out of therapy?

THERAPIST: Yeah—that's actually true for many people who come to therapy. Usually people know what's going on in their lives that they don't like but they are not exactly sure how to change that. That's something you and I will start to work on together today but that's also something that will be an important part of your therapy!

CLIENT: Okay—well, when do I start therapy then? I thought I was starting today!

THERAPIST: Well, in a way you are starting. It's just that today I'm collecting information from you so we can decide if our clinic is the right place for you. Remember how I sort of explained earlier that no therapy can guarantee success? Well, different clinics can deal with different problems and in our clinic there are some problems we can't deal with. So today it's my job to figure out if we can help with the problems that you think are important in your life right now.

CLIENT: *(Still looks puzzled)*

THERAPIST: For example, we can't really work with people here who come in because they are very addicted to drugs. A person with a drug problem often needs detox and residential treatment and those are things we just can't do here. Or some people may want to kill themselves. They may need to be in a hospital to be safe—again that's something we can't do. Does that make more sense?

CLIENT: Yeah—now I understand. You want to find out if you can handle what I have to say.

THERAPIST: Yeah—I guess so! And then once I decide on that and you decide you want to keep doing this, we'll schedule you for an intake. And that's really the start of your therapy. How does that sound to you?

CLIENT: That's fine.

THERAPIST: Okay—then let's get started. What led you to decide to come to therapy at this time?

CLIENT: Well, I have been having problems sleeping and I have had some trouble keeping up with my work. My wife says I'm depressed but I'm not sure about that. I think I'm just having a hard time with my new boss. He's a real jerk.

And they're off. The next step is to explore the presenting concern and then to decide if the clinic or clinician can deal with the client. This feedback is then given to the client, and an intake session is scheduled if the client is accepted to the clinic. Assuming the presenting problem of this client is in line with what the clinic in the above example can manage, this might be how the session for this client ends.

THERAPIST: All right, now that we've reviewed why you are here and what you are hoping will change for you, I can tell you with confidence that we can work with you here at our clinic. The kinds of concerns that you have voiced today are well within the realm of things that we deal with here regularly, and we have several clinicians who have experience working with people like you. So if you would like to pursue therapy here, we can go ahead and get you scheduled for an intake. What would you like to do?

CLIENT: Yeah—I think I'd like to keep coming. Just talking to you about what's going on helped today. I actually have a better idea now than I did of why I'm here. So what happens next?

THERAPIST: Well, as soon as we leave the room here, you can go to the receptionist and tell him that you need to schedule an intake with one of our therapists.

Whoever the receptionist assigns you will be the person that you will work with from now on. The first appointment that the receptionist will schedule for you will be pretty long—about an hour and a half. But then once the intake is done, your sessions will generally be exactly fifty minutes long. You'll schedule your regular therapy time with your therapist directly at the end of your intake. The reception-ist only schedules screenings and intakes. After that you and your therapist work out a schedule that works well for the two of you. All right?

CLIENT: Sounds good.

THERAPIST: Okay—then that's it for today. Thank you very much for coming in. *(The therapist gets up, walks toward the door, slowing the pace to accommodate the client; once the client is up and ready to go, the therapist opens the door.)*

CLIENT: Thanks a lot!

THERAPIST: Take care.

CLIENT: Bye.

(The client leaves, and the therapist stays in the room.)

This transcript demonstrates that the screening interviewer needs to take care to let the client know what will happen next. It also shows some of the limits an in-terviewer and therapist may set with a client in terms of clinic procedures. For ex-ample, the therapist signals to the client that the session is definitely over by getting up and leading the client to the door. Once at the door, the therapist stops talking to the client about anything confidential. Similarly, should the client continue to talk about personal issues, the therapist would at that time ask the client to refrain from doing so to protect this person's privacy. The transcript also pointed out that thera-pists do not usually accompany their clients to see the receptionist. This is prefer-able because it clearly communicates that the interaction with the interviewer is over, and it eliminates social chitchat. Finally, the therapist chooses a closing that expresses concern and caring for the client.

SUMMARY AND CONCLUDING THOUGHTS

Successful initiation to therapy relies on a number of factors, including conducive therapist traits, an accepting office atmosphere, and a clear therapeutic and clini-cal structure. Therapist traits are important to the rapport building purpose of all interviews with clients. The office atmosphere assures that the client feels com-fortable and respected. Therapeutic structure models a lack of chaos and empha-sizes predictability, both being circumstances that are often problematic in clients' lives. It also protects the therapist from ethical charges and personal burnout. Ini-tiation of a client into therapy always begins with the assessment of the presenting concern and an evaluation of service eligibility in a certain setting and by a certain clinician. There are several models that accommodate these purposes. The one presented here consists of the movement from a screening interview (or mental health triage) to an intake assessment and finally to the transition into therapy. As a final note, some books have been written to facilitate the decision to enter the counseling profession and journey toward becoming a counselor (Blackstone, 1991; Brems, 1994; Hazler & Kottler, 1994; Kottler, 1997; Skovholt & Ronnestad, 1995). These books might be helpful to beginners who are still not sure about their chosen profession.

DOCUMENTATION AND RECORD-KEEPING

After the first contact with the client, the therapist must take care to open a case file or record for the client and to document properly any agreements that have been made with the client thus far, plus any assessments that have been conducted and conclusions drawn, any paperwork signed by the client, and any information received about the client from other sources. At a minimum, the record of the client at this point will contain a signed informed consent, a screening report, any signed releases of information about prior or related treatment or services, and documentation of the fee agreed on. The following is a sample of a screening report. This sample will provide the clinician with an idea of the type of information that must be recorded in this first report about a client after a screening has taken place.

Sample Screening Report

Client Name: Frederick X.   Screener Name: Mary Jones

Date of Birth: 23 June 1957   Screening Date: 23 August 1994

Address: 2319 Chugach Drive #3B   Phone Number: (907) 993–5678

Fee Arranged (see fee schedule): $60   Screening Tests Administered: MMPI-2

Informed Consent Signed: yes X no __   Informed Consent Verified: yes X no __

Definition, Scope, and History of Presenting Concerns (PCs)

Client Definition of the PCs

1. current acute depression marked by poor sleeping patterns (with initial and terminal insomnia leading to less than five hours of sleep per day), loss of appetite and sexual drive, dysphoric mood, poor concentration and attention, low energy
2. chronic low-grade depression since childhood manifested through low self-esteem, indecisiveness, lack of self-confidence, fear of loneliness, and constant dysphoria
3. social isolation, chronic with acute exacerbation

Circumstances and Scope of the PCs

1. when does the problem arise
   - at all times of day, with sleep disturbance being most bothersome at night
   - at all times of day, both current and chronic
   - at all times of day, both current and chronic
2. where does the problem arise
   - in all situations currently
   - in most situations, though it has not affected work or academic adjustment
   - in his social life; also manifests at work and the university, but not with problematic content attached
3. how does the problem arise
   - through major life stress precipitants that disrupt interpersonal relationships (e.g., deaths of intimate friends)
   - chronically manifested, through lifestyle or personality traits
   - when placed in social situations
4. with whom does the problem arise
   - pervasively with all people he comes in contact with
   - pervasively with all people he comes in contact with
   - pervasively with anyone with whom he has not developed a close, intimate friendship or relationship
5. how often does the problem arise
   - in response to major stressors only, at unpredictable time intervals
   - chronically
   - chronically
6. how intense is the problem
   - severe
   - moderate
   - severe in some circumstances; mild in others

History of the PCs

1. how long has the problem been occurring
   - two weeks
   - lifelong
   - lifelong
2. how has the problem changed over time
   - represents an acute recurrence of a problem manifested five years ago
   - no change
   - minimal change over the life span with a brief period of improvement five to seven years ago
3. when is the first time the problem was noticed
   - two weeks ago by significant other
   - five years ago when a major depression revealed the coexistence of a lifelong dysthymia
   - uncertain; perhaps in elementary school

4. when is the last time the problem was not at all present
  - more than two weeks and less than five years ago
  - not known; lifelong pattern
  - not known; lifelong pattern

Precipitating Event for the PCs

1. suicide of brother
2. no specific precipitant; lifelong familial predisposing factors (possibly including emotional and physical neglect)
3. no specific precipitant

Precipitating Event for Seeking Services

The suicide by his oldest brother two weeks ago stimulated acute depressive symptoms; these led the client's significant other to encourage him to seek therapy.

Other Information about the Client Available at This Time

History   (e.g., family history, social history, academic/occupational history, medical history, treatment history)

distant family relationships with possible history of physical and emotional neglect; family history (mother) of depression requiring inpatient treatment; socially isolated; stable academic and occupational history; positive relationship with significant other

Behavioral Observations

dysphoric behavior with restricted range of affect; good cognitive skills; no perceptual disturbances; cooperative though shy; responsive to questions though not spontaneous; well-groomed and dressed with no unusual mannerisms or body language; psychomotor retardation; some attention deficits; some depressive logic; denied suicidal ideation at this time (acknowledged suicidal thoughts five years ago)

Releases of Information (ROIs) Collected and Signed

ROI #1 for: N/A

ROI #2 for: N/A

ROI #3 for: N/A

Diagnostic Impressions

Axis I: R/O Major Depressive Disorder, Recurrent

  R/O Dysthymic Disorder

Axis II: R/O Dependent Personality Disorder with avoidant traits

Axis III: sleep and appetite disturbance

Axis IV: suicide of brother; social isolation

Axis V: 60—moderate symptoms

Recommendations for Acceptance

         __X__ definitely accept for services

         _____ accept only for further assessment

         _____ do not accept for services because _____

         _____ other: _____

_____   _____

Signature of Screener   Signature of Supervisor

2

THE INTAKE INTERVIEW

Our appearance, our words, our actions are never greater than
ourselves. For the soul is our house; our eyes its window;
and our words its messengers.
—KAHLIL GIBRAN

The intake interview is often the first time the assigned therapist and the client meet (unless the therapist conducted the screening as well). Thus this session has multiple purposes that must be attended to by the therapist. The intake is used (1) to establish a therapeutic relationship, (2) to gather information, and (3) to formulate a preliminary case conceptualization and treatment plan. It requires skills and procedures that are distinct from both screening and therapy sessions and therefore follows a format that requires the therapist to take an active and directive role. This reality requires some adjustment of procedures and clarification of the client–therapist relationship once the intake is complete and therapy begins.

Establishing a therapeutic relationship (rapport) is a critical component of the intake process. To help the client feel heard and understood, the therapist must be able to collect the necessary data from the client while remaining sensitive to the client's needs and feelings. The empathic skills that are necessary to build therapeutic rapport and facilitate the therapeutic process will be addressed in detail in Chapter 5 (and only briefly in this chapter). The focus of the current chapter will be on the type of information to be gathered during a routine intake exam. The reader must keep in mind that if a client presents with a crisis, suicidal or homicidal tendencies, or child abuse issues (in which the client is the perpetrator), the intake may need to be suspended and the therapist may need to switch to a crisis assessment and intervention mode. If this happens, the relationship between the client and therapist will change, though rapport building remains possible and is, in fact, critical. Further, case conceptualization merely begins in the intake interview and requires adjustment if additional assessments are necessary. Indeed, case conceptualizations are best viewed as evolving and dynamic because they are flexibly adapted to the constant flow of newly emerging information provided about the client as therapy progresses. How to go about conceptualizing a case will be detailed in Chapter 4.

PROCESS OF AN INTAKE INTERVIEW

The intake interview is generally very lengthy and is conducted in either a single lengthy session or over the course of two weeks. In general, it is best to plan up to two hours of time to accomplish the task of data gathering (see Seligman, 1996). The intake, not unlike the screening but very unlike therapy proper, is directive and highly focused. However, what makes the intake different from the screening is the fact that the intake is also strongly concerned with establishing therapeutic rapport and hence is much more client-centered than the screening (Kottler & Brown, 1992). The therapist takes a supporting role in the intake and is willing to make a detour in the plan for data gathering to accommodate the needs of the client, should painful emotions or important details emerge (see Beutler & Berren, 1995; Giordano, 1997). The intake is concerned with the whole client—that is, with all aspects of the client's history—in contrast to the screening, during which the therapist merely focuses on the specifics of the presenting concern. In the intake, the therapist wants to know about the client in that person's entire familial, social, and cultural context (see Cormier & Cormier, 1991; Cormier & Hackney, 1987; Morrison, 1995a). This curiosity about the entire interpersonal matrix of the client as well the client's intrapsychic state or personal style make the process both exploratory and explanatory. The exploration and explanation, however, remains largely unverbalized by the therapist. Instead, aspects of the process verbalized and expressed by the therapist at this stage are interest, caring, concern, and the desire to help; therapeutic interventions will come later (Cormier & Hackney, 1987). Conceptualizing the intake interview requires an evolving, process-oriented approach, not a static, mechanistic one. In fact, in the intake, the "how" of information delivery by the client is as important as, if not more important than, the "what" (Lemma, 1996).

The therapist will need to explain the nature of the intake to the client so that the client can understand the reason for all the questions (Morrison, 1995a; Seligman, 1996). This is particularly important because the therapist will request a significant amount of highly personal and sensitive information from the client. If the client does not understand why these questions are asked, and if the questions are not formulated carefully and respectfully, the client may resist and may even lose interest in the therapeutic process (Choca, 1988). A good introduction to the intake process is presented in the sample therapy transcript that follows.

Therapy Transcript: Intake Interview Introduction

(This is done at the very beginning of the intake interview.)

THERAPIST: Before we begin today, I wanted to explain to you what I am about to do. I am going to be asking you a lot of questions about a lot of things. We're not just going to talk about why you decided to come here, though that will be a part of it, but I am also going to ask you questions about your family background, your friends, your job, your school experiences, and your health. I am going to ask about all these things to try to help both of us understand how and why the concerns you have might have developed. How does that sound to you?

CLIENT: Well, I already talked a lot about why I'm here when I talked to the person who did the screening. Why do we have to cover that again?

THERAPIST: Well, I know it's a bit redundant for you but I would like to hear from you why you are here rather than just having read about it in your file. Plus it's been a couple of weeks since you were here the last time, so I'm also going to be curious about any changes that may have happened.

CLIENT: Well, nothing has changed.

THERAPIST: All right. How do you feel about my asking you a lot of other questions about your family and such?

CLIENT: I kind of figured you would. . . . *(shrugs)*

THERAPIST: Today will also be a little different from how things will go in the future because I do have all of these questions. Once I have asked you all about you, and you and I have decided on a course of action, you will be much more in charge of what we talk about. It will be up to you for the most part to bring up things and to decide what you want to talk about, and then I may be a bit quieter than I will be today. Today I'm going to ask a lot of questions and be pretty focused. Do you have any other questions, or should we start? Like do you have any more questions about confidentiality or any of the things you talked about during the screening?

CLIENT: No. Let's get started!

THERAPIST: I know you talked about this during the screening, but please fill me in anyway. What led you to decide to seek therapy at this time?

CLIENT: Well, I have been having trouble . . .

Once the opening introduction has been successfully communicated, the remainder of the intake interview will focus on the purposes of gathering data and building the client–therapist relationship. After all data have been gathered (the data to be gathered will be outlined in the next section), the therapist will do a summary of this understanding of the client's concerns, as well as a preliminary understanding of the case dynamics. Based on the perceived case dynamics, the therapist will also make several preliminary treatment recommendations and will discuss these with the client to make sure that therapist and client coincide with regard to what they hope to accomplish in treatment.

The therapist's role is also to pay attention to the client's emotional state and to assure that the client feels comfortable, not only throughout the interview, but especially during the closing comments (Kottler & Brown, 1992). The therapist should solicit from the client whether the client feels comfortable with the therapist or whether the client might prefer to work with someone else (Choca, 1988). The therapist needs to give the client an opportunity to ask questions about the upcoming therapy and about any content that emerged during the current session. If the client reveals previous therapeutic intervention or is currently under the care of a physician for what might be therapy-related symptoms, proper releases of information (ROIs) need to be collected at the close of the intake session.

Once therapists have concluded the summary, the client check-in, ROIs, and preliminary treatment recommendations, they must take some time to schedule the standing appointment with the client that they will have for the next few months. The therapist needs to stress that this 45- or 50-minute session will take place weekly, at the same time, and in the same place. A strong commitment must be elicited from the client to make the appointment time one that is convenient and appropriate for the client. Careful discussion of this issue may prevent client no-shows and cancellations. In addition to discussing issues of appointment scheduling, other structuring activities (see thorough discussion thereof in Chapter 1) may be engaged in by the therapist (although some of this may already have occurred during the screening process). For example, therapists must reassure themselves that the client is knowledgeable about fees, cancellation policies, the lack of a guarantee for success, the possibility of some negative emotions and side effects of therapy, and the requested commitment for therapy (Cormier & Cormier, 1991; Hutchins & Vaught, 1997; Morrison, 1995a). Finally, as partially outlined by Scissons (1993), by the end of the intake session, the therapist should be able to answer the following questions:

- Do I understand the issues of the client?
- Can I help this person competently?
- What are the client's therapy goals?
- What is the direction to take with this client?
- Which strategies are going to be most useful?
- Is the client motivated for treatment?
- Have I helped the client gain enough composure to leave?

Similarly, the client should have an understanding of a variety of issues as well (Scissons, 1993; Seligman, 1996). Namely, the client should:

- understand what therapy is about
- have a beginning sense of trust in and safety with the therapist
- believe in the therapist's interest and concern
- be satisfied with the therapist's competence
- have a positive sense toward therapy
- know what will happen next (what to expect)
- have a sense that treatment planning is well underway
- have a sense of closure

Therapy is most likely to succeed if therapist and client agree on the goals and processes of therapy and if they are well-matched with regard to values, philosophies, and ways of viewing the world (Beutler, Clarkin, Crago, & Bergen, 1991). If these connections can be made in the intake, therapy will begin positively.

RAPPORT BUILDING ISSUES

Throughout the data gathering process, the therapist must remember that rapport building is as important as data gathering. The essential components of therapeutic rapport that need to be established over time are: the therapist's commitment to the client and vice versa; the client's trust in the therapist as a caring human being and a knowledgeable expert in mental health issues; both the client's and therapist's belief in hope for change and improvement in the client, though this is felt foremost by the client; the client's belief in the therapist's good will and basic benevolence; the client's sense of safety that the therapist will not violate that trust, either through violations of confidentiality or through value judgments; the therapist's empathy for the client's situation and self-expression; the therapist's understanding of the client's unique situation; and the agreement of both on a structure for the relationship that keeps healthy boundaries and limits, and one that facilitates growth and change. Given these components of rapport and their importance, therapists must use their clinical judgment about when to abandon data gathering during an intake to maintain a good relationship with the client. For example, if very painful contents are discussed, it may be important to slow down and check with the client to make sure that they are not being overwhelmed with emotions or racing thoughts. This empathic listening and questioning style is critical and cannot be understated. Of course, it would be asking the impossible of the therapist to develop all components of therapeutic rapport in a single session. A therapeutic relationship develops over a long period of time; however, the foundation for it is often laid in the initial hour of interaction with the client, while the client's feelings of vulnerability are heightened by the newness of the situation.

The types of questions a therapist asks even during the intake session can set the tone regarding how therapist and client will work together. Even though the intake session involves a higher percentage of questions and a lower percentage of some of the more traditional therapeutic strategies (such as reflections, reframing comments, active listening, and so forth), it uses essentially the same skills as a therapy session (Seligman, 1996). In that sense, the intake truly sets the stage or lays the foundation for the therapy. To facilitate the best possible rapport, the therapist tries to avoid questions that antagonize the client; ones that can be perceived as having a value judgment about something the client has self-disclosed; ones that may embarrass, humiliate, or shame the client; and ones that are too vague or too specific to be of value. Vague questions tend to frustrate the client or heighten an anxious client's anxiety (Choca, 1988). Questions that are overly specific or ones that are closed do not help the therapist greatly in getting to know the client better. Vague questions can upset the client; overly specific questions can waste time. It is also best to ask questions in such a way that the client has much to say in response. Such open-ended questions, which often serve to clarify issues, assure that the client has plenty to say and share between questions. This will avoid "machine gunning" questions toward clients (Choca, 1988, p. 42). Although silence can be an excellent therapeutic strategy, it has limited utility in an intake. Silence is often used to raise anxiety in the client and/or to provoke a genuine response from the client. Raising anxiety in an intake session is not a good idea. Most clients come to the intake somewhat uneasy and concerned to begin with. The intake is best used to alleviate this unease and to put the client's worst fears to rest.

The best questions for an intake are open-ended questions about a specific topic or clarifying questions in response to something the client has revealed (Cormier & Hackney, 1987). Such questions clarify that the therapist has an agenda (i.e., wants to cover certain topics), yet is flexible enough to allow the client the necessary room within each topic to make shared information heard and understood. It is often possible to elicit more information from a client about a given topic by using nonverbal means of communicating understanding and interest, or by merely probing mildly about a statement the client has made. The therapist conducting the intake interview does not need to bombard the client with lists of questions to have hundreds of questions answered. This is a skill that may take some practice to develop, but it can be done. In choosing an approach for the intake, the therapist best remembers that the desired outcome of the intake for the client is that the client feels understood by the therapist, relieved by having obtained some catharsis, hopeful about the ability to change or improve, and motivated to begin work (Cormier & Hackney, 1987; Kottler & Brown, 1992). An intake has somehow gone awry if the client leaves feeling more anxious and/or emotionally vulnerable than before the intake, interrogated by having been approached as a nonperson, and/or evaluated by having been judged by the therapist (Cormier & Hackney, 1987).

For an intake interview, the hope is that the client leaves feeling at least slightly better than before, if only for the hope that was raised about potential change. This is different from therapy sessions, in which clients at times leave feeling worse than when they came in because of the content that may have been uncovered during a session. This deterioration in affective state can be tolerated by the client in later stages of treatment because by then the relationship with the therapist has been cemented and the client has begun to trust in the therapist's good will and knowledge about the procedures needed to help the client change or improve. However, it is rare that this level of trust and safety is developed by the end of an intake session. In other words, therapists, although asking numerous questions and eliciting a great deal of information, limit themselves in the amount of challenging, explaining, confronting, or interpreting done in the intake review. These catalysts of therapeutic change are saved for a later stage in the therapist–client relationship.

Another issue related to rapport building in the intake interview is that of taking notes while with the client. Although this is a common practice, it is not recommended (Seligman, 1996). Even Freud suggested that taking notes tends to create an emotional distance between client and therapist and often draws the therapist's attention away from the client. The therapist becomes so concerned with getting things down on paper that the person can miss essential emotional nuances in the client (especially those communicated nonverbally) and become an unempathic listener. Taking notes is appropriate only in settings where therapeutic rapport is not of issue; if a relationship is to be established, taking notes interferes. If therapists are worried about not remembering the content of an intake session with a client, then they should tape the session and review the tape when writing case notes or the intake report. Writing detailed notes and a report based on the history gathered in the intake is critical for several reasons. First, it forces the therapist to organize the information that was collected in a way that often facilitates case conceptualization. Second, it clarifies for the therapist where the client provided essential bits of information, thus providing the therapist a stimulus for further exploration of an area in a later session. Third, the therapist can later refer back to the notes and report to refresh the memory about essential historical aspects of the client. Such renewal of a therapist's memory is extremely helpful because clients truly appreciate therapists who can remember what the client has told them. This can often facilitate rapport and trust greatly as the client feels heard (and even understood).

CULTURAL SENSITIVITY

An issue essential to, but nevertheless separate from, rapport building needs to be discussed here—namely, the development of cultural sensitivity. This is of equal relevance to rapport building throughout the therapeutic process, the special assessment process, and any crisis procedures. In fact, without exercising sensitivity to cultural issues, rapport building is not possible. Therapists must evaluate their level of cultural sensitivity and must challenge themselves to think about their perceptions of other cultural groups. Gaining the skills and knowledge necessary to deal with a racially, ethnically, and culturally diverse clientele is as important to a therapist's education as gaining the basic skills and knowledge of assessment and therapy itself (Iijima Hall, 1997).

To begin the process of becoming culturally sensitive, it is important for the new therapist to learn a few specific definitions of terms commonly applied in the context of cultural sensitivity and awareness: namely, the labels of race, ethnicity, and culture. The term *race* refers to a biological classification that is based on physical and genetic characteristics. The three primary races identified belong to the groups Caucasoid, Mongoloid, and Negroid. *Ethnicity* refers to a shared social and cultural heritage as may be identified, for example, for Asian Americans or Alaska Natives. Finally, *culture* refers to learned behavior that is shared and transmitted within a group. Such transmission can occur across generations through the teaching of shared values and rules, or it can be conducted very consciously with new members, as can occur in gay and lesbian cultures. For example, members of the Jewish faith constitute an ethnic group with a shared social, cultural, and religious heritage, though they do not constitute a race. White members of society also constitute an ethnic group in the United States. Like most ethnic groups, this group has a number of cultures within it, such as Irish Americans, Italian Americans, German Americans, and so forth, each of which shares a learned set of behaviors. Although ethnic or cultural status often overlaps with minority status of a group of people, this is not always so. A comprehensive approach to multigroup or multicultural sensitivity therefore must encompass not only ethnicity and culture, but also minority status. Minority status as relevant in the therapy context is not related to the actual number of people within a specific group. Instead, a minority group is best defined as

> A group of people who, because of physical or cultural characteristics, are singled out from others in the society in which they live for differential and unequal treatment, and who therefore regard themselves as objects of collective discrimination. . . . Minority status carries with it the exclusion from full participation in the life of the society (Wirth, 1945, p. 347).

This definition characterizes a number of groups in U.S. society who are oppressed and, as a result, are not able to participate fully in society as a whole. It also makes the conceptual identification of a minority one separate from the numerical concept. For example, in most countries, women suffer from oppression at the hands of males, rendering them a conceptual minority, despite being a numerical majority. Using this definition, other minorities include individuals with physical disabilities, the elderly, gays and lesbians, and individuals who are economically disadvantaged. Thus the therapist in a culturally diverse society works not only with individuals who vary in terms of ethnic or cultural background, but also in terms of the various avenues of oppression.

The term race, properly defined, is purely biological in nature and hence does not have direct psychological consequences. It is often perceived as derogatory, it carries significant stereotypes with it, and thus it has generally fallen into disuse. Ethnic and cultural differentiations, as well as minority status, on the other hand, have social and psychological relevance by contributing greatly to the self development of their members. Often members of a specific ethnic, cultural, or minority group cannot be understood properly if taken out of the contextual or multicultural matrix of relationships. Thus ethnic, cultural, and other group variables have great impact on social and psychological issues and must be considered with regard to their implications for diagnostic and therapeutic work.

In recognition of the diversity of the population inside and outside the United States and the need to provide mental health services adequately and appropriately to all ethnic, cultural, and minority members of a given society, the American Psychological Association and other professional mental health organizations have expressed strong support of the need for therapists to be culturally sensitive and for training programs to help meet this need. For example, the American Psychological Association's ethical guidelines clearly require that, "psychologists are aware of cultural, individual, and role differences, including those due to age, gender, race, ethnicity, national origin, religion, sexual orientation, disability, language, and socioeconomic status" (American Psychological Association, 1992, p. 1599). Similarly, the need to include cultural issues in all therapists' training was advanced by the National Conference on Graduate Education in Psychology (American Psychological Association, 1987) when this committee stated that, "psychologists must be educated to realize that all training, practice, and research in psychology are profoundly affected by the cultural, subcultural, and national contexts within which they occur" (p. 1079). Thus there is a growing recognition from professional organizations, as well as from individual practitioners, for therapists to become culturally sensitive, thereby to meet the needs of a culturally diverse population (see Iijima Hall, 1997; Ponterotto, Casas, Suzuki, & Alexander, 1995).

Cultural sensitivity can be learned and has a number of specific components, most importantly awareness, knowledge, and skills. Simply put, awareness is gained through self-reflection and respect for others, as well as through the strong recognition of and belief in the notion that difference does not equal deviance (Namyniuk, 1996); knowledge can be accumulated through clinicians' familiarizing themselves with cultural, anthropological, historical, and related events involving or affecting all cultural and ethnic groups with whom they anticipate working (see Chapters 5 through 9 in Ponterotto, Casas, Suzuki, & Alexander, 1995); and skill is developed through learning about alternative approaches to intervention, reducing prejudicial or stereotyped use of language, and becoming politically active (Ivey, 1995). Therapists who strive to be culturally sensitive need to be able to claim that all three of these traits are part and parcel of their repertoire of skills and beliefs. Each of the three categories is best defined through subcategories and examples. The following listings provide this information (adapted from Johnson, 1993).

Culturally Aware Therapists:

- are aware of and sensitive to their own cultural heritage
- are conscious and embracing of all minority groups of which they are members
- value and respect cultural differences
- are aware of their own values and biases and their effect on therapy
- are sensitive to neither overemphasizing or underemphasizing therapist–client cultural differences
- feel comfortable with cultural differences between themselves and their clients
- demonstrate sensitivity to situations that may require referral of a minority client to a member of the same cultural heritage

Culturally Knowledgeable Therapists:

- understand how the sociopolitical system in the United States treats minorities
- know about the presence and various manifestations of racism, sexism, and heterosexism and their effects on minorities
- are familiar with the history of mental health treatment for minorities and potential biases of traditional psychotherapy theories
- have an awareness of cultural definitions of mental illness and perspectives on mental health services
- are knowledgeable about cultural and minority groups in the United States
- possess specific knowledge about particular groups with whom they are working

- have clear and explicit knowledge and understanding of the generic characteristics of therapy
- are familiar with cross-cultural applications of psychotherapy skills
- are aware of the effects the therapy setting and office can have on minority clients
- are knowledgeable about institutional barriers that prevent minorities from using mental health services

Culturally Skillful Therapists:

- are adept at adjusting communication and therapeutic style to match individual clients' needs
- know how to place the appropriate amount of attention on the role of culture
- do not categorize individuals according to stereotypes and prejudices
- are respectful and flexible in providing services to meet the individual needs of clients
- exercise intervention skills as the needs of the client dictate and as appropriate to clients' personal contextual backgrounds
- act as social change agents to help reduce or eliminate racism, sexism, and heterosexism
- use language that is devoid of prejudice and bias

Not only can cultural sensitivity be learned, it can also be measured (Ponterotto & Alexander, 1996). This measurement is based in the belief that regardless of how well-trained counselors are in certain multicultural skills or how well they choose techniques or tests based on their clients' cultural and ethnic backgrounds, ultimately any tool is only as good (i.e., as multiculturally competent) as the persons using it. In other words, "what is of paramount importance is the clinician's multicultural awareness, knowledge, and interpretive skill" (Ponterotto & Alexander, 1996, p. 651). A number of instruments (for example, the Cross-Cultural Counseling Inventory-R [LaFramboise, Coleman, & Hernandez, 1991], the Multicultural Awareness–Knowledge–and–Skills Survey [D'Andrea & Daniels, 1991; D'Andrea, Daniels, & Heck, 1991], and the Multicultural Counseling Inventory [Sodowsky, Taffe, Gutkin, & Wise, 1994]) exist for this purpose, and the interested reader is referred to Suzuki, Meller, and Ponterotto (1996) for more information.

Once therapists have mastered the art of building rapport successfully, respectfully, and efficiently, they are ready to begin the data gathering phase of the intake process. The data collection phase of the intake process should proceed efficiently and effectively as long as therapists are continually aware of their impact on their clients. Respect, empathy, concern, and sensitivity to clients' needs greatly facilitate the process of soliciting information from clients. They communicate to clients that despite the difficult and sensitive nature of information that is being sought, therapists can assure the clients' safety and integrity, as well as their ability to leave the intake session intact and hopeful.

DATA GATHERING IN THE INTAKE INTERVIEW

Significant consensus exists in the literature with regard to the type of data that needs to be gathered in the intake session. In fact, this consensus is so great that no sources will be referenced in this part of the intake discussion. The interested reader can refer to Cormier and Cormier (1991), Choca (1988), Kottler and Brown (1992), Morrison (1995a), Palmer and McMahon (1997), Beutler and Berren (1995), and Seligman (1996) for more information and additional reading. The flow of the session as outlined here has been developed through clinical experience. It is a logical flow that is less choppy than some outlines that have been suggested elsewhere.

The Presenting Concern

The intake session, and thus therapy in general, begins most concretely with the opening question of "What led you to decide to seek therapy at this time?" The response to this question becomes the client's presenting concern. From there, the therapist needs to explore the presenting concern in detail. How many questions are necessary will depend entirely on the client. Some clients respond to the opening question with a great deal of detail; some give a very brief and unelaborated response. The goal with regard to the presenting concern is to be able to answer a series of questions about it (see below). However, this does not imply that the therapist would ask exactly these questions of the client or would even approach them in exactly the sequence with which they are presented here. Rather, the therapist will attempt to have information about these questions by the end of this segment of the intake. In other words, there may be great variation with regard to the sequencing of questions pinpointing the presenting concern, but the actual subsections of intake inquiry remain distinct. This is true for all intake subsections. Within each section, questions may follow outlines like the ones provided here or they may meander, but the overall sequencing recommended below should be adhered to by novice therapists to ensure that all information is gathered. More seasoned clinicians will learn to be even more flexible in their data gathering, asking questions as they emerge in the interview and remembering what has been asked and what has not. The main point is to gather all the information, yet not become a slave to the outline format suggested here.

Issues to Be Addressed about the Presenting Concern

1. What is the primary presenting concern?
2. What are the circumstances?
   - When does the problem arise?
   - Where does the problem arise?
   - How does the problem arise?
   - With whom does the problem arise?
   - How often does the problem arise?
   - How intense is the problem?

3. What is the history of the presenting concern?
   - How long has the problem been occurring?
   - How has the problem changed over time?
   - When is the first time the problem was noticed?
   - When is the last time the problem was not at all present?
4. What does the client want from therapy?
5. How would the client's life be different, if the presenting concern were to disappear right now?
6. Why is the client seeking treatment now (what was the precipitating event)?

These questions will demonstrate that the presenting concern is seen as complex and interpreted in a detailed manner. It is not enough to know why the client came; it is as, if not more, important to know how the presenting concern is manifested in a variety of situations, how it developed over the years, and how it may have changed and intensified. Understanding the various components of the presenting concern often lays the groundwork for understanding the client and for conceptualizing the case. Although it often has direct implications for treatment as well, analyzing the presenting concern is necessary, but not sufficient. More data about the client are generally needed to make a confident decision about treatment and conceptualization. The precipitating event for seeking treatment often provides great insight into the client's motivation for therapy. If the precipitating event is a spouse threatening divorce unless the client changes, the motivation for treatment is external, not internal, and may not be as powerful as if the client saw a strong internal reason to change. Similarly, if the client begins therapy because of a court order, the client's own interest in the request for help in changing a behavior cannot be taken for granted.

Asking the client how life would change often helps the therapist gain an appreciation of what life circumstances may be maintaining a client's presenting problem. People may say they want to change, but may not always mean it completely. For example, a client may arrive for counseling who has been mildly suicidal and depressed for several years. He relates various symptoms of depression and talks about how this has taken a toll on his marriage, has led to many fights with his wife, and has even caused occasional trial separations. Each time, his wife returned to live with him because of a suicidal gesture. What will this man's motivation for change be if he believes one of the things that will change should he improve will be a potential divorce from his wife (who will no longer be "trapped" in the relationship by his suicidal behavior)? Such secondary gain from presenting symptoms is not unusual, though it may not always be as overt or monumental; mild reinforcers for symptoms exist in many clients' lives. Sometimes enablers are present in persons' lives who make excuses for clients when they fail at something; sometimes rescuers intervene when things go particularly badly for clients. Sometimes the changes anticipated by clients, of course, are healthy and positive. When the latter is the case, a powerful motivator has been offered to clients and therapists to make therapy work.

The "why now" question is perhaps the most important question with regard to understanding whether the presenting concern is a long-standing problem or a temporary situation. Clients who complain that their problems have been present for years but are only now seeking treatment need to be questioned further to explore what changed recently to motivate them to seek services. The precipitating event can be used to gain a better understanding of what is happening to these clients in the short run and may serve to clarify why they did not seek therapy sooner. Often, it also gives clues about interpersonal problems that were precipitated in an interpersonal situation.

Family History (Origin and Nuclear)

Often, questions about the history and circumstances of a presenting concern provide a logical segue to the exploration of family-of-origin concerns. It is the rare client for whom no connection exists at all between the presenting concern and family dynamics. Sometimes the connection is presented as a causative one (e.g., "I think it all started when my mother and father divorced when I was five. I remember hiding in the closet because I was so scared during the fight they had about it. I don't think I ever quite recovered my confidence."). Sometimes it is a relational one (e.g., "I hated my father because he treated me like dirt. He drank all the time and we just didn't get along. Then when I turned 18, I moved out. Now I don't see him at all, but I think about him all the time, wondering what he would do or say about what's going on with me."). Sometimes familial patterns are being repeated ("I'm told that my mother was sexually abused by her stepfather too. It seems so strange that she didn't want to believe me when I told her about it—but maybe she just couldn't deal with it yet.").

Consequently, most of the time clients are not at all surprised when the questions about presenting concerns suddenly lead to questions about family. In fact, often the connection is so close that the topic can be changed without client or therapist feeling as though they have changed topics at all (e.g., by following up with: "When did you first know that there were problems in your parents' marriage?"; "What else do you remember about your father?"; "How old was your mother when it happened to her?"). From these basic questions that are clearly and intimately related to the client and therapist's discussion regarding the presenting concern, the conversation can then turn to a more detailed analysis of the family history of the client. By the end of this exploration, the therapist should have at least some basic information about family-related issues, such as those listed below. It must be noted that no intake is ever complete. Information gathering continues throughout a client's therapy, and new data will continue to emerge (see Basch, 1980; Kohut, 1984). This is due in part to reluctance on the client's part to share all information with this new person who is the therapist, due in part to the client's memory lapses, sometimes due to repression and denial, and sometimes at least partly due to how the therapist may have asked the question(s) the first time. Thus data gathering does not end with the intake session. The intake interview is merely an efficient way of getting a start on this important process.

Issues to Be Addressed about the Client's Family

1. all family members with whom client interacted in childhood (family of origin)
2. family interactions during childhood and adolescent years
   - interactions with siblings, step-siblings, half-siblings, and so on
   - interactions with parents, step-parents, foster parents, and so on
   - structure of family (persons, relationships, communication, etc.)
   - generational boundaries, coalitions
3. family experiences during childhood and adolescent years
   - parenting styles experienced
   - communication styles and patterns
   - memories of the family setting
   - family trauma (including, but not limited to, history of abuse, domestic violence witnessed)
4. parental family background
   - parental family trees
   - parental family experiences
   - parental experience of childhood and adolescent trauma
   - parental medical and psychiatric history
5. genogram or family genealogy (optional)
6. current interactions with family of origin
7. nuclear family members in client's adult life
8. nuclear family interactions
   - interactions with significant others (SOs), former SOs, other adults
   - interactions with own children, step-children, foster children, and so on
   - interactions with family of SOs
   - structure of family (persons, relationships, communication, and so on)
   - generational boundaries, coalitions
9. nuclear family experiences
   - parenting styles exercised with own children
   - memories of the family setting
   - family trauma (including, but not limited to, domestic violence, perpetration of abuse)
   - communication styles and patterns
10. functionality of the family

Exploring family of origin is generally best done in a chronological order, starting with early childhood and progressing to adulthood and current relationships with family-of-origin members. Often, it is easier for the client to talk about siblings first, because these relationships may not be as emotionally laden. It is also generally easier for people to speak of generalities (overall relationships, parenting styles) before discussing specifics (e.g., domestic violence). Exploring family memories can serve to refocus the client more positively if need be by asking for good family memories and about things the family used to do together that they enjoyed. These questions can give the client a brief reprieve in what for some may be a painfully introspective exercise.

Collecting data about parents is often somewhat easier for the client as well, because they tend merely to report data that they have been told about and are not dealing with topics that they themselves experienced directly. Constructing a genogram can be enlightening for clients because it can help them recognize family patterns. However, this also takes a long time and often leads to therapeutic interventions. Thus this strategy is often saved for one of the first therapy sessions. It is mentioned here, however, because it can provide a tremendous amount of data for conceptualizing a case. The process of constructing a genogram is dealt with in Chapter 3.

The segue into the current nuclear family is generally easy and follows logically from the exploration of the family of origin. Many of the same dynamics and patterns are explored as the therapist tries to understand how the client relates to significant others and children. A parenting history may need to be collected if the therapist is unsure about the client's level of parenting skill. In routine intakes, however, only a general brush stroke profile is taken in this regard. If a parenting assessment is necessary, this may be scheduled outside of the intake interview during one of the first therapy sessions. Like the genogram constructions, developing a parenting profile can be an emotional process that opens many doors to therapeutic interactions. Chapter 3 covers parenting assessments in more detail.

Overall functionality of a family refers to the level of health experienced by both the nuclear family and the family of origin. Most families have some problems—few are maximally functional. In assessing functionality, the therapist evaluates how well the family communicates, how well they maintain clear boundaries and avoid collusions and coalitions, how well they share emotions, and how well they allow for both individuation and togetherness. The therapist can attempt to differentiate between centripetal families that function as an enmeshed unit (i.e., that cannot allow separation and individuation), centrifugal families (i.e., that have no cohesiveness or sense of unity), and average families (i.e., that can tolerate unity as well as separation).

Sexual History

The exploration of relationships with nuclear family members (that is, with significant others or spouses) generally provides an easy lead-in to examining the client's sexual history. Occasionally, if a family-of-origin member has sexually abused a client, taking a sexual history may be embedded in the family interview. If this is the case, some care must be taken by the therapist to assist the client in differentiating between healthy and normal versus unhealthy and abusive sexual relationships. This is also true if the therapist suspects rape within the client's nuclear family (i.e., in the relationship with a significant other).

Many new therapists have some difficulty addressing the issue of sexuality with their clients. Most of the time, however, once they delve into the topic they realize that the client is less worried about this topic than the therapist. Most people who seek therapy expect that they will be asked about sex. If Freud has offered nothing else to psychology, he has made sexuality a topic that people expect to talk about with their therapist. That does not mean that the issue should be taken lightly or dealt with casually. Sexuality is a very private topic, and if a client is extremely uncomfortable about it, this discussion can be delayed until later in the therapy when the therapeutic relationship is stronger. Except in cases of sexual abuse or rape (or perhaps as an aspect of couples therapy, which is not a focus of this book), sexuality is often not a central issue in the client's case conceptualization or development (apologies to Sigmund). Thus exploring the topic generally does not greatly affect case conceptualization or treatment planning.

Issues to Be Addressed about the Client's Sexual History

1. sexuality in current intimate relationship
   - quality
   - frequency
   - enjoyment, compatibility
2. sexuality in other relationships
   - quality
   - frequency
   - enjoyment, compatibility
3. first sexual experience (as a lead-in to possible sexual abuse)
4. later sexual experiences
   - quality
   - frequency
   - masturbation
   - enjoyment, compatibility
5. sexual abuse (incest, molestation, rape)
   - perpetrator(s)
   - specifics about the abuse (type, form)
   - age, frequency, and duration
   - events surrounding the abuse (e.g., where, when, threats made)
   - presence of a protector/confidant

Dealing with the topic of sexuality is most important during the intake if the client has been a victim of some form of sexual abuse (e.g., incest or rape). If this is the case, sexuality, plus its manifestation and development, may be quite central to the client's presenting concern. Nevertheless, the topic needs to be broached carefully and empathically, not forcing the client to move too fast (and thus revictimizing the client). It is also very possible that the therapist may suspect sexual abuse that the client denies. The intake session is neither the time nor place for therapists to share their speculations about sexual abuse of the client (nor is therapy, really). The issue of repressed memories is a touchy one, and therapists are generally best advised not to suggest the presence of abuse if no concrete evidence exists. Forcing clients into accepting a therapist's opinion about this topic is extremely counterproductive to treatment, if not unethical.

Exploring the specifics surrounding events of sexual victimization needs to be done respectfully, slowly, and caringly. This topic, perhaps more than any other topic that will be explored during an intake, is generally loaded with emotion and importance to the presenting concern (whether acknowledged by the client or not). Exploration needs to proceed slowly and, with some clients, the actual details may not emerge or be broachable until later in therapy. If the client denies that disclosed sexual abuse is relevant to the presenting concern, the therapist has no right to force the person into discussing the issue as if it were. The client's opinion must be respected, although the therapist may indicate to the client that they will return to the topic at some future point in time. If clients have made the connection between their victimization and their presenting concerns, they may be more willing to talk about details as soon as the intake. Clients need to be allowed to set the pace and take the lead in this exploration. If therapists believe their clients are able to discuss this topic in some detail during the intake, the data gathered should deal with circumstances and facts, not feelings. The emotional charge and repercussions of this topic will be addressed in therapy at a later time.

Social and Sociocultural History

The discussion of sexual relationships and experiences often leads relatively naturally into the exploration of social relationships because most sexual experiences discussed by clients will be discussed in the context of some type of social relationship. The social history is best traced chronologically and may move from the most to the least important relationships clients have had over their lifetimes.

The social history extends beyond social relationships per se, and also includes hobbies, interests, and recreational activities. Whether these are solitary or social should be explored and noted. The issues to be addressed in taking a social history of clients follow.

Issues to Be Addressed about the Client's Social History

1. number and description of close friends
   - current
   - past
2. acquaintances and colleague relationships
   - current
   - past
3. interests, hobbies, recreational activities, and interests
   - current
   - past
4. number and level of involvement in memberships or groups (e.g., Sierra Club, NRA)
   - current
   - past
5. religion and spirituality

6. sociocultural issues
  - socioeconomic variables
  - cultural background
  - ethnic background
  - minority status
  - level of acculturation
  - context of acculturation (forced versus voluntary)
  - world views

The issue of social relationships is important to explore during the intake session because it gives the therapist information about the client's social support network. Clients without friends and few meaningful acquaintance relationships present much more of a danger for harming themselves than ones who have developed strong interpersonal friendships. Social isolation versus connectedness may also play a role in the prognosis of cases because clients who are highly isolated may face more obstacles than clients who have people around them whose resources they can draw on during difficult times.

As important, if not more so, the social history gives the therapist occasion to appreciate the client's cultural and socioeconomic background. This assessment will allow the therapist to make a judgment about whether a more detailed, special assessment is needed for clients whose background is not in mainstream culture. Level of acculturation and acculturation stress may need to be assessed for these clients (see Dana, 1993). If acculturation emerges as important in the therapeutic intervention of a client, the issue must be addressed thoroughly and thoughtfully. Acculturation assessments per se are rarely done in the intake session, but if indicated, these should be done very early on in therapy—perhaps in the next scheduled therapy session with the client. This applies to most follow-up assessments such as parenting skills assessments, genograms, substance use assessments, and so on.

Acculturation is defined as the degree to which individuals adopt the dominant society's social and cultural norms to the exclusion or inclusion of their own cultures' social and cultural norms (Dillard, 1983). Acculturation is typically not a matter of endorsing one set of cultural norms versus another, but rather it refers to the degree to which values or attitudes derived from both cultures are incorporated. Many factors exist that may affect a person's level of acculturation, including socioeconomic status, number of generations that have been part of a given cultural group, educational and employment opportunities, and geographic location. Gauging persons' level of acculturation is an important part of getting to know them and involves an evaluation of several factors, including the degree to which traditional cultural practices are followed and the native language is used in thinking and speaking (see Gibbs & Huang, 1989). Four levels of acculturation have been identified (e.g., Dana, 1993): traditional (adherence to the "birth" culture), assimilated or nontraditional (adherence to the majority culture), bicultural (adherence to the birth and the majority culture), and marginal (lack of adherence to either culture). Acculturation is closely related to, if not identical with, the concept of racial identity that explores the degree to which a person identifies with and feels part of a given cultural group (see Kohatsu & Richardson, 1996).

To assist clinicians with the process of assessing acculturation or racial identity, several scales have been developed. These are very specific to the cultural background of the client, and they exist for each of the most populous cultural groups represented in the United States. For example, the Developmental Inventory of Black Consciousness (DIB-C; Milliones, 1980) and the Racial Identity Attitude Scale (RIAS; Parham & Helms, 1985; Ponterotto & Wise, 1987) can be used. For Hispanic clients, a variety of scales exist that must be carefully chosen according to the subgroup of U.S. Hispanics to which the client belongs (e.g., the Acculturation Scale for Mexican Americans [Cuellar, Harris, & Jasso, 1980]). Unfortunately, some ethnic subgroups exist in the United States for whom satisfactory acculturation scales have not yet been developed, despite a number of attempts in the literature. Examples of such subgroups are Alaska Natives of Eskimo descent (e.g., Yupik and Inupiat; Dana, 1993). For clients from cultural backgrounds for whom good acculturation measures have not yet been developed, a clinical interview in which the relevant issues are at least discussed (e.g., language, lifestyle choices, exposure to majority culture, adherence to traditional ways) is of critical importance (Kohatsu & Richardson, 1996).

Clients' levels of acculturation will affect how they interact with members of both the original and mainstream cultures and may have an influence on diagnostic and therapeutic issues. For example, if Native American clients appear very committed to their Native culture, then therapy might make more use of storytelling, a commonly used technique in Native culture, to resolve problems. Dana (1993) has argued that in addition to assessing clients' levels of acculturation (i.e., assimilation, biculturalism, traditionalism, or marginality), it is also critical to note whether their acculturation occurred voluntarily or involuntarily. The presence of a support network (as, for example, exists for most Alaska Natives) is a positive prognostic indicator, whereas the lack of a support network (e.g., as in the case of a single refugee) may pose an increased risk for the client.

Another important sociocultural variable is that of world view (incorporating values, attitudes, beliefs, cultural self-concept, etc.). This variable can be assessed by a thorough interview and/or on the examiner's knowledge of clients' primary cultural groups, as well as through interactions with clients and knowledge of clients' larger social contexts, such as individuals from their families and communities. These individuals can provide important insights into the values and beliefs of the groups to which clients belong, even when clients themselves may not be able to verbalize these concepts. It is important never to assume that clients adhere to the world view of the larger cultural group to which they appear to belong (i.e., assumptions about group membership are never to be based on external factors such as skin color). In fact, world view itself is often moderated by the degree of acculturation of the client. For example, even if clients are African American, if they reveal through the acculturation assessment that they are fully assimilated and do not adhere to their traditional African American culture, the assumption of White (majority) values, beliefs, and attitudes may need to be ruled out.

Academic and Professional History

The movement from assessing the social history to gathering the academic and professional history of the client is generally easily accomplished. There is a logical connection between social context and work for most people. In fact, for many people the social and work-related arenas overlap greatly, with people making friends at work or finding jobs through friends. This may be one area in which the intake moves in reverse chronological order, going from the client's current job situation back in time to prior jobs, vocational preparation, and then the school years. As in all intake subsections, the following list of issues should guide the therapist's inquiry. A model for such an adult intake session is provided here.

Issues to Be Addressed about the Client's Academic and Professional History

1. description of current job situation
2. career plans and aspirations
3. jobs and/or occupations in the past
4. adult academic or vocational preparation background
   - degrees or certificates
   - performance (i.e., grades, level of success)
   - problems (e.g., learning disabilities or physical impediments)
5. school (K to 12) background
   - graduation
   - performance (i.e., grades, level of success)
   - problems (e.g., learning disabilities, peer relationships)

Query regarding career and schooling can be rather quick and to the point unless, of course, this is an identified problem area. It is important, however, to pay some attention to how the person describes significant relationships in these settings. Most importantly, observe how the person does and did relate to authority figures (i.e., teachers and bosses) and to peers (i.e., fellow students and colleagues). If there are or were conflicts, their nature needs to be explored in some detail, even if the client did not associate them with the presenting concern. A connection may exist of which the client is unaware. The issue of career and school performance often is also closely related to issues of self-esteem and life direction. Clients who are at a loss about where their life will lead them may feel freer to talk about that in the intake than in any other context.

Health and Developmental History

The transition from the academic/professional history to the health history is often not quite as smooth as the earlier transitions. Thus it is often best introduced by suggesting that the therapist will now shift the client to a different area of concern. One similarity between the preceding and this subsection of the intake, however, is the fact, that both sections tend to be quick, straightforward, and relatively easy to deal with as they focus on more concrete data. The health history is important for the therapist to gain appreciation of the client's current and past health status. It is also an area that needs to be explored, because many clients do not readily associate their physical and mental health. Hence, they may not spontaneously disclose information about physical symptoms, medications they may be taking, and accidents they may have had. Yet all of these issues may be absolutely crucial to gaining an accurate understanding of the client's presenting concern.

The therapist, unfortunately, is not a health care provider and may not have enough knowledge to make these connections easily. However, if the question of a possible health-related concern arises in the mind of the client or the therapist, a referral to a physician should be initiated immediately. It is also good practice for the therapist to note any symptoms and medications mentioned by the client and to look them up after the interview to find out their connections to mental health. For example, if clients relate that they are taking a particular type of heart medication, their therapists must take the time to inform themselves of the side effects of this medication in the most recent edition of the *Physician's Desk Reference*, which covers all prescription medications, their implications, side effects, and other issues. Many useful reference guides exist for psychotropic drugs that are very useful for the nonmedical practitioner (e.g., *Current Psychotherapeutic Drugs* by Klein & Rowland, 1996). If the client reveals a particular physical diagnosis, the therapist should refer to the *Merck* manual or a similar publication to read about the disease and learn of potential emotional/mental health-related symptoms. In all cases, the therapist also needs to secure releases of information to obtain the client's medical records and to talk to the client's physician if a potential connection between the physical and emotional presentation exists.

Issues to Be Addressed about the Client's Developmental and Health History

1. developmental history
   - mother's pregnancy (i.e., *in utero* development and exposure)
   - birth information
   - developmental milestones
2. previous mental health treatment
   - prior therapy or counseling
   - prior psychological testing or assessment
   - school assessments
   - vocational assessments
3. medical trauma
   - injuries, recent and past
   - accidents, recent and past
   - head injuries, recent and past
4. physical health
   - current physical symptoms or complaints (e.g., chronic fatigue, dizziness)
   - current acute diagnosed illness
   - current chronic or severe diagnosed illness
   - past acute illness

- date, circumstances, and findings of last physical examination
- name of physician and other health care providers
- hospitalizations, recent and past
- current medical treatments other than medications
5. current medications

The information about medical trauma is sought because it can deliver clues about recent behavior or personality changes, as well as about a history of child abuse or neglect. A recent head injury in a client who is presenting with memory problems would prompt an immediate referral to both a neurologist and a neuropsychologist for further assessment. A series of accidental injuries in childhood that have a suspicious pattern of occurring in the presence of a parent or ones due to unavailability of a parent may suggest that the issue of childhood abuse and neglect may need to be revisited. A series of recent injuries that are suspicious in terms of the client's reaction to them (e.g., indifference, suggesting a reduced will to live) may be early indicators of suicidal ideation or may be related to borderline personality adjustment. The issue of suicidal thinking (if it was not addressed through exploring the presenting concern) may well surface during the review of the client's medical history. For instance, repeated hospitalizations due to the need to have a stomach pumped for "accidental" reasons and similar self-inflicted injuries or illnesses can signal acting out suicidal impulses.

The medical history is important to differentiate the diagnosis of a physical disorder with psychiatric symptoms from one that is a purely psychiatric disorder. A number of physical illnesses have primarily psychiatric manifestations, and a skilled clinician will inquire about enough medical detail to know when to refer the client for a complete medical evaluation. The most common medical illnesses that have primary psychiatric or psychological symptoms include, but may not be limited to, hypo- and hyperthyroidism, Addison's disease, Cushing's syndrome, hypopituitarism, hypocalcemia (mainly an issue among child clients), hypercalcemia, temporal lobe epilepsy, pancreatic cancer, Wilson's disease, posterolateral sclerosis, systemic lupus erythematosus, mitral valve prolapse, multiple sclerosis, and hypoglycemia (Klonoff & Landrine, 1997).

Finally, the medical history can also assist in identifying psychosomatic illnesses and hypochondriacal conditions, as well as serious conditions such as Munchhausen disorder. However, clients with these types of psychiatric diagnoses are more likely to come to the attention of medical professionals than therapists. Finally, a variety of physical symptoms and patterns of misuse of medications (both prescription and over-the-counter) can be related to substance use, demonstrating the need to assess that aspect of a client's history.

Substance Use and Nutritional History

The perfect lead-in to the assessment of substance use is the discussion of medications taken in the past and at present to explore the use of prescription and over-the-counter medications. Once the subject of medications has been broached, it is easy to follow up with questions about the regular use of any other mind-altering substances, including alcohol, caffeine, and tobacco. Asking questions about these legal drugs is a primer for the client to expect follow-up questions about the use of possible illegal substances. It is best if the therapist names a few specific drugs to ask questions rather than to ask generically if the client has ever used street drugs. That is, it may be better to ask, "Have you ever used marijuana, even just tried it, or experimented with it?", followed by "How about cocaine or crack?", "Or maybe amphetamines or hallucinogens like LSD?", than to ask "Have you ever used any street drugs or illegal drugs?"

If the client answers affirmatively to any of the legal or illegal substance use questions, the therapist must follow up with questions about the recency, frequency, and intensity of their use. If the use is in the past and has been resolved, additional detailed assessment may not be necessary, unless the therapist suspects that the client is not entirely truthful about the current use. If the use of caffeine or tobacco products is current and severe, follow-up questions about their impact on the client's life are important. The therapist needs to find out about the client's attitudes about the use of tobacco and caffeine and whether the client perceives it as a problem. Further, some assessment of the client's knowledge of the medical implications of their use may be helpful. If the client reveals current use of alcohol that goes beyond well-controlled or moderate social or recreational use, or uses any of the illegal drugs, a substance use assessment is necessary to evaluate the significance of the client's substance use. This assessment is discussed in detail in Chapter 3. In general, therapists should feel satisfied that by the end of this subsection of the intake they can address the following issues with regard to the client's substance use:

Issues to Be Addressed about the Client's Substance Use History

1. prescription drug use
   - type(s)
   - recency
   - frequency
   - amount
2. over-the-counter drug use
   - type(s)
   - recency
   - frequency
   - amount
3. use of legal drugs: alcohol, tobacco products, caffeine
4. use of illegal substances (e.g., marijuana, cocaine, amphetamines, hallucinogen, barbiturates, inhalants)
5. family history of substance use
   - medications (prescription and over-the-counter)
   - legal drugs (alcohol, tobacco, caffeine)
   - illegal substances (e.g., marijuana, cocaine, amphetamines, hallucinogen, barbiturates, inhalants)
   - issues related to adult children of substance users

Follow-up questions about a family history of substance use is particularly important if the client reveals their use. It should be a standard question for all clients, because it is generally recognized that people with family histories of substance use may have certain personality styles or traits they learned in this environment, even if they themselves are not using drugs of any kind. However, family history is most usefully gathered in some detail if clients themselves reveal a history of use. It is also often true that clients may admit to substance use in their family before they admit to problematic substance use themselves. Thus questions about family substance use can often lead to more insight about the client's own stance vis-à-vis drug and alcohol use. If family members are reported to have heavy use during the client's childhood, it is important that the clinician explore how this use affected the client.

Finally, the use of food and exercise is included in this category because it is often related to addictive behaviors, because this category is concerned with substances clients ingest, and because it reveals how clients treat their bodies. It is good clinical practice to ask about food and exercise directly, because clients may not feel that these behaviors contribute to the presenting concern when indeed they do. Further, eating disorders are not always obvious (e.g., a bulimic person may have a perfectly normal physiognomy), but they can wreak havoc on a person's physical health and they certainly have implications for the person's emotional health and family dynamics. Similarly, exercise can be used to mask an eating disorder when overused. Questions that must be answerable after the intake include, but may not be limited to, the following issues:

Issues to Be Addressed about the Client's Nutrition/Eating Habits History

1. daily food intake, exploring timing and quantities
   - breakfast
   - lunch
   - dinner
   - snacks and desserts
2. special diets
   - diets for physical illnesses (e.g., for diabetes or hypoglycemia, for heart or cardiovascular disease)
   - vegetarian diets
   - macrobiotic diets
3. daily liquids intake, exploring timing and quantities
   - water
   - juices
   - soft drinks
   - hot drinks
4. daily exercise routine
5. awareness of nutrition and exercise needs
6. inappropriate use of food (e.g., under- or overeating; bingeing and purging)
7. inappropriate use of exercise
8. family attitudes about foods, liquids, and exercise

Awareness of nutrition and its possible effects on mood and energy level are important issues to be explored with clients. Merely asking questions about food and liquid intake often raises the recognition in the client that these behaviors can be related to psychological symptoms and presentations. Careful questioning is important in this regard, because clients may misrepresent what they actually eat and drink in the course of the day. Rechecking with the client, especially of their snacking and liquid intake, is often essential. Exercise routines need to be explored, both for excessiveness and lack thereof. Family attitudes about food, drink, and exercise can further illuminate clients' perception of their roles and the importance of these factors to mental and physical health.

Strengths

Finally, the intake interview needs to result in an appreciation of the person's strengths. These issues can be addressed by directly questioning the client, as well as through behavioral observation and inference. It is always interesting to ask clients what they perceive as their unique strengths or abilities. The absence of an answer to this question may speak volumes as well. Therapists' focus on this issue also ascertains that they appreciate the wholeness of the person and are not just focusing on the presenting concerns. The strengths identified in the client can also be used for treatment planning and formulating a case and a prognosis. This is also often valuable feedback for clients themselves, especially for clients who have some tunnel vision about their own worth. Although there is no way to provide a complete listing of potential client strengths, a few examples are provided below to steer the clinician in the right direction. It must be noted that this list of examples is included to give therapists an idea about the wide range of client characteristics that can be assessed, not to limit them to exploring these particular issues.

Examples of Client Strengths Identified by the Therapist

1. good cognitive skills
   - well-educated
   - a good memory
   - abstract reasoning skills
   - no severe cognitive disturbances (such as delusions or ruminations)
2. adequate support network
   - stable intimate relationships
   - some contact with the family of origin
   - a loose network of acquaintances
3. history of hard work and perseverance
   - a stable work history
   - the chosen educational track completed
   - follow-through on prior medical treatment regimen
4. absence of significant childhood trauma
   - no report of having been a victim
   - no report of having been a perpetrator

5. no current health problems
6. no history of substance use
7. some evidence of interpersonal/social skills
8. the ability to express a range of emotions
9. the absence of psychotic symptomatology
10. hope about the possibility that therapy will be helpful
11. self-motivation and interest in psychological issues

Behavioral Observations

This aspect of the interview usually requires no questioning of the client but rather is conducted by the therapist nonverbally throughout the interview. Essentially, this requires the therapist's attention to client aspects that are communicated nonverbally and to the client's verbal responses to the standard questions outlined above. As such, the therapist wants to be able to provide information about the client regarding the following features:

Client Features to Be Described by the Therapist

1. appearance
   - dress
   - grooming
   - posture
   - gestures and facial expressions
   - manners and habits
   - characteristic physical features
2. cognitive functioning
   - estimated intellectual level
   - attention and concentration
   - stream and clarity of thought and speech
   - long- and short-term memory
   - level of abstraction versus concreteness
   - level of cognitive flexibility versus rigidity
   - distorted thought content (e.g., fixed beliefs, obsessions, delusions)
   - distorted thought processes (e.g., ruminations, loose or strange associations)
3. affect and mood
   - primary mood (i.e., subjective feelings)
   - primary affect (i.e., expressed or observed feelings)
   - range of affect
   - appropriateness of affective expression
   - congruence between affect and topic of conversation
   - congruence between affect and mood
4. sensorium and perception
   - reality testing/appraisal
   - perceptual disturbances (e.g., illusions, hallucinations)
   - orientation to time, place, person, and self

- judgment
- alertness

5. interpersonal style
   - level of self-assurance displayed
   - quality of interaction (e.g., hostile, challenging, trying to please, submissive, passive)
   - ability to engage and self-disclose
   - level of trust (i.e., ranging from paranoia to overly trusting)
   - need for acceptance

6. other observations
   - changes in behavior over the course of the interview
   - psychomotor movement
   - speech patterns

This description of the client is essentially an informal or abbreviated mental status exam, as routinely conducted in psychiatric hospital settings (Beutler & Berren, 1995). Occasionally, it may be necessary to conduct a formal mental status exam—namely, if problems are noted either in the area of cognition, sensorium, perception, or possibly affect. How to conduct a formal mental status exam is out-lined in Chapter 3. As a rule of thumb, though, behavioral observations that can address the above-listed features of the client are usually sufficient to describe a client adequately (Morrison, 1995a).

CLOSING THE INTAKE INTERVIEW

Once all data have been collected, the intake interview must be closed, regardless of how comfortable the therapist currently is with a specific case conceptualization or long-term treatment plan. In closing the interview, the therapist needs to help the client regain composure, should the client become upset in some way (Kottler & Brown, 1992). Once the client seems to be in a receptive frame of mind, the therapist will summarize the major findings. The therapist will offer a perspective on the presenting concern, a way of understanding the concern in the total context of the client as provided during the interview, and suggest a preliminary treatment plan (Brems, 1993; Seligman, 1996). The client is then given the opportunity to ask questions and is asked to voice any particular concerns about the plan outlined by the therapist. In an optimal situation, client and therapist agree in concept about what is going on with the client, what has led up to the presenting concerns, and where to go from here (Cormier & Hackney, 1987). Nevertheless, it is helpful to have clients verbalize their expectations about what therapy will be like and how the work together will progress. The therapist should also assess the client's level of hope about progress and attempt to kindle some hope in the person should this not have been spontaneously expressed (Kohut, 1984; Kottler & Brown, 1992). An example of a session closing that includes a therapist's formulation of the case and suggested treatment plan is provided in Chapter 4.

SUMMARY AND CONCLUDING THOUGHTS

The intake interview serves multiple purposes, all of which deserve a great deal of attention by the therapist. It is during the intake that the stage is set for therapy, data are collected to conceptualize the client's presenting concern, information is consolidated to make a treatment plan, and a relationship is built between client and therapist that will become the foundation of successful treatment. The data to be collected are vast and detailed, and it is generally best to schedule an intake session for either up to two hours in a single session or for two consecutive weeks in regular sessions. The intake interview culminates in a feedback loop wherein therapists inform their clients of how they understand the client's presenting concern and how the therapy should proceed. This feedback to clients is essential to set the stage for successful progress in the future and must be done carefully, respectfully, and in a manner that is easily understood by the client. The client should leave the intake session feeling more reassured, hopeful, and insightful than before.

The intake interview is an opportunity for the therapist to learn about the client without preconceived notions and to form a mental picture of the client, one that is brought about by the interaction and process that the client and clinician have engaged in together. This knowledge of the client is, of course, subjective. It is nevertheless an excellent means of appraising clients and learning about their presentation, idiosyncrasies, problems, and strengths. The intake process as proposed here is an epistemological process, in the same way Lemma (1996) describes psychological assessments as an epistemological means of learning about clients. Specifically,

all knowledge is a process by which the knower actively organizes and shapes what is given to perception and thought and thereby constructs what is known. Knowledge of a client then represents the outcome of a dynamic interaction between knower and known, between subject and object. The therapist carrying out an assessment thus needs to be mindful of the fact that the knowledge gathered from the assessment is inevitably subjective. This view of assessment [or intake interviewing] stands in contrast with a "medical model" approach which focuses on "history-taking." What is being proposed here, rather, is an emphasis on "history-making" (Lemma, 1996, pp. 39–40).

DOCUMENTATION AND RECORD-KEEPING

After the intake interview is complete, the client's case has been conceptualized, goals have been set, and a treatment plan has been made, the clinician needs to prepare an intake report that becomes part of the client's permanent clinical record.

This report needs to reflect all the data that were collected over the course of the intake as well as the therapist's understanding of what these data mean (the conceptualization), what needs to change in the client's life (the goals and objectives), and how this change can be catalyzed (the treatment plan). If the clinician still has some open questions that can only be answered through future assessments by other professionals, this needs to be noted, along with additional data that remain to be collected. This section of the report includes recommendations for referrals (if they are not already incorporated into the treatment plan). The recommended sections of the intake report are as follows:

- identifying information
- description of the presenting concern (including its history and precipitating event)
- family history
- sexual history
- social history
- academic and professional history
- health and developmental history
- substance use history
- strengths of the client
- behavioral observations (including mental status exam results if indicated)
- conceptualization
- goals and objectives
- treatment plan and selected strategies
- additional data collection needed

If any additional assessments were conducted by the interviewer (e.g., a parenting assessment or substance use assessment), this information should be incorporated into the relevant sections of the intake report (e.g., a parenting assessment would be included in the family history section; a substance use assessment in the substance use history section). If a genogram was constructed, it can be attached to the intake report, though it may also be briefly summarized in narrative form in the family history section. The process for special assessments is covered in Chapter 3.

Following is a sample of a partial intake report for the same client used in the sample screening report in Chapter 1. This sample provides the clinician with an idea of the type of information that must be recorded in the client's file after an intake is complete. This intake report sample, however, is incomplete, taking the reader merely through the sections that record the information outlined in this chapter. A complete intake report will also contain a conceptualization, goals and objectives, and a treatment plan. Samples for these sections of the intake report are contained in the relevant later chapter of this book (using the same client).

Sample of a Partial Intake Report

Client Name: Frederick X.   Clinician: Chris Brems

Date of Birth: 23 June 1957   Intake Date: 1 September 1994

Fee Arranged (see fee schedule): $60   Tests Administered: none

Informed Consent Signed: yes X no __   Informed Consent Verified: yes X no __

Identifying Data

The client is a 37-year-old Native American (Cree) and European American (Irish) male who lives with his significant other of 13 years in an apartment in Anchorage, Alaska. He currently works part-time as a carpenter's assistant and is also a full-time student at the local university, studying wildlife biology at the graduate level.

Definition, Scope, and History of Presenting Concerns (PCs)

The client presented to therapy because of severe symptoms of depression that had their onset five years ago, but recurred acutely two weeks prior to the client's contact with the clinic. At the current presentation, the client reported numerous symptoms of major depression, including poor sleeping patterns (with initial and terminal insomnia leading to less than five hours of sleep per night), loss of appetite and sexual drive, continuously dysphoric mood, poor concentration and attention, and low energy. The client reports the presence of these symptoms for the past two weeks and indicates that they represent a significant deterioration in his functioning as compared to before that time. The client also indicated that in the past two weeks he has begun to isolate himself even further socially, has missed several classes and class assignments, and has called in sick at work for four out of ten working days. He revealed a five-pound weight loss in the past two weeks due to his inability to eat. The client himself was not motivated to call for therapy, but his partner (significant other) finally convinced him to do so because she realized that he had once again slipped into a depression as severe as the one five years ago. It was the partner who attempted to make the client's original screening appointment for him (clinic procedure required him to make the appointment himself), although the client currently appears motivated to be in treatment.

The client reported that approximately two weeks ago he received news of his brother's suicide and believes that this stressor is tied to his current deterioration in functioning. He indicated that his severe depression five years ago was similarly precipitated because it occurred after the accidental death of his best friend. He related that this depression was very similar in nature to his current depression, involving virtually the same symptoms though of slightly greater severity. He also revealed that he has had low grade symptoms of depression, low self-esteem, indecisiveness, lack of self-confidence, and fear of loneliness throughout his entire life and that his adjustment after the resolution of his severe depression five years ago reflects one of the highest levels of functioning he has ever attained. The client reported that he is a relatively isolated individual who has little motivation for social activities and few interests that involve interaction with others. Despite this self-ascribed social isolation, however, he has never lived alone (see social history below) and has never experienced any significant difficulties at his current place of employment (see occupational history below).

Family History

The client is the youngest of five children born to the same biological parents. He had two older brothers (who would be aged 43 and 40), and two older sisters (aged 40 and 38). The two 40-year-old siblings were twins who were born 4 weeks prematurely. All children were the products of planned pregnancies by parents who had planned to have seven children. However, the client's mother had two miscarriages after the client was born and had a hysterectomy (due to suspected but unverified cancer of the uterus) when the client was three years old. The client grew up in a somewhat emotionally cool home in which his mother and father held traditional roles in the family; his mother was responsible for child care and the household, and his father was a self-employed carpenter who owned a small business. The client's parents are alive and remain married. They still live in the original family home in Lawton, Oklahoma, where the client and all his siblings grew up.

His father, Gregory (now age 70), retired four years ago and is reportedly doing well despite some initial difficulty in adjusting to retirement. Gregory was an active man throughout his lifetime, who spent most of his energy working and maintaining his business. He was interested in his children and willing to help with child care and household chores when he was home, but was generally out of the home most of the day. His business kept him busy from 7 A.M. until 7 P.M. most days, and he often worked not only on Saturdays but also on Sunday afternoons. The client believes that his father worked long hours to avoid his family, despite the client's belief that the father genuinely loved his children. The client speculated that his parents' marriage was never entirely satisfactory, though he indicated that he had never actually spoken with them about this. The client is unaware of the circumstances of his parents' dating relationship, wedding, and early years of marriage and indicated that his family does not discuss such matters.

The client's mother, Jane (now age 65), reportedly became severely depressed after her hysterectomy and had to be hospitalized for several weeks (the client could not recall how long). The client remembers her absence and that his paternal grandmother moved in with the family to take care of the children and the household during his mother's absence. He described this grandmother as mean and angry and remembered being afraid of her most of the time. He did not recall being physically abused by her but expressed the belief that she had beaten his two older brothers severely. He was uncertain about her relationship with his two sisters, but merely recalled that they had to help with household chores despite being quite young at the time. The client indicated that when his mother returned from the hospital, she was different and less interested in her children. He expressed the belief that she might still have suffered from depression at that time, a fact that was to be true of the mother throughout most of the client's childhood life. According to the client, his mother finally resolved her depressive symptoms ten years ago after another yearlong hospitalization. This hospitalization had been precipitated by a significant deterioration in her functioning that included severe suicidal ideation and a suicide attempt by taking sleeping pills.

The client described his childhood years in his family as uneventful. However, there are indications that he may have suffered from mild to moderate emotional neglect given the mother's emotional difficulties and the father's frequent physical absence. Corroborating this possibility is the client's recollection that his teachers were often concerned about him and his siblings and called his mother and father for parent–teacher conferences on a regular basis. He also recalled walking to school in cold weather without warm clothing, often being poorly groomed and ridiculed by others because of his disheveled and unclean appearance, and never seeing a physician or dentist until his teenage years. He indicated that his brothers and sisters were very independent, often spending time away from home with friends. He revealed that his mother put no limits on the children's staying away, and she sometimes did not even notice if one of the children was absent from family meals.

The client's oldest brother forged a close relationship with the father by starting to work in the family business at age 12 after school, and full-time (quitting school altogether) at age 14. He never married, and he became addicted to alcohol at age 20. He recovered and had been sober for five years before he killed himself two weeks ago. The second oldest brother left home at age 16 to live with the family of a close friend. He later went on to enlist in the military and was killed during the Vietnam war. His twin sister also left the home at age 16 to marry a much older man. She is still married to this husband, has two children of her own, and has cut all ties to her family of origin. The youngest sister had remained in the home and become the person who essentially took care of the household for and with the client's mother. She is still living in the family home and has never made career plans or plans for an independent life.

The client related that he perceived his relationships with his siblings as relatively distant—there was little encouragement for interaction in the family home. He indicated that he generally kept to himself, seeking refuge in the basement of the family home. He initially shared a room with his two brothers, but at age five he started sleeping on an old couch in the basement, the place where he also spent most of his days. He learned to read at an early age and remembers reading voraciously as a child. The client was unable to give thorough descriptions of his siblings. He indicated that he never knew them well and has had little contact with them in his adult life. He did indicate that he was closest to his oldest brother, who seemed to have taken some interest in the client after he had moved out of the family home at age 18. This oldest brother continued to work with his father until the father's retirement, when he took over the family business. He is the brother who killed himself two weeks ago. Since his death, the family has implored the client to return home to take over the family business. The client has refused but feels distraught by their request and his refusal of it.

The family had close contact with the maternal grandfather until he died when the client was eight years old. The maternal grandmother had died in childbirth when the mother's only sibling (a brother) was stillborn. The maternal grandparents had married late in life and the client's grandmother was already in her forties when the client's mother was born; the grandfather was in his late fifties. The maternal grandmother was Cree and had met her husband in Oklahoma, where he was stationed in the military. The grandfather was second generation Irish American and had lived a fairly rough-and-tumble life. The client was unable to provide any additional history about his maternal family.

The family had limited contact with the paternal grandparents who lived in Oklahoma City. The most extended contact was during the mother's hospitalization when the client was age three. They were also of Irish American descent and had had eight children; the client's father was the seventh, and the eighth died two weeks after birth. The client indicated that the family visited rarely and that these grandparents died when he was an adolescent. The client also indicated that there were few extended family contacts. He alluded to the possibility that the paternal family was dissatisfied with the client's father's choice of wife and hence had broken off contact with him.

Currently, the client is living with his significant other, Sandra; they have known each other for 15 years and have lived together for 13 years. They have no children and plan to remain childless. They have no intention for marriage, being satisfied with their relationship status as it is. They met through the client's best friend, who was killed in an accident five years ago. The client revealed that both are relatively shy and socially isolated but take care of each other's emotional needs. He is very close to Sandra and the couple appears to share many interests and personality traits. The client did indicate that he has noted that recently Sandra appears more dissatisfied with their relationship and has begun to form a social support network outside of her relationship with the client. She has begun making some friends at work and to go out with them on weekends, not including the client. As yet, the client denies that this is a problem, though he appeared somewhat threatened and worried about this development.

Sexual History

The client reports that his sexual relationship with Sandra is generally satisfying though currently nonexistent due to his decreased sexual drive. Sandra was his first sexual partner and the couple had some sexual difficulties early on in their relationship, partly accounted for by Sandra's history of sexual abuse by her father from the ages of four to ten. The client indicated that the couple had sex approximately once every two weeks for most of the past five years, with the exception of the last month, during which time they have not had sex at all. However, he indicated that they were and have remained very affectionate in a nonsexual manner. The client did not indicate that he perceived his sex life (current or past) as a problem area and indicated that Sandra is equally satisfied.

Social History

The client was a socially isolated and lonely child who had no friends whatsoever before starting first grade. He indicated that there was little opportunity or desire for interaction with other children and said that he had enough contact with children by having four siblings. When he started school he made one friend, Jason, who lived on the same street and who had just moved into the neighborhood from Arizona. He described this friend as very quiet and shy and interested in the same things as the client. The two boys reportedly started playing together after school and remained close throughout their lifetimes; this friend was killed in an accident five years ago.

The two boys had moved through all of elementary and high school together. After high school graduation, Jason had moved to Phoenix, Arizona, where he studied wildlife biology, his lifelong interest. The client remained at home and learned the carpentry trade from his father and brother. He had remained there for two years and then decided to move to Phoenix to be close to Jason. The two men moved in together at that time and the client began taking some classes with Jason at the university, while working as an assistant to a local carpenter. The two men spent most of their free time together, going hiking and rafting by themselves. They met Sandra at the family reunion of Jason's extended family when the client was 22 years old. Sandra was a second cousin of Jason's whom he had never met before. Sandra also lived in Phoenix, and the three became friends. Sandra joined Jason and the client on their frequent hiking and camping trips, and the client and Sandra became increasingly close. Two years after having met, Sandra and the client decided to move in together. Jason was very hurt by the client's decision to move out, and he began to distance himself from the client for a while. However, perhaps due to his limited social network, he reapproached the couple after about a year and the three rekindled their close relationship. After graduation Jason moved to Alaska where he worked as a park ranger in Denali National Park. Sandra and the client visited shortly after Jason moved and decided to move to Alaska themselves. They finally did so when Sandra graduated with her degree in elementary education seven years ago.

In the meantime, Jason had married and his wife became part of the close circle of friends. The two couples camped and hiked together in the summers, and they skied and snowshoed together in the winter. They also became slightly more sociable and occasionally included acquaintances from work or school in their activities. Their social circle was beginning to increase and the client indicated that this was the best time in his life. Two years after the client had moved to Alaska, Jason was killed by a drunk driver in downtown Anchorage during a visit from Denali to see the client and Sandra. The client has made no new friends since that time; in fact, he seems to have isolated himself even more, breaking off several of the new contacts the friends had made before Jason's death. Sandra and the client have remained close to Jason's wife even though she moved back to her home state of California after her husband's death.

Although he is currently taking classes in wildlife biology at the local university, the client reports no increase in his social life. He does not participate in study groups or after-school activities with peers or colleagues. However, he maintains collegial and cordial relationships with peers at the university and colleagues at work.

Academic and Professional History

The client was an excellent student all throughout elementary and high school. He taught himself how to read by age five, and even though he did not go to kindergarten, he was ahead of his classmates in first grade in overall achievement. The only school problems he related were linked to teachers' concerns about his disheveled and poorly groomed appearance, his inadequate dress during cold temperatures, and his lack of proper nourishment before school. Although he related being relatively socially isolated during his school years, this was never a concern raised by his teachers, perhaps because he and Jason were such close friends.

The client had taken college courses in Phoenix in a variety of subjects but never chose a major subject of study. He took classes as varied as calculus, organic chemistry, physics, astronomy, and geology. Seven years ago, immediately after moving to Alaska, he started taking courses in biology, and within two years he completed a B.S. in biology with a GPA of 4.0. One year ago he was accepted to a graduate program in wildlife biology. He has been carrying a full course load since that time and achieving well.

The client learned the carpentry trade from his father and brother in Oklahoma but never received any formal vocational schooling. He worked part-time as a carpenter's assistant in Phoenix for several years. After moving to Alaska, he worked as a seasonal worker for the Parks and Recreation Department for a little over a year though was unemployed when no seasonal work was available. He then (about six years ago) found a full-time construction job that utilized his carpentry skills, a position he has maintained throughout the past five years. This meant he had to cut back to part-time work (approximately 20 hours per week) when he entered the graduate program.

Health, Developmental, and Substance Use History

The client claimed that he is and always has been very healthy and had no major illnesses, no chronic diseases, and no surgeries in his lifetime. He had a successful and unproblematic vasectomy one year ago. He had the normal childhood illnesses (including measles and mumps). He is uncertain about his developmental milestones and was unable to secure this information from family members. He was unaware of any problems during his mother's pregnancy or delivery and assumed that his childhood development was normal. He did reveal some symptoms of emotional and physical neglect during early and late childhood, but he expressed the belief that this did not affect his physical health or development. However, he also related that even when he was ill as a child, his parents did not take him to see physicians; rather, they made the diagnoses themselves and decided how to proceed with treatment.

The client did not seek treatment for his depression five years ago. He was unable to pinpoint exactly how his depressive symptoms were resolved at that time, but he indicated that it took at least one year before he noted improvement. He also related that his significant other was a significant source of support and strength for him at that time and that he had kept a journal. The client's depression was never diagnosed at that time.

Other than the mother's two hospitalizations for depression and single hospitalization for a hysterectomy, no family history of significant illness (physical or emotional) was revealed. The client was not a good historian for family medical issues and claimed that this was information to which he did not have access.

Currently, the client reports an adequate omnivorous diet that includes some unhealthy foods and habits. Specifically, he likes fast food and often lacks the energy to cook or prepare meals. Additionally, he drinks caffeinated soft drinks up to four times per day and has a high intake of refined sugar products. He does not drink coffee and denies excessive use of alcohol, though he drinks alcohol occasionally (about the equivalent of two drinks per week). He denies ever having experimented with illegal substances and does not use over-the-counter medications. He is not currently taking any prescription drugs. He reports little to no exercise in the past four weeks; however, he usually hikes and backpacks regularly during the summer months and skies and snowshoes during the winter months. He has no formal or routine exercise program.

Behavioral Observations and Mental Status Exam

The client presented as a man taller than average, well-groomed and neatly dressed, who looked his age. He is slightly underweight for his height but is muscular and healthy. He evidenced no unusual mannerisms or gestures, though his psychomotor movements appeared significantly slowed and he sat slouched in his chair. His mood was subdued throughout the session and was restricted in range to the experience of negative, depressive affects. Even when he related positive events in his life, his mood remained unchanged and hence appeared somewhat incongruent. His rate of speech was slow and thought production was equally delayed. He appeared occasionally distracted and unable to concentrate on the questions, responding almost randomly at times. However, his vocabulary, grammar, and syntax suggested high average to above average intelligence and good cognitive abstracting ability. His logic was sound and he appeared capable of abstract reasoning, even at this time of significant cognitive distractibility and psychomotor retardation. His thoughts appeared preoccupied with his concern over his brother's suicide, as well as over the recent changes in his relationship with his partner, despite denying that the latter was his presenting problem.

He was oriented to time, place, and person and there was no evidence of psychotic symptomatology; the client also denied having any hallucinations or delusions in the past. He denied current suicidal ideation but did admit that the thought had occurred to him five years prior following his best friend's death. He denied all substance abuse, past and present, and seemed a credible source for this information. His judgment, though clouded by his dysphoric mood, appeared to be largely intact and receptive to external input and feedback. He disclosed freely though not spontaneously in response to questions, a fact most likely related to his low energy. His interpersonal style was reticent and cautious though not pathologically or excessively so. He was not disturbed by the interpersonal demand of the therapy situation and did well with the relationship-building aspect of the intake interview. He did not appear excessively shy or constricted and had good interpersonal or social skills. He did evidence some signs of dependence, frequently asking for advice by phrasing statements as questions and giving indications of helplessness. He had some difficulty making simple decisions (such as scheduling a convenient time of the next appointment; completing the intake form) and generally did not initiate action.

Strengths of the Client

This client presents with several significant strengths in the cognitive, interpersonal, and behavioral area. He is bright with good reasoning and abstracting skills; he is open to and understands verbal feedback and input; he has a strong educational and occupational background; he is free from perceptual or sensory disturbances; he has no major cognitive distortions; and he has the potential for adequate concentration and attention. He has developed social skills and interpersonal skills despite his social isolation; he has some forms of social support through his relationship with his significant other, his work, and his university studies; he has the ability to form close and intimate relationships with both men and women; he is appropriately self-disclosing; and he is capable of understanding social situations and contexts. He has adequate eating and exercise habits; he is physically healthy; he has a steady employment history; he has an excellent academic history; he has the skills to persevere and delay gratification; he has successfully resolved a major depression in the past; he has a solid economic and financial situation; and he brings some motivation to receive treatment.

3

GATHERING ADDITIONAL INTAKE INFORMATION

*Other people teach us who we are. Their attitudes to us are the
mirror in which we learn to see ourselves, but the mirror is
distorted. . . . We copy emotional reactions from our
parents. . . . Society is our extended mind and body.*
—*ALAN WATTS*, THE BOOK

As indicated in Chapter 2, although the majority of cases can be conceptualized based upon a standard intake protocol, there are times when additional information about a client needs to be collected. Circumstances when this needs to occur may include, but are not limited to, the following:

- when the client has a particularly complex family history with relationships that are difficult to trace or with apparent patterns of pathology → genogram construction
- when the client has particular difficulty in the area of parenting, either due to a volatile parenting history or due to current problems with children → parenting assessment
- when the client has a significant history of substance use that may require referral for substance use treatment before outpatient psychotherapy can become an option → substance use assessment
- when the client presents with symptoms that suggest an unusual mental status, such as perceptual disturbances (e.g., hallucinations), unusual cognitive processes (e.g., delusions), or severe affective disturbances (e.g., history of manic behavior) → formal mental status examination

The recommended specialized assessments associated with these circumstances, although out of the range of ordinary intake procedures, can be mastered by most psychotherapists and are not only in the realm of specialized mental health care providers. However, all intake workers who undertake a given special assessment should gain significant practice and the experience should be supervised. A multitude of references will be provided for each type of assessment below to give the interested therapist plenty of resources for further readings and detailed information. Referrals for such specialized assessment are generally not necessary, unlike assessments that are medical or specialty oriented (e.g., speech and language assessments, psychological testing).

GENOGRAM CONSTRUCTION

One suggested format for collecting data from the client who has a particularly complex family history (i.e., with relationships that are difficult to trace or where there are apparent patterns of pathology) is the construction of a genogram. In a genogram, clinician and client plot out the client's family history by creating a family tree showing all family members on both the maternal and paternal side of the client. The tracing goes backward to grandparents, great-grandparents, and aunts and uncles, as well as forward to siblings, children and grandchildren, and nieces and nephews, if applicable. For all family members mentioned salient information is taken down. Although this section will quickly describe how a genogram is constructed, therapists who plan to use this technique regularly with clients would be well-served to read more thorough descriptions of the process of constructing and interpreting genograms as presented by McGoldrick and Gerson (1985) and Scarff (1987).

Although genograms are frequently used by a variety of mental health service providers, there is little agreement among clinicians with regard to exact components, symbols, or procedures needed. McGoldrick and Gerson (1985) have proposed the most well-defined and well-thought-out genogram construction process. Hence, the genogram construction directions provided here follow this approach most closely, despite the fact that the idea of genogram development (i.e., of family mapping) was first formulated by family therapists such as Bowen (1978) and Satir (1967; see also Minuchin, Lee, & Simon, 1996). McGoldrick and Gerson (1985) point out that genograms are extremely clinically helpful because they "display family information graphically in a way that provides a quick gestalt of the complex family patterns and a rich source of hypotheses about how a clinical problem may be connected to the family context and the evolution of both problem and context over time" (p. 1). Genograms help therapists trace relationships and patterns of behavior across generations in a visual manner that can be easily scanned throughout the work with the client. Often the genogram construction also results in significant insights on the part of clients about their families; this is often the first time that clients have taken the time to think through fully all of their relationships and interactional patterns with all family members at once. Often clients begin to see patterns of which they were previously unaware and which begin to illuminate the possible etiology of their presenting concerns. Thus, although this is an intake procedure, the construction of genograms is often an excellent means of ushering in a therapeutic process and of introducing the type of thinking and analysis representative of therapeutic work.

The model for genogram construction suggested by McGoldrick and Gerson (1985) consists of three discrete levels: mapping a family structure, recording information about the family, and delineating relationships. Mapping is the basis for the genogram. It outlines who the family members are and, most basically, represents the family tree. Information that is added to the map consists of items such as demographics, functional data, and critical events or incidents. Relationship delineation refers to the family systems approach of defining relationships as enmeshed or fused, disengaged or distant, conflicted or poor, and so forth (see Minuchin & Fishman, 1981).

All three levels of the genogram are constructed through the interview with the client who has presented for treatment. It must be noted that this practice will no doubt introduce some bias because the therapist only receives information about the family and its relationships from one family member. Nevertheless, the genogram is a useful tool because it allows clients to react to their families from their unique biases about them. The interview with the client to construct the genogram can follow the order of the three levels. In other words, it first shows on paper who all of the members are and how the basic family tree appears. It then describes additional information that may be relatively concrete in nature. It concludes by adding relationship definitions based upon the descriptions rendered about various family relationships by the client. A genogram can be used repeatedly over the course of treatment and can be modified and expanded as new information emerges. It can also be used strictly for assessment purposes to give both client and therapist an initial understanding of the client's family background.

Mapping the Genogram

Drawing the family tree requires a large piece of paper mounted on an easel or on cardboard. It consists of drawing a family outline (the family structure as it manifests through different family members in relation to each other) with common symbols that can be read easily by the therapist, the client, and any future clinicians who may work with the client. Thus learning about mapping mainly consists of learning about the various symbols that are used in drawing the family tree. A

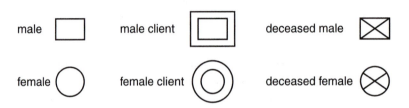

FIGURE 3.1   Basic Symbols in the Genogram

box is used for males; a circle for females. Lines are doubled for the identified client and a large X is placed in any box of a person who has died (see Figure 3.1).

Connections between various individuals are represented by lines drawn to connect their boxes to reflect their biological or legal relationships. A marriage connection is indicated by a hanging horizontal line; a broken line in the same orientation would signify an intimate, but nonmarital relationship. The line is double-slashed vertically if the relationship has been severed by separation or divorce (see Figure 3.2).

Multiple marriages are connected on the same horizontal line, preferably moving chronologically from left to right. If current or prior spouses or significant others have had prior intimate relationships, these are indicated through a second line that is drawn slightly above the current marital line (see Figure 3.3).

Horizontal lines generally imply marital or intimate relationships and vertical lines imply parental relationships. Thus a couple with children would be connected

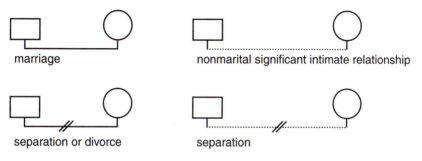

FIGURE 3.2   Simple Relationships in a Genogram

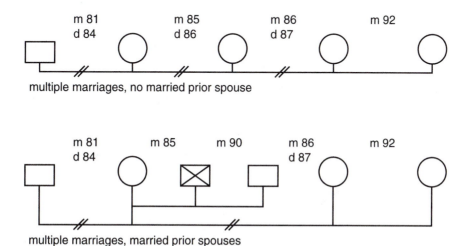

FIGURE 3.3   Multiple Marriages in a Genogram

with each other by a horizontal line; their children would be represented with boxes attached to vertical lines hanging from the marital relationship line. Twins are connected at the origin of the horizontal line if fraternal, and also to each other if identical. A solid vertical line is used for biological children; a broken line for adopted or foster children. A stillbirth is indicated by a solidly colored box. A circle or a dotted line is drawn around the various members who share a household at the current time or at the time of interest (see Figure 3.4).

Multiple past or future generations are added in the same manner by plotting out each nuclear family in the same manner described, using the same symbols, and connecting them to the client's current nuclear family with vertical lines. Past generations are drawn above the client's current nuclear family; future generations (i.e., children's families) are drawn below.

Recording Family Information

Once the map of the family has been completed to the best of the client's knowledge, family information can be added to flesh out the complexity of the family above and beyond their merely biological and legal ties. Demographics are added for ages, geography, education, and so forth, and therapists can add as many demographics as they are interested in. McGoldrick and Gerson (1985) suggest that at

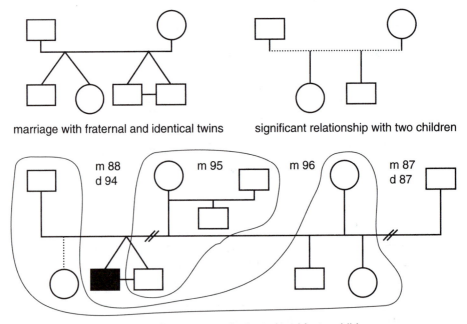

marriage with fraternal and identical twins

significant relationship with two children

complex family with remarried spouses and adopted and foster children

FIGURE 3.4   Family Relationships in a Genogram

a minimum the following demographics be included: ages, dates of birth and death, locations, occupations, and educational levels. It would probably be advisable to add cultural or ethnic backgrounds, as well as housing or living arrangements.

Additionally, functional data are added for all persons included in the genogram. These data can vary widely; they can range from information about medical conditions and concerns to emotional factors (including psychiatric conditions and symptoms such as depression, schizophrenia, substance use, and so forth) to behavior (including behavioral patterns in relationships, at the workplace, during the person's academic/school years, hobbies, interests, and so forth). It is important to focus clients not only on problematic functional data, but also on helping them identify strengths of various family members.

Finally, it is helpful to include critical family events such as "important transitions, relationship shifts, losses, and successes" (McGoldrick & Gerson, 1985, p. 19). Dates for marriages, separations, divorces, moves, and job changes are included here. McGoldrick and Gerson (1985) also suggest keeping a separate listing of these events in chronological order because the linear nature of events may be lost in the map format of the genogram. Keeping track of family events in both dimensions can help identify chronological sequences as well as intergenerational patterns or repetitions.

The collection of family information clearly overlaps greatly with taking the family history during the intake interview. Thus it is most useful to combine the genogram with the family portion of the intake if the therapist is inclined to do a genogram at all. Being prepared with paper and pencil during an intake is good practice so that the therapist can begin to draft a genogram on the spur of the moment, should the client reveal a large family with a complex web of relationships.

Delineating Family Relationships

The delineation of family relationships requires interviewing skills as well as knowledge of several special symbols, which again are based on the formats suggested by McGoldrick and Gerson (1985). A variety of types of relationships can be identified in a genogram to show family systems theory. Specifically, a triple line is drawn to signify a fused or enmeshed relationship between the two individuals involved; a double line represents a very close relationship. A conflicted relationship is drawn as a zigzag line, whereas a distant relationship is represented by a dotted line. If a relationship is completely estranged or even cut off, two vertical lines are placed in the middle of the horizontal line connecting the two individuals (see Figure 3.5).

To identify the relationships correctly, therapists must not only know the appropriate symbols provided above, but must also be able to identify the relationships of the clients and their family members as enmeshed, disengaged, negative, and such. Some knowledge of family systems theory is helpful in this regard. A brief overview of the types of relationships that are identified by this school of thought are provided. However, further reading is necessary for the therapist to become more familiar with this way of thinking about relationships.

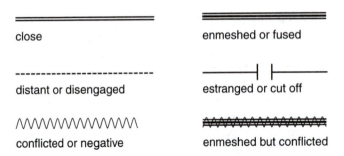

FIGURE 3.5   Symbols Qualifying Family Relationships in a Genogram

Family systems theory describes relationship in the context of defining family structure; however, relationship definitions are only one subset of the larger concept of family structure. Specifically, family structure refers to at least three distinct concepts: family boundaries and alliances, attachments in family relationships, and family affect relations. Even though McGoldrick and Gerson (1985) have singled out family relationships as an important component of the genogram, all three family structures can be delineated in the family map with no new symbols necessary. For example, family boundaries and alliances can be delineated through the use of the same family relationship lines, but the lines may be drawn between two family members that are not necessarily directly adjacent to each other on the family map (see Figure 3.6).

From a family systems perspective, family structure deals with family functioning as far as boundaries and alliances among family members are concerned. It addresses a family's stability, cohesiveness, divisiveness, closeness, and distance. All families need several sets of boundaries that are acknowledged and respected by all family members. Not always are these boundaries considered healthy or productive from a therapist's point of view, but they always do exist (see Teyber, 1997). Healthy boundaries delineate appropriate subgroups (called holons) of a family. For instance, children should not be part of the spousal holon; there should be a clear dividing line that the children in the family are not allowed to traverse. Thus if there is a conflict in the spousal unit or holon, the boundary would not permit the children to be drawn into this conflict. In problem families, this healthy boundary often does not exist. Frequently an unhealthy boundary or cross-generational alliance replaces it. For instance, one of the spouses might actually engage in an alliance with a child against the other spouse, thus rearranging the boundaries within the family. Obviously, the boundaries and alliances that exist then often go hand in hand in families and can be used to estimate the level of psychological health of the system (Minuchin & Fishman, 1981). Boundaries have a direct impact on who is close to whom and on how family members interact. Alliances function in much the same way.

Family structure and boundary issues also deal with how various members of the family are attached. Levels of attachment vary widely from relationships that

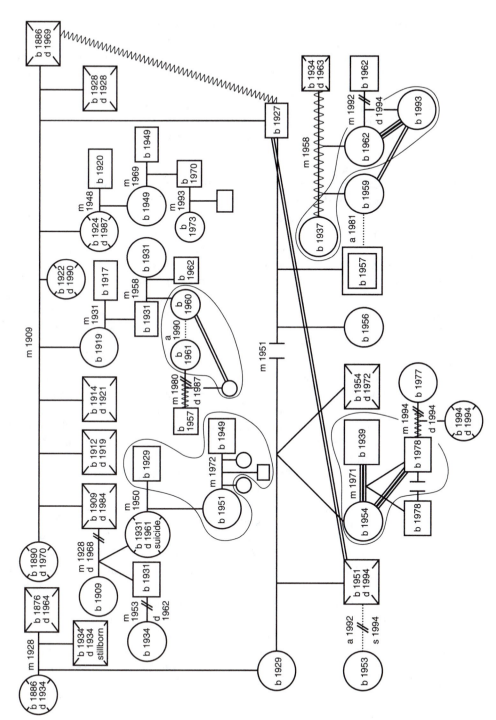

FIGURE 3.6 A Completed Genogram

are overly attached to relationships that are insufficiently attached. In some systems there may be overengagement, or enmeshment, between two members, whereas another member might be quite disengaged from the family. Disengagement can be defined as a relationship between two family members that has become distant and uninvolved although it was once close and emotionally connected or charged. Disengagement implies rather concretely that two people have disengaged from one another and that, for such disengagement to have taken place, they must once have had a meaningful connection. Distanced relationships, on the other hand, refer to relationships that are distant that have never been close, even though traditionally these may be expected to be close relationships. An often-cited example of the disengaged member is the parent who has withdrawn from the family and from a spouse to whom the person was once close and has redirected this energy to work activities instead. An example of a distant relationship may be the relationship between a parent and a child that never flourished.

Enmeshment (or fusion) can be defined as overinvolvement between two people in a relationship. An enmeshed relationship can have a very healthy beginning as a close intimate or emotionally involved relationship. However, the relationship fails to stabilize at a healthy level of involvement and become closer and closer until the two partners in the relationship can no longer function independently. Alternatively, an enmeshed relationship can be the result of a healthy attachment that fails to loosen to accommodate the developmental needs of one of the partners in the relationship. The latter type of enmeshment is best exemplified by the enmeshed parent who has trouble letting go of a child even after that child has reached adulthood and is attempting to leave home (Haley, 1980). The former type of enmeshment may be exemplified by a spousal relationship that has become so close that the two partners no longer interact with anyone outside the relationship, make no decisions independent of one another, or are otherwise incapable of or fail to function as autonomous individuals. Closeness is not the same as enmeshment. Two relationship partners can be close (double line in the family map) without being enmeshed (triple line). Closeness implies emotional connection; not emotional overinvolvement or lack of autonomy. Closeness is achieved in an emotionally healthy relationship that has mastered attachment that is solid without being intrusive (Teyber, 1997).

Although more intuitively associated with disengaged or distant relationships, conflict can occur in enmeshed or fused relationships just as easily, or perhaps even more commonly. Two relationship partners can be enmeshed; in other words, they can be fused with regard to decision-making and functioning but have severe conflicts between them. They may not be able to function independently, but they may have severely different opinions and approaches; hence, they fight constantly about what to do and how to approach a given situation. In disengaged or distant relationships, such conflict is also possible. However, given the disengaged (i.e., emotionally distant) nature of the relationship, the conflict may never be expressed as directly or intensely as in the enmeshed or fused relationship.

Finally, family structure also has to do with a family's affective status. Their interwoven character, or emotional state within the family system, is often quite obvious. Specifically, just as individuals can be angry, anxious, depressed, reluctant, and so forth, so can families. It is interesting to be alert to the family's overall affective state and then to compare that state to the affective states of the separate holons, and particularly to those identified with the client. Such affective information can easily be included in the family map in the same way other family information was mapped in the second step of the genogram construction process (this is demonstrated in Figure 3.6 for the same sample client shown in Chapters 1 and 2). In fact, this family information has already been discussed and will be included at that stage. Certainly, much more can be said about family structures and their effects on the mental health of the members of that family. The interested reader is referred to the vast family therapy literature for a more in-depth discussion of this topic.

Final Notes about Genograms

Constructing a genogram is an excellent ancillary to taking a client's family history. It has the advantage of clarifying family patterns very concretely to both therapist and client, thus becoming an excellent therapeutic technique that is appropriate even at the time of intake. Construction of a genogram is relatively simple, and genograms can facilitate communication across therapists if a common set of symbols is used. However, interpreting a genogram that was constructed by another therapist requires that caution be exercised. It is best that therapists who are not thoroughly trained in the use of genograms not draw extensive family system or psychodynamic conclusions based on a genogram they did not construct with a client. However, even relatively novice therapists can construct and interpret genograms that they have built with their clients during family interviews. A completed genogram is shown in Figure 3.6. This sample is provided to help therapists learn how to draw genograms with their clients, not to suggest that therapists should try to make systems or dynamic interpretations based on it. Once therapists have attempted to construct a genogram for the first time (perhaps mapping their own family), they will note the complexity involved in drawing a family map, especially one for a family with a wide-reaching web of relationships. This process will help clarify for therapists why it is best to interpret genograms only if they were involved in their construction. The reader who is interested in learning more about genogram interpretation should read McGoldrick and Gerson (1985) and Scarff (1987).

PARENTING SKILLS ASSESSMENT

If a client presents with particular difficulty in the area of parenting, either due to a volatile parenting history or due to current problems with children, it may be wise to collect more detailed parenting information. When collecting such additional data, the therapist needs to be fairly systematic and well-informed about the issues that commonly face parents in their relationship with their children. Specifically, at a time when child abuse statistics continue to rise in most of the nation's states, it is essential for a therapist to have some background in basic parenting issues, including the understanding and means to explore and classify parenting (or discipline) strategies, parenting philosophies, and goals of clients who are parents (Darling & Steinberg, 1993).

All therapists need to be aware that how parents deal with their own children is often strongly associated with how these persons were parented themselves; parents often either adapt their own parents' strategies or rebel against them (see Booth & Booth, 1994; Dietzel, 1995). Thus an exploration of strategies, goals, and philosophies or values is often conducted twice—once with regard to the parent's own parenting history (i.e., the client's experience as a child) and again with regard to the client's current beliefs and attitudes (i.e., the parent's behavior or practice toward the child or children). In the following section, brief definitions and references for more information will be provided for various parenting strategies, parenting philosophies, and parental goals, along with the means of querying parents about them. All questions can be asked for two aspects of parenting—experience and practice—though they will not necessarily always be stated that way below.

Parenting Strategies

The range of parenting or discipline strategies that has been developed and written about is vast and varied and cannot be covered fully in this chapter. Many traditions in psychology have developed their own unique approaches to parenting. These include, but are not limited to, the individual psychology of Adler (represented by Dreikurs' system of logical and natural consequences), the humanistic psychology of Rogers (represented by Gordon's parent effectiveness training), and behavioral theory as proposed by Skinner (represented by Krumboltz and Krumboltz's system of parenting). These three systems, although not necessarily all-inclusive, incorporate the large majority of parenting strategies and will suffice as a background for conducting parenting assessment. They have been applied and tested repeatedly and have been incorporated into comprehensive parent education programs (e.g., Brems, 1990; Brems, Baldwin, & Baxter, 1993; Dietzel, 1995).

Logical and Natural Consequences

The Adlerian system is based on the belief that all behavior has a purpose or a goal, and that the psychological and behavioral movement of individuals—including children—is always toward a higher goal or a more advanced level of functioning. The nature of this higher goal is largely, if not entirely, determined by the fundamental human need for belongingness. Thus all individuals are seen as striving for the betterment of society or for the social interests of the groups to which they desire to belong. Factors internal and external to each person help determine whether this socially appropriate goal is maintained or whether an inappropriate goal is substituted that leads to maladaptive behavior. In other words, people are viewed as actively interacting with their environments rather than passively responding to them, and as molding their behavior according to the feedback they receive. Actual environmental factors, as well as individual interpretations thereof, help determine their behavior and responses.

If the environment and the child's interpretation thereof is healthy and accurate, this striving will result in actions that are in the greater social interest and to the benefit of all. However, if the child misinterprets the environment, or if the environment is nonresponsive or inappropriately responsive, the child's striving will be derailed in a negative way. It is then up to a clinician to help parents redirect the child and to help the child regain the healthier, socially-oriented development. This can be done by using natural and logical consequences, encouragement, and democratic family functioning strategies (Dreikurs & Grey, 1968), all of which are strategies parents learn through parent education according to this model of human behavior. The two most important strategies of this school of thought are natural and logical consequence interventions. Parents who use this strategy of training children rely on using naturally occurring or parentally predetermined consequences to the child's behavior to modify the child's actions. Specifically, natural consequences are the experiences or events that follow a child's behavior or action in the absence of parental intervention, ones that follow a child's action naturally, and ones that influence the child's future behavior (Dreikurs & Soltz, 1964). For instance, the natural consequence of touching a hot stove is receiving a painful burn that will teach the child not to touch a hot stove.

Obviously, although natural consequences are powerful teaching tools, they are not always acceptable. Specifically, they are not appropriate in situations in which the child could be harmed, in which the natural consequence may be so far in the future that the child cannot make a logical connection between the behavior and the consequence, and in situations that do not have a natural consequence. When the use of natural consequences is either not possible or not appropriate, logical consequences are designed to take their place. Logical consequences are the experiences or events that follow a child's behavior or action as determined previously by a parental decision to affect the child's behavior in a certain way. They are events designed by parents to make the child's actions safer or more acceptable to family or social values. For example, a mother who does not tolerate lateness for dinner may set up a logical consequence wherein the child who is late for dinner must eat the leftovers alone and must clean up the dishes afterwards. Logical consequences are presented as choices that the child is allowed to make and are presented in either–or, or when–then format. In other words, the parent presents the consequences in a manner that neither implies a restriction nor a punishment.

For instance, if children are supposed to clean their rooms before being allowed to watch TV, consequences would be presented as follows: "*When* you have cleaned your room, *then* you may watch TV." The parent would neither say, "You cannot watch TV until you have cleaned your room," as this would imply a restriction, nor say, "If you don't clean your room, there is no TV for you today," as this would imply a punishment. Instead, the focus is placed on giving the child a choice. Logical consequences work only if they can be enforced and if they are used consistently. If the child does not follow through, the parent must be prepared to enforce the rule. As parents enforce the consequences, they also point out again that the child has made a choice. A bargain is made between child and parent, and when the child fails to follow through, the parent responds according to the terms that were set up beforehand. The parent does not respond to the child angrily, nor does the parent give nonverbal cues of misgivings or disrespect. Instead, the consequences are merely reiterated and enforced respectfully, yet firmly.

In setting up consequences, parents have to be firm but respectful, and they must follow through consistently. Setting consequences and not following through firmly leaves the child doubtful about the parents' authority and their ability to provide strength and guidance. This firmness, however, must be accompanied by encouragement to help children discover their strengths and competencies (Dinkmayer & McKay, 1976). This encouragement may not only be verbal, but also be reflected in the parents' voice, body posture, and other nonverbal cues. Appropriate consequences are best arranged to provide the child with routine and predictability in most instances, yet to give parents flexiblity within appropriate limits. It is best to use consequences when parents wish to avoid giving attention inappropriately (i.e., without reinforcing the wrong behavior); to avoid power struggles; to avoid conflict that results in retaliation and revenge; and to avoid discouraging the child, which then leads to feelings of inadequacy and incompetence.

Parent Effectiveness Training

Humanism, the second school of thought to result in a parent education program, led to the development of Parent Effectiveness Training (Gordon, 1970; Gordon & Sands, 1978). Rogers had a deep faith in the tendency of humans to grow in a positive and constructive manner, as long as respect and trust develop and are provided in their lives. He perceived people as basically rational, socialized, forward moving, and realistic. He believed that behavior is motivated either by urges within the person, or by the environment, which strengthens or weakens certain actions. He regarded the disagreement between personal urges and socially condoned behaviors, affects, and needs as the root of all conflict for humans. Specifically, behavior that is designed to help persons move toward self-actualization, as they have defined it for themselves, at times clashes with environmental sanctions. The resulting changes in behavior prevent persons from being the way they would really like to be. This results in the formation of a false sense of self, or a self that is not congruent with the person's ideal self or way of being. Hence, Rogers believed that for people to become self-actualized, and thus be emotionally and psychologically healthy, they would need environments that were accepting of them—that would allow them to interact with genuineness and where their free and uncensored expressions of affect could be explored. Such empathic responsiveness of the environment to the individual is perceived as critical to the development of a healthy self.

Applying these humanistic principles to children means that as children grow up and interact with their environment, they are viewed as striving to become self-actualized human beings and to achieve their unique definitions of their ideal selves. As children grow up, feedback from the environment increases in meaning, and the child uses this to determine the appropriateness of behaviors and affects. If the environment is accepting of and empathic with the child's expressed urges, a healthy self can develop that is congruent with the child's ideal self. However, if the environment is not accepting, is rejecting, or is indifferent to the child, a self will develop that is not congruent with the child's own urges, but rather with the perception of the surrounding environment. This results in an incongruence between what the child does and wants to do, what the child really feels and actually expresses, and what the child needs and asks for. Rogers perceives this incongruence as the source of all psychological and emotional problems. It can be dealt with through therapy for the child, as well as through educating parents about the importance of becoming more aware of their child's genuine needs, desires, and affects, and stressing the importance of being accepting of and empathic with these manifestations of the child's developing self. Two primary strategies developed for parents for this purpose are active listening and I-messages (Gordon, 1970).

Active listening is a five-step process designed to help parents understand their children better, especially in situations in which children have identified that they have problems. It is a process through which the parent expresses caring and concern, as well as acceptance and the genuine attempt to understand the child and to help the child arrive at a solution to the problem. It is done without giving advice and without lecturing. The first step in the process of active listening is listening attentively. Parents are taught to open conversations and to listen not only to the actual content of the child's verbalization, but also to watch the child to listen for feelings that may be expressed more readily through nonverbal communication. The second step of active listening is listening for feelings. The parent is encouraged to listen for the child's expression of affect and is reminded that feelings can never be wrong or inappropriate. In addition to listening to the feelings, the parent must also acknowledge to the child that the feelings were heard, understood, and most importantly, accepted. In the third step, the parent reflects the child's feelings back to the child in an attempt to connect the child's feeling to the content of the situation or problem that the child is describing. This step is often difficult for parents because many are not used to talking about feelings, much less identifying them. Once the parent has understood the affect, has reflected it back to the child, and has placed it in a context for the child, problem solving can begin.

Problem solving, looking for alternatives and predicting consequences, is the fourth step in the active listening process. This is not to imply that parents give advice or commands at this time. Quite to the contrary, in this step parents help the child learn to solve problems by helping the child identify alternatives or consequences. Children are not told what to do, but are encouraged to develop their own courses of action. This is best done by asking children questions about what they think or would like to do, how they may have tackled similar problems in the past, what potential consequences might occur, and what could be done to change a given situation. Children are asked these questions to stimulate their own problem solving and creativity, not to steer them toward specific solutions. The final step of active listening, and the one most frequently forgotten, is follow-up. To round out the active listening process, the parents must follow up with the child to investigate whether the child successfully implemented the solution and whether the implementation led to the desired results. Regardless of the success of the intervention, praise and encouragement are critical components of the follow-up stage. If the solution was unsuccessful and the child's problem was not solved, the active listening process can begin anew at this stage.

I-messages serve to inform the child about the parent's feelings; these are the inverse of active listening tactics that helped the parent understand the child's feelings. An I-message is delivered in one statement that has four components, all of which must always be included when I-messages are used. The first component of an I-message describes to the child the behavior or situation that causes the parent a problem without making a judgment about the behavior or situation. This part of the I-message usually begins with "When you . . .". The second component explains to the child how the parent feels when faced with the behavior or situation outlined in the first component of the message. It always begins with "I feel . . .". The third component informs the child of the reason why this feeling occurs and how it interferes with the parent's well-being or peace of mind. As the explanatory section of the I-message, it always begins with "because . . .". The fourth, and final, section of the I-message describes an alternative behavior or situation that the parent would prefer for the child and that in the parent's opinion would solve the child's problem. This component is necessary, because children need to know how they can change or what is expected of them. Merely telling the child that they are doing something wrong without suggesting an alternative may leave the child struggling with what to do next. If at all possible, parents should give the child a choice with regard to what can be done to take care of the problem. This gives the child a level of control and helps the child feel more included in the decision-making and problem-solving process. This section of the I-message often begins with "I would like you to . . . or . . .".

Humanist theory also suggests that at times a problem is best dealt with through environmental modification. In this instance, a problem may occur neither because of the child's or the parent's direct behavior nor because of a parent's response to a child's behavior, but rather due to environmental factors that are less than positive. The best strategy in such a case is to change a variable in the environment to take care of or remove the problem.

Behavioral Techniques

Finally, behaviorism has been used by a number of parent educators, including Krumboltz and Krumboltz (1972) and Becker (1971). B. F. Skinner firmly believed that theories such as Adler's and Rogers's were unnecessary and not very economical. He proposed instead that all behavior is learned strictly as a result of the events or consequences that follow it. This operant conditioning approach implies that behavior is not intrinsically determined, but rather is a response to environmental contingencies. Thus behaviors can be changed, taught, and eliminated by applying the correct environmental response. All behaviors are acquired in the same manner, and hence there is no such thing as normal versus abnormal behavior. Instead, behavior is merely seen as more or less functional or dysfunctional. Both functional and dysfunctional behaviors are learned and can be changed through the application of four principles. These principles, or primary responses, as outlined by behaviorists are:

positive reinforcement, negative reinforcement, punishment, and extinction. All four principles are generally highly familiar to most therapists and hence will not be explained here. One word of caution is necessary though. Punishment, especially if physical in nature (e.g., a slap in the face, a jerking of an arm), is generally not an acceptable discipline strategy; many alternatives to punishment exist and are preferable. Parents need to be aware of the principles of punishment, however, to know when they are using it inadvertently so that they can modify their behavior.

Applied to parenting, behavioral principles imply that if the parent knows how to apply or not to apply the four responses correctly, the child's behavior can be modified as desired by the parent. This approach clearly implies much more control and direction on the parents' part than the other approaches to parent education that are more concerned with the child's self-expression and acceptance. Primary parenting strategies for the behavioral model are outlined in detail by Krumboltz and Krumboltz (1972) and are identical to those applied by a clinician in therapy.

A number of sophisticated strategies have been improvised to develop, maintain, eliminate, and modify behaviors and emotional responses, and these can be used by parents to modify a child's behavior. Just as reinforcement can be used in a therapy room to increase the frequency of a desired behavior, so too can a parent use a similar reinforcer in the home to modify the child's response in that environment. Parents can help children develop new behaviors through the processes of modeling or shaping, and they can recognize and appropriately reinforce the child's successive approximations to a new behavior. Parents can use alternatives to punishment such as extinction and reinforcement of incompatible behaviors to eliminate undesirable behaviors. Parents can make use of reinforcement schedules and succeed in modifying behaviors by timing and selecting reinforcers appropriately. They can be aware of the powerful uses of modeling and how their own children may control their own responses.

Assessment

These three sets of parenting strategies have become commonly accepted as the basis of most parent education programs. Hence, it makes sense for therapists to be sufficiently familiar with them to assess a client's familiarity with and use of these strategies. In assessing parenting strategies, therapists must remember a number of points. First, most parents have never taken classes that teach parenting strategies and are merely operating on belief systems that stem from their own respective childhoods (Dietzel, 1995). Thus they may not be familiar with all the different types of parenting strategies, their appropriate applications, and complex components of parenting. Second, given that parents have often had no particular parenting education, they may either be inconsistent or rigid in how they implement the parenting strategies with which they are familiar (Brooks, 1994, 1996). It is possible that they may be overly rigid or overly inconsistent with regard to when, how, or with whom they apply their parenting techniques, who enforces or implements them, and how their use and appropriateness is negotiated in certain situations (Darling & Steinberg, 1993). Third, disagreements between co-parents about what constitutes adequate disciplinary strategies are not at all uncommon (Johnson, Fortman, & Brems, 1993). When this is the case, it is equally likely that the children are aware of the conflict and use it to their advantage (though generally neither consciously nor maliciously so). Finally, there are many groups of parents who may have limitations or special challenges with regard to parenting, and these have to be addressed separately (e.g., learning disabled parents, Booth & Booth, 1994; single parents, Roberts, 1994; or step-parents).

Given these realities about parents, it is generally necessary to ask very specific questions of clients to gain an understanding of how they (and their co-parents) parent and discipline their child or children. It is also generally worthwhile to investigate whether the same strategies are employed with all children, by all co-parents, in all situations, and at all times. Whenever clinicians ask about whether their clients know of certain strategies, they should also ascertain that the clients know the correct definition and application of that technique. Knowing about a strategy and using it correctly are often two completely different things. If a client is unfamiliar with a given strategy, the therapist needs to define it briefly, because it is often true that a parent may use a certain strategy without being aware of its label. Throughout this line of questioning the therapist needs to be sure to check with the client about the degree of agreement across all co-parents involved. Finally, it is often very illuminating to ask clients about their favorite and best parenting strategies, as well as about what they perceive to have been their worst interventions as parents. A question about what strategies seem to work and not work with their children can be helpful.

A listing of necessary information to evaluate a client's parenting skills is provided below to guide the therapist's exploration of parenting strategies employed by a given client. This list is only a guide; a therapist should develop a flexible and logical set of questions that can be applied in the specific context of each client in the most appropriate manner (Kamphaus & Frick, 1996). As mentioned above, each area of information listed below can be asked in two ways: first, with regard to how clients experienced it as a child (i.e., how clients were parented); and second, with regard to how clients currently put it into practice with their own children.

Knowledge of Strategies

1. Adlerian tradition
   - natural consequences
   - logical consequences
   - choices for logical consequences
2. Rogerian tradition
   - active listening
   - I-messages
   - choices for I-messages
   - environmental modification
3. behavioral tradition
   - positive reinforcement

- negative reinforcement
- extinction
- punishment
- reinforcement of incompatible behavior
- modeling
- shaping (reinforcement of successive approximations)

Implementation of Strategies

1. context
   - appropriate to developmental age of child
   - appropriate to historical factors
   - appropriate to a specific situation
2. consistency
   - consistent with established rules
   - consistent with history
   - consistent within child
   - consistent across children
   - consistent with co-parent

To explore these areas of information, the therapist can phrase questions in a multitude of ways; questions should be tailored to the particular style of each therapist and to the needs of each client. One suggested list of relevant questions is provided in Brems (1993), and a few sample questions are excerpted here to give the reader an idea of how these informational areas can be tapped through questions that do not sound too technical.

Sample Questions

1. How do you reward good behaviors of your children?
2. Can you explain what active listening is and how you use it?
3. When do you use active listening with your children?
4. Would you explain what time out is and when best to use it?
5. How and when do you show logical and natural consequences of your children's behaviors?
6. Do you ever spank your child?
7. Where on the child's body do you hit?
8. Do you ground your child for misbehavior?

Another way to assess use of parenting strategies is through the development and use of an informal questionnaire that can be easily administered to a client. An example of such a questionnaire is provided in Johnson, Fortman, and Brems (1993). Item 9 is excerpted below to give the reader an idea of how such a questionnaire may be structured. The excerpted question is written to assess parenting experience, not practice, but could easily be rephrased to assess practice, not experience.

Sample Questionnaire Item

9. What kind of discipline strategies did your primary parents use? In other words, did your primary parents (mark all that apply):
   - make you feel guilty for misbehavior? If so, under what circumstances and how?
   - use corporal punishment (i.e., hit you)? If so, where did they hit you and how often? How bad of an offense did you have to commit for a parent to resort to hitting?
   - use time out (i.e., make you stand in a corner or go to a secluded spot in the house) to correct behavior?
   - use logical or natural consequences of behaviors (i.e., make you feel the consequences of your misbehavior; for example, if you refused to wear your coat, you got cold; if you lost your bike, you had to earn money to buy a new one)?
   - talk to you to help you understand what you did wrong?
   - ignore you when you tried to get their attention in inappropriate ways (e.g., if you had a tantrum in a grocery store, did they just walk off and let you come to your senses)?
   - reward you in some way if you behaved well?
   - let you know they appreciated it when you behaved well?
   - praise you for good behavior?
   - notice good behavior?
   - only pay attention to you when you misbehaved?
   - make you feel terrible for your behavior?
   - hold you or another sibling out as an example of how a child should or should not behave to alter your behavior?
   - yell at you to get you to do things?
   - humiliate you in front of other people to get you to change your behavior?
   - talk poorly about you behind your back?
   - ground you or take away privileges as punishment (e.g., take away your allowance; not allow you to watch TV; refuse the nightly bedtime story)?

Parenting Philosophies

Another important aspect of parenting that needs to be assessed with the client who has parenting difficulties is that of parenting values or philosophy (Brooks, 1996; Elkind, 1995). Parenting philosophy can translate into at least three styles: authoritarian, permissive, and authoritative (Baumrind, 1971, 1973, 1983). Authoritarian parents tend to be restrictive, expecting their children to follow rules without questioning. They are generally strict disciplinarians who have little tolerance for negotiating a compromise or for letting the children work toward their own solutions to problems. These parents have strict rules and expect the child to abide by them. Violation is punished without asking about purpose or reason for the transgression.

Permissive parents, on the other hand, have loose rules and the child is often not clear about what is expected. What few rules there are, are not consistently enforced, and limits are notoriously unclear. This leaves little room for structure and often has the child guessing about appropriateness of behavior and acceptability of affect. Because children are not born with an innate sense of rules, this permissive style can be quite unsettling and anxiety provoking for the child. Permissive parents often tend to develop a peer relationship rather than a parental relationship with the child. Thus because children need adults in their environment to help them figure out what is right and wrong in their society and neighborhood, they are often left guessing and unsure of themselves.

Authoritative parents have developed a compromise between having no rules, like permissive parents, and having too many rigid rules, like authoritarian parents. They generally have several sensible rules that are explained to the child and are often agreed on and renegotiated as the child develops and matures. Even though these parents are still in charge of the family, they are tolerant of input from their children and are more likely to run a fairly democratic household in which every member is perceived as having input about what is appropriate and acceptable and what is not. Authoritative parents are not personally threatened by a child's misbehavior or stubbornness, but rather see it in perspective and can deal with it constructively. Of the three parenting styles, the authoritative is the most psychologically sound approach to parenting. Therapists need to assess which styles are favored by their clients, and whether their co-parents have the same style. Disagreements in styles are a major problem that often results in conflict and arguments for parents.

One related aspect of parenting is the setting and clarification of rules in a household. A well-functioning family has to have rules that are explicitly stated and that have certain predictable consequences associated with violating them (Brems, 1993). These explicit rules, as well as the consequences of violating or transgressing them, need to be investigated. Further, most families also have several implicit rules. Even though these are more difficult to assess directly, they are still worthwhile pursuing. The origin of all rules needs to be explored, as well as the parents' willingness to renegotiate them according to the developmental needs of their children (Elkind, 1995; Teyber, 1997). For instance, rules about bedtime are very appropriate and common in most families. However, they need to be renegotiated as children grow older, and they need to be different for different children in the same family depending on their ages. As one way in which parents express their general values about parenting and about children, rules are an issue that must be assessed. Values that need to be looked at include, but are not necessarily limited to, attitudes about gender roles for children, beliefs about the basic goodness or badness of human beings, traditional ways of looking at children's relationships with authority figures, concern about children's career and other goals, need for parental collaboration versus the strict gender division of parenting roles, and basic attitudes about moral and ethical issues (see Brooks, 1996; Dietzel, 1995).

To explore parenting styles and values, the following areas of information need to be considered by the therapist, again by phrasing questions in a meaningful, nontechnical manner that is neither threatening nor overwhelming for the client. Therapists should read as much about parenting as they can, even though they may not plan to conduct the parent education directly (e.g., Booth & Booth, 1994; Brems, 1993; Brooks, 1994, 1996; Dietzel, 1995; Roberts, 1994).

Parenting Philosophy

1. authoritarian parenting style
2. permissive parenting style
3. authoritative parenting style

Household Rules

1. explicit rules
2. implicit rules
3. clarity of rules
4. negotiation of rules
5. clarity of consequences in case of rule violation
6. appropriateness of rules
7. appropriateness of consequences
8. appropriateness of negotiation of rules

Parenting Values

1. attitudes about children
2. attitudes about gender roles
3. beliefs about human value
4. beliefs about parent–child relationships (authority structure)
5. ability for parental collaboration
6. need for control of children's behaviors, thoughts, attitudes, and so on.

A few sample questions (excerpted from Brems, 1993) are provided here, along with a few sample questionnaire items (Items 2, 6, and 10; excerpted from Johnson, Fortman, & Brems, 1993). The questionnaire items are again phrased to explore parenting experience in childhood, but can be easily rewritten to assess parenting practice.

Sample Questions

1. Do you take into consideration what motivated a child's behavior?
2. Do you think that all strategies work equally well with all your children regardless of their ages? Explain.
3. Do you think that all strategies work equally well in all situations? Explain.

Sample Questionnaire Items

2. What were your primary parents' attitudes and beliefs about children? For instance, did they believe (mark all that apply)
   - that children should be spoiled?
   - that children should be seen and not heard?
   - that children should take care of their parents?

- that children are the most important aspect of family life?
- that children have the same rights as adults?
- that all children in the household have the same rights and responsibilities regardless of age differences?
- that children cannot understand most important issues (e.g., finances) and are therefore to be kept in the dark about any problems the parents are encountering?
- that children need to be informed of all family problems, including conflicts in the parents' marital relationship?
- that children are basically bad?
- that children are basically good?
- that all children are alike?
- that boys and girls should be treated differently?
- that children's rights should supersede parents' rights?
- that one's children should always be included in all activities the adults engage in?

6. What were the important messages your primary parent gave you about yourself?
   - Were you a good child or bad child?
   - A smart child or dumb child?
   - A wanted child or endured child?

10. What kind of philosophy did your parent have about parenting? In other words, using the definitions below, was your parent authoritarian, permissive, or authoritative?

   Authoritarian: parent is the boss and the child has to follow the rules and has few rights; discipline is strict and there are few, if any, rewards for good behavior; there are many rules that are applied rigidly and excuses are not tolerated

   Permissive: child is the boss and decides what she or he wants to do with little interference by the parent; the parent rarely, if ever, punishes the child; there are few rules in the household and those are there can be easily broken without repercussions for the child

   Authoritative: parent has clear rules for the child and applies them flexibly and caringly; parent is willing to talk with the child and pays attention to good behavior; corporal punishment is rarely used; parent and child tend to communicate well and respect each other's rights

Parenting Goals and Related Issues

Parents have various goals for their children and themselves as parents. These goals are worthy of exploration because they often play a significant role in how parents and children interact and because they may lead to problems in the parent–child relationship. For example, a parent who plans to make the child successful in academics may put excessive stress on that aspect of the child and ignore the child's emotional development. Such partial recognition of this child (also called partial mirroring; see Kohut, 1984) can have grave consequences for the child's development of a healthy self and can lead to significant conflict between the parent and child.

Goals also have to be developmentally appropriate and have to reflect children's needs at various ages (Roberts, 1994; Stern, 1985). Tailoring parenting strategies to age and need is critical and reflects sensitivity and caring to the children. Parenting scales that have been developed (largely for research purposes) often address this dimension of developmental appropriateness and how it relates to parental empathy and intervention, (e.g., the Adult Adolescent Parenting Inventory by Bavolek, 1984; and the Child-Rearing Practices Report by Block, 1965). A very promising new scale that investigates the relationship between child and parent on several dimensions is the Child–Parent Relationship Inventory by Gerard (1994). Any or all of these scales can be administered as a follow-up to conducting this parenting assessment interview, though they should never replace it. If scales are used, they should become the foundation of a discussion with clients about their parenting skills and should not be administered without feedback. They can become an objective basis for intervening and making recommendations to parents who are being seen in individual treatment, especially if parent education is one important aspect of their therapy. They can also become the basis for a referral for additional parent education outside of individual therapy (see also the questions listed below).

Finally, if the child spends considerable time with other adults who have parental or disciplinary roles vis-à-vis the child, the clinician needs to inquire about these individuals' parenting or discipline strategies and styles as well. Just as conflict between two co-parents affects the child, so does conflict between parents and other adult caretakers that are important in the child's life. Collaborative parenting needs to be explored for agreement in parental philosophies and parenting styles. A client may present with problems in the parenting area, not because of conflict with a child but because of disagreements with a co-parent. The therapist conducting the parenting assessment must tease out this difference. Some sample questions (from Brems, 1993) and questionnaire Items 17, 18, and 3 (from Johnson, Fortman, & Brems, 1993) are provided below to help guide the new therapist in assessing this aspect of parenting.

Sample Questions

1. Who is the primary parent in your home? That is, who spends the most time with the children?
2. How do you discuss disagreements about rules with your co-parent?
3. What are your goals for your children, and how did you develop these goals?

Sample Questionnaire Items

17. Did your parents seem to collaborate on the task of parenting? In other words, did they make major decisions together about the children, or was one parent the decision maker and the other the follower?
18. What did your parents do when they disagreed about a parenting decision?

3. What were your primary parents' goals for their children? In other words, what were the messages that you received about what you ought to become or would become once you were an adult? For instance, did your primary parent seem to hope or imply that you and your brothers and sisters would grow up to be (mark all that apply):

- followers?
- leaders?
- independent thinkers?
- free spirits?
- spitting images of their parents?
- unique?
- people who fit in under any circumstances?
- people who have their own opinions?
- people who follow the opinions of others?
- people who adapt or conform?
- people who challenge the system and break some rules every now and then?
- perfect?
- losers or failures?
- people who always win regardless of how they go about doing so?
- people who put the needs of others ahead of their own?
- religious?
- smart?
- achievers?
- just like their parents?
- better than their parents?
- those things the parents themselves could not become?

Final Notes about Parenting Skills Assessment

Assessing parenting practices (see Darling & Steinberg, 1993) and parenting philosophies or styles (Baumrind, 1973) is the most critical aspect of conducting a parenting intake. Most problems reported by clients with their children stem either from unfortunate choices of parenting strategies or from unsuccessful parenting philosophies. The combination of the two has also been implicated in helping determine parenting success or failure (Darling & Steinberg, 1993). In other words, some parenting strategies may be more or less successful depending on whether they are used by a permissive or an authoritative parent. Similarly, parenting goals and other parenting issues may need to be calculated into the equation. A parent with unrealistic goals for a child may abuse the logical consequences strategy by defining consequences that are consistent with the parent's goals for the child but may be inconsistent with the child's needs.

Thus only a thorough assessment of all three aspects of parenting will provide data that are sufficiently complete to help the therapist determine the possible roots of the parent–child conflict presented by the client. If such a conflict is identified through this expanded intake assessment, the therapist then must take care to address this issue in the treatment plan. This can be accomplished in myriad ways. For example, it is possible to build parent education into the individual treatment of the client or to refer the client out for additional psychoeducational treatment groups that have parent education at their core. Alternatively, a client can be recommended for family therapy in addition to individual treatment to learn to negotiate conflicts between the client and a child. Deciding which specific treatment route to take will no doubt be learned if assessment follows the recommendations outlined above.

SUBSTANCE USE ASSESSMENT

Substance use is one of the most common mental health problems in the United States. Epidemiological Catchment Area (ECA) studies funded by the National Institute of Mental Health (see Regier et al., 1990), found that 13.5% of the general population reported a lifetime occurrence of alcohol abuse or dependence and 5.9% to 6.1% reported drug abuse or dependence (Helzer & Przybeck, 1988; Regier et al., 1990). Conducted in 1991 to 1993, the National Comorbidity Survey (NCS) found very similar rates, with 14% of respondents reporting lifetime symptoms of alcohol abuse or dependence and 7.5% reporting lifetime drug dependence (Kessler et al., 1994; Warner, Kessler, Hughes, Anthony, & Nelson, 1995). Relative to alcohol abuse or dependence, age of onset for 80% of all ECA cases was before 30 years of age, and 40% had their onset between ages 15 and 19; women reported a slightly later onset than men and had lower overall prevalence rates (4.6% versus 23.8%; Robins, Helzer, Przybeck, & Regier, 1988).

To point out the prevalence of substance use disorders, their rates in the general population are best compared to rates of other DSM-IV disorders. Regarding other mental disorders, the highest lifetime prevalence rates for the general population are reported for phobias (12.6%), simple phobias (10.0%), major depression (5.9%), agoraphobia (5.2%), social phobia (2.8%), and antisocial personality disorders (2.6%; Regier et al., 1990), according to the ECA survey. The NCS reports the highest lifetime rates for major depression (17%), followed by social phobias (13%), simple phobias (11%), and dysthymia (6.4%; Kessler et al., 1994). This comparison clearly indicates that alcohol and other drug use and dependence rank among the greatest mental health risks in the country.

The importance of this finding is underscored further by observing reviews of the psychological health of individuals who have reported alcohol or other drug use. In the general population, 47% of ECA respondents who reported drug abuse or drug dependence also reported another lifetime DSM-III diagnosis, with higher co-occurrence rates for drug abusing or drug dependent individuals than for alcoholics. Specifically, 53% of drug users in the general population had psychiatric co-occurrence, as compared to 37% of alcohol abusers. Whereas having an alcohol problem doubles the likelihood of having a mental disorder, a drug disorder increases the likelihood of co-occurrence sevenfold (Regier et al., 1990). The NCA survey found similar patterns: 52% of respondents with a lifetime diagnosis of alcohol abuse or alcohol dependence had a psychiatric disorder, as did 59% of respondents with lifetime drug abuse or drug dependence (Kessler, 1994). Given these co-occurrence figures, it is not surprising that the general mental health practitioner is often confronted with the need to assess a client for substance use.

Because general mental health practitioners may not have spent a lot of time thinking or reading about substance use, they are often not properly prepared to assess and treat the substance using client. However, given the strong likelihood that a substance using individual will present for treatment in a mental health setting, every therapist must have a basic awareness of the types of drugs that are commonly abused, must have some knowledge of diagnostic issues, must know how to conduct a thorough substance use assessment, and must be able to use this information appropriately for referral and treatment.

Types of Drugs

The Diagnostic and Statistical Manual of Mental Disorders, Fourth Edition (DSM-IV; American Psychiatric Association, 1994) provides diagnostic guidelines for eleven discrete categories of substances. For most of these substances (the only exceptions being caffeine and nicotine), the manual outlines diagnostic criteria for two types of substance use disorders (i.e., abuse and dependence) and a range of substance-induced disorders (e.g., delirium, withdrawal, intoxication). The eleven substances that are listed in the DSM-IV are alcohol, amphetamines, caffeine, cannabis, cocaine, hallucinogens, inhalants, nicotine, opiates, phencyclidine (PCP), and sedatives (including hypnotics and anxiolytics). Given the acceptance of the DSM-IV as the organizing principle for diagnoses in the mental health field, these eleven groups of substances will be briefly reviewed to give the therapist some idea about their nature and effects. All definitions, intoxication symptoms and signs, and withdrawal symptoms presented below are based on the DSM-IV (American Psychiatric Association, 1994).

Alcohol

Although a legal substance, alcohol is the most commonly abused drug in the United States, as the figures provided above have already revealed. Alcohol is a depressant with very specific intoxication and withdrawal symptoms. Alcohol intoxication symptoms include maladaptive behavioral and psychological changes, along with a variety of signs (such as slurred speech, incoordination, unsteady gait, nystagmus, attention and memory impairment, stupor, and even coma). Alcohol withdrawal symptoms include autonomic hyperactivity (e.g., sweating, increased pulse rate), hand tremor, insomnia, nausea, vomiting, hallucinations or illusions, agitation, anxiety, and even seizures.

Alcohol may present the most difficult scenario when deciding whether a substance use disorder diagnosis is appropriate, that is, when making the clinical judgment that a person's behavior constitutes a disorder. This is so given the general social acceptance of alcohol consumption in a wide variety of social and even professional settings. In fact, the DSM-IV reports that 90% of all adults have had some experience with alcohol, and 60% have had one or more adverse life events due to alcohol consumption (American Psychiatric Association, 1994). The continuum of alcohol use ranges from appropriate social use that does not represent a problem to the overconsumption of alcohol that greatly interferes with the person's functioning. Generally speaking, the consumer who falls on either end of this continuum does not present a diagnostic puzzle for most clinicians. However, the consumer who falls anywhere in the middle range of use can be a challenge to the therapist who has to decide on a diagnosis and treatment plan (Kitchens, 1994). Assessing alcohol use hence becomes critical and must be done with care and consideration. Clinical interviews, structured interviews, and questionnaires are available for assessing alcohol use.

Amphetamines

Most amphetamines (a class of stimulant substances that includes amphetamine, dextroamphetamine, and methamphetamine) are taken orally or intravenously, with the exception of methamphetamine, which can be snorted (i.e., taken nasally) or, if in its purest form called "ice," can be smoked. Some amphetamines can be obtained legally through prescription (for obesity, narcolepsy, or attention deficit disorder), though most are obtained illegally. Amphetamines have specific intoxication and withdrawal symptoms. Amphetamine intoxication may be recognized through symptoms such as maladaptive behavioral or psychological changes, and by numerous signs, including tachycardia and bradycardia, dilation of the pupils, changed blood pressure, perspiration or chills, nausea, vomiting, weight loss, psychomotor changes, muscular weakness, confusion, seizures, and even coma. Withdrawal symptoms include fatigue, unpleasant dreams, insomnia or hypersomnia, increased appetite, and psychomotor changes.

Caffeine

This stimulant substance is highly available to and used by the general public. Caffeine is not only present in its most well-known form (coffee and caffeinated soft drinks), but is also hidden in many other commonly consumed substances such as prescription and over-the-counter medications, candy bars, and some teas. Caffeine has specific intoxication symptoms that include restlessness, nervousness, excitement, insomnia, flushed face, diuresis, gastrointestinal disturbance, muscle twitching, rambling flow of thought, cardiac arrythmia, agitation, and periods of inexhaustibility. Although not formally recognized as a diagnosable disorder, caffeine withdrawal symptoms have also been noted. These include headaches, drowsiness, anxiety, depression, nausea, and vomiting.

Cannabis

This group of substances is derived from the cannabis plant and includes products such as marijuana (the dried leaves, tops, and stems of the plant that are rolled into cigarettes), hashish (the dried resinous substance that is exuded from the tops and leaves), or hashish oil (a distillate of hashish). All forms of cannabis are most commonly smoked, though they may be taken orally in other ways (e.g., mixed with food or drink). Although cannabis intoxication has been formally recognized, no cannabis withdrawal disorder has been identified. Intoxication symptoms include maladaptive behavioral or psychological changes along with a number of physiological signs (conjunctival infection, increased appetite, dry mouth, and tachycardia). Cannabis has been found helpful in alleviating symptoms associated with chemotherapy for cancer and with AIDS, and legalizing cannabis has been attempted repeatedly in the absence of evidence of its addictive nature.

Cocaine

Cocaine, a stimulant, is derived from the coca plant and can take a minimum of four different forms for consumption: coca leaves, coca paste, cocaine hydrochloride, and cocaine alkaloid. The former two forms of cocaine are most commonly used by native populations in Central and South America, where the coca plant grows. The latter two preparations are more commonly used in other parts of the world. Cocaine hydrochloride is usually snorted as a powder or is dissolved in water and injected. Cocaine alkaloid (known as crack in the United States) is easily vaporized and hence inhaled. Cocaine can induce both intoxication and withdrawal disorders. Intoxication symptoms include symptoms of maladaptive behavior and psychological changes, as well as signs such as tachycardia, bradycardia, dilation of the pupils, changes in blood pressure, perspiration or chills, nausea, vomiting, weight loss, psychomotor changes, muscular weakness, respiratory depression, confusion, dyskinesia, and even coma. Withdrawal symptoms include fatigue, unpleasant dreams, changes in sleep patterns, increased appetite, and psychomotor changes (agitation or retardation).

Hallucinogens

This group of substances is highly varied; it includes LSD, morning glory seeds, mescaline, and psilocybin. (Not included are PCP and cannabis, though these may also have hallucinogenic effects; these are discussed separately because they are otherwise significantly different from this class of substances.) These substances are used to induce altered sensations, emotions, and perceptions. They are most commonly ingested by smoking and orally, though injection is occasionally favored by some. Hallucinogens produce specific intoxication symptoms; these include maladaptive behavioral or psychological changes, perceptual changes despite full alertness (e.g., intensified perceptions, depersonalization, derealizations, illusions, hallucinations), and physiological signs such as dilation of the pupils, tachycardia, sweating, palpitations, blurred vision, tremors, and incoordination. Also associated with hallucinogen use is what is termed hallucinogen persisting perception disorder, better known as flashbacks. This refers to re-experiencing the perceptual disturbances noted during intoxication in the absence of having ingested the drug. Common triggers for flashbacks are dark environments, fatigue, stress, or ingestion of other drugs. Flashbacks may occur for several weeks or up to five years after use. No other withdrawal disorders or symptoms are noted.

Inhalants

Inhalants include primarily aliphatic and aromatic hydrocarbons (e.g., gasoline, glue, spray paint, paint thinners) and secondarily halogenated compounds (e.g., cleaners, correction fluids, spray can propellants) that are inhaled (sniffed) for their intoxicating effects. These may be inhaled by holding a fluid-soaked cloth in front of the mouth and nose or breathing in the fluid vapors from a container. Some users heat the fluid to accelerate vaporization of the inhaled substance. Only a specific intoxication disorder has been identified for inhalant use. Intoxication symptoms include maladaptive behavioral or psychological changes, along with signs such as dizziness, nystagmus, incoordination, slurred speech, unsteady gait, lethargy, depressed reflexes, psychomotor retardation, tremor, muscle weakness, blurred vision, stupor, euphoria, and coma.

Nicotine
Nicotine use includes smoking cigars, cigarettes, and pipes, as well as using chewing tobacco or snuff and prescription medications containing nicotine (nicotine gum and the nicotine patch). No intoxication disorder has been specified, but withdrawal can be diagnosed. Withdrawal symptoms include dysphoric mood, insomnia, irritability, frustration, anger, anxiety, difficulty concentrating, restlessness, decreased heart rate, increased appetite, and weight gain.

Opiates
Opiates include illegal as well as legal substances that are used to reduce pain or induce relaxation. Opiates such as morphine (a natural opioid) and codeine (a synthetic form) can be legally obtained by prescription as analgesics, anesthetics, antidiarrheal agents, or cough suppressants. The most commonly used illegal opioid is heroin. Heroin is usually injected, though it may also be smoked or snorted. Prescribed opioids are generally taken orally. Both intoxication and withdrawal disorders can be diagnosed for opioid use. Intoxication symptoms include maladaptive behavioral or psychological changes and pupillary constriction (or dilation if overdose induces anoxia), as well as several signs such as drowsiness, coma, slurred speech, and impairment in attention and memory. Opioid withdrawal is indicated by symptoms including dysphoric mood, nausea, vomiting, muscle aches, dilation of pupils, lacrimation, rhinorrhea, diarrhea, yawning, fever, and insomnia.

Phencyclidine (PCP)
Originally developed as synthetically produced anesthetics, these substances became street drugs in the 1960s. PCP-type drugs are taken orally, injected, or smoked. Although not the only drug included here, PCP (also called angel dust, hog, or peace pill) is the most commonly used one. Only intoxication is recognized for PCP. It includes the following symptoms: maladaptive behavioral or psychological changes, nystagmus, hypertension, tachycardia, numbness, decreased responsiveness to pain, ataxia, dysarthria, muscle rigidity, seizures, hyperacusis, and coma. At times hallucinations and/or illusions may also occur. Illusions are less severe than hallucinations and refer to a misperception of a real stimulus (e.g., perceiving a shadow of a tree as a burglar).

Sedatives

This grouping of substances includes sedatives, anxiolytics, and hypnotic drugs such as benzodiazepines, barbiturates, and hypnotics. These brain depressants or tranquilizers can be obtained legally in the form of sleeping medications and anti-anxiety medications (anxiolytics). Intoxication and withdrawal disorders have been identified. Intoxication symptoms include maladaptive behavioral and psychological changes, and signs such as slurred speech, incoordination, unsteady gait, nystagmus, attention and memory problems, stupor, and coma. Withdrawal symptoms include autonomic hyperactivity, hand tremors, insomnia, nausea, vomiting, hallucinations and illusions, psychomotor agitation, anxiety, and grand mal seizures.

Diagnostic Issues

The DSM-IV outlines two types of substance-related disorders: substance use disorders and substance-induced disorders. In turn, substance use disorders have two subcategories, namely, substance abuse and substance dependence. These diagnoses apply to nine of the eleven substances listed above. The two exceptions are caffeine and nicotine. No substance use disorder (neither abuse nor dependence) can be diagnosed for the consumption of caffeine; only substance dependence can be diagnosed for nicotine. Abuse is diagnosed if the client evidences "a maladaptive pattern of substance use leading to clinically significant impairment of distress" (American Psychiatric Association, 1994, p. 182). Clinically significant impairment is defined as the presence of at least one of four identified symptoms over the past 12 months. The four possible symptoms are: (a) recurrent use that results in a failure to fulfill a major life role (e.g., work, school, or home); (b) recurrent use in situations in which it is physically dangerous (e.g., driving); (c) recurrent use-related legal problems (e.g., citations for driving under the influence); or (d) continued use despite persistent negative social or interpersonal effects (e.g., fights with partner). Abuse is only diagnosable in comparison with dependence—lifetime and current absence of dependence on the same substance constitutes abuse.

Dependence always subsumes abuse and is also defined as "a maladaptive pattern of substance use leading to clinically significant impairment of distress" (American Psychiatric Association, 1994, p. 181); however, in this case clinically significant impairment is defined through the presence of at least three symptoms from a list of seven, again occurring over a 12-month span. The seven possible symptoms show a greater severity of use than those listed in the abuse category and thus point the therapist toward a pattern of use that has continuously increased over time. These include: (a) tolerance (evidenced either through the need for increased amounts of the substance to reach the desired effect or through diminished effects when the same amount is ingested over time); (b) withdrawal (either through the presence of withdrawal symptoms or through the use of the known substance to prevent such symptoms); (c) use of the substance in larger amounts or for longer time periods than originally intended; (d) persistent desire for the substance or the unsuccessful attempt to cut down on its use; (e) a large time investment to procure the substance, use it, or recover from its use; (f) reduction of time spent on other activities to make time for substance use-related activity; and/or (g) continued use despite awareness of its negative effect on major life areas.

Some substance use treatment professionals have taken exception to the classification of substance use disorders by the DSM-IV. They have argued that substance use cannot be forced into two arbitrary categories of abuse or dependence, but rather should be viewed as a continuum that ranges from nonuse to dependence. Lewis, Dana, and Blevins (1988) have suggested that the continuum of use should be conceptualized as ranging from no use to moderate use with no associated problems; to heavy use with no associated life problems; to heavy use with associated moderate problems; to heavy use with serious problems; and finally to dependence with serious life and health problems. Similarly, authors within the National Institute on Drug Abuse suggest that the current DSM system is not sufficiently specialized to take into consideration all components of substance use and dependence needed to make a reliable functional diagnosis (Blaine, Horton, & Towle, 1995). They too suggest that a "sharper definition and criteria for abuse, hazardous use, or mild problems" (p. 13) are necessary in the future to provide clearer conceptual definitions and diagnostic criteria. They also support a model presented by Skinner (1990) that takes into consideration consumption and related problems and suggests (like Lewis, Dana, & Blevins, 1988) that dependence should be diagnosed only when heavy consumption and severe problems converge and that abuse needs to be graded further to differentiate different levels of use and their complications. The argument that level of use ranges widely and that it is sometimes difficult to make a judgment regarding proper diagnosis has definite validity. However, the differentiation between abuse and dependence appears to be valid, though this does not offer sufficient criteria to determine treatment planning. The continuum of use must still be taken into consideration when deciding on a course of treatment with a client; however, it does not preclude diagnosis.

The second category of substance-related disorder specified in the DSM-IV is the category of substance-induced disorders. There are three types of substance-induced disorders: intoxication, withdrawal, and substance-induced other mental disorders (e.g., delirium, amnestic disorder, mood disorder, psychotic disorder). Intoxication is marked by the "development of a reversible substance-specific syndrome due to the recent ingestion of (or exposure to) a substance . . . [and] clinically maladaptive behavioral or psychological changes that are due to the effect of the substance on the central nervous system and [that] develop during or shortly after use of the substance" (American Psychiatric Association, 1994, p. 184). The specific syndrome or change varies from substance to substance (e.g., alcohol intoxication may involve slurred speech, incoordination, and/or unsteady gait, whereas cocaine intoxication may manifest as tachycardia, confusion, nausea, and/or pupillary dilation). Withdrawal is diagnosed if the following two conditions are met: (a) "development of a substance-specific syndrome due to the cessation of (or reduction in) substance use that has been heavy and prolonged" (American Psychiatric Association, 1994, p. 185) and (b) a "substance-specific syndrome [that] causes clinically significant distress or impairment in social, occupational, or other important areas of functioning" (American Psychiatric Association, 1994, p. 185). As with intoxication, actual manifestation of withdrawal symptoms depends on the drug of choice (e.g., amphetamine withdrawal results in fatigue, unpleasant dreams, sleep disturbance, appetite changes, and/or psychomotor changes; nicotine withdrawal results in restlessness, decreased heart rate, and/or increased appetite and weight gain). Not all substances result in withdrawal syndromes (e.g., cannabis); and some have very specific withdrawal symptoms that manifest a disorder in and of itself (e.g., hallucinogen persisting perception disorder [flashbacks]).

The final DSM-IV category of substance-induced disorders varies widely in terms of manifestation (or associated symptomatology), both across substances and even within specific substances. Essentially, this category refers to any other mental disorder the symptoms of which can be traced directly to the use of a substance (e.g., alcohol intoxication delirium; amphetamine-induced mood disorder; inhalant-induced persisting dementia). Being able to recognize the symptoms of what may be a variety of mental disorders (ranging from organic brain/cognitive disorders to mood disorders, psychotic disorders, and so forth) as a substance-induced disorder is a critical skill for all therapists. For this reason, a thorough substance use assessment is critical if a client gives any indication of regular drug use. Not assessing clients' substance use and its potential effects on their lives (and behavior, cognition, and affect) may mean misdiagnosing the client as depressed, psychotic, or otherwise impaired, when in reality they are experiencing these symptoms as a result of their drug use. Clearly, for example, the implications for treatment are significantly different depending on whether certain symptoms are manifestations of a true mood disorder or a substance-induced mood disorder.

Assessment Strategies

Given the importance of correct diagnosis, substance use assessment clearly has its place in the repertoire of skills the therapist must bring to the intake assessment of each client. To assure the success of such an assessment, it must be conducted matter-of-factly, not with an accusatory or moralistic tone (Boylan, Malley, & Scott, 1995). It is the goal of the therapist to conduct the assessment in such a manner that an easy and honest flow of information develops that will allow for reliable and valid diagnosis and treatment planning (Boylan, Malley, & Scott, 1995). The assessment will most likely consist of an extension of the intake interview (i.e., a clinical interview) that incorporates a range of specialized questions that pinpoint the client's history of substance use. However, it is also possible to expand that assessment through the use of collateral informants and biochemical analyses (Carey & Teitelbaum, 1996), as well as the use of questionnaires (Kitchens, 1994). The first two procedures are rarely practical or possible in outpatient work, though the third has good utility with many options. A variety of substance use questionnaires have been developed that can be helpful to the clinician. However, most of these instruments are not as valid and reliable as one would like them to be because they have psychometric properties that are less than adequate. Thus, the cautious therapist never relies exclusively on these questionnaires, but always uses them as mere supplements to the clinical interview.

Whether therapists administer questionnaires, use structured interviews, or rely on both, they need to be aware that substance-abusing or -dependent clients may not be the most reliable and forthcoming historians. Meyer and Deitsch (1996) have outlined several specific behavioral observations therapists can make following intake to help them decide whether a substance use assessment was valid. Namely, these authors indicate that if the client is not currently using a substance, does not perceive any objective or interpersonal coercion for treatment (i.e., is neither court-referred nor urged by a significant other), is certain about confidentiality and trusting of the therapist, is willing to have self-report data checked against more objective reports (e.g., urinalyses or family reports), and is generally compliant, not antisocial, and intrinsically motivated for treatment, only then is a valid substance use assessment possible. However, if the client is still actively using the substance, has been coerced into treatment, is poorly aligned with the therapist, is antisocial, and is generally noncompliant or has little intrinsic motivation for treatment or change, then therapists who conduct assessments must be aware that the information gleaned is, in all likelihood, neither reliable nor truthful. The same is true for any questionnaires that were administered; the same variables that affect responding truthfully to the interview will also affect openness in responding to questionnaires.

A range of questions needs to be asked of the client suspected of substance use to make proper diagnosis and correct treatment planning possible. These questions need to cover a range of information that includes specific data about the substance use (e.g., frequency, recency, intensity, duration, age of onset), associated behaviors and problems (e.g., blackouts, intoxication symptoms, withdrawal symptoms), and general effects on the client's life (e.g., impact on work history, intimate relationships, social interactions). Below is a list of the areas of functioning that need to be evaluated in the interview. This list is followed by some discussion of each area of data collection, as well as some information about possible questionnaires that can be used to supplement the interview.

Issues Related to Substance Use to Be Addressed through Assessment

1. types of substances used (List each specific drug, and address all related items for each individual drug.)
   - age of onset
   - recency
   - duration
   - frequency
   - intensity
   - time of day of use
   - drug of choice
   - intoxication symptoms
   - withdrawal symptoms

2. common related symptoms
   - attention and/or memory impairment
   - blackouts
   - blurred vision
   - changes in appetite and/or weight
   - disorientation and/or decreased alertness
   - flashbacks
   - heart arrhythmias (e.g., tachycardia, bradycardia)
   - incoordination and/or unsteady gait
   - insomnia or hypersomnia
   - nausea and/or vomiting
   - nystagmus (rhythmic movements or tremors of the eyes)
   - palpitations (unusually rapid or irregular beating of the heart)
   - perceptual disturbances
   - perspiration or chills
   - psychomotor agitation or retardation
   - pupillary dilation or constriction
   - seizures
   - slurred speech
   - tremors or twitching
3. circumstances around use
   - situational triggers for use
   - solitary use or use with someone else
   - attempts at quitting
   - periods of sobriety
   - securing of money to pay for drugs
   - criminal behavior related to drug use or procurement
   - time spent on drug procurement, use, and aftereffects
4. common affected areas of functioning
   - family relationships
   - social relationships
   - employment history
   - academic history
   - coping skills
   - decision-making and problem-solving abilities
   - physical health
   - financial situation
   - criminal record
5. common associated psychiatric symptoms
   - mood disorder (including suicidal ideation and action)
   - psychotic disorder
   - cognitive disorder
   - anxiety disorder
   - impulse control disorder

Substance Use-Related Questions

It is eminently important to explore all suspected substances used independent from one another and not to place them all in a single category of abused drugs (Hood & Johnson, 1997). Vastly different patterns in use are possible across different drugs, and research shows with great consistency that the trend of substance use is one toward poly-substance abuse (i.e., the use of more than one substance at a time or in a lifetime). Exploring each substance for its frequency of use (how many time per day, week, month, year), recency of use (e.g., within one day, one week, one month of the intake interview), intensity of use (i.e., how much at each incidence of use), and duration (i.e., for how long each time) is critical. It is also helpful to determine how long a particular substance has been used—that is, to inquire about age of onset of occasional and then regular use. Once all suspected substances used have been explored, it is often helpful to ask clients to identify their drug of choice. This is often, but not always, self-evident from frequency and intensity of use. Clients may identify cocaine as the drug of choice despite having used alcohol more frequently, recently, and intensively. This is a pattern that may suggest that the client uses alcohol in part because cocaine is less readily available or because of its higher cost.

Questions regarding intoxication and withdrawal symptoms are also important because the duration and frequency of these symptoms may help the therapist determine a proper diagnosis of abuse versus dependence, or lend credence to additional diagnoses for substance-induced disorders. It is helpful for therapists to have some knowledge of common substance intoxication and withdrawal symptoms so that they may ask pointed questions about symptoms, depending on which drugs the client identified as drugs of choice and/or of frequent use. However, lacking this knowledge, the therapist can ask about the list of generic common symptoms provided above, which is a relatively comprehensive list of possible intoxication and withdrawal symptoms. The therapist can then later determine the proper diagnosis by comparing the list obtained from the client to the lists provided in the DSM-IV for each individual substance.

The circumstances or context surrounding drug use are also important to explore because they may help the therapist identify situational triggers for use (Carey & Teitelbaum, 1996; Hood & Johnson, 1997). Whether a client uses a substance alone or with others can be valuable information, especially if a pattern develops; such a pattern may consist of isolated use or use with a certain group of friends. The presence of friends who do not use the substance has good prognostic implications, whereas the loss of all nonusing friends is a negative one. What the client expects as consequences of alcohol and other drug use can show the reinforcing factors that maintain substance use (Carey & Teitelbaum, 1996), as in a case where the client expects greater social ease and camaraderie through use. Exploring whether there have been attempts at quitting that have been unsuccessful or periods of nonuse is important. A client who has attempted to quit many times without success and without assistance may have some motivation for change, whereas a client who has never thought of quitting may still not be inclined to do so. A client with no extended periods of sobriety may have a worse prognosis than one who has been able to abstain for one reason or another (e.g., women who abstain during pregnancy).

The issue of illegal activity is an important one that often has direct implications for the severity of the use. A client who has had repeated criminal convictions due to use-related behavior (e.g., DUIs, disorderly conduct) may be more severely addicted than one who has never experienced such symptoms. Similarly, the amount of time invested in the substance use habit may also provide some insight into the severity of use. A client whose entire day is somehow preoccupied with drug procurement, use, and recovery is less likely to be treatable on an outpatient basis than a client with a mild habit that involves time only on weekends.

Ancillary Symptom Questions

Commonly associated difficulties can emerge in a multitude of areas of functioning —including, but not limited to, family relationships, social contexts, employment and career settings, and academic settings (Boylan, Malley, & Scott, 1995; Meyer & Deitsch, 1996). The client's financial situation and physical health are also often affected, as well as the client's involvement with law enforcement. Assessing how vastly clients' networks of relationships (both intimate and superficial) have been affected by their drug use provides great insight into clients' level of addiction and the possible level of motivation for treatment. Often family relationships are severely affected, with clients turning away from nonusing parents or spouses. Even more complicating, however, may be the family in which the client uses a substance together with a spouse or intimate partner, in which case drug use may be a major cementing feature of the relationship. Violence within the intimate relationship needs to be explored, because this is often related to drug use. In terms of social relationships, the therapist must explore whether there are drugs in the client's social network; that is, whether there are friends who use and whether there are any left who do not. With regard to employment history, it is important to find out if clients have used on the job, are arriving at work intoxicated or are withdrawing, and whether their ability to work has been affected by the use. This is of particular importance (in the sense of physical safety) if the client's work involves operating heavy machinery or otherwise requires attention and concentration to safety.

Finally, it is important to find out if clients' financial situations have suffered due to drug use, if they have experienced changes in physical health, and if they have become involved with the criminal justice system. Relatedly, any mental health symptoms that are revealed by clients must be put in the context of their substance use to be able to make accurate diagnoses of mental illness per se versus substance-induced mental illness.

Supplemental Questionnaires

Once therapists have completed the clinical interview, they can decide on administering additional questionnaires to elicit even more information or to corroborate findings. A number of instruments have been developed for this purpose, though none are entirely satisfactory as far as validity and reliability are concerned. The most commonly used instruments appear to be the Michigan Alcohol Screening

Test (MAST), the Addiction Severity Index (ASI), and the Substance Abuse Subtle Screening Inventory (SASSI). Many others exist (e.g., subscales of the MMPI-2); the interested reader may refer to Allen and Columbus (1995) and Litten and Allen (1994) for more information.

Michigan Alcohol Screening Test   The MAST (MAST; Selzer, 1971) was developed as a "rapid and effective screening for lifetime alcohol-related problems and alcoholism" (Allen & Columbus, 1995, p. 386) for a variety of populations. It consists of 25 brief items that are self-administered in approximately 10 minutes and responded to on a true–false basis. Scoring is accomplished after reverse-scoring four of the 25 items and assigning weighted scores. These weighted scores are then summed; the sum represents a total score reflecting the client's severity of alcohol-related problems. A total score of "five points or more would place the subject in an 'alcoholic' category. Four points would be suggestive of alcoholism, three points or less would indicate the subject was not alcoholic" (Allen & Columbus, 1995, p. 391). Psychometric studies (e.g., Hedlund & Vieweg, 1984) report adequate internal consistency but marginal construct validity. Nevertheless, the MAST has been recommended as a screening tool by the National Institute on Alcohol Abuse and Alcoholism (see Connors, 1995).

Addiction Severity Index   The ASI (ASI; McLellan et al., 1985) was developed to measure seven key problem areas associated with drug use. The ASI rates each problem area with regard to severity and provides information that will assist with treatment planning. The ASI is a structured interview that can be completed in about 45 minutes (including scoring time); this can be used in conjunction with a clinical interview, as described above. Its interrater reliability and test–retest reliability are reported to be excellent, and it has acceptable concurrent validity. It can be administered repeatedly throughout treatment to assess progress. The seven areas tapped by the ASI are drug and alcohol use, medical status, employment status, illegal activity, family and social relations, and psychiatric conditions over a lifetime and within the last 30 days. Each area is assessed via 20 to 30 questions, the answers to which are scored objectively and subjectively. Thus the ASI is more comprehensive than the MAST, but it is also more difficult and more time-consuming to administer. However, training aids for interested users are available from the National Institute on Drug Abuse. The ASI is rated by the National Institute on Drug Abuse as one of the most widely used drug screening instruments for treatment and research purposes (National Institute on Drug Abuse, 1994).

Substance Abuse Subtle Screening Inventory   The SASSI (SASSI; Miller, 1985) was developed as a subtle measure of substance use disorder with the purpose of classifying respondents as chemical abusers or nonabusers. The SASSI provides a subtle means of assessing substance use disorder; in other words, it screens test takers without using obvious substance-use items. It is this feature of the SASSI that makes it particularly useful in non-substance use treatment settings (see Department of Health and Human Services, 1993). It is also this feature that requires that the SASSI be used in conjunction with a clinical interview once a categorization of substance abuse or dependence has been made. The SASSI consists of 52 true–false items and can be scored to provide subscales that render a substance use profile. Administration time averages 10 minutes. The subscales of the SASSI show the following: the FVA measures use of alcohol; the FVOD assesses use of other drugs; the OAT assesses more obvious attributes of substance use; the SAT measures subtle attributes of substance use; the DEF identifies defensiveness in test-taking behavior and can be followed up on with the DEF2; the COR measures current risk for substance abuse; and the RAP serves as a validity scale. Six of the scales are used in a formula to provide a dichotomous determination of whether the respondent is substance dependent. The current scale has good internal consistency and validity (Miller, 1985).

Final Notes about Substance Use Assessment

Thorough substance use assessment is critical for many reasons, not the least of which are proper diagnosis and treatment planning. Much controversy still exists in the minds of some mental health professionals about the ultimate treatment goal for a substance using client. Nystul (1993) and Nugent (1994) argue that it is not clear whether no use or controlled use should be the goal; others, however, believe that only no use can be a proper treatment goal (e.g., American Psychiatric Association, 1994; Meyer & Deitsch, 1996). This controversy will not likely be put to rest any time soon, so until that time clinicians will have to make personal decisions about the issues that fit with their own conceptualizations of substance use and moral values. There are other treatment decisions that have to be made that are not always clear-cut. The therapist must decide whether any substance using client should be treated on an outpatient basis or whether inpatient treatment is necessary for all. Certainly, if there is an anticipated period of withdrawal after severe and prolonged use, the client may need to detoxify in a controlled medical environment. However, even after detoxification, the client may need inpatient treatment to prevent relapse. A consistent argument has been made that clients should not be seen in outpatient treatment while they are still under the influence of or actively using substances. A client who is still actively and severely addicted and using a substance needs to be referred for inpatient evaluation and treatment. If a client is seen in outpatient treatment after inpatient treatment has been completed or because substance use was not judged severe enough to warrant inpatient services, auxiliary services should also be recommended. Common referrals in that regard include referring clients to physicians to monitor and assess physical health, to support groups (e.g., AA or NA) to help them establish non-using social networks, and perhaps to psychoeducational programs conducted by service providers specializing in substance use treatment. The latter is particularly indicated if the client still manifests significant denial or a profound inability to stop substance use (Hood & Johnson, 1997).

Substance use, even once stopped, generally implies that there will be a number of related presenting concerns that need to be addressed in the treatment plan. These tend to include, though they may not be limited to, legal problems, relationship problems, educational and career interferences, need for social skills training and social support development, physical health and fitness problems, need for alternative coping strategies to deal with stress, development of leisure skills, treatment of psychological symptoms (ranging from symptoms to disorders), and relapse prevention (Nystul, 1993). Additionally, there is significant consensus in the literature that substance use does not occur in a vacuum, but rather always has implications for family members. Hence, treatment planning with substance using individuals should always address the idea that their families may need therapeutic support in one form or another as well (Nugent, 1994).

MENTAL STATUS EXAMS

Conducting a mental status examination (MSE) is a skill every mental health service provider should have because it provides a context in which to gather certain types of information. A mental status exam structures the types of behaviors, affects, cognitions, perception, and client features a therapist considers when working with a client. Because there are several well-accepted components of a mental status exam, its conduct also facilitates communication among professionals because it provides a focus for questioning and a structure for reporting (Morrison, 1995a; Simmons, 1987). A formal mental status examination is indicated when a client presents with symptoms that suggest psychotic symptomatology, brain or other neurological dysfunction, or other severe psychopathology (Choca, 1988; Cormier & Cormier, 1991).

Despite the very distinct categories of information covered by the MSE, it is an interview that can be conducted in a very structured or a very informal manner, depending largely on the style of the individual clinician and the needs of the client. A brief outline of the crucial components of the mental status interview is provided here, although readers anticipating the need for MSEs in their practice on a regular basis (e.g., clinicians working with a population of severely or chronically mentally ill clients) should also refer to Beutler and Berren (1995) and Morrison (1995a) for more detailed information. The primary categories of a mental status exam include (not necessarily in this order) appearance and level of physical activity, mood and affect, sensorium and perception, cognitive functioning, interpersonal style, and coping strategies or psychological defenses. For each of these broad categories, several subsections of exploration and assessment exist.

Appearance and Level of Physical Activity

This category involves a good deal of information that need not be sought, but rather is gleaned from behavioral observations. It focuses attention on factors such as height and weight, grooming and hygiene, manner and style of dress, eye and hair color, posture, gait, psychomotor movement, speech patterns, and physical attributes such as scars, bruises, physical handicaps, and prosthetic devices. Several of these characteristics are simply descriptive, whereas others can be evaluated for their appropriateness or can be rated and further defined. Traits such as eye and hair color are simply described. Height and weight can be evaluated and related to expected healthy or normative ranges. Hygiene and grooming can be rated by whether they approximate given societal health standards and grooming habits. Motor movement must be further defined as agitated, fidgety, unusual, normal, or as including tics, tremors, or motor abnormalities. Speech patterns can be described as slowed, pressured, or otherwise unusual (e.g., stuttering or cluttering). Gestures and facial expressions can be assessed for their congruence with the verbal content of conversation as well as the level of activity or agitation they may suggest. Any unusual or characteristic mannerisms and habits of a person should also be noted, such as tics, repetitive verbalizations, or nervous gestures or laughter.

Assessing deficiencies in appearance suggests where the client's self-care skills are lacking, which in turn may help the clinician make some assessment of the client's social competence and social judgment (Beutler & Berren, 1995). Observing motor movements can lead to conclusions about the client's state of alertness and can help the clinician form diagnoses related to alertness (such as delirium and dementia) as well as diagnoses related to psychomotor issues (e.g., bipolar disorder).

Mood and Affect

This information can be gleaned through observation as well as through some cautious questioning of the client. It assesses primary emotions, paying attention to clinical sign of depression, anxiety, fears, and phobias (mood); it also assesses clients' expressions of emotion (affect)— that is, how cheerful, optimistic, angry, irritable, hostile, friendly, or antagonistic they are during interactions with the clinician (Morrison, 1995a). The stability of a client's affects needs to be described, especially if the clinician notes that they appear to fluctuate widely and change quickly. The client's range of affect and its appropriateness to the topic of conversation also needs to be rated and should be described by its most outstanding features. As such, the therapist needs to judge whether affect is blunted or restricted, labile or rigid, dramatized or constricted, exaggerated or overly controlled. Restricted or blunted affect is not be confused with the appropriate ability to keep affect in check as required by circumstances. To inhibit crying may not signal restriction of affect as much as it may signal persons' abilities to hold affect in check when they judge a situation as inappropriate for its expression (Beutler & Berren, 1995).

Similarly, affect and mood need to be assessed for their congruence. First, affect needs to be congruent with mood. For example, a depressed client (mood) who laughs throughout the interview (affect), evidences incongruence. Second, affect needs to be congruent with the topic of conversation. For example, a client who discusses the death of a loved one while making jokes and laughing a lot, evidences incongruent affects. It is also important to note whether the client is comfortable expressing affect. It is not uncommon for some clients to have familial backgrounds in which there were unwritten rules about the appropriateness of some expressions of affect over others. Thus, a person may be quite at ease with affects that are positive and may show appropriate expression in that realm. However, as the same client encounters negative affects, expression may be inhibited and clearly uncomfortable for the person.

Affect is often easier to describe than mood. Affect is the expression of feelings or emotions, whereas mood refers to their experience. Affect is obvious; mood is subtle (Cormier & Cormier, 1991). Mood is sometimes inferred from verbalizations, sometimes judged from expressed affect. For example, clients who talk about their inability to sleep, poor appetite, decreased enjoyment of life, and similar symptoms can be judged to be depressed (mood). A client who is aggressive and hostile toward the examiner (affect) and relates a history of physical fighting and arguments can be evaluated as angry (mood). Mood can be denied by clients who seek to keep emotions hidden from themselves or from the clinician. Mood can at times also be inferred from somatic symptoms. Such clients may refuse to admit they are depressed or anxious despite obvious symptoms of either disorder and may be unaware that their reports of headaches, stomachaches, and tension may be related to their mood state.

Sensorium and Perception

This realm of functioning can range from a simple assessment of the functionality of clients' senses to a complex assessment of their level of contact with reality and orientation to their surroundings (Choca, 1988). Morrison (1995a) suggests that this aspect of the mental status exam always be included in a general intake because therapists can never assume that persons are unimpaired just because they do not spontaneously report related symptomatology. Perception and sensorium can be assessed through observation, as well as directly questioned. To be oriented and aware, clients need to have a basic awareness of where they are in time and space, as well as of who they and their significant others are. They should be able to provide name, age, residence address, current location (including clinic name and therapist), and time of day (the month, the year, and within approximately 30 minutes to the hour). Clients should be able to share information about themselves that goes beyond mere biographical data.

Before assessing contact with reality, the functionality of the client's senses must be assessed. In other words, the therapist must inquire about the client's ability to hear, see, feel, speak, and taste. If any question arises about the physiological functioning of any of the client's senses, an appropriate medical referral needs to be initiated before potentially rash judgments about contact with reality and diagnosis are made. It is also interesting to note any obvious preferences of certain senses. Some preferences are developmentally driven. Infants, for instance, prefer to use their sense of taste in exploring new surroundings. Clearly, this preference in a four-year-old would be somewhat disturbing. Similarly, whereas the sense of touch is an important one for the eight-year-old who explores the new therapy environment, an adolescent is more likely to explore simply through the sense of vision (see Sigelman & Shafer, 1995).

Further, and perhaps more importantly, the therapist must ascertain that the client can differentiate fantasy from reality and that there is no hallucinatory process in any of the client's realms of sensing. Hallucinations are important to rule out through direct questioning if the presenting problems include concerns such as excessive fantasy life, distractedness that appears and disappears suddenly, night-mares or night terrors, and physical concerns or strange physical sensations. Hallu-cinations are best assessed through direct questioning about voices or visions in the absence of a person who produces them (e.g., "Do you ever hear voices or other sounds when there is no one around to produce them? Do you ever see things other people don't see?", Morrison, 1995a, p. 122). Hallucinations range in severity. For example, auditory hallucinations range from (least to most severe) vague noises to mumbling, to understandable words, to phrases, to complete sentences (Morrison, 1995a). Sometimes clients may also relate isolated incidents of hearing their names spoken. These are illusions that are often stress-induced, not hallucinations. Illu-sions generally refer to events that are misperceived (e.g., mistaking and being con-vinced that a suit hanging in a dark room is a burglar) and are also more likely to occur during times of mild sensory deprivation or while moving in or out of sleep. It is important to differentiate between illusions and hallucinations by inquiring about the circumstances around the experience of these phenomena. If a client re-ports hallucinations, it is a good practice to assess their reactions to them. In other words, therapists need to inquire whether clients know when they hallucinate, how they react to the hallucinations (e.g., are frightened by them), and when they occur. The content of the hallucinations also needs to be explored.

Visual and auditory hallucinations are the most common perceptual distur-bances seen in psychotic disorders. However, they are also often related to substance use disorders (e.g., experienced during intoxication or withdrawal). Tactile, olfac-tory, and gustatory hallucinations, on the other hand, are more commonly associ-ated with a brain disorder with an etiology that may include brain injury, tumors, or toxicity. Thus the presence of hallucinations in and of itself does not suggest a spe-cific diagnosis. It merely alerts the therapist to the potential presence of a range of possible syndromes that need to be explored further. Generally, the presence of hal-lucinations suggests that the therapist who is not a medical professional needs to ini-tiate a referral to a psychiatrist for differential diagnosis and appropriate care.

Finally, the client's level of consciousness must be assessed through questions about loss of consciousness, such as fainting or blacking out. The intrusiveness of certain environmental stimuli into clients' consciousness must be assessed to give clues about their level of distractibility and ability to pay attention. Dissociations or similar lapses in consciousness need to be recorded, and the presence of seizure disorders must be inquired about. Alertness ranges from full awareness of the en-vironment with the ability to respond quickly, to sensory input, to drowsiness or clouding that can be transient or chronic, to unconsciousness (stupor or coma). General outpatient mental health workers will not often evidence levels of alert-ness that are beyond drowsiness or clouding, though they may work with clients who have reported stupor or coma in the past. Reports of impaired alertness in the past should prompt the therapist to ask for releases of information from previous health care providers to find out more about the circumstances of these periods of time in the client's life.

Cognitive Functioning

The first category of information within the realm of cognitive functioning includes intelligence, cognitive complexity, concentration and attention, and memory. The amount of formality used to make these assessments can range from applying intelligence and other cognitive testing to making judgments based on the client's verbalizations, grammatical correctness, and logic of thought during the interview. To test concentration and attention, the clinician can ask the client to perform simple tasks such as counting backwards from 100 to 0 by intervals of threes or counting forward by sevens. Abstracting ability can be evaluated by asking the client to interpret simple proverbs such as those included in the Wechsler Adult Intelligence Scale and by observing the client's problem-solving skills and problem awareness during the interview. Memory can be assessed by asking the client to recall birthdays, the breakfast food on the day of the interview, and similar questions; it can also be assessed by asking the client to remember three words said by the therapist and checking later in the interview whether the client recalled them. A very crude test of intelligence assesses the client's fund of information through simple conversation that challenges the client to converse in different topic areas. While conducting interviewing centered around academic and vocational achievements, the therapist pays attention to vocabulary, grammar, and similar skills. Related to the issue of intelligence is the client's ability to process language. Specifically, the therapist pays attention to the client's ability to comprehend instructions and conversation; to the fluency of the client's speech and thought processes; to any problems with naming common items; and to the client's ability to read and write easily (e.g., as is required to read an informed consent form or fill out an application for admission). Relatedly, the mental health professional should pay attention to the spontaneity of the client's speech, the adequacy of word choice and word finding, and the age and context appropriateness of a person's language.

Once these general cognitive processes have been assessed, it is also necessary to evaluate the presence of cognitive features (content and processes) that may be pathological in nature, such as delusions, preoccupations, and obsessions (Cormier & Cormier, 1991). Thought content needs to be further specified by the topic that is prevalent. Common themes that may emerge include guilt, violence, religion, spirits (demons, ghosts, devils), worthlessness, persecution by peers, and physical complaints. Thought content can be mildly distorted (e.g., overgeneralization, catastrophizing, black–white thinking, perfectionism), moderately dysfunctional (obsessions, ruminations, or other cognitive preoccupation), or grossly delusional. A delusion is defined as a "fixed, false belief that cannot be explained by the patient's culture or education" (Morrison, 1995a, p. 119). Delusions can vary greatly with regard to content and include grandiose themes, persecutory themes, or guilt themes (for a comprehensive listing of themes and examples, refer to Morrison, 1995a). Delusions are generally associated with thought disorders (psychoses such as delusional disorders or schizophrenias) or very severe mood disorders.

Additionally, the client's thought processes must be evaluated for coherence, circumstantiality, tangentiality, neologisms, echolalia, unusual associations (e.g., clang associations), and blocking or evasiveness (Beutler & Berren, 1995). Circumstantial logic suggests that the client is temporarily easily distracted from the topical focus but can ultimately reorient and reconnect with the focus of conversation. Tangential logic departs from the focus of conversation but with some logical connection between the thoughts that follow from one to the other. Loose associations (also referred to as derailment or flight of ideas if very severe) are deviations from the topic of conversation that are not obviously logically or topically related. Like delusions, severe disturbances in thought process are generally associated with psychotic or extremely severe mood disorders (with psychotic symptoms).

Finally, the effects of cognitive processes on judgment and level of insight must be estimated (Morrison, 1995a). Insight is the person's ability to understand and express the problem or presenting concern with which they have come to the therapist. Judgment, on the other hand, refers to the client's ability to set realistic goals, to plan an appropriate course of action, and to verbalize realistic expectations.

Interpersonal Style

Interpersonal style can be evaluated based on observations, more so than on specific interview questions (Beutler & Berren, 1995). The therapist observes the client's patterns of reacting to the therapist to evaluate the client's ability to form relationships, level of effort made to relate, ability to self-disclose appropriately, physical proximity or personal space, patterns of defense and expression, and manifestation of personality traits. The therapist can assess the clients' level of self-assurance displayed, as well as their ability to engage in speaking and self-disclose. Level of trust (which can range from paranoia to being overly trusting) can be judged, as can the need for acceptance. Finally, the quality of the interaction between client and therapist can communicate much about the general quality of a client's relationships with others. A client who meets the therapist with inexplicable hostility is likely to express such an attitude in general. Similarly, patterns of interpersonal interaction with the therapist that suggest challenge, attempts or need to please, submissiveness, or passivity can be similarly interpreted. Finally, this category also includes a thorough assessment of peer, adult, and family relationships (Cormier & Cormier, 1991). Because this aspect of the mental status exam is redundant with the type of information that should already have been collected during the intake interview, it will not be discussed in further detail at this time.

The therapist can also include in interpersonal relationships the issue of psychological defense and coping, because these are often behaviors exercised in social situations. Defense and coping are particularly relevant in unfamiliar environments and relationships, as in the new encounter with the therapist. Thus observation of the client in the new therapy situation may provide clues not only about whether the client is capable of coping, but also about the preferred types of strategies used. Capacity for coping is evidenced by the person's ability to tolerate and adapt to new situations and strangers, to express difficult needs and desires and accept them as important, and to express even strong or difficult affects as they emerge and to deal with them (e.g., diffuse them) successfully.

Clients do not always cope successfully, and sometimes rather then coping, they use defenses to deal with difficult situations. Kohut (1984) has reconceptualized defenses as protective mechanisms that are used by people to protect vulnerabilities within themselves. This conceptualization of the defensive process appears extremely appropriate. There are large numbers of defenses or protective mechanisms that have been identified in the literature, and it is impossible to define and mention all of them here. The reader is referred to works by Anna Freud (1946) and Laughlin (1983) for details. However, a few defensive strategies are common enough to warrant providing some discussion and examples. The mental status examiner must not only note whether a client has the capacity to cope, but also know the types of self-protective (defensive) strategies a person employs in various coping situations.

Many clients will try to use avoidance, evasion, or diversion when difficult coping situations arise. A client failing to respond to a question, suddenly changing topics, or attempting to direct the interaction or questioning to avoid a certain subject matter are examples of such maneuvers. Sometimes diversion also involves somatization when the chosen diversion may be a physical complaint (e.g., the client suddenly develops a headache and wants to cut the session short). Withdrawal is a common defense among clients and may range from quite severe manifestations to lesser forms of shunning contact. Often people engage in a defense called undoing. Clients may reveal some information that was too difficult for them to deal with at this time and then may deny that they said it or referred to it. These clients try to undo their verbal actions by covering them up. Acting out is another common defense. However, it does not always occur in the context of negative or angry affect, but might also be used to relieve anxiety or fear. Other defenses that are frequently used include denial, rationalization, internalization, projection, and projective identification.

Final Notes about Mental Status Exams

The MSE provides a range of information that can be helpful, though not necessarily conclusive, for the diagnostic process. Using this formal interview is particularly implicated if the client presents with concerns of extreme mood disturbance, thought disorders or other cognitive problems, potential perceptual disturbances, or severe problems in coping and interpersonal relating. Many of the symptoms and processes assessed by the MSE are signs of severe psychopathology, such as psychotic disorders or mood disorders. However, many of the signs and symptoms are also often present in substance use disorders and neurological disorders and hence cannot be conclusively diagnosed without the appropriate additional assessments and referrals. Some clinicians insist that formal MSEs, at least of the cognitive and perceptual areas of a client's functioning, should be included in routine intake interviews (e.g., Morrison, 1995a). Others suggest that MSEs are only needed when particular questions that relate to psychosis, neurological disease, or related severe pathology emerge in an intake interview (e.g., Choca, 1988; Cormier & Cormier, 1991). Ultimately the decision about the length and depth of a mental status exam rests with each individual clinician. However, it appears that an abbreviated form of a mental status exam can be easily incorporated into a general intake interview and can be quickly expanded when needed (this suggestion is commensurate with information provided in the Behavioral Observation section of the intake interview presented in Chapter 2). Such an abbreviated version may include questions about hallucinations and illusions, as well as thought processes and contents that may be unusual, without spending undue time on these issues if their presence is denied and if no other symptomatology exists.

SUMMARY AND CONCLUDING THOUGHTS

A number of special assessments are often indicated by circumstances presented by the client at intake. Many of these special assessments can be conducted by the well-informed therapist and do not require referral to other mental health or medical providers. Most common among these special assessments are genograms, parenting assessments, substance use assessments, and mental status exams. It must be noted, however, that these special assessments do not always answer all questions, but instead, on some occasions may actually raise more concerns. Skilled therapists know when to initiate referrals and when their skills are insufficient for adequate diagnosis and/or treatment of the client.

DOCUMENTATION AND RECORD-KEEPING

Information gathered through special assessments to supplement the intake data that were collected prior to or concurrent with the intake is generally recorded in the intake report. As mentioned in Chapter 2, parenting assessment data and genogram data could be incorporated into the family section. Any special documents that were prepared in the process of these special assessments are attached to the intake report (e.g., the genogram itself). Data obtained from the substance use assessment clearly fit into the intake report section on the client's substance use history; the mental status exam findings are incorporated in the behavioral observations section.

Occasionally, special assessments are not conducted early on in treatment because the concern did not emerge until after the client had been seen for a while. In this case, it is best to record the collected information in two ways: first, as part of the regular progress notes that are being written for the session, and second, as an Intake Report Addendum. The addendum approach assures that these critical data do not get lost in the progress notes should the case be taken over by another clinician or should a release of information be received about this client. In other words, new therapists—and the information mailed out in response to a release of information—generally focus on reports only (progress notes are rarely released). Thus if the new data are not somehow attached to the intake report, another service provider who could benefit from them may well not notice them.

4

CASE CONCEPTUALIZATION
AND TREATMENT PLANNING

*The things we see are the same things that are within us. There is
no reality except the one contained within us. That is why so
many people live such an unreal life. They take the images outside
them for reality and never allow the world within to assert itself.
You can be happy that way. But once you know the other
interpretation you no longer have the choice of following
the crowd. The majority's path is an easy one.
—HERMAN HESSE, DEMIAN*

So far this book has addressed data collection and exploration of historical events
about psychotherapy clients. It now moves into the less defined yet even more important area of case conceptualization, and moves from there to goal setting and
treatment planning. Conceptualizing a case is a bit like helping the client identify
a true self and the motivations that fuel it—the therapist attempts to recognize the
client's reality as a means of deciding how best to help the client with growth,
change, and healing. This is often not a straightforward process. It begins with
what the therapist knows about the client thus far (the outer image), and continues
with finding out what motivates this outer presentation (the inner world). It then
progresses through interpretations of what the combination of inner and outer
worlds mean for the client. This interpretation dictates the treatment plan and continues throughout treatment until the client is ready to terminate. In other words,
although the clinician gives the initial conceptualization much thought and prepares it carefully, based on all the history that has been collected, it generally is
open to minor revision as therapy continues on its way. Even more importantly,
therapists must be open to revising goals (in collaboration with their clients) and
to be flexible in their use of treatment strategies. This is not to say that therapists
will continually change course; generally, it is best to settle on a chosen approach
and then to stick with it for some period of time to see if it produces the desired re-

sults. However, within this approach, the therapist must remain flexible to use techniques, strategies, and catalysts as they appear appropriate and helpful.

It may be important here to define a few terms. Treatment approach refers to the overall conceptual model (or school of thought) chosen by the therapist, such as a psychodynamic approach, a humanistic approach, an existential approach, or a family systems approach. Strategies or techniques refer to actual complex intervention procedures (often derived from a specific school of thought) in which the therapist engages to assist the client in the growth and healing process, such as relaxation training, guided imagery, metaphors, dream analysis, and so forth. These techniques, though derived from a specific theoretical way of thinking about human behavior, tend to be usable in multiple therapy approaches by therapists of various schools of thought. For example, even though relaxation training is derived from a classical conditioning (i.e., behavioral) background, it is frequently used by psychodynamic therapists. Finally, catalysts are therapist behaviors that facilitate growth and change in the client and that are considered theory free (i.e., are used by therapists of all schools of thought); examples of catalysts are empathic responding, reflection, catharsis, and similar basic therapy and helping skills.

The process of planning and conceptualizing treatment always proceeds through five stages. First, the therapist diagnoses the client; this is followed by conceptualizing the client's case; then treatment goals are set and negotiated with the client; goal setting is followed by treatment planning that consists of selection of approach, strategy, and techniques; and finally the process is completed through feedback to the client. These five steps must be followed in all cases to ensure that proper care is provided to the client. Treatment without the benefit of a guiding conceptualization and without clearly identified goals and treatment plans is bound to flounder because therapist and client lack direction and clarity about the therapeutic process.

DIAGNOSIS

Two issues are attended to in making a diagnosis; first, the therapist prepares a problem list that reflects all potentially relevant problems, whether they were identified as problems by clients themselves or not; second, the problem list is used to make a DSM-IV diagnosis to satisfy epidemiological and third-party reimbursement needs. Therapists who are concerned about the drawbacks of diagnostic labeling can skip the DSM-IV diagnosis. However, even if clinicians choose to skip the DSM-IV diagnosis, they should be familiar with what it involves and how to do it. Then if circumstances are encountered where a diagnosis is essential, the therapist is prepared to provide it.

List of Therapist-Identified Problems

Often, as an intake assessment progresses, the clinician will make note of a number of problems that are not mentioned by clients as part of their reason for seeking treatment. These problems noted by the clinician often are related to other areas of clients' lives, not merely to those that motivated the appointment. Specifically, several areas of functioning need to be explored for potential problems that may not be addressed by the client directly—namely, psychological, social or cultural, medical or physical, occupational or academic, and family-related problems. Although not all problems the clinician has become aware of during the intake may be obviously related to the presenting problem, all need to be listed.

Psychological Problems

Psychological problems are those that involve the client's emotional, psychological, intrapsychic, and interpersonal adjustment. Emotional adjustment involves affect and mood, including fears, moodiness, depression, variability in affect, and so forth. Psychological adjustment refers to the client's functioning with regard to pathology in perception, cognition, awareness, or development, including hallucinations, delusions, lapses in consciousness, delays in development, and thought disturbances. Intrapsychic adjustment refers to issues of self-perception, self-understanding, conflict with self, and life direction, including low self-esteem, lack of interests or hobbies, obsessive hand-washing, conflicted expression of affect, indecisiveness, and similar problems. Interpersonal adjustment refers to problems that manifest in the context of relating to others such as family and friends, including difficulties in peer relationships, fighting with significant others, ambivalence about attachment and trust, or job-related problems.

Social or Cultural Problems

This category refers to the client's social situation, including environmental, socioeconomic, cultural, religious, and similar issues. Environmental problems may include issues such as inappropriate shelter or nourishment, whereas living in a deprived neighborhood may represent a socioeconomic issue. Although the two are often directly and inextricably related, sometimes environmental problems may not be as obvious as socioeconomic ones. For instance, exposure to pollution is an environmental issue that can have psychological implications, but it may not be at all tied to socioeconomic status. Cultural problems may include such issues as intolerance by others of certain behaviors that are acceptable within the client's cultural group, or unfamiliarity with the cultural expectations, values, and rules of a group into which the client is trying to integrate, as may be the case with a rural young adult who is beginning university studies in a major urban area. Religious problems may involve ostracism because of religious affiliation, rejection by a peer group because of atheism, or conflict over religious beliefs incompatible with those of parents.

Medical and Other Physical Problems

Medical or physical problems refer to the client's general level of health, health consciousness, and accident proneness. Medical problems can vary from severe (e.g., frequent hospitalizations for a chronic illness) to mild (e.g., seasonal allergies). Regardless of severity, they should be listed here. Developmental deficits and delays (although occasionally not physical or physiological in nature) are placed into this category, as are family history of mental or other illness. It is also wise to note obvious medical problems of other family members here because of their potential impact on the client. Neurological and neuropsychological problems can be listed here if they have been formally assessed. Dietary and nutritional issues should be noted if problematic, as should exercise or lack thereof.

Occupational and Academic Problems
This grouping of problems refers to issues that emerge in the job or educational setting, but it focuses primarily on actual occupational or academic performance, such as changes in functioning, poor or exceptional performance, grades, learning disabilities, and job stress. There may be some overlap with psychological problems in that there may be interpersonal problems, such as peer or authority relationships that are confined to the occupational or academic setting. It is an arbitrary decision by the therapist as to where to list these types of problems, as long as they are listed somewhere.

Family-Related Problems
Family-related problems refer to conflicts that arise in the family setting. As with occupational problems, they may overlap with psychological concerns. This category should focus on a detailed description of the family problem, not merely make a statement of a conflict among family members. For instance, triangulation (in which a third person is pulled into a dyadic conflict), crossing generational boundaries, frequent fighting in the marital dyad, lack of trust, history of divorce, and similar issues are appropriate problems to include. Problems should be listed separately for the current nuclear family and the family of origin. Issues of child abuse or neglect, both that experienced and that perpetrated, are included in this category of problems.

It is best to make a list of problems within each of these areas rather than to attempt to deal with them in narrative form. The problems are often closely related to the issues and dynamics outlined in the psychosocial history of the intake report; hence the problem list will have some overlap with the information in the intake report. It is generally not included in the intake report, but rather is used to guide diagnosis and to begin to give the therapist some direction in identifying goals and objectives. In this regard, it serves to point out areas in the client's life where improvements may be desirable.

To help put problems identified into a time context and into a time-referenced relationship with one another, it helps to note age of onset and duration or acuteness. These timing issues can be noted by indicating the number of weeks since a problem or behavior emerged; by noting a problem or behavior as chronic; by showing it has a long history and is still occurring; or by noting an issue is acute, if the onset is recent and of particular importance or salience in the present. Problems that wax and wane should also be noted in some form, as should problems that occurred recently but are currently resolved. An example of a problem list is shown in Table 4.1. Here it is also linked to a DSM-IV diagnosis as a means of demonstrating the usefulness of the problem list in the diagnostic process.

TABLE 4.1 Problem List and Associated DSM-IV Diagnosis for a Depressed Adult Client

Problem Category	Onset/Type	Specific Concerns	Diagnostic Code
Psychological	2 weeks ago	initial and terminal insomnia	296.32
	2 weeks ago	less than 5 hours of sleep per night	296.32
	2 weeks ago	loss of appetite	296.32
	2 weeks ago	loss of sex drive	296.32
	2 weeks ago	psychomotor retardation	296.32
	chronic	low-grade dysphoria	300.40
	acute	severe dysphoria	296.32
	2 weeks ago	poor concentration and attention	296.32
	chronic	low energy	300.40
	chronic	does not initiate action	301.60
	chronic	helplessness	301.60
	chronic	low self-esteem	300.40
	chronic	indecisive	300.40, 301.60
	chronic	lack of self-confidence	301.60
Social/Cultural	chronic	social isolation	
	chronic	fear of loneliness	301.60
	chronic	has never lived alone	301.60
	5 years ago	death of best friend	
Medical/Physical	chronic	poor physical health care during childhood	
	chronic	reluctance to seek health care in adulthood	
	4 weeks ago	no regular exercise	296.32
	in 2 weeks	5-pound weight loss	296.32
	chronic	some unhealthy dietary habits	
Occupational/Academic	for 2 weeks	missing classes and class assignments	296.32
	for 2 weeks	calling in sick to work	296.32
Family-Related	2 weeks ago	brother's suicide	
	resolved	brother's history of alcoholism	
	resolved	mother's history of depression requiring hospitilization	
	chronic	father's relative absence during childhood	
	chronic	mother's emotional absence	
	chronic	victim of neglect, emotional and physical	
	chronic	loose family ties at present	
	chronic	absence of extended family in childhood	
	acute	perceived distancing from significant other	

Diagnostic Impressions

Axis I	all criteria met	Major Depressive Disorder, recurrent, moderate severity	296.32
	all criteria met	Dysthymic Disorder, early onset **(primary diagnosis)**	300.40
Axis II	all criteria met	Dependent Personality Disorder with avoidant traits	301.60
Axis III		sleep and appetite disturbances	
Axis IV		suicide of brother, social isolation	
Axis V		60—moderate symptoms	

DSM-IV Diagnosis

Diagnosis in this context refers to DSM-IV diagnosis and must be carefully differentiated from a conceptualization. The Diagnostic and Statistical Manual of Mental Disorders (4th ed.; DSM-IV; American Psychiatric Association, 1994) is the result of the American Psychiatric Association's long struggle to develop a psychiatric nosology that accurately and reliably captures the primary psychiatric syndromes presented by clients to their health care providers. The DSM's widespread use and application has been severely criticized (e.g., Kirk & Kutchins, 1992) and has been equally intensively defended (e.g., Spitzer & Williams, 1987) Regardless of whether a clinician is on the critical or supportive side of the issue, the current reality is that the DSM-IV has a number of drawbacks but remains the only consistent psychiatric nosology in use today. As such, it is the standard that is applied and used for a variety of purposes (as will be outlined below), and every mental health care provider must be familiar with it. The manual takes a multifaceted approach to psychiatric illness, by classifying problems along five dimensions (or axes). It is symptom-based, relatively standardized, and as objective as possible.

The five dimensions of the DSM-IV guide the clinician toward making evaluations along the lines of clinical syndromes (Axis I), mental retardation or personality disorders (Axis II), physical disorders (Axis III), psychosocial stressors (Axis IV), and overall level of functioning (Axis V). Axis I and Axis II diagnoses are symptom driven and structured somewhat like checklists. If the therapist has developed a thorough problem list for a client, it should provide all the information necessary to make a diagnostic decision. Nevertheless, very thorough familiarity with the manual (American Psychiatric Association, 1994) and related resources (e.g., Morrison, 1995a, 1995b; Reid, 1989; Spitzer, Gibbon, Skodol, Williams, & First, 1994) is required for its successful and responsible use. In fact, formal classroom training in its use is preferable to merely studying the manual and related books. An example of a DSM-IV diagnosis is provided in Table 4.1, along with a client's associated problem list. This example shows the usefulness of a carefully prepared problem list in making a DSM-IV diagnosis.

Axis I—Clinical Syndromes

Axis I of the DSM-IV is focused on the identification of major clinical disorders, such as depression, anxiety, and schizophrenia that generally have periods of florid symptomatology and do not necessarily begin in childhood nor necessarily continue in stable form across the lifespan. More likely, these disorders have later onsets, as well as fluctuations in the severity of their symptoms across time. This fluctuation is not to be mistaken for the absence of chronicity. It merely indicates that although the disorder itself may be chronic, its actual manifestation through obvious symptoms may wax and wane. As will be evident, the definition of Axis I disorders is written in such a manner as to differentiate it from Axis II. It is possible for a client to warrant more than one diagnosis on Axis I. Further, sometimes a client may meet most of the criteria necessary for a given diagnosis but does not fulfill all. It is then possible to note this diagnosis as a "rule out" category, implying that this diagnosis is a possibility, but that more information must be gathered before it can be established for certain.

There are fifteen distinct categories of major clinical syndromes, each with a number of disorders contained within it. One of these categories is less relevant to the adult therapist but remains of great importance to child clinicians—namely, the category of disorders first diagnosed in infancy, childhood, and adolescence (e.g., learning disorders, tic disorders, elimination disorders). The remaining fourteen categories are as follows (each presented with a few distinct examples of actual diagnoses):

- *Delirium, Dementia, and Amnestic and other Cognitive Disorders* (e.g., Dementia of the Alzheimer's Type; Substance-Induced Amnestic Disorder)
- *Mental Disorders Due to a General Medical Condition* (e.g., Catatonic Disorder due to [specific medical condition]; Personality Change due to [specific medical condition])
- *Substance-Related Disorders* (e.g., Alcohol Dependence; Cocaine Withdrawal)
- *Schizophrenia and Other Psychotic Disorders* (e.g., Schizophreniform Disorder; Shared Psychotic Disorder)
- *Mood Disorders* (e.g., Dysthymic Disorder; Bipolar I Disorder)
- *Anxiety Disorders* (e.g., Social Phobia; Obsessive–Compulsive Disorder, Post-Traumatic Stress Disorder)
- *Somatoform Disorders* (e.g., Conversion Disorder; Hypochondriasis)
- *Factitious Disorders* (e.g., Factitious Disorder with Predominantly Physical Signs and Symptoms; Factitious Disorder with Predominantly Psychological Signs and Symptoms)
- *Dissociative Disorders* (e.g., Dissociative Fugue; Dissociative Identity Disorder [formerly multiple personality disorder])
- *Sexual and Gender Identity Disorders* (Sexual Aversion Disorder; Premature Ejaculation)
- *Eating Disorders* (e.g., Anorexia Nervosa; Bulimia Nervosa)
- *Sleep Disorders* (e.g., Primary Insomnia, Sleep Terror Disorder)
- *Impulse-Control Disorders Not Elsewhere Classified* (e.g., Kleptomania; Pyromania)
- *Adjustment Disorders* (e.g., Adjustment Disorder with Anxiety; Adjustment Disorder with Depressed Mood)

Axis II—Mental Retardation and Personality Disorders

As opposed to Axis I disorders, Axis II disorders always have to have their onset during the developmental period of life (i.e., birth to age 18). They are always either called Personality Disorders or Mental Retardation; they are considered chronic and their symptoms are stable. The fluctuations in symptomatology that are characteristic of Axis I disorders are not present in Axis II disorders. The Axis I versus Axis II differentiation was originally made by the authors of the DSM-III (American Psychiatric Association, 1980) to ensure that clinicians will never be satisfied looking only at the most florid or obvious symptoms, but also at less obvious but more stable and chronic symptomatology of long-term disorders that have their onset early in life. It is not uncommon to have diagnoses on Axis I and Axis

II for the same individual. If this is the case, the clinician is urged to make a judgment with regard to which diagnosis is the primary one—that is, which diagnosis is viewed as chiefly responsible for the referral of the client. This diagnosis becomes the principal diagnosis, and it theoretically guides treatment planning (see criticisms in this regard below). Finally, as is true for Axis I, more than one diagnosis can be made on Axis II, and a "rule out" category can be provided.

There are five types of mental retardation (MR) and ten distinct types of personality disorders that can be specified on Axis II (as well as a category for non-specific personality disorders). The five types of MR are mild, moderate, severe, profound, and severity unspecified. The ten distinct personality disorders and their most prominent associated features are as follows:

- *Paranoid Personality Disorder* (distrust, suspiciousness)
- *Schizoid Personality Disorder* (detachment from social relationships, restricted emotional expression)
- *Schizotypal Personality Disorder* (discomfort in relationships, eccentricities in behavior, distortions in perception and cognition)
- *Antisocial Personality Disorder* (disregard for others, violation of others' rights)
- *Borderline Personality Disorder* (impulsivity; instability in interpersonal relationships, self-identity, and affect)
- *Histrionic Personality Disorder* (excessive emotionality and attention-seeking)
- *Narcissistic Personality Disorder* (grandiosity, need for admiration, lack of empathy)
- *Avoidant Personality Disorder* (social inhibition, feelings of inadequacy, hypersensitivity to criticism)
- *Dependent Personality Disorder* (submissiveness, clinging behavior, need to be taken care of)
- *Obsessive–Compulsive Personality Disorder* (preoccupation with orderliness, perfectionism, and control)

All of these personality disorders have the following features in common: they reflect an enduring pattern of inner experiences and behaviors that deviates markedly from the individual's cultural expectations, and these affect at least two of the four areas of human functioning (i.e., cognition, affectivity, interpersonal functioning, and impulse control); they reflect a pattern that is pervasive and rigid, and one that permeates a broad range of personal and social situations; they lead to significant distress or impairment in various areas of functioning, such as social, occupational, or personal functioning; their onset can be traced to childhood or adolescence; the pattern cannot be accounted for by another clinical disorder (on Axis I), and is not due to substance abuse or a physical condition.

Axis III—Physical Disorders
Axis III allows for the formal coding of any physical condition or disorder that is seen as relevant to the diagnoses on Axis I and/or Axis II. In other words, the physical condition is relevant either etiologically or in terms of its impact on the person's mental health. Sometimes the condition is a result of the mental disorder;

sometimes it is a predisposing factor for the mental condition; and sometimes it is only loosely or potentially associated. Technically, Axis III *diagnosis* is under the purview of physicians only; however, all clinicians have the responsibility to note physical disorders or symptoms already identified (by history and records or by the client's self-report) on this axis. Obviously, whenever there is a notation on Axis III, there must have been and will need to be some involvement of a physician in the assessment and treatment phase of a case (either by studying previous treatment records or by a thorough referral). Including Axis III assures that mental health care providers look at possible physical and medical factors that can play a role in the person's psychological and mental state, and it assures that providers pay some attention to the physical aspects of the client.

Axis IV—Severity of Psychosocial Stressors
Axis IV requires notation regarding the presence, absence, and severity of psychosocial and environmental stressors in the client's life that may affect the etiology, prognosis, or treatment of the disorders noted on Axes I and II. Psychosocial stressors include negative or positive life events, environmental deficiency or stressors, family-related problems or concerns, inadequate social support, culturally-related experiences, or any other stressful life events. Common categories of stressors are listed in the manual and include the following (American Psychiatric Association, 1994, pp. 29–30):

- *problems with primary support group* [e.g., death of a family member, divorce, physical abuse, inadequate discipline]
- *problems related to the social environment* [e.g., loss of a friend, difficulty with acculturation, discrimination, isolation]
- *educational problems* [e.g., illiteracy, academic problems, educational deprivation]
- *occupational problems* [e.g., unemployment, stressful work schedule, altercations with superiors]
- *housing problems* [e.g., homelessness, discord with neighbors]
- *problems with access to health care services* [e.g., inadequate insurance, no transportation]
- *problems related to interaction with the legal system/crime* [e.g., arrest, litigation, crime victim]
- *other psychosocial and environmental problems* [e.g., exposure to war or disaster, discord with caregivers, lack of social services, discrimination or prejudice]

Multiple stressors may be present and all should be listed on Axis IV. Stressors often contribute either to the development, maintenance, or recurrence of a disorder. Occasionally, however, they can be the consequence of a disorder (for instance, enuresis may result in a disturbance of peer relationships).

Axis V—Global Assessment of Functioning
This axis is rated on a scale of 0 to 90 to indicate an individual's overall level of functioning; it considers social, occupational (professional/academic), and psychologi-

cal aspects. A zero is given only for inadequate information and is equivalent to the absence of such a rating. The higher the index, the better the client's functioning. Thus a rating of 90 would indicate minimal symptoms of disorder and good functioning in all three areas mentioned above. A rating of 1, on the other hand, would indicate extremely severe pathology with persistent danger of suicide, severe disruption in communication, or gross inability to care for oneself. Ratings are made for the client's presentation at intake based on the idea that the person's current level of functioning will better reflect the need for treatment. Examples of ratings are provided in the manual (American Psychiatric Association, 1994).

Controversy about DSM-IV Diagnosis

Although the issue of DSM-IV diagnosis has been controversial in some psychology camps (especially among counseling psychologists), all mental health care providers need to be familiar with the diagnostic process. The controversy about diagnosis arises from fears about labeling clients as a potential drawback, concerns about the psychometric properties of the DSM-IV manual, and criticisms of the DSM-IV diagnoses as culturally biased and therapeutically useless. Specifically, problems that have been identified with the diagnostic process include, but may not be limited to (Helmchen, 1991; Iijima Hall, 1997; Kleinke, 1994; Kottler & Brown, 1992; Matsumoto, 1994a):

- labeling that results in stigma or self-fulfilling prophecies
- implications about deficit or disease requiring medical treatment
- opportunity for clients to excuse their behavior
- opportunity for clients to develop new false identities or definitions of self
- pigeonholing clients
- dehumanizing clients
- poor diagnostic reliability of DSM-IV diagnosis
- poor validity of DSM-IV diagnosis
- poor recognition of comorbidity occurrence and issues
- poor cultural sensitivity and awareness
- poor predictability of treatment needs
- irrelevance to treatment planning and strategy selection

The first few of these issues (from labeling to dehumanizing clients) are certainly real, but they are not sufficient reason to refrain from diagnosing clients. With diagnosis comes responsibility, and the therapist must make a judgment about whether to inform clients of their diagnostic label. Many times such sharing is counterproductive and therapeutically not indicated. Any client who has an uncertain self-definition or who is struggling for an identity, while at the same time showing evidence of externalizing defenses (e.g., projection, blaming), is generally not well-served by being told a diagnostic label. These clients use the label as a new self-identity that can be used to explain, and perhaps defend or excuse, unhealthy behavior. The concern about the deficit or disease implications of a diagnosis appears warranted for the same reason. A diagnosis should not be made to imply that the client is sick or somehow in need of medical treatment; giving a DSM-IV diagnosis does not mean that the client will need to receive the services of a psychiatrist or physician. The problem of dehumanizing and pigeonholing clients must be combatted, not by avoiding diagnosing clients, but by ascertaining that therapists do not respond to clients with prejudicial and stereotypical attitudes. If there is a problem with pigeonholing clients, it most likely stems from the therapist's inadequate training and not from the diagnosis itself. Confusing the process of applying prejudice with the process of making a diagnosis is an error; the diagnosis does not label, dehumanize, or pigeonhole; insensitive therapists do. Thus to prevent clinicians from abusing diagnoses means to train them better in their appropriate use.

The psychometric problems about reliable and valid DSM-IV diagnoses carry more weight than criticisms related to labeling. There are definite problems with the DSM-IV nosology as it exists today (Kirk & Kutchins, 1992). Although the DSM-IV has become the standard of care for the diagnostic process and actually reflects a rather careful revision of the prior editions of the same manual, its reliability and validity problems will linger as long as the syndromes listed in the DSM-IV remain heterogeneous (which is highly likely). The therapists' best approach to this problem that is currently available is for them to be aware that the diagnoses derived from the DSM-IV are not the complete or final answer. As is true for the entire conceptualization and treatment plan process, clinicians must remain open to making revisions and adjustments. Further, therapists must be knowledgeable about the diagnostic process and must avoid common diagnostic mistakes. Thorough familiarity with the DSM-IV manual, careful consideration of differential diagnoses, and a comprehensive listing of symptoms and related problems are necessary for optimally reliable and valid diagnoses. Common mistakes need to be avoided. For example, Patterson and Welfel (1994) and Morrison (1995a, 1995b) point to the following common mistakes clinicians must avoid:

- Do not ignore potential physical or medical explanations for the symptoms presented by the client through a preemptive focus on social, psychological, and interpersonal factors.
- Do not miss multiple or superior diagnoses by being satisfied with the first diagnosis that appears to fit a client.
- Do not view DSM-IV diagnoses as static and unchangeable.
- Do not overuse data collected during a crisis because these can distort or mask what is really going on with a client.

Instead, the clinician needs to be careful to use the manual correctly and to follow the suggestions contained in it and in books written to accompany it (e.g., American Psychiatric Association, 1994; Meyer & Deitsch, 1996; Morrison, 1995a, 1995b). These resources make the following suggestions:

- Be thoroughly familiar with the entire DSM-IV manual before beginning to use it.
- Use the decision tree provided in the DSM-IV manual.

- Rule out cognitive disorders and medical conditions first.
- Consider and carefully rule out all differential diagnoses listed in the differential diagnosis section of the DSM-IV manual for the favored diagnosis for the client.
- Carefully consider social and cultural factors that may affect final diagnosis.
- Give as few diagnoses as possible without missing all that are appropriate.
- Use the history presented by the client and all prior records to supplement current data.
- Value recent history more than past history.
- Prefer signs (behavior observable by the clinician) to symptoms (client-described symptoms or behaviors) in making diagnostic determinations.
- Prefer objective assessment (e.g., concrete and observable data) to subjective assessment (e.g., interpretive and intuitive data).

The issue of comorbidity deserves to be addressed here briefly. DSM-IV proceeds with little recognition of comorbid diagnosis (the coexistence of more than one diagnosable clinical syndrome or the coexistence of Axis I and Axis II diagnoses), whereas epidemiological and clinical studies have shown comorbidity rates to be extremely high (e.g., Kessler, 1994; Regier et al., 1990). In fact, researchers have shown that as many as 40% of clients presenting with generalized anxiety disorder also have a major depression, and over 20% have a dysthymic disorder (Wittchen, Zhao, Kessler, & Eaton, 1994); as many as 70% of substance use disordered clients have coexisting clinical disorders or personality disorders (Brems & Johnson, 1997; Regier et al., 1990); as many as half of the clients who present with post-traumatic stress disorder also have a major depression (Kessler, Sonnega, Bromet, Hughes, & Nelson, 1995); and the list continues (see Kessler, 1994). Failure to recognize that clients may meet the criteria of more than one disorder results in misdiagnosis and ignores an important reality about the client that has definite etiological, prognostic, and treatment implications. The competent clinician will heed the advice given above not to stop with the diagnostic process once a single disorder has been diagnosed, but to continue until all symptoms or problems have been accounted for. Yet this same clinician must also take care not to over-diagnose clients, giving diagnoses that are unnecessary if symptoms have already been accounted for by another label that supersedes others (e.g., a borderline personality disorder label may not be appropriate for a female client with a strong history of sexual abuse during childhood who meets criteria for post-traumatic stress disorder; the PTSD label accounts for all of her symptoms and hence is the driving force behind her presentation, even though she may also theoretically meet criteria for BPD; see American Psychiatric Association, 1994). The issue of comorbidity also has specific etiological and treatment implications. Etiologically speaking, it has been hypothesized that pure disorders have different sets of predisposing factors than the same disorder when it coexists with another (e.g., Blazer, Kessler, McGonagle, & Swartz, 1994). With regard to treatment, it has been suggested that more complex choices will need to be made in terms of selection of treatment approaches and strategies (e.g., Brems & Johnson, 1997; Brown & Barlow, 1992; Namyniuk, Brems, & Clarson, 1997), a fact that will be revisited again below. Further, comorbidity tends to increase many risk factors associated with treatment and presentation, such as increasing suicide and risks of harm to others, and has implications for a client's prognosis or treatment outcome (e.g., Cornelius et al., 1995).

The cultural criticisms of the diagnostic process weigh heavier still. Cultures vary greatly in what they consider a problem or an appropriate strategy for coping in a given situation (see Castillo, 1997; Dana, 1993; Iijima Hall, 1997). Thus what may constitute abnormality in one culture may be acceptable, if not mainstream behavior, in another. Different cultures may also express the same type of problem in different ways, choosing different idioms to describe an essentially identical level of emotion and type of pain (Matsumoto, 1994a). As such, depression among mainstream White clients may conform to the criteria outlined in the DSM-IV, whereas depression among the Chinese is manifested through a different set of highly somatized symptoms, such as constipation, loss of appetite, and fatigue, and with little expressed dysphoric affect (Castillo, 1997; Dana, 1993). Additionally, some disorders appear to be culture-bound; these appear (or are predominant) in some but not all cultures (American Psychiatric Association, 1994; Suzuki, Meller, & Ponterotto, 1996). This latter phenomenon may be explained by the observation that different cultures reinforce different traits and behaviors. Because any traits or behaviors taken to an extreme may result in pathology, different cultural groups will have different manifestations of pathology based on the types of traits it emphasizes in its healthy population (Alarcon & Foulks, 1995; Iijima Hall, 1997). For example, eating disorders appear to be a phenomenon of industrialized, Western cultures where there is a strong focus on being thin (especially for women) and where there is an abundance of food (American Psychiatric Association, 1994; Castillo, 1997); *frigophobia*, a disorder characterized by irrational fear of being exposed to the cold and of freezing to death, is only identified among the Chinese, where somatic concerns are prevalent in the culture (Dana, 1993); *amok*, a disorder characterized by a period of brooding, followed by a violent outburst, and usually ending with exhaustion and amnesia of the event, appears limited to Southeast Asian men (Castillo, 1997); and *ataques de nervios*, a disorder that includes symptoms such as hyperemotionality accompanied by trembling, palpitations, and general hyperkinesis, occurs primarily among Puerto Rican women who are culturally encouraged to express distress through somatization and who are encouraged to be highly emotional (Rivera-Arzola & Ramos-Grenier, 1997).

Personality disorders are particularly vulnerable to cultural influences because they are more bound to psychological and environmental factors and are by definition interpersonal in nature (see Castillo, 1997; Fabrega, 1992). Further, what complicates a universal standard for diagnosis, especially of personality disorders, is "the observation that different cultures have tended to emphasize different traits of personality as ideal" (Alarcon & Foulks, 1995, p. 6). This may lead to behaviors that are acceptable, even admired in some cultures, and ones that are considered inappropriate or even pathological in others. For example, persons of Mediterranean and Latin descent are most commonly mislabeled as histrionic due to the cultural emphasis on emotionality, dramatic interpersonal style, novelty seeking, and tendency toward somatization; Asian and Asian American clients are frequently mis-labeled as dependent because of the stress placed by their culture on politeness, deference, acceptance of others' opinions, and passivity (Castillo, 1997; Johnson, F., 1993). Talmudic scholars may be misdiagnosed as obsessive–compulsive because of their cultural encouragement to be conscientious and scrupulous with regard to morality, restricted affective expression, and striving for perfectionism; Hindu yogis may be mislabeled as schizoid (Castillo, 1997; Witztum, Greenberg, & Dasberg, 1990).

Although the DSM-IV has addressed cultural issues more thoroughly than its predecessors, and has incorporated discussions of cultural issues for almost all categories of disorders—this by providing culturally relevant examples of Axis IV stressors (e.g., prejudice, migration), adding culturally sensitive V-Codes (such as Acculturation Problems), and providing examples of culturally specific (or culture-bound) disorders (such as the ones exemplified above)—it continues to have a number of shortcomings in the area of cultural relevance and sensitivity (Hohenshil, 1994; Smart & Smart, 1997). It fails to deal with the diagnosis and treatment of individuals in a culturally unbiased fashion and presenting cultural-bound taxonomies in a manner that suggests that they are exotic and unusual manifestations of psychopathology (Levine & Gaw, 1995). It fails to discuss cultural traits relevant to various diagnostic categories in sufficient detail, and it continues to use the White mainstream experience as the norm (refer to Mezzich, Kleinman, Fabrega, & Parron's [1996] edited volume for a more complete discussion of the DSM-IV cultural sensitivity and relevance issue). To use the DSM-IV responsibly, clinicians "must develop a critical awareness that every diagnosis, however appropriate or inappropriate, always occurs in a broad sociocultural, linguistic, political and economic context. The current prevailing model (DSM-IV) reflects a good deal of careful thoughts and preparation, yet [remains] biased toward the North American culture in which it has arisen" (Smart & Smart, 1997, p. 397). Therefore, to be a responsible diagnostician, it is absolutely essential for a therapist to know about the sociocultural norms of the client's cultural group in terms of what constitutes mental health and what defines abnormality or clinical disorder (Matsumoto, 1994a). When working with clients from other cultural groups, the therapist must have an appreciation of the type of language to expect from the members of this cultural group to describe various psychological or emotional symptoms. Not knowing the cultural subtleties may result in misdiagnosis, overdiagnosis, or underdiagnosis of members of specific cultural groups. Fortunately, the DSM-IV itself has made some strides over its predecessors in this regard, at least acknowledging the culturally-bound nature of some of the disorders or behavioral manifestations of distress in the differential diagnosis sections of various disorders listed in the manual (American Psychiatric Association, 1994; Matsumoto, 1994a). The multiaxial system first introduced in DSM-III was also an improvement in that it directed the clinician's attention to factors other than symptoms and labels, this by introducing a diagnostic process for social issues and an evaluation of the person's overall level of functioning. The DSM-IV further improved on this approach. It made cultural issues a central theme within Axis IV, which is concerned with the social context of the client and included a diagnostic criterion for the personality disorders diagnoses (Axis II) that specifies the need to consider the cultural acceptability of the person's pervasive pattern of behavior and experience.

Nevertheless, the manual remains primarily focused on disorders and syndromes derived from observation of Western cultures through mainstream values and current research that is known to be culturally biased and gender biased (Matsumoto, 1994b). Hence, each individual therapist still needs to take care to avoid misdiagnosis of clients of non-mainstream culture (and of all clients, for that matter). When diagnosing clients from non-mainstream or non-Western cultures, it may behoove clinicians to include in the diagnostic section of their reports a stipulation that outlines the cultural biases contained in the diagnostic tools; alternatively, the therapist may choose to omit the DSM-IV diagnosis from the intake report altogether.

Throwing out the whole idea of making a DSM-IV diagnosis because of its potential drawbacks appears impossible at the current time because of external forces imposed on clinicians. Specifically, great pressure is placed on mental health professionals to provide DSM-IV diagnoses to third-party payors, such as managed care companies, health management organizations, insurance companies, and Medicare and Medicaid. These businesses have a vested interest in the diagnostic procedures. Diagnoses are used to determine service eligibility, service length, service types, and reimbursement schedules. This practice is unfortunate indeed, given that one of the gravest criticisms of the DSM-IV diagnosis is its utter failure in predicting treatment needs and strategies (e.g., Basch, 1980; Beutler & Berren, 1995; Gelso & Fretz, 1992; Helmchen, 1991; Kleinke, 1994; Kottler & Brown, 1992).

Third-party payors use a medical model of psychiatric diagnosis with DSM-IV. This medical model relies on the fact that in medicine, diagnoses usually tell the clinician a relatively unbiased story about the etiology, prognosis, and treatment protocol of a disorder. Insurers assume that this is true for DSM-IV diagnoses as well, but this is simply not so (see Brems, 1993; Helmchen, 1991; Kottler & Brown, 1992; Meyer & Deitsch, 1996). Psychiatric diagnoses, such as DSM-IV diagnoses, are based on extremely heterogeneous clusters of symptoms that reduce reliability of diagnosis, very unlike medical diagnoses, where symptom clusters are often much more homogenous and clearly defined. Further, in psychiatric diagnosis, the diagnosis itself says little to nothing about the etiology of the disorder or the symptoms presented by the client. Two clients with almost identical symptoms of depression may have developed these symptoms through entirely different sets of predisposing factors, precipitating factors, and perpetuating factors. Similarly, prognosis is usually unreliable to nonexistent (some of the more chronic DSM-IV diagnoses exempted). Finally, psychiatric diagnoses have no standard treatment protocol associated with them, although attempts (as yet unsuccessful) have been made to that effect. Instead, there is great agreement among mental health practitioners that DSM-IV diagnoses have few or no implications for how to treat and intervene with clients—again, given the great heterogeneity of symptoms, the lack of implications for etiology, and the lack of implications for how to help persons change, grow, or heal (see Gelso & Fretz, 1992; Helmchen, 1991). DSM-IV diagnoses have been called too heterogeneous, too arbitrary, and too poorly predictive to be of any use at all in treatment planning (Helmchen, 1991; Kleinke, 1994).

Usefulness of DSM-IV Diagnosis

The vastness and vehemence of these criticisms lead to the question of why mental health professionals continue to use DSM-IV diagnoses at all. There is a variety of more or less satisfying answers to this question. First of all, DSM-IV diagnoses still do provide care providers with a fairly systematic means of organizing symptoms into syndromes, and this process makes communication among professionals somewhat easier (Kottler & Brown, 1992). Namely, most mental health profession-als, when they are told of a client who has been diagnosed with schizophrenia, will have a certain mental picture of what this diagnosis means and what it implies in terms of symptoms, prognosis, and treatment. This, of course, is also a potential pit-fall if one's mental picture is rigid and overly confident (leading directly to the crit-icism of pigeonholing and dehumanizing clients mentioned above). The solution is to allow the diagnostic label to facilitate communication about a basic idea (in the example of the client with schizophrenia, the basic idea would be that the person is struggling with a chronic mental illness) without allowing it to produce precon-ceived notions about the client's actual current presentation, etiology, and potential as a human being. Again, it is the proper training of the clinician that will prevent the misuse of the diagnosis, not the nonuse of diagnoses altogether.

Other uses of DSM-IV diagnoses include epidemiological purposes and ser-vice allocation decisions. DSM-IV diagnoses are of great assistance to program planners and legislators, who must make decisions about service allocations, and to administrators, who must plan services for their potential clientele. Having epi-demiological data that are organized in some nosological fashion (i.e., by using the DSM-IV) makes it easier for legislators, for instance, to know how many chroni-cally mentally ill patients live in their community and will require services that are tailored to severe mental illness. Similarly, having DSM-IV diagnostic data for their primary clientele helps agency directors make decisions about whether to implement groups for depression, anxiety, or other primary syndromes. Without some organized nosological system, these decisions would be made based on im-pressions or clinician judgments instead of sound data (Helmchen, 1991). In other words, the most redeeming quality of DSM-IV diagnoses may be their epidemio-logical and greater community service planning implications, not their contribu-tion to the individual treatment planning for actual clients. Finally, as pointed out above, currently DSM-IV diagnoses are the only accepted organized system that can help clients receive third-party reimbursement for mental health services (the confidentiality problems of this issue have been discussed in a prior chapter).

Concluding Thoughts about the DSM-IV and the Diagnostic Process

To summarize, consensus appears to exist that DSM-IV diagnoses are here to stay and have some usefulness in the greater scheme of community-wide or agency-wide service planning and epidemiology. However, they are not necessarily good predictors of clients' treatment needs and, hence, cannot be used exclusively to help the clinician make a proper individual treatment plan. What is needed in-stead is a dynamic or etiological conceptualization of the client. This etiological conceptualization considers factors about the client that are generally ignored by DSM-IV diagnoses. Namely, it

- considers presenting problems that are not necessarily verbalized by the client directly, but which are observed by the clinician (Basch, 1980)
- follows a contextual model that can be continually revised as new data emerge (Brems, 1993)
- considers the actual symptom clusters presented by the client (Brems, 1993)
- explores the course of the disorder, including features such as age of onset, duration, stage, and premorbid traits (Helmchen, 1991)
- explores potential predisposing factors, precipitating factors, and perpetuating factors (Lemma, 1995)
- considers accompanying risk factors, such as coexisting disorders, age, and lifestyles (Brems & Johnson, 1997)
- weighs issues such as problem severity, coping styles, problem complexity, and client cooperation (Beutler & Berren, 1995)

ETIOLOGICAL CONCEPTUALIZATION

The conceptualization that will be used to determine an individual treatment plan is a process, not a single static decision; as such, it is highly contextual and flexible. It must be clearly differentiated from the diagnosis or the diagnostic process; the terms diagnosis and conceptualization should never be used interchangeably, though many writers unfortunately continue to do so (e.g., Kottler & Brown, 1992). The dynamic or etiological conceptualization begins by exploring the three Ps: predisposing factors, precipitating factors, and perpetuating factors. It then continues to outline the dynamics of the case by detailing intrapsychic, interpersonal matrix, and family-related dynamics. It is not finished until it accounts for all problems, behaviors, cognitions, and affects presented by the client (Weiss, 1993). This conceptualization considers the context for each presenting problem and each therapist-identified problem, integrating all apparently separate parts of the client's history into one cohesive and holistic network of events and experiences that can explain even apparent inconsistencies or contradictions (Karoly, 1993). It takes care to avoid biases or stereotypes to enter the process of understanding the client and keeps all attributions logical and rational (Olson, Jackson, & Nelson, 1997). In the words of Basch (1980), "a therapist should not make a diagnosis simply on the basis of the main complaint, nor should he [or she] center on a patient's symptom. The therapist should consider the context in which the complaint is made or in which the symptom occurs, for it is the context that often leads to an understanding of what is going on with the patient and of what needs to be done for him [or her]" (p. 121).

The Three Ps

In preparing for such a thorough, contextual, and integrative conceptualization, the mental health professional needs to begin to appreciate the circumstances, forces, and occurrences in a client's life that may have contributed to the problems that are presented by the client and identified by the clinician. The therapist gains this appreciation by considering factors that may have *predisposed* (the first P) the client to the development of symptoms, such as psychological concerns experienced in childhood, family dynamics that derailed development, social concerns that interfered with healthy adjustment, medical problems that contributed to psychological pain, or cultural factors that resulted in painful emotion. Further, the clinician must gain an understanding of why symptoms developed at a given point in time and why the client chose to present for treatment at this time. This exploration is essentially preoccupied with the identification of *precipitants* (the second P)—that is, with factors that may account for a sudden stress reaction or onset of distress. Finally, the clinician must look at the client's environment to assess whether circumstances are present that serve to *perpetuate* the symptoms and any other problems identified by the therapist (the third P). These three Ps (predisposing factors, precipitating factors, and perpetuating factors), in combination with observed problem areas in the client's life, will provide the clinician with direction for goal setting and treatment planning, as well as give the clinician a sense of understanding and empathy for why the presenting problems developed.

Predisposing Factors

A variety of factors that can predispose people to mental illness or emotional problems have been identified in the therapy literature. They have been explored in general and have been related to particular disorders. They are not to be confused with causative factors (of which few to none have been clearly identified), but rather must be viewed as those variables in a person's life that have contributed to the noted problems developing without necessarily having caused them. This concept of a predisposing factor suggests that certain factors in persons' lives can render them vulnerable to the development of clinical disorders through stress, by encouraging symptoms, or for other reasons.

Predisposing factors can be societal, environmental, social, familial, parental, personal, biological, and genetic. For each area, the clinician must look at the possibility of influences on the person's mental health and current presenting problems. Often such factors are quite obvious, but only rarely can all of them be assessed accurately. A comprehensive listing of all possibilities for any given client will exhaust any possible component that may have contributed to the client's psychological development and adjustment. Rarely will any single factor account for all of the symptoms identified at intake.

Societal Factors

Societal factors can include issues such as Zeitgeist and moral attitudes, prejudice and discrimination, ostracism of certain population subgroups, or media-induced societal values. Eating disorders are known to have a strong societal predisposing component because of the strong focus on certain body types as acceptable in our society. In an attempt to conform to such body typing, many women may fall into unhealthy eating habits or patterns (e.g., Nagel & Jones, 1992; Paxton & Sculthorpe, 1991). Adolescent suicide behavior among Alaska Native children may have a strong societal predisposing factor, because the Native culture is currently lacking in sufficient numbers of heroes or role models from within its own culture (Sullivan & Brems, 1997). This dearth of positive role models or ideals, combined with being bombarded through the media with unhealthy (non-Native) role models, leaves adolescents wanting for self-esteem and a sense of life direction, and this results in depression and hopelessness that not uncommonly culminates in suicide. Similarly, the combined experience of prejudice and discrimination is said to be related to the development of personality traits often included in a variety of personality disorders, such as vigilance, paranoia, lack of trust, and so forth (Alarcon & Foulks, 1995).

Environmental Factors

Environmental factors can range from issues such as moving to a new neighborhood or starting a new job, to surviving a major environmental event such as an earthquake or a tornado, to experiencing an environmental trauma such as war. A grave environmental factor that may predispose people for maladjustments of numerous types, including depression (e.g., in the elderly) or elective mutism (in children; American Psychiatric Association, 1994) is absence of stimulation in the environment, such as might occur in an institutional setting. Adjustment disorders by definition have a strong environmental predisposing component, in which the client is responding strongly to a minor to severe environmental (or interpersonal) stressor. Finally, environmental factors are crucial to the development of post-traumatic stress disorder, for which a major environmental stressor (e.g., participation in a war, becoming the victim of a violent crime) is a required part of the diagnostic picture of the disorder.

Social Factors

Social factors are often closely related to environmental issues. They include malnutrition, neglect, influences due to a person's living situation (such as living in a rural versus an inner-urban area), socioeconomic status, stress levels in daily living situations, and similar influences. Social concerns such as poor economic conditions and inner-city lifestyles are considered important predisposing factors in developing disorders such as drug or substance abuse (e.g., Pentz, 1994). Further, disorders involving aggressive behavior, impulse control disorders, and certain personality disorders are correlated with socioeconomic status, which suggests a potential predisposing link between this social factor and subsequent pathology (Meyer & Deitsch, 1996). Malnutrition may be involved in Pica behaviors, as well as being related to developmental disorders (American Psychiatric Association, 1994). The possibility of these factors as important influences on a client's behavior or affects should never be underestimated.

Familial Factors

Familial factors refer to issues such as parental divorce and discord experienced in childhood, inappropriate generational boundaries in the family of origin, problems in the current nuclear family related to marital discord, or discipline problems with children. It is important to explore such factors within clients' families of origin as well as within their current nuclear families or intimate relationships. Particular attention needs to be paid to concerns involving crossed generational boundaries, blurred intergenerational boundaries, triangulation, and similar concerns in both families. Such structural family difficulties have been associated with authority problems, individuation difficulties, entitlement and aggrandizement, and parentification of children (Minuchin & Fishman, 1981; Teyber, 1997). Other familial concerns involve attachment relationships between parents and children, again both in the nuclear family and the family of origin. Both over- and underattachment are problematic. Overattachment between a parent and child may lead the adult to look for having needs met through the child, often a sign of personality disorder in the adult and a precursor of individuation difficulties for the child. Underattachment generally implies a lack of a nurturing and supportive relationship in the parent–child dyad, and this is strongly related to personality disorder in the adult and attachment disorder in the child (Teyber, 1997).

Parental Factors

Parental factors are closely related to the familial factors; in fact, the two often go hand in hand. They are, however, differentiated from family factors in that they are strictly concerned with parenting issues and leave out the spousal dyad and overall family structural issues such as triangulation or generational conflicts. Parenting styles have been discussed previously in some detail. To reiterate, authoritative parenting styles are most likely to be associated with healthy development in a person's offspring, whereas both authoritarian and permissive styles tend to be highly associated with a variety of emotional problems (Baumrind, 1983). It is important to explore parenting both in terms of parenting received and parenting delivered. Other parental issues involve interactions between parent and child that are designed to be shaming and critical of the child, that are perceived as rejecting or judgmental by the child, and that may lead to abandonment or fears of abandonment (Teyber, 1997).

Biological Factors

Biological factors include neurological deficits, biochemical disturbances, handicaps of various types (e.g., physical, sensory), a range of severe or chronic illnesses (e.g., temporal lobe epilepsy, encephalitis), psychoactive substance use or abuse by the mother during pregnancy (e.g., alcohol, caffeine, sleeping pills), and frequent illness or allergies. Fetal Alcohol Syndrome is considered a primary predisposing factor for a number of mental illnesses or behavior disorders in children, including (but not limited to) mental retardation, attention deficit hyperactivity disorder, and learning disabilities (see Streissguth et al., 1991; Streissguth et al., 1994). Biological factors have been identified in the development of dementia and delirium (American Psychiatric Association, 1994) and depression (Thase & Howland, 1995). Genetic factors have been identified as playing a role in schizophrenia (see Cromwell & Snyder, 1993), bipolar disorders (e.g., Orvaschel, 1990; Sevy, Mendlewicz, & Mendelbaum, 1995), attention deficit disorders (e.g., Silver, 1992), and others. Possible biological predisposing factors are best traced through family histories of medical illness, mental illness, and psychological disturbances.

Precipitating Factors

Precipitating factors are those circumstances that triggered either the client's symptoms or presentation for treatment. Some precipitants may be as simple as a fight with a spouse; some may be as severe as a rape. The precipitant can at times be an external factor, rather than the reflection of the client's internal motivation for treatment (e.g., as may be the case with a court-referred client or a client who is mandated by child protection services to seek therapy to maintain custody of the children). Precipitants are often most helpful for the client in understanding why they are presenting for treatment when they do, especially when their problems have existed for some time.

Precipitants may not only be responsible for triggering clients' decisions for treatment, but also for causing a particular symptom to manifest. For example, a rape may have resulted in severe anxiety symptoms that are pernicious and apparently out of the control of the client. In this example, the event that brought the client to treatment had also led to the symptom. When a precipitant can be directly linked to the formation of a particular symptom, it can at times be difficult to discern whether the factor was a predisposing or precipitating one. Most simply put, a client will react to a precipitant with immediate symptoms that are generally acute in nature; a client will respond to a predisposing factor through the gradual onset of a problem that tends to be more chronic in nature. An interaction between predisposing factors and precipitating factors is possible as well. For instance, if a person experienced childhood sexual abuse and then witnesses or experienced a rape, the person may be significantly more traumatized than another person who is a rape witness or victim but who did not have history of abuse. In such an instance, the predisposing factor of childhood abuse magnified the reaction to the current situation, leaving the person more vulnerable to responding strongly to the precipitant (i.e., the rape).

Perpetuating Factors

There are two types of perpetuating factors. First, there are factors that have also been called reinforcing factors or secondary gain factors (see Brems, 1993). These events, behaviors, or circumstances serve to maintain a problem by providing the person with some form of reward (secondary gain) for the symptoms or problems. Therefore, the clinician needs to assess the potentially reinforcing or rewarding aspects of a problem situation that may perpetuate the problem or may encourage a symptom to be expressed. For example, a client may present with frequent physical complaints that have resulted in many days of missed work. If this same client also reports conflict at the workplace, the possibility that the physical complaints are a perpetuating factor may need to be explored, as they serve to keep the client out of a noxious environment. In this example, another symptom (the frequent physical complaints) is actually a perpetuating factor that points to the complexity of symptom development and maintenance. Some reinforcing factors are external—

that is, they arise out of interactions with the external world that reinforce the client's symptomatology. For example, clients who are highly dependent may be reinforced for their behavior by their spouses, who subsequently make all major decisions and take charge of crisis situations. Similarly, clients who are depressed may be reinforced for their symptoms by bosses who are overly accommodating, who allow them to take excessive time off work or to come late and leave early. Substance using clients may be reinforced (enabled) by partners who cover up for them by calling bosses and making excuses for the substance using persons' absences or illnesses.

This discussion of reinforcing factors is not meant to imply that the therapist blames the client for the symptom or even believes that the reinforcing factor or symptoms is produced voluntarily and thus allows the rewarding condition. Quite to the contrary, the therapist needs to view the perpetuating factor as yet another problem (or symptom) that requires intervention, because there is often a quite unconscious connection between the reinforcing factor and the symptoms it maintains (Lemma, 1995).

A second type of perpetuating factors is a behavioral pattern that has been called a "vicious cycle." In this type of perpetuating factor, clients often develop very specific patterns of behavior and emotion in response to symptoms or predisposing factors. These factors unfortunately turn out to become perpetuating factors in that they maintain problems in others areas of the client's life. Teyber (1997) has identified several such behavioral patterns (partially based in Karen Horney's neopsychoanalytic theory) that fit this definition of perpetuating, or vicious cycle, factors. Specifically, Teyber points out that clients often develop one of four reactions to childhood predisposing factors (especially familial and parental factors) that result in vicious cycles: they may block unmet needs, move towards others, move away from others, or move against others. Clients who block their unmet needs may do so in a variety of ways. They may reject their own emerging emotional needs that were not met appropriately during childhood through repression, denial, or other psychologically self-protective mechanisms. In so doing, they reject their own developing self, a reality that only serves to perpetuate problems in identifying the self, choosing a direction, and setting life goals. Alternatively, they may choose to do unto others what was done to them, becoming as unresponsive to the needs of their own children as their parents were to them. These clients identify with their parents and reject others, a vicious cycle that perpetuates a sense of rejection, isolation, and emotional impoverishment. Thirdly, clients may block their emerging emotional needs by selecting people for relationships who are as rejecting as the clients' parents were in childhood. By choosing, for example, equally rejecting mates, such clients unconsciously perpetuate this cycle of rejection and emotional isolation in their lives.

Clients who have chosen a style of reacting to predisposing factors in childhood that incorporates movement toward others will essentially try to please others at the expense of their own desires and wishes. They become overly compliant, submissive, and nonassertive to win approval and emotional acceptance. They generally expect adulation, reassurance, and approval for their submissive behavior, though this reality often does not come to pass. When their need for approval is thus once again frustrated, the cycle of problems and symptoms is perpetuated. Clients who have chosen to try to adapt to predisposing factors of childhood by moving away from others will tend to show symptoms of avoidance, withdrawal, and self-sufficiency linked to isolation and false independence. They expect demands and criticisms from others to be absent and are greatly frustrated and emotionally traumatized when this expected reality does not come to pass. Thus the unrealistic expectations for others in response to the patterns these clients have developed serve to preserve and strengthen their sense of rejection and emotional isolation in a vicious cycle. Finally, clients who have responded to childhood patterns and deprivations by moving against others have developed a pattern of aggression, threats, and coercion. They expect others to respect them, to show allegiance to them, and to yield leadership to them. When these expectations are not met, these clients are reinforced in their belief in a hostile world and their symptoms and beliefs are perpetuated.

To summarize, in exploring perpetuating factors in a client's life, it behooves the clinician to look for patterns of behavior that keep the client trapped in the experience of symptoms and problems either through reinforcement/reward for the symptom or through development of a vicious cycle. Again, it must be understood that all of these situations in which the client derives either secondary gain or is stuck in a vicious cycle of behavior are generally not consciously set up or manipulated by the client. Instead, the clinician must be aware of these perpetuating factors prior to treatment planning as important dynamics in the client's life, because they are often the very factors that prove to be the great stumbling blocks or points of resistance in the therapy process. A sample listing of the three Ps is provided in Table 4.2 for the same client used to prepare Table 4.1.

Case Dynamics

The three Ps can help the therapist gain insight into the dynamics presented by the client. They can be used to come to some understanding of the intrapsychic experiences of their clients, clients' family-related conflicts and events, and their interpersonal matrix. Most commonly, each of these three areas concerned with case dynamics contains several predisposing factors, precipitating factors, and perpetuating factors, though there appears to be some correlation between certain factors and certain case dynamics. Specifically, familial and parental predisposing factors appear most commonly related to family dynamics; social predisposing factors appear commonly linked to interpersonal matrix dynamics; perpetuating factors seem primarily related to intrapsychic dynamics and secondarily to interpersonal matrix dynamics; and precipitating factors often arise from the interpersonal matrix, with an external motivator pushing the client into treatment. Not surprisingly, the three Ps and the case dynamics presented in this section often have a large degree of content overlap. To reduce redundancy in the intake report, the three Ps are generated by the therapist without being listed in the report. Instead, strictly the case dynamics aspect of the conceptualization process is included in the intake report, traditionally labeled case conceptualization or formulation.

TABLE 4.2   The Three Ps: Contributing Factors in the Case of a Depressed Adult Client

Issues and Patterns	Predisposing Factor	Perpetuating Factor	Precipitant
brother's suicide			X
significant other perceived as dissatisfied with relationship			X
best friend's suicide	X		X
father's relative absence during childhood	X		
mother's emotional absence	X		
family-of-origin isolation	X		
victim of neglect, both emotional and physical	X		
absence of extended family in childhood	X		
brother's history of alcoholism	X		
mother's history of depression requiring hospitalization	X		
reluctance to seek health care services	X		
loose family ties at present	X	X	
perceived distancing from significant other	X	X	
social isolation	X	X	
poor internal coping skills and resources	X	X	
few hobbies or interests that involve others		X	
indecisiveness		X	
lack of initiation of action		X	
significant other who assists with decision making		X	
helplessness		X	
reliance on significant other for decisions and action choices		X	
strong dependency needs		X	
strong social avoidance traits		X	

Intrapsychic Dynamics

Not all clinicians will emphasize the same contents, nor perhaps this entire aspect of a conceptualization, in the same manner. Of all parts of the case conceptualization, perhaps this one most strongly reflects the clinician's primary theoretical approach; therefore, it may vary greatly depending on the approach used, whether psychoanalytic, psychodynamic, person-centered, cognitive–behavioral, or any other system of psychotherapy. However, all therapies observe the individual and the individual's personal adjustment (though behaviorally-oriented therapists may take offense at the "intrapsychic" label) and make this an integral part of the formulation of a case. Whether the conceptual framework focuses on interpreting belief systems, values, interests, behavioral patterns, development, reinforcement histories, or other facets of the client's psychological being is determined by the choice of theoretical approach of the clinician. The common themes, however, always center around the attempt to understand clients from their unique personal perspectives and to appreciate how clients have dealt with and adjusted to their living situations. For example, behaviorists will look at persons' reinforcement or learning history, assessing how they have learned various behaviors or symptoms and how well they are coping. Cognitive–behaviorists will emphasize aspects such as distorted thought patterns exhibited by clients, irrational beliefs they endorse, and automatic thoughts that may affect their moods. Developmental theorists will assess the developmental phase of clients and the developmental tasks and challenges they are facing. Psychodynamic theorists, on the other hand, will assess clients' ego strengths, developmental stages, conflicts, defenses, development of self, and similar forces.

It is impossible to dictate a particular approach for this aspect of the case conceptualization, nor would it be prudent to do so. Over the years, research has indicated that there is no *single* theoretical approach that is clearly superior to any other for conceptualization and treatment, though a specific problem may indeed warrant a specific technique or strategy (Mash & Barkley, 1996). However, it has been established that *having* a firm theoretical background of any type is crucial to successfully completing treatment. Thus clinicians who are about to embark on their careers involving the conduct of psychotherapy need to take a look at their beliefs with regard to human functioning (those encompassing thoughts, feelings, and behaviors, as well as interpersonal relationships) and should try to approach their cases from consistent theoretical points of view. Knowledge of various systems of psychotherapy is crucial, and therapists need to choose to which theoretical system or systems to ascribe. Changing this conceptual understanding of a case midstream, and thus the practical approach to treatment, is likely to be confusing not only for the therapist and the supervisor, but also and primarily for the client. Such a change midstream in treatment suggests that the therapist is floundering and that the therapy does not have a clear sense of direction. Because clients are often in treatment when their lives and families do not have consistency and direction, such traits in the therapy are clearly counterproductive.

In other words, careful formulation of a client's intrapsychic processes is a necessary prerequisite to successful treatment because it dictates its overall approach (though not necessarily specific techniques or strategies). Using a self psychological perspective about human functioning and therapeutic process, the intrapsychic dynamics of the client presented in the examples in Tables 4.1 and 4.2 (as well as in the documentation sections of Chapters 1, 2, and 3) could be summarized as follows:

Intrapsychic Dynamics in the Case of a Depressed Adult Client

This client presents with an underdeveloped self that shows significant deficits in the mirroring (self-appraisal, self-esteem, self-confidence, and self-nurturance) and idealizing pole (life direction, goals, strength, and stability). As such, it is not surprising that he evidences symptoms that suggest unrealistic self-appraisal, inhibited ambitions, delayed decision-making with regard to life direction and goal setting, interpersonal difficulties, and depressive mood.

Given the client's poorly internalized strength and guidance skills (i.e., deficit in the idealizing pole of the self), it is not surprising that he does not have solid internal coping skills. Instead, he feels overwhelmed and stretched to the limit most of the time, using all the psychic energy he has available just to make it through regular day-to-day tasks. When additional stressors were added (e.g., the death of his friend, the suicide of his brother), he became unable to cope. If these stressors carry potential abandonment or rejection themes, the client may well become emotionally incapacitated as well as suicidal.

Given the poor internalization of realistic self-appraisal and self-worth (i.e., deficits in the mirroring pole of the self), the client remains unsure of himself with regard to self-esteem and self-confidence and is unable to take care of his emotional and psychological needs. He is unable to believe in his own ability to nurture himself and views himself as less than competent, reliable, and successful. The self-doubts coupled with these negative self-perceptions contribute to his depressed mood, and these flavor his entire perception of the world and himself.

The two deficits (mirroring and idealization) together explain why the client is uncertain about what to do with his future and unable to commit with finality to a relationship. Further, his limited interactions with others throughout his life most likely also led to an underdevelopment of skills and talents which would, in turn, assist him with successful coping and thus would lend him a sense of self-esteem, self-efficacy, and competence. Fortunately, the client is very bright, hence has always been able to rely on his intellect to see him through most day-to-day situations. However, his achievement and performance could be significantly improved if he could develop healthy interpersonal relationship (twinship skills) and could complete his self-development by internalizing adequate mirroring and idealization skills.

Family Dynamics

As was true for the formulation of intrapsychic processes, all clinicians must and do integrate the family context of a client to arrive at yet another component of the case conceptualization. Given that most people are firmly embedded in an interpersonal matrix of significant others and that developed out of an interpersonal matrix of parenting adults, the role of such family members can neither be ignored nor underestimated. Their impact on the client's life, their interactions with the client, their effects on the client's behavior, and their own psychological makeup are crucial to the understanding and context of the client's symptomatic presentation. Family processes can be phrased in terms of a number of theoretical approaches, and again, no one superior approach has emerged in the literature. However, there appears to be much less divergence across clinicians from various systems of psychotherapy in their understanding of family systems, and most therapists take an interactive or interpersonal systems approach to this section of the conceptualization. Generally, the focus is twofold. First, attention is paid to how the behaviors, attitudes, mental health, and interactions of the client's primary caretakers in childhood influenced and continue to affect her or his psychological adjustment and behavior. Second, current nuclear family dynamics are explored to assess them for repetitions of old patterns that stem from the family of origin, to gain an appreciation for the amount of conflict in these intimate and significant relationships, and to begin to understand the client's and her or his nuclear family members' roles in the presenting concern. Extended family influences are also considered if there is frequent interaction. The family dynamics, consistent with a self psychological perspective, of the client presented in the above examples can be summarized as follows:

Family Dynamics in the Case of a Depressed Adult Client

It appears that the mirroring aspects of the client's self were unable to develop completely after the depressive disorder of his mother, which resulted in her physical and emotional absence from the home. The absence of a nurturing and rewarding supportive parent who would attend to the client's developing self-esteem and ambitions interfered with his ability to internalize a strong sense of confidence, esteem, competence, and realistic self-evaluation. The absence of his father further complicated the picture, because it resulted in the absence of a strong guiding person in the household who could have helped the child internalize a sense of strength, direction, and safety. The client was left to his own devices from early childhood on and learned during these early years not to trust the presence of supportive others to last. The absence of consistent strong role models (idealizable others) and supportive others (mirroring others) left him vulnerable to feelings of rejection and abandonment because he was unable to explain the absence or departure of these potential supportive others in ways other than to look at his own possible contributions. The fact that his siblings all appear to have some emotional difficulties and interpersonal problems confirms that the client's symptoms are of a chronic nature and were developed within the family-of-origin setting.

Current family dynamics remain essentially emotionally distant and unfulfilling. The client has little contact with siblings or extended family. The fact that the closest person in his family (i.e., his brother) recently died of a suicide attempt further complicates the family picture, reinforcing his belief that the family is not a safe place for attachments, and this exacerbated his depression and self-doubt. Each time the client has made an attachment in the family (e.g., to his mother in early childhood), the person in whom he trusted and to whom he attached disappeared, either emotionally (like his mother and father) or physically (like his brother). In his current relationship with his significant other, the client expresses strong dependency needs that have cemented their relationship in a potentially unhealthy way. How this dynamic has developed and is currently played out will be addressed in more detail below in the context of the client's interpersonal matrix dynamics.

Interpersonal Matrix Dynamics

Family dynamics, as outlined above, are but one aspect of a client's interpersonal matrix. Adults interact with other adults, children, colleagues, educators, authority figures, friends, acquaintances, and many other individuals every day. All of these people represent potential sources of conflict or assistance, and must be considered part of the client's overall life. Exploration of the interpersonal matrix is driven by the therapist's theoretical framework, and may be considered more important by some than by others. However, most mental health professionals do tend to agree that interpersonal relationships are an important aspect of a person's mental health and day-to-day functioning. After all, ultimately, any gains made in therapy are hoped to generalize to the client's interpersonal matrix. The interpersonal matrix also must consider the client's cultural embeddedness, social context, and community ties. As such, it goes far beyond the tight interpersonal relationships with people with whom the client interacts regularly to include casual and incidental relationships in her or his larger environment. The interpersonal matrix dynamics of the case of the client presented thus far follow below, again taking a self psychological perspective. The intrapsychic, family, and interpersonal sections make up the complete case conceptualization; they are integrated and sequenced (in the order and as they were presented here) in the intake report under the heading of "Case Conceptualization."

Interpersonal Matrix Dynamics in the Case of a Depressed Adult

Given his young age at the time of his mother's depression and father's regular physical absence from the home, the client was not provided with consistent encouragement or opportunity to interact with others (children or adults), because he remained distant from parents, siblings, extended family, neighbors, and others. The social isolation, lack of connectedness with an extended family, apparent absence of community or cultural cohesiveness, and social distance of the entire family contributed to the fact that the client is likely never to have internalized a sense of belonging and has felt disconnected and isolated from the rest of humanity from an early age on.

The family dynamics of isolation and the emotional as well as physical absence (if not neglect) during the client's early childhood contributed to, if not caused, the development of two (what on the surface appear to be) contradictory interpersonal traits. On one hand, the client is highly socially isolated, having great difficulty making friends and reaching out to people. On the other hand, once he forges a relationship he becomes dependent and most likely strongly relies on and needs emotional and psychological support from the other person. These reactions are actually just flip sides of the same coin. Namely, the client is unable to rely on internalized sources of support and strength, and hence he is highly dependent on external sources for meeting any of his emotional and dependency needs. Thus once he enters (however reluctantly at first) into an intimate relationship, the intensity of the needs that are aroused is so strong and overwhelming to him that he becomes highly dependent on the other person. Given the fact that he experienced what he perceived as rejection and abandonment in childhood, this dependency is both frightening and essential. It is essential because it represents the only means for this client to meet his emotional needs (given the lack of internalized mirroring skills); it is frightening because the client is anticipating rejection and abandonment because this is an early experience he came to live through and then expect in his family.

Because of his strong dependency coupled with a significant fear of abandonment, the client enters into relationships only hesitatingly, remaining isolated and distanced from most people. Only after he has developed trust in another person does he become close to her or him. Once close, he quickly transfers all of his emotional needs onto the other person and becomes emotionally dependent. This reality most likely sets up a vicious cycle that prevents the other person, who has some of the same dependency needs, to come to rely on the client in a mutually dependent way (which may explain why he had two successful intimate relationships, one with Jason and one with Sandra). However, in most other relationships, the client is more likely either to remain alienated and distant because of the mistrust that is driven by rejection and abandonment fears, or he ultimately drives people away because of excessive dependency that ultimately again leaves him isolated and reinforces his belief that people cannot be trusted to stay around for any length of time. It is this latter dynamic that might explain the current distancing initiated by his significant other, who may be becoming overwhelmed by the client's dependency needs that have probably increased steadily since the death of his best friend five years ago.

Concluding Thoughts about the Conceptualization

Once the case conceptualization has been prepared, clear avenues for intervention will (hopefully) begin to occur to the clinician. The conceptualization is a direct precursor to setting goals and planning treatment to determine the direction therapy will take. Outlining a therapeutic approach and selecting strategies without previously having formulated a case conceptualization is doomed to failure because the plan is bound to be incomplete or haphazard. Further, formulating a case based on one therapeutic approach or system of psychotherapy and then using a different approach during the actual intervention is inconsistent and is likely to be confusing and replete with mistakes and misunderstandings. The need for consistency between conceptualization and the treatment approach, however, does not imply that once a treatment plan has been developed, it is written in stone. Nothing could be further from the truth. Throughout the work with the client, the therapist will glean new information and gain new insights. The therapist is encouraged to modify the conceptualization, therapy goals, and treatment strategies as appropriate to these new understandings. However, any reconceptualization should remain consistent with the original theoretical approach that was chosen by the mental health care provider. In other words, updating treatment plans does not imply changing direction; it merely implies implementing new techniques and possibly revising some of the therapy goals that had been set. Only rarely is the initial conceptualization so inadequate that a major therapeutic shift is necessary. Case conceptualization will reflect the therapist's clinical orientation most clearly, and therapists may consult several new textbooks to help them understand the differences in case conceptualization across a variety of theoretical orientations (i.e., Berman, 1997; Eells, 1997).

GOAL SETTING

As mentioned previously, goals need to be directly relevant to the client's presenting concerns and the therapist's conceptualization of the case. Given this importance of goals, both to the client and the therapist, it is important that the goal-setting process be a collaborative one that results in some level of agreement between client and therapist about what they will be working toward (Egan, 1994). Goal setting has a number of purposes that serve therapy process and progress. Specifically, according to various writers (e.g., Cormier & Cormier, 1991; Cormier & Hackney, 1987; Egan, 1994; Seligman, 1993), goals have educational, motivational, and evaluative purposes. More concretely, they

- give clients new ideas about what their behavior, thoughts, affects, and relationships could be like
- can induce change merely by clarifying what the client wants to achieve
- focus the attention and action of the client and therapist
- provide an endpoint of treatment to strive toward
- motivate a search for strategies by both client and therapist
- mobilize the client's energy and effort
- mobilize the client's and therapist's attention toward identifying resources and processes that help the client improve or grow
- increase the client's and therapist's persistence
- provide a sense of direction and purpose to the treatment process
- lead to specific strategy selection
- help clinicians determine whether they have the requisite skills needed in the treatment of a given client
- are helpful to outcome evaluations
- demonstrate therapist accountability

Through the collaborative goal-setting process, the therapist assists clients in defining what they would like to gain from therapy. As such, therapists can ask their clients about what they want from treatment, what they need from treatment, and what they would like to achieve through treatment (Egan, 1994). These questions can help determine goals and will often assist the client in identifying and clarifying why therapy is being sought. The collaborative process is important because goals that are made together have a greater motivating force than goals that are set for the client by the therapist. Collaboration helps assure that the goals are owned by the client (Cormier & Cormier, 1991). However, the collaborative process of goal setting with clients requires a word of caution. Weiss (1993) has correctly pointed out that clients cannot always be taken at their word when it comes to setting goals. The goals they identify early in treatment may not be the true goals they have set for themselves, because denial and rationalization may still run high at that time. For instance, it is possible that when clients present for treatment, they indicate that they are coming to treatment to save a relationship, when after some work in therapy it turns out that they are seeking to leave that relationship. Therapists need to be careful of such possibilities and need to revise treatment plans and goals accordingly.

Although "no universally accepted formula for writing treatment goals" exists (Berman, 1997, p. 4), to be optimally effective, goals need to have a number of specific traits. According to most writers and practitioners (e.g., Cormier & Cormier, 1991; Cormier & Hackney, 1987; Egan, 1994; Hutchins & Vaught, 1997; Parsons, 1986), goals need to be

- behaviorally specific, not broad
- realistic, not unreasonable
- achievable, not unfeasible
- meaningful, not trite
- stated in positive, not negative terms
- measurable, not vague
- specific to condition, not generalized
- tied to a time frame, not open-ended

Goals need to be set in such a way that they can be realistically achieved and then sustained once they are achieved. They need to reflect the values and beliefs of the client, while being acceptable to the therapist. It is best to tie concrete behavioral outcomes to goals, because this makes evaluation easier and more obvious for the client. Because it is likely that the behavior, affect, or cognition that is to be changed does not necessarily occur in all settings and at all times, it is helpful to write goals in such a manner that they clarify where, when, and with whom the change is to be expected. The level of change is important to quantify, because some clients may need to achieve a greater degree of behavioral change than others. Level of change is also related to time frame—the more change that needs to be achieved, the more time needs to be allowed. Egan (1994, pp. 255–256) has suggested that most treatment plans should include "now" goals that can or must be achieved almost immediately (such as immediate relief from panic attacks); "soon" goals that change within a short period of time (such as changing appearance through a new haircut or improved grooming habits); "shorter term" goals that can be achieved within a reasonable and foreseeable time frame (such as planning to enroll in university courses at the beginning of the next semester), and "longer term" goals that will require a significant amount of time (such as major personality or interpersonal style changes).

To make goals sufficiently specific, it is best to break them down into smaller components, a process that has been called hierarchical treatment planning (Makover, 1992). Through this process, desired outcomes are broken down into their subcomponents, and each aspect of a desired outcome is specified and quantified. This process is helpful because the smaller steps are more easily and quickly obtainable, and they give both client and therapist a sense of accomplishment. Various labels have been used for this process—the differentiation between goals and objectives, aims and goals, and goals and subgoals remains unclear. Regardless of labels, it is important to have larger and smaller goals. For simplicity, the terms chosen here will be goals and objectives, with goals referring to the larger (broader) aims of treatment, and objectives referring to the more specific desired outcomes. Goals are defined as the larger desired outcomes that will require more time to achieve; objectives are defined as the "stepping stones" (Parsons, 1986, p. 13) toward treatment goals; these are shorter term and more measurable than goals, and often they are more idiosyncratic to the client than the larger treatment goals formulated.

In addition to differentiating between goals and objectives, it is important for the clinician to realize that several types of goals can be specified. Namely, there are process goals and outcome goals (Cormier & Hackney, 1987). Process goals refer to goals the therapist identifies as important to the therapeutic process and that are needed to facilitate outcome goals. Examples of process goals are aims such as establishing trust between client and therapist, developing a sense of safety for the client in the treatment room, the therapist developing empathy and understanding for the client, establishing rapport, and so forth. The general warning not to confuse strategies and goals is particularly important with regard to process goals (Makover, 1992). For example, establishing trust as a goal then needs to have specific treatment strategies assigned to it, such as being sensitive to the client's needs, providing a predictable environment, and being prompt for sessions. Process goals are not verbalized and worked out collaboratively with the client. Instead, they are goals set by the therapist to facilitate the achievement of outcome goals.

With regard to outcome goals, various guidelines and suggestions have been provided. Some theorists believe that there are three types of outcome goals: goals that help the client think differently, goals that help the client feel differently, and goals that help the client behave differently (e.g., Corsini & Wedding, 1997). Hutchins and Vaught (1997) also outline three types of outcome goals: goals that cluster around stopping undesirable behaviors, goals modifying less than satisfying behaviors, or goals for learning new behaviors. Goals formulated can also be related to the three Ps; these would focus on relinquishing unsuccessful coping strategies or perpetuating factors; removing or overcoming the effects of precipitating factors; and accepting, changing, or coming to terms with predisposing factors (Lemma, 1995; Teyber, 1997). Nathensen and Johnson (1992) suggest five types of outcome goals, each tied to one of the five axes of the DSM-IV. As such, they suggest setting goals tied to acute symptoms (Axis I goals), goals tied to long-term symptoms (Axis II goals), goals tied to the client's medical and physical presentation (Axis III goals), goals tied to social concerns and stressors (including cultural issues) faced by the client (Axis IV goals), and goals tied to the client's level of functioning (Axis V goals). This type of goal setting forces therapist and client to evaluate every aspect of the client's life and therefore tends to lead to very comprehensive treatment planning. A similar approach is suggested by Karoly (1993) without being tied to DSM-IV. He suggests that goals need to be contextual rather than preoccupied with the client's presenting concern, which suggests that clients do not necessarily present all problems at intake. This issue was discussed in some detail when the idea of a problem list was introduced. Karoly's approach is consistent with this approach and integrates short-term treatment goals of acute presenting symptomatology with long-term treatment planning that attends to other concerns and etiological factors.

The approach to goal setting that is advocated here is a combination of several of the above approaches; it differentiates between client goals, therapist goals, and shared client–therapist goals. Shared goals are goals that are outcome goals (and related objectives); these are negotiated and discussed with the client and are to be used for motivational, educational, and evaluative purposes; therapist goals incorporate process goals as well as outcome goals (and objectives) that are based in the theoretical approach chosen by the clinician for the client's treatment; client goals are outcome goals that are formulated by the client that the therapist does not necessarily endorse wholeheartedly, but neither opposes nor finds unacceptable.

As client and therapist negotiate goals and objectives, they must outline the possible consequences of these goals for the client. Therapy goals do not necessarily always have exclusively positive consequences; it is entirely possible that certain desired therapeutic changes will result in undesirable side effects. For example, it is not uncommon for clients who grow and change to outgrow current intimate relationships. Also, some therapeutic goals may carry with them the need for work that will be painful to the client as this person begins to work toward resolving problems. For example, a client who formulates a goal (and the related objectives) of overcoming the effects of childhood sexual abuse must come to understand before treatment commences that this aim can and often does involve a painful process that may make the client's current symptoms worse before they begin to improve. Outlining and discussing these possibilities with the client as goals are being set will prevent the client from being caught unaware by any temporary deterioration in functioning, environmental responses that may be less than supportive, or withdrawal by others as the treatment progresses.

Shared Goals

Most commonly, the shared goals of therapy will relate to resolving the client's presenting problems and the related problems identified by the therapist (and client) during the intake. This category of goals is independent of the therapist's theoretical orientation; it represents the essence of the treatment plan that is discussed and negotiated with the client and that is used as a measure of progress. It is most desirable that client and therapist agree on all of the outcome goals they select for a client's treatment. Their shared goals must be compatible, must honor the client's wishes, and must reflect the therapist's assessment of the client's needs (Cormier & Cormier, 1991).

Shared goals can be formulated from any or all of the approaches sampled above (e.g., addressing affect, behavior, and cognition; or addressing elimination, change, or development of certain behaviors; or following the five DSM-IV axes; or corresponding to the client's context; or using any other format preferred by a given therapist). Regardless of the types of outcome goals and objectives chosen around the guiding principle, formulating clear objectives is most important for the category of shared goals. This category of goals should have the following characteristics:

- Goals and objectives should be grouped logically (either from a contextual or temporal perspective).
- Goals and objectives should be stated hierarchically and sorted with regard to priority.
- Each set of objectives within a goal should be stated to allow movement from broadest to most specific.
- Objectives need to be specific about defining levels of change so the client and therapist can recognize when a goal or objective has been reached.
- Objectives need to be specific when defining contexts of change so client and therapist can recognize when a goal or objective has been reached.
- Objectives need to be realistic and attainable within a reasonable and specified time frame.

Therapist Goals

Therapist goals are generally formulated to reflect the desired process and outcome goals selected by the clinician to guide treatment from a particular theoretical perspective. As such, they are much more theoretically bound than shared goals or client goals and may vary greatly across therapists from different schools of thought. In general terms, this set of goals provides the framework for the treatment approach selected by the therapist and will be most important in guiding the selection of specific treatment strategies. This category of goals is not discussed or negotiated with client but rather represents privately formulated theoretically-bound treatment objectives to be used by the therapist in planning and evaluating treatment process and progress. It is also this procedure of listing the goals that is most likely to encounter some minor revision as new facts emerge throughout therapy. This set of goals is most likely to attempt to address modifying perpetuating factors, precipitating factors, and predisposing factors in the client's life and seeking the rehabilitation, growth, or development of the client's self.

Therapist goals may be defined in slightly broader terms than shared goals, though they are still accompanied by objectives that define behaviors, affects, cognitions, and interpersonal dynamics that can be used as evidence that a goal has been reached. They consider the individual and the broader familial and social contexts of the client, appraising these issues in terms of their implications for etiology, prognosis, and treatment planning. In other words, it is in this aspect of goal setting that the therapist considers external and internal influences present in the client and the client's life that may affect therapy directly or indirectly. Such influences can hinder or facilitate the therapy process and generally best require optimum preparation. For example, in this goal section, a therapist will consider the presence of a dominating spouse who does not want the partner in treatment and has some investment in preventing the client's change. Such a possible hindrance to therapy will be reflected here in devising a goal that addresses this external influence to neutralize it.

Client Goals

The issue of client goals raises the possibility that a client may desire outcomes that are unacceptable to a therapist, to which the therapist must respond. Although most of the time client goals will fit into the general concept or plan developed by the therapist, occasions arise when the client has additional goals that are not captured by the therapist's assessment of the client's situation. In such instances, client goals can be formulated that the therapist does not necessarily share, but which the therapist does not object to and is willing to incorporate into the treatment process. These goals are rarely broken down carefully into accompanying objectives, unless the client is inclined to do so, because they are not seen as integral to the treatment plan and process by the therapist. Occasionally clients will formulate goals that are either disadvantageous for them or that conflict with the therapist's conscience, ethics, or legal obligations. Client goals that "cannot be embraced" by the therapist include the following possibilities (Hutchins & Vaught, 1997, p. 150):

- the goal to harm or kill oneself
- the goal to harm or kill someone else
- the goal to continue to maintain a harmful relationship with a child or dependent under the client's care (e.g., perpetuation of neglect or abuse of an elderly parent)
- the goal of developing or maintaining particular lifestyles that are incompatible with the therapist's world view (e.g., being an active member of a militia group; becoming a member of the Ku Klux Klan)
- the goal of joining or remaining part of a religious group or affiliation that is incompatible with the therapist's judgment of what is safe for the client or for others in the client's life (e.g., joining a cult, involving one's children in satanic rituals)
- the goal of pursuing illegal activities that are incompatible with the therapist's perception of safe and healthy conduct (e.g., drug trafficking, illegal arms sales)
- the goal of expressing attitude-related behaviors that are incompatible with the therapist's ethics, morals, or perceptions of what is safe (e.g., prejudice and discrimination against a particular identified ethnic, racial, or cultural group)
- the goal of achieving unsafe behaviors or physical states (e.g., planning to lose unhealthy amounts of weight, planning to engage in unhealthy or dangerous physical activities)

When the client verbalizes goals such as these, the therapist must discuss their appropriateness with the client. If the client insists on these goals, the therapist may need to take steps to protect the client and others in the client's life, such as invoking the duty to warn, protect, and report. In cases in which therapists do not have the legal responsibility to intervene, but cannot reconcile clients' goals with their own conscience or ethics, clients may need to be refused for treatment and referred if a compromise position cannot be negotiated.

A sample list of goals (including shared, therapist, and client goals) is provided in Table 4.3 that draws on the same case used throughout this chapter so far. This list of goals demonstrates the characteristics and format of a hierarchical goal statement.

TABLE 4.3   Goals and Objectives Formulated for a Depressed Adult Client

Goals Shared by Client and Therapist (Resolution of Presenting Concerns)

Goal A: Resolve Major Depressive Symptoms
Priority Rating: Number One
Time Frame: One Month
Objectives:
1. Improve sleeping patterns
   a. Resolve initial insomnia by falling asleep earlier
   b. Resolve terminal insomnia by sleeping later
   c. Increase number of hours of sleep per night
2. Improve appetite and food intake
   a. Eat regular meals regardless of appetite
   b. Eat healthy foods
   c. Reduce intake of fast foods
   d. Reduce intake of refined sugar products
   e. Regain five pounds
3. Improve energy, drive, and attentional processes
   a. Exercise mildly to moderately three times per week
   b. Resume a sexual relationship with significant other
   c. Go to classes regularly
   d. Go to work regularly
   e. Concentrate and attend adequately
4. Resolve grief issues
   a. Resolve grief and concern over brother's suicide
   b. Grieve and resolve sadness over best friend's suicide

Goal B: Resolve Symptoms Related to Chronic Dysthymia
Priority Rating: Number Two
Time Frame: One Year
Objectives:
1. Improve mood
   a. Decrease severity of depression
   b. Decrease frequency of depression
   c. Feel hopeful and joyful more often than feeling depressed
2. Improve self-esteem and self-confidence
   a. Feel more competent with regard to making decisions
   b. Feel more able to be alone
   c. Feel more comfortable suggesting action plans
   d. Decrease sensitivity to critical feedback
   e. Improve sense of self-worth
3. Improve drive and energy (see Objective A-3 above)

Goal C: Resolve Symptoms Related to Personality Style
Priority Rating: Number Three
Time Frame: One Year
Objectives:
1. Initiate action and improve decisiveness
   a. Make one minor and one major decision per day
   b. Decide about one action plan per day
   c. Motivate one action per day
2. Decrease helplessness
   a. Rely on self for an off work or school-related action or decision at least once per day
   b. Attempt to solve one personal concern or problem per day without first asking for assistance
   c. Help someone else with a problem or concern at least once per day

Continued

TABLE 4.3 *Continued*

3. Decrease social isolation
   a. Engage in one social activity per week that involves at least one other person (not including Sandra)
   b. Attend one social event per month that involves several other people (e.g., a party, performance, or dance)
   c. At least once a month invite an acquaintance for lunch or a shared activity to get to know the person better
4. Resolve fear of loneliness
   a. Once a week engage in an activity outside the home without Sandra
   b. Once a month spend an entire day away from Sandra
   c. In a one-year period, take an overnight (single or multiple) without Sandra
   d. Spend at least one hour per day at home without Sandra
5. Improve self-care skills
   a. Seek health care services regularly as needed
   b. Develop internal coping skills
   c. Improve nutrition and exercise
6. Improve relationship with significant other (also see Objective C-4)
   a. Become less dependent on Sandra
   b. Make fewer requests of Sandra for assistance and support
   c. Give Sandra needed space for her social activities
   d. Initiate more actions relevant to the relationship
   e. Improve sexual relationship

Additional Client Goals

Goal A: Improve Relationships at Work
Priority Rating: Low
Time Frame: One Month
Objectives:
1. Apologize for missed work days
2. Work more regular hours to help boss with scheduling

Additional Therapist Goals (Rehabilitation of Underlying Dynamics and Self-Structure)

Goal A: Process-Related Goals
Objectives:
1. Develop healthy therapeutic rapport
   a. Foster comfortable self-disclosure
   b. Foster emotional expressiveness and catharsis
   c. Prevent dependency
   d. Attend to fears of abandonment and rejection
2. Develop trust and attend to trust issues
3. Develop predictability and stability
4. Develop a psychologically safe holding environment
5. Facilitate generalization of change
6. Facilitate ancillary treatment options (especially regarding couples work)

Goal B: Outcome-Related Goals
Objectives:
1. Develop insight regarding the interplay of personality style and dysthymia
2. Clarify childhood factors in the development of dependency and dysthymia
3. Resolve abandonment and rejection fears

Continued

TABLE 4.3   *Continued*

4. Improve internal coping resources and skills
5. Improve external coping resources
6. Facilitate healthy development of self
    a. Improve mirroring pole of self (self-esteem, self-appraisal, self-confidence)
    b. Improve idealizing pole of self (decisiveness, action planning, direction, life goals)
    c. Improve twinship feelings (social connectedness, skill development, interpersonal ease)

TREATMENT PLANNING

Once the goals for treatment have been negotiated and agreed on, the therapist concludes the conceptualization and treatment plan process by selecting treatment strategies. The general approach to treatment has already been chosen by this time because it is reflected in the case dynamics section of the report (especially the intrapsychic dynamics section) and in the therapist's goals in the goal listing. The choice of strategies is still left, however, and that becomes the treatment plan proper. It has been pointed out that the diagnosis of a client, though often the most dreaded aspect of the process of conceptualizing and planning treatment, is actually the easiest; the toughest part is actually selecting strategies, because the therapist must juggle all variables considered and identified in the process up to this point (see Makover, 1992). It is important to recognize that treatment strategy selection must reflect flexibility and must be highly idiosyncratic for each client: "A theory of techniques that prescribes roughly the same approach (or range of related approaches) for every patient is not sufficiently flexible. It may be well suited to the treatment of some patients, but not to the treatment of others" (Weiss, 1993, p. 59).

It must also be stressed once more that the cultural context of the client must be considered again in this last phase of the preparation for therapy. Specifically, treatment strategy choice may in part be dictated by what the therapist has learned about the client in a variety of circumstances, but especially in the context of culture (Matsumoto, 1994a). People from different cultures (these not necessarily tied to race or ethnicity) may prefer different styles of intervention, and the therapist best makes strategy choices by integrating techniques that optimize the likelihood of treatment compliance and success. Much has been written about strategy preferences by different groups of clients, and detailed information about this issue is beyond the scope of this book. However, the interested (and responsible) reader is referred to books such as Dana (1993) and Ponterotto, Casas, Suzuki, and Alexander (1995). To optimize overall strategy selection, several issues must be considered by the conscientious therapist (see Beutler & Berren, 1995; Brems, 1993; Cormier & Cormier, 1991; Cormier & Hackney, 1987; Meyer & Deitsch, 1996; Weiss, 1993):

1. therapist factors:
    • therapist's theoretical approach or school of thought
    • therapist skills, competencies, training, expertise, and familiarity with specific strategies

2. client factors:
   - preference for a given theoretical approach
   - client preferences for interpersonal styles (e.g., lifestyle approaches, activity versus passivity)
   - cognitive capacity
   - reactance (i.e., cooperation and compliance with the treatment plan)
   - motivational distress
   - coping style
3. environmental factors:
   - community or agency service availability
   - insurance coverage
   - level of family support
   - clinic equipment
4. symptom-related factors:
   - research that suggests which techniques work best with what types of symptoms
   - problem severity
   - problem complexity
   - comorbidity of syndromes and disorders
5. goal-related factors:
   - cognitive changes or modifications
   - affective/emotional changes or modifications
   - behavioral changes or modifications
   - interpersonal changes or modifications
   - spiritual changes or modifications

Therapist-Related Factors

Strategy choices must be made ethically and responsibly—a requirement that suggests that the therapist's skill level must be taken into consideration (see American Psychological Association, 1992). Therapists cannot provide services for which they were not trained. As such, clinicians cannot attempt to use biofeedback strategies, hypnosis, and similar strategies that require specific skills training if they never received thorough and comprehensive education and supervised experience in these techniques. Also relevant to strategy selection, though less decisively so, is the therapist's theoretical orientation. An exclusively psychoanalytically oriented therapist may well not do the best work attempting to use behavior modification with a client; similarly, a behaviorist may not do well with dream analysis. Notably, it is more the clinician's skill level and training that determines strategy choice in this instance than actual theoretical orientation. For example, a psychodynamically oriented therapist who has had training in using systematic desensitization or guided imagery can use these techniques appropriately, even though they stem from a different school of thought. It is clearly up to therapists' conscience and professional ethics to decide what they are competent to try. The best rule of thumb is having received both education and supervised experience in the techniques in question.

Merely having read about a technique or having been taught it in a purely didactic way generally does not suffice to make a clinician competent in its use; however, a course that included actual application with subsequent feedback and opportunity for skill improvement may adequately prepare the clinician. Optimally, the therapist must have received course training *and* supervised practicum experience for any given strategy to be qualified to use it.

If a therapist is not skilled with a certain technique but is convinced that it would be greatly helpful to the client, two choices exist. The therapist can make a referral to a clinician who is trained in this particular strategy, or the therapist can discuss with the client the fact that the therapist is not yet qualified for this work but is in the process or has the desire to learn it and could implement the technique under supervision. The client can then make an informed choice to transfer to a different clinician or to remain with the current therapist who would then implement the new technique under the close supervision of a skilled consultant with the explicit understanding of the client that this is being done.

Client-Related Factors

Occasionally clients will present to treatment seeking intervention within a particular school of thought. If this is the case, it is the overall treatment approach more than actual technique selection that is affected. Depending on the match between the client's desires and the therapist's skills and theoretical orientation, the client's request can either be honored or not. If the match is good, client and therapist can work together; if the match is poor, a referral may need to be initiated. Certain client characteristics may dictate a particular style of interaction or choice of strategies. For example, some writers have suggested that clients from certain ethnic groups fare better with a more directive than a psychodynamic approach to treatment. Other client characteristics that may affect strategy selection include interpersonal styles and cognitive capacity. A client who is extremely shy and reticent would probably not do well with Gestalt techniques that require a lot of role playing and direct therapist–client interaction. Similarly, a client who is extremely outgoing and excitable may not do well on a psychoanalytic couch. Cognitive limitations of the client may also rule out certain types of interventions. A client with borderline or significantly below average intelligence may not deal well with an exploratory, insight-oriented set of strategies that requires logical thinking and cognitive complexity. A client who is highly cognitively complex and an independent thinker, on the other hand, may take offense with a highly directive and overly concrete style. It is also important to make use of existing client skills and strengths (Lauver & Harvey, 1997) and incorporate these into treatment as appropriate. For example, a client with an art background may enjoy and use art techniques very well; a client who is an avid reader may benefit from incorporating some bibliotherapy techniques; a client who is emotionally expressive may find it useful to engage in the use of metaphors and storytelling.

Client reactance refers to the client's level of cooperation and compliance with treatment (Beutler & Berren, 1995). Highly reactant clients are those who are generally noncompliant and uncooperative because they perceive their clinicians as threatening the clients' freedom. Such reactant clients will be likely to exhibit resistant and oppositional behaviors that may best be dealt with through para-doxical and nondirective strategies. Clients with low reactance are generally co-operative and compliant; they tolerate a high degree of intervention by clinicians because they do not perceive external control as a threat. Such clients will tolerate clinician-directed interventions quite well. Clients manifest high reactance symp-tomatically by complying with direction, accepting interpretations and sugges-tions, tolerating events outside their control, seeking direction, submitting to authority, being open to feedback, and being nondefensive in their interpersonal styles. Clients' high reactance is characterized by their intense need to maintain autonomy, refusing interpretations and rejecting feedback, dominating behavior, resisting, having a history of social conflict, having a history of incomplete treat-ment, and resisting external influences (Beutler & Berren, 1995).

Clients' motivational distress refers to their degree of distress expressed about the presenting symptoms. If clients perceive that their symptoms do not result in significant distress or anxiety, motivation for treatment will be lower than if clients perceive their problems as highly distressing. Motivation and reactance may be highly correlated because compliance may increase with distress. Clients who have high degrees of motivational distress may be more motivated for treatment but may also exhibit such high levels of arousal that their response to intervention is in-terfered with by their anxiety level. In such cases, strategies need to be selected early on in treatment that will reduce clients' level of arousal (e.g., relaxation tech-niques, reassurance, emotional support, thought stopping, focusing). On the other hand, clients with low levels of motivational distress may be best treated with arousal induction strategies that create some level of self-awareness and that may result in insight about the symptoms and subsequent increase in distress that they become a motivating force for complying with treatment (e.g., silence, interpreta-tion, Gestalt work, dream work, self-monitoring, directed imagery). High distress is indicated by symptoms such as motor agitation, difficulty maintaining concentra-tion, unsteady voice, autonomic symptoms, hyperventilation, excitation, and in-tense emotions. Low distress manifests as reduced motor activity, low energy level, low investment in treatment, blunted or constricted affect, unmodulated emotional expression, and slow verbalizations (see Beutler & Berren, 1995).

A client's coping style can be seen as externalizing or internalizing in terms of how the person manages conflict and anxiety. Clients who internalize are generally well-served with insight-oriented, awareness-producing techniques that require in-trospection and self-analyses. Clients who externalize, on the other hand, do not like to introspect and hence respond less well to insight-oriented work. They tend to respond better to setting limits, building skills, and other behaviorally focused approaches (Beutler & Berren, 1995). Internalizing styles are recognized by features such as social withdrawal, somatization, social introversion, emotional overcontrol or constriction, delay of gratification, self-blame and self-punishment, and inter-nalizing defenses such as reaction formation, introjection, identification, undoing, intellectualization, denial, and repression (see Beutler & Berren, 1995). Externaliz-ing styles are recognized by features that include stimulation seeking, manipulative behavior, social extroversion, low frustration tolerance, blaming others, aggressive behavior, poor impulse control, and defenses such as projection, avoidance, acting out, and other externalizing maneuvers (see Beutler & Berren, 1995).

Environmental Factors

Considering environmental factors in the selection of techniques is generally an issue that does not require much discussion because it is dictated by common sense. Clinicians will not recommend or seek to use techniques for which they do not have the resources (e.g., therapists will not plan to use biofeedback if they have no biofeedback equipment). Important in this context are other factors as well, such as community service availability. A suicidal client may receive different treatment depending on whether a community has a crisis hotline or not. If the client appears on the verge of becoming actively suicidal, a clinician may choose to hospitalize the client sooner if no such service is available. Similarly, the prescription of participating in support or self-help groups is only sensible if clients have access to these, either through their availability in the community or through clients' ability to transport themselves to them. Strategies that require family support can only be recommended if the family is indeed supportive of treatment and does not work to undermine the client's work with the therapist. Finally, insurance coverage may dictate some treatment planning, depending on the amount of coverage and financial solvency of the client. If clients seek services that can be covered completely by their insurance, short-term treatment may need to be planned, and this has definite implications for strategy selection. A therapist and client faced with only 10 to 12 weeks of work together will embark on much more directive and focused work than the same dyad would with unlimited time available.

Symptom-Related Factors

Strategies must also be selected with some attention to the research literature that suggests certain techniques for certain symptoms. For example, Cormier and Cormier (1991) provide the following research-based guidelines for pairing symptoms and strategies:

- phobias → systematic desensitization
- anxiety → relaxation training, meditation
- anger → reframing, cognitive restructuring, stress inoculation
- depression → imagery, reframing, supportive strategies
- skill deficit → psychoeducation, specific skills training, modeling
- shyness → assertiveness training
- obsessive–compulsiveness → reframing, Gestalt work, paradoxical interventions

In perusing Cormier and Cormier's (1991) suggestions, the cogent therapist recognizes that they are only that—suggestions. The psychotherapy literature to date is not sufficiently advanced to be able to prescribe treatment approaches based on specific contents of symptoms (although attempts have been made with limited success; e.g., Chambless et al., 1993, 1996). In fact, severe criticisms have been rendered in response to attempts to do so. These correctly and eloquently suggest that prescriptive psychological treatment choices are inadequate and are not in line with the most advanced techniques of the mental health professions (Silverman, 1996). Silverman provides convincing, research-based arguments showing that researchers do not yet know why psychotherapy works and have not yet identified any single approach that is superior to another. Therapy does appear to work, but perhaps due more to idiosyncratic interactions between each client and therapist rather than due to specific therapeutic approaches.

Hence, more important to the client's recovery than the specific content of the symptoms is their severity and complexity. Problem severity is defined as the intensity of the problem, the degree to which it interferes with day-to-day functioning, and the availability of social support (Beutler & Berren, 1995). Problem severity can dictate intensity as well as appropriate modality of treatment, these ranging from inpatient or outpatient treatment to making choices about psychosocial and/or medical interventions (e.g., medication referrals). High problem severity is marked by interference with the client's functioning during the interview and, in general, the client's inability to concentrate, distraction by minor events, difficulty functioning (to the point of being incapacitated), difficulty maintaining interpersonal interaction, and impairment in multiple areas of functioning. The severity of the problem can also be gleaned from the client's level of impairment, as rated on Axis V of the DSM-IV, by test scores on psychological screening tests, and as shown in the range and severity of Axis I, II, and III concerns. Low problem severity is marked by a presentation opposite that outlined for severe problems (see Beutler & Berren, 1995). The more severe the problem, the more restrictive or directive the intervention.

Problem complexity refers to behaviors and patterns that endure across time and situations. If symptoms are presented as enduring across time (i.e., chronic) and across situations (i.e., pervasive or characterological), they are likely to be reflections of underlying psychic conflict or developmental delay. If, on the other hand, they are temporary or highly situational, there is not likely to be underlying chronic pathology or developmental concern. In the former case, strategy selection must reflect the chronicity and complexity of the problem and may involve complex intervention due to the client's need for complex life theme and lifestyle pattern changes. In the latter situation, interventions may be direct and focused, being oriented toward simple symptom removal without pattern or lifestyle changes necessary (Beutler & Berren, 1996).

Both complexity and severity are often involved when the therapist considers comorbidity of syndromes or diagnoses. Clients with comorbid clinical disorders and personality disorders often report more complex and severe problems than clients without such a label. Not surprisingly, comorbid clients need to be approached with a more complex set of treatment strategies, and at times with a specific treatment approach (see Brems & Johnson, 1997; Brown & Barlow, 1992; Namyniuk, Brems, & Clarson, 1997). Their treatment may need to be more directive, focused, and specific to deal with one set of symptoms, whereas it may call for insight-oriented, affect-oriented, and experiential strategies for another. How to combine such apparently disparate techniques can be a great challenge and may explain in part why comorbid clients tend to have less positive treatment outcomes. However, this combination of strategies is possible and is best put in a temporal context (Brems & Johnson, 1997). As such, more directive and focused techniques may be used early on in treatment to deal with acute symptom resolution; once the client has experienced some relief from these symptoms, treatment may shift to a more insight-oriented modality that accounts for the more chronic and severe problems.

Goal-Related Factors

Goal-related issues also need to be considered in final strategy selection. If goals are predominantly affect-oriented, techniques need to be chosen that work best with this aspect of human functioning; if intervention is most important with regard to changing cognitions, appropriate techniques must be selected. The same idea is obviously true for behavioral or interpersonal changes. The following guidelines for this approach to technique selection practices have been suggested (e.g., Cormier & Hackney, 1987; Corsini & Wedding, 1997; Hutchins & Vaught, 1997):

If cognitions are to be changed, use

- insight-oriented self analysis
- rational emotive therapy strategies
- self-talk
- cognitive behavioral strategies (e.g., ABC chains)
- bibliotherapy
- psychoeducational interventions
- journaling
- modeling
- symbolic learning (e.g., dream work)

If emotions are to be changed, use

- person-centered techniques
- existential techniques
- humanistic techniques
- experiential exercises
- Gestalt techniques
- classical conditioning-based strategies
- insight-oriented strategies
- facilitation of emotional expression
- exercises to enhance emotional awareness

If behaviors are to be changed, use

- behavior modification and operant conditioning
- classical conditioning
- insight-oriented strategies
- physical action
- exercises to change physical and somatic change (e.g., relaxation training)

- role play
- modeling
- rehearsal

If physical symptoms need to be addressed, use
- medication
- exercise
- relaxation training
- meditation
- biofeedback
- medical treatment
- diet and nutritional strategies

If interpersonal symptoms need to be addressed, use
- role play
- Gestalt techniques
- insight-oriented strategies
- paradoxical interventions
- systems therapy strategies (e.g., sculpting)
- logical consequences
- environmental changes
- conjoint therapy

Clearly there is some overlap in terms of strategies across the areas of human functioning. However, some techniques are obviously more appropriate for some goals than for others. Choosing a theoretical approach and supplementing it with a variety of strategies that are relevant to the goals that have been set is a prudent approach to treatment. It is beyond the scope of this book to acquaint the reader with all possible treatment strategies and systems of psychotherapy. Therapists who would like to incorporate specific treatment strategies (e.g., Gestalt techniques, relaxation training, cognitive–behavioral strategies, and so forth) in their work need to consult primary references and receive specialized training to do so successfully. Some texts covering specific strategies that may be recommended for the purpose of in-depth training include, but are certainly not limited to, the following list.

- Gestalt Therapy Integrated (Polster & Polster, 1973)
- Dream Work in Psychotherapy and Self Change (Mahrer, 1989)
- Cognitive Therapy: Basics and Beyond (Beck, 1995)
- International Handbook of Behavior Modification and Therapy (Bellak, Herson, & Kazdin, 1990)
- Process Experiential Psychotherapy (Greenberg, 1994)
- The Practice of Rational–Emotive Therapy (RET) (Ellis & Dryden, 1987)
- The Will to Meaning: Foundations and Applications of Logotherapy (Frankl, 1969)
- Focusing (Gendlin, 1981)
- The Practice of Multimodal Therapy (Lazarus, 1981)

- Paradoxical Psychotherapy (Weeks & L'Abate, 1982)
- Ericksonian Methods: The Essence of the Story (Zeig, 1994)
- Flash of Insight: Metaphor and Narrative in Therapy (Pearce, 1996)

Concluding Thoughts about Treatment Plans

Thorough treatment planning proceeds by carefully considering numerous variables, each one of which makes a unique contribution to the way the client presents, sets goals, and responds to treatment. Selecting strategies carefully using as many of these factors as possible increases the likelihood that the client will cooperate with treatment, will see treatment as valuable, and will ultimately become an active partner in change. Table 4.4 provides an example of a treatment plan for the sample client that has been followed throughout this chapter.

A good treatment plan not only matches strategies to therapist, client, environment, symptoms, and goals but also reflects a client's strengths, healthy traits, potential, and positive contributions to the therapy process. Considering these strengths, the treatment plan attempts to render a prognosis that helps both client and therapist evaluate how long treatment will take and what the likelihood of success will be. This allows therapist and client to be realistic with regard to goal setting and outcome expectations. Further, a good and comprehensive treatment plan incorporates referral recommendations for ancillary services such as medications, self-help groups,

TABLE 4.4 Treatment Strategies Selected in the Case of a Depressed Adult Client

Strategies Selected	Client–Therapist Goals Addressed (refer to Table 4.3)
Primary Treatment (once a week outpatient psychotherapy–50 minutes)	
1. tracking behaviors and affects through journaling	A-1 through A-3, B-2, C-5
2. relaxation training	A-1
3. guided imagery	A-1, A-4, B-2, C-2
4. experiential exercises (e.g., localizing feelings)	A-1 through A-4, B-1, C-4
5. symbolic work (e.g., dream analysis)	A-1 through A-4, B-2, C-1 through C-6
6. insight-oriented work (e.g., interpretation, self-analysis, introspection)	B-1 through B-3, C-1 through C-6
7. supportive strategies (e.g., reframing, normalization, reassurance, support)	A-1 through A-4, C-2, C-4
8. cognitive work (e.g., action planning)	C-1 and C-2
9. continued monitoring of suicidal ideation	A-3, B-1, C-5
10. continuous monitoring for need for medication	A-1 through A-3
Ancillary Treatments (as often as possible)	
1. relationship therapy	C-4 and C-6
2. referral to a physician	A-1, A-2, C-5
3. exercise	A-1 through A-3, C-5
4. relaxation exercises and meditation at home	A-1, B-2, C-5
5. referral to a nutritionist	A-2, C-5
6. membership in relevant clubs or organizations (e.g., Sierra Club)	C-3 through C-6

support groups, and social resource development (Seligman, 1993), instead of merely relying on doing all the necessary therapeutic work within the confines of a weekly 50-minute hour. Ancillary services that can always be considered with the client include, but may not be limited to, the following (see also Choca, 1988; Seligman, 1996):

1. environmental changes or modifications
   - separation or divorce
   - foster placement of children
   - moving to a new house
   - moving to a different state
2. alternate living arrangements
   - halfway house
   - shelter
   - group home
   - foster home
3. consideration of medical, physical, and health-related needs
   - physical exam
   - medication referral
   - nutrition referral
   - exercise or yoga
   - substance use treatment referral
   - meditation
4. skill building and education
   - tutoring
   - study skills development
   - GED preparation
   - academic skills preparation
   - job-seeking skills development
   - vocational interest and aptitude assessment
5. personal growth skills development
   - assertiveness skills
   - communication skills
   - values clarification
   - anger management
   - relaxation
6. social support development
   - peer support groups
   - symptoms support groups
   - self-help groups
   - clubs and special interest groups
7. social resource development
   - referral to social work or case management
   - appointment with social services agency
   - information regarding relevant community support systems

8. professional services
   - legal assistance
   - financial planning
   - divorce mediation

Even the best treatment plan, however, is potentially useless if it is neither shared nor discussed with the client. As mentioned in the goal-setting section, goals are negotiated with a client to arrive at shared goals and a sense of direction for treatment. Similarly, treatment strategy choices, information about prognosis, time commitment, and the therapist's understanding of the client must be communicated. The specifics of all phases of feedback are presented below; these represent the conclusion of the conceptualization and treatment planning process.

FEEDBACK

Feedback during the process of conceptualizing and planning treatment is most important with regard to sharing the therapist's perceptions of case dynamics and negotiating treatment goals. Sharing case dynamics must be accomplished by using simple language that excludes jargon as much as possible. The conceptualization needs to be presented in understandable, layperson's terms that make sense to the client. In presenting the case dynamics the clinician must show compassion and understanding as well as empathy for how the client may feel on hearing the therapist's understanding of the client's situation (Morrison, 1995a). From the discussion of case dynamics, therapist and client will move on to goal setting, a process that is more of a dialogue than a presentation of the conceptualization to the client. Goals need to be clearly spelled out, and advantages and disadvantages may be discussed for each goal. It is likely that the therapist will still maintain a relatively active role in this process and will be called on by the client to make suggestions about appropriate goals. However, in setting goals it is always best to ask the client to generate ideas first, to be corroborated, elaborated, and expanded on by the clinician. As this is done, the clinician needs to be careful to give a rationale for each suggestion and to emphasize the client's strengths and resources.

After discussing goals, therapist and client need to discuss treatment options briefly and only in as much depth as the clinician believes will be helpful to the client. Both client's and therapist's roles need to be reiterated and possible drawbacks of each suggested intervention need to be discussed. If a client disagrees with the course of treatment suggested by the therapist, the two people then must explore what is unacceptable to the client and need to try to compromise. Compromise may best be achieved by exploring areas of agreement and any suggestions the client is willing to try. If client and therapist cannot come to a satisfying resolution about how to proceed with treatment (a rare occurrence), a referral may be necessary (Morrison, 1995a).

SUMMARY AND CONCLUDING THOUGHTS

Making a treatment contract with a client is the bridge between assessment and therapy (Makover, 1992) and plays an important role in getting treatment underway in a positive and helpful way. Collaboration with the client during this process is likely to increase motivation and compliance because the client will feel part of the process, will own the goals and decisions that were made, and is informed about what to expect. Disclosing specifics about diagnosis and strategy selection is left to the discretion of the therapist. It is often not helpful to inform clients of diagnostic decisions because these are generally not entirely relevant to treatment planning. Further, although the general approach to treatment is discussed with the client, specifics about catalysts and strategies need not be discussed—this information may be rather meaningless to the client. The most important collaborative aspects of this process have to do with feedback about the conceptualization and negotiation of acceptable, shared goals. Once the treatment plan is in place, client and therapist are ready to begin therapeutic work. This work presupposes that the therapist is familiar with therapeutic catalysts and has mastered a variety of treatment strategies. The next chapters will introduce the most important catalysts for change and will outline how to deal with challenging therapeutic situations. From there, the therapist is ready to embark on therapy with the client.

DOCUMENTATION AND RECORD-KEEPING

Documenting the treatment planning process only roughly parallels the actions taken by the therapist. Although the therapist makes a problem list, this list is not included in the intake report, but rather is a separate document that may be filed as a progress note or a separate notation that can be attached to the intake report. The diagnosis derived from the problem list is provided in the intake report unless the clinician has reason to exclude it (e.g., due to cultural concerns or other misgivings about diagnostic labeling). If providing the diagnosis in the report, it is helpful to support the decisions made on each DSM-IV axis with a brief outline of related problems and concerns.

The case conceptualization requires some preliminary work that is not reflected in the intake report; namely, the listing of predisposing factors, precipitating factors, and perpetuating factors is not included in the report, but rather is filed as a progress note or as a separate document to back up the intake report. Only the case dynamics (intrapsychic, family-related, and interpersonal matrix-related) are reported in the intake report under the heading of Case Conceptualization.

Goals are not noted in detail, but merely in summary form, in the intake report. Treatment recommendations are noted in detail (see documentation sample below). The goals and treatment strategies can be listed in a separate treatment plan document that is attached to the intake report. Given that examples of all of these aspects of the conceptualization and treatment plan have been provided throughout this chapter, they will not be repeated here, with the exception of the Recommendations section (i.e., the treatment plan summary) which appears below as it would be written for an Intake Report.

Recommendation Section of the Intake Report

Given the complexity and severity of the client's problem, a multifaceted approach to treatment is recommended. First and foremost, it is recommended that the client be seen once a week in long-term, insight-oriented psychotherapy. This particular type of therapy is viewed as most compatible with both problem complexity and client variables, such as internalizing coping style, current level of distress, and anticipated level of cooperation with treatment. Therapy will take an overall psychodynamic (self-psychological) approach (supplemented with a range of eclectic strategies) that will be geared toward symptom resolution as well as personality change and self-development and growth. A supportive and stable working relationship will need to be established with the client that will foster self-disclosure, trust, catharsis, and insight while preventing inappropriate levels of dependency. The therapist will use the transference relationship with the client to develop such therapeutic rapport; traditional therapeutic structure will be used to create a stable and predictable environment within which the client can deal with his fears of abandonment and rejection. Additionally, a variety of ancillary interventions are indicated that will reach beyond the individual approach. These strategies are recommended to facilitate generalized change, to enhance the development of new skills and resources, and to support the individual treatment strategies.

Primary Treatment Recommendations

1. To address the client's immediate distress and several of the symptoms that affect the client's physiological arousal state (e.g., sleep disturbance, low energy), the therapist will use relaxation strategies in session and will teach these to the client for use outside of session.
2. To address depressive symptomatology (including self-esteem and self-confidence issues), the therapist will use guided imagery.
3. Experiential exercises are recommended to assist the client with creating self-awareness, enhancing emotional awareness and expressiveness, and confronting loneliness issues.
4. The therapist will use symbolic work along with insight-oriented strategies to facilitate the client's cognitive insight, self-awareness, and introspection that will lead to improving his depressive symptoms as well as self-esteem and concerns related to self-development.
5. The therapist will use supportive strategies during periods of severe distress and early on in treatment while the client is still dealing with acute symptoms of major depression. These strategies will also be useful for dealing with the client's sense of helplessness, hopelessness, and indecisiveness.
6. The therapist will employ cognitive strategies to assist the client with action planning that is to improve his decision-making skills and overall internal coping skills. These strategies will also be used to a lesser extent to supplement strategies that will address his unrealistic self-appraisal.
7. The therapist will consider the possibility of journaling to track the client's symptoms more fully and to provide direct feedback about behavioral, affective, and cognitive changes over time.

8. It will be important for the therapist to continue to monitor the client for suicidal ideation, given the acuteness of his symptoms and the family history of depression and suicide.
9. Although medication does not appear indicated at this time due to the chronic nature of the client's depression, the therapist will consider this possibility throughout the first few weeks of treatment until the major depressive symptoms have resolved.

Ancillary Treatment Recommendations

1. The therapist will refer the client to a nutritionist to assist with improved dietary and nutritional planning, given the possible impact of diet on mood.
2. The therapist will refer the client to a physician for a complete physical exam, given that he has not been examined for years and has never been evaluated for the possibility of physiological factors that may contribute to his depression.
3. The therapist will teach the client relaxation strategies in his individual therapy to use at home, but will also refer the client for meditation and additional relaxation or relaxation-related classes (e.g., yoga).
4. The therapist will encourage the client to develop a consistent exercise program that may assist with reducing depressive symptoms (especially sleep- and energy-related symptoms) and that may create a greater sense of well-being and independence.
5. The therapist will encourage the client to seek out social activities that supplement individual therapy, such as joining a club that may be of interest (e.g., Sierra Club). Such activities may also be supportive to the client's relationship with his significant other because it may reduce his dependency in that context.
6. The therapist will raise the possibility of couples therapy for the client and his significant other. The therapist will make appropriate referrals if the client agrees to the need for such intervention.
7. The therapist will consider the possibility of participating in a therapy group for the client once he has firmly committed to and made some progress in individual therapy (no sooner than six months into individual therapy).

It is anticipated that the client's acute depressive symptoms will resolve within one month unless new stressors emerge in the client's life before new and more adequate coping skills have been internalized. The client remains vulnerable to stressors related to his fear of abandonment and rejection, and these issues will need to be monitored to assure that the most appropriate treatment strategies will be selected as treatment progresses. It is anticipated that treatment will require at least one year to achieve enhanced self-development and growth.

5

CATALYSTS FOR CHANGE

Das Amt des Dichters ist nicht das Zeigen des Weges,
sondern vor allem das Wecken der Sehnsucht.
(The duty of the poet is not to show the way,
but above all to awaken the yearning.)
—*HERMANN HESSE*

It is not a therapist's job to give advice or to point clients toward specific solutions to the presenting problems they bring to treatment. Instead, it is the job of the skilled clinician to help the client rekindle hope that a better life and a healthier solution to life's problems is possible (Kohut, 1984). This rekindling of hope can be achieved through a multitude of processes and skills; that is the foremost concern of this chapter. The characteristics and tools of a therapist and therapy setting that are used to rekindle hope and awaken yearning for change and growth can be called catalysts. As borrowed from the biochemical literature, the term catalyst refers to an agent that can serve to modify (generally by increasing the rate of) a chemical reaction without being consumed in the process. In other words, a catalyst is an agent that has a great effect even if used in small amounts; it sets off a reaction or speeds up a reaction that otherwise might not have occurred or would have occurred at a much slower rate. This is a very apt comparison because therapeutic catalysts (as the term will be used in this chapter) are used to bring about or accelerate change in the client with the clear recognition that the catalyst (or therapist using the catalyst) is a means of triggering a process that may also occur naturally. There has been documentation that certain symptoms presented by clients may resolve themselves independently, without intervention. However, therapy accomplishes the faster or more complete resolution of these same symptoms, much as a biochemical process is sped up, enhanced, or otherwise modified through the introduction of a catalyst. In some cases, the catalyst is also critical to make the reaction happen to begin with, another reality reflected in the treatment of some clients who would not have experienced change without an external agent that rekindled hope and facilitated growth.

Stated in another way, then, therapeutic catalysts are the basic skills, techniques, and rules employed by every clinician that facilitate growth and development and that form the foundation of therapy. They are largely independent of a therapist's specific theoretical framework (e.g., behavioral, humanistic, psychodynamic) or preferred intervention strategies (e.g., metaphors, dream work, relaxation training, imagery). Therapists will develop their own preferred repertoire of these catalytic tools and rules; their variety and style of use will differ widely from clinician to clinician. However, a basic set of these rules and tools are familiar to most, if not all, clinicians. Even though they may vary with regard to how often they use any one of these, all therapists are knowledgeable about and capable of using any of them.

There are three groupings of catalysts: first, there are catalysts for a therapeutic environment; second, there are catalysts that facilitate forming a therapeutic relationship; and third, there are catalysts that move therapy forward by involving the client in the therapeutic process. Although they are summarized again briefly below, catalysts for a therapeutic environment and relationship have been discussed in detail in Chapters 1 and 2 under the headings of therapist traits, rapport building, and structure building. The primary focus of this chapter is on the third grouping of catalysts—namely, catalysts that facilitate therapy process.

CATALYSTS FOR A THERAPEUTIC ENVIRONMENT AND RELATIONSHIP

The catalysts in these two categories are essentially prerequisites for treatment. In their absence, a client will neither feel safe nor attached and hence is not likely to remain in therapy. It is because of their essential importance to therapy and assessment that these catalysts have already been dealt with in detail throughout earlier chapters of this book. They are summarized briefly here, but readers who do not remember this information should take the time to refer back to earlier chapters to reacquaint themselves with these concepts of structuring, rapport building, and treatment-enhancing therapist traits.

Catalysts for a therapeutic environment are concerned with safety in two regards: physical safety and psychological safety. Physical safety is provided through thoughtful and respectful surroundings that take individual differences and needs into consideration and that are safe in that they are areas free of violence and aggression as well as free of prejudice and stereotype (see Chapter 1 for detail). Psychological safety is established by providing a firm and predictable therapeutic structure that remains stable across time. This therapeutic structure was discussed at length in Chapter 1. To reiterate briefly, therapy structure is achieved by a length of sessions agreed on and adhered to (most commonly 45 or 50 minutes); regular and agreed upon intervals between sessions (usually one week); a predictable structure within sessions (e.g., opening questions, client disclosure with feedback and involvement, closing process); sameness of the setting (i.e., use of the same room every week, no major environmental changes if possible); clearly spelled-out rules and clinic guidelines (e.g., fee schedules, payment arrangements, rules about missed appointments); confidential and respectful atmosphere; and continuity of the therapist's physical and emotional presence (i.e., same therapist every week, alert therapists who are focused on and familiar with every client they see).

Catalysts for creating a therapeutic relationship refer primarily to the traits of the clinician that are helpful to the therapeutic process. They include factors such as the therapist's willingness and ability to listen attentively and patiently, the treatment's exclusive focus on the client that precludes self-disclosure by the therapist, the presence of stable rules in the absence of unnecessary or rigidly enforced rules, a comforting and reassuring style and personality of the therapist, the ability of the therapist to tolerate silence, the willingness on the part of the clinician to allow the client to lead and set the agenda within reasonable and appropriate limits, self-awareness and control over countertransference on the part of the clinician, and flexibility and cognitive skills that help the therapist understand and conceptualize the client and therapy. Thorough discussions of these traits are provided in Chapter 1.

CATALYSTS THAT FACILITATE THERAPY PROCESS

There are three types of catalysts that move therapy forward by facilitating a connection between therapist and client, enhancing communication, and supporting change and growth. First, there are those skills of the therapist that facilitate communication. These include competencies such as attending, listening, and basic responding to clients and are skills that are sometimes referred to as the microskills of a therapist or clinician (e.g., see Evans, Hearn, Uhleman, & Ivey, 1993, for detailed discussion and programmed instruction). Second, there are those basic skills that facilitate a client's affective self-awareness and internalization of change. These strategies are somewhat more complex than the microskills that enhance communication and may require more practice on the part of the therapist before they are mastered satisfactorily. Third, there are those skills and techniques that facilitate cognitive self-awareness and promote change through insight. These skills are highly complex and require some practice before they can be used successfully. Further, they may need to be used sparingly at times and also require more skill in terms of proper timing and phrasing. The following is a list of the catalysts that move therapy forward.

1. catalysts that facilitate communication
   - attending to nonverbal communication
   - listening to verbal communication
   - responding
2. catalysts that facilitate affective self-awareness and internalization
   - catharsis
   - empathy and understanding (vicarious introspection)
   - affect acceptance, identification, and expression
   - identification of sources of feelings

3. catalysts that facilitate cognitive self-awareness and insight
   - imparting information
   - pointing out patterns
   - asking clarifying questions
   - confrontation
   - here-and-now process comments
   - interpretation

Catalysts That Facilitate Communication

The most important aspect of the client–therapist relationship is open and accurate communication. The communication process is comprised of three components that, although discussed as discrete entities in separate sections below, are interdependent and circular. Communication begins with attending skills that are focused on the nonverbal communication and understanding of the client. Our first impression of people tends to come from their appearance, not from what they are saying. Thus therapists need to be fully aware of what different nonverbal behaviors of a client may say and how therapists themselves communicate with the client through body language. Second, communication always involves listening skills. Therapists must have active listening abilities that remain as undistorted and unbiased as possible. Finally, the communication cycle is not closed (i.e., successful) unless the clinician also responds to the client. Sometimes these responses are designed to stimulate further disclosure; sometimes they have more complex purposes.

Attending to Nonverbal Communication

Basic nonverbal attending skills have been summarized as consisting of facing the client *S*quarely, maintaining an *O*pen posture, *L*eaning in toward the speaker, making *E*ye contact, and being *R*elaxed (memorized through the acronym SOLER; Egan, 1994). Although this mnemonic device is appropriate in making sure that clinicians direct some of their attention to nonverbal attending, it is somewhat simplistic. The nonverbal attending process consists of more than just obeying or following these suggestions. It also includes recognizing body language presented by the client and body language expressed by the therapist. A number of the client's and therapist's nonverbal behaviors need to be focused on. Most important, clinicians must be aware of their clients' and their own eye expressions, eye contact, body movements, body posture, body position, mouth, facial expressions, skin, voice, and appearance (Okun, 1997). For example, it is important to note whether eyes are open, closed, teary, or twitching; if eye contact is steady, shifting, or avoidant; if body movement is fidgety, includes tapping or shaking, or is jerking; if body posture is stooped, slouched, or erect; if body position is tense, relaxed, or rigid; if the mouth is open, tight-lipped, smiling, or drooping; if the skin is clammy, flushed, blushing, pale, or sweaty; if the voice is loud, fast, clear, or unsteady; and if appearance is neat, sloppy, disheveled, or well-groomed. Attention needs to be paid not only to how the client presents but also how therapists present themselves to the client. Knowing what certain body traits may express (or how they may be interpreted by the receiver) helps the therapist avoid body traits that are not conducive to rapport or relationship building.

Lowered eyes may indicate preoccupation with a thought or task not at hand; steady eye contact indicates readiness to work; darting eyes may suggest anxiety; tight lips often portray anger; quivering lips reveal sadness; lip chewing is often related to anxiety; a flushed face may suggest embarrassment; a pale, drained face can give evidence of depression or exhaustion; a nodding head generally communicates agreement; a hanging head implies sadness; folded arms convey distance and avoidance; clenched fists speak of anger; foot tapping implies anxiety; stiff muscles suggest uptightness and being closed to contact; a rocking body reflects worry; a whispering voice is related to difficulty disclosing or with painful emotions; a hesitating voice expresses discomfort. With regard to voice, it is important to note that three qualities are addressed by this one body trait: pitch, volume, and speech rate. A voice can also be used to verbally underline statements by giving vocal emphasis to certain words or phrases (Ivey, 1994). Many body traits can be described and interpreted; the most complete listing is contained in Cormier and Cormier (1991).

Given the common interpretations of body traits, therapists can use their own body to communicate important information to clients (Patterson & Welfel, 1993). To convey comfort, they can use a calm, soothing voice along with a relaxed posture and an open face. To communicate patience, the clinician can use speech that is slow, can avoid impatient gestures, and can make sure not to allow attention to drift. To welcome the client, the therapist can use encouraging gestures (nodding, smiling, open gestures) and can adopt an open body posture (no folded arms or crossed legs). To reflect empathy, the therapist can lean forward, make eye contact, face the client, and match the client's posture. To express genuineness, the clinician makes appropriate eye contact (not too steady, not too shifting), smiles when appropriate, leans forward, and makes body actions match voice. To convey warmth, the therapist adjusts the tone of voice and facial expressions, maintains a relaxed body posture, but leans inward, makes respectful eye contact, has open and inviting gestures, is physically close, and may occasionally use gentle touch. To express understanding, the clinician can match the client's posture, breathing, voice volume, and rate of speech. If this strategy is used, the clinician must be careful not to overdo the matching to the point at which the client feels imitated or ridiculed.

In using any of these nonverbal strategies to communicate with a client, the therapist must be aware that there are significant personal and cross-cultural differences in how body language is received. Some cultures stand much closer to each other during conversation than others (Ivey, Ivey, & Simek-Morgan, 1997). For example, Middle Eastern and Arab cultures tend to have a personal space during conversation that is only six to twelve inches apart—in other words, is almost eyeball-to-eyeball. People from Asian cultures also stand relatively close, but farther away than Middle Eastern cultures. North Americans keep their distance to about arm's length, whereas British and some other European cultures prefer an even greater distance (see Ivey, 1994). Within each of these cultural groups there are significant variations in personal preferences. Hence, although these cultural ideas can be used as guides, they cannot be perceived as rigid rules. Cultural and personal differences may also emerge with regard to eye contact. Some Native American and Alaska Native cultures do not make eye contact when intimate information is shared; most cultures seek more eye contact while listening than while talking, whereas some display the reverse pattern (e.g., African Americans may make more eye contact while speaking than listening). Some clients, regardless of culture, are less likely to make eye contact when talking about difficult or highly intimate information (Ivey, 1994). Body posture also has a cultural component. For example, leaning forward and being seated face-to-face is a Western way of communicating. However, there are some Native cultures that prefer to be seated side by side while discussing intimate issues (Ivey, Ivey, & Simek-Morgan, 1997). In other words, although some generalizations can be made about how to use body language to communicate attention, interest, warmth, and so forth, therapists must always be aware whether their nonverbal message is received as intended. If it is not, a modification in usual patterns of nonverbal communication may need to be made to accommodate cultural or personal preferences.

Listening to Verbal Communication

The listening process contains two important elements: a message has to be received (perceived) and processed (understood). Reception is accomplished by attending (including attending to the nonverbal communications of the client as outlined above), hearing (i.e., having hearing aids as required for accurate perception), watching, and sensing (i.e., using some intuitive processes that may enhance understanding). In other words, perception must be geared toward taking in both content (overt) and affect (overt and covert; Okun, 1997). If therapists' primary focus is on content or cognition that is overt and direct, their perception may be limited. The relationship between client and clinician may remain somewhat distant and unexplored because an important aspect of the client may have been ignored. It is important also to perceive affect (especially covert or latent affect) to ensure that the relationship with the client will be one marked by nearness of experience (see Kohut, 1984). As therapists process or understand what is heard, they give it meaning and do not distort this meaning through personal values, judgments, assumptions, expectations, and presuppositions. Breakdowns in listening are most likely to occur in the processing stage for these reasons of possible distortion. However, other breakdowns in the listening process are also possible.

Specifically, Egan (1994) has identified a number of potential pitfalls that can interfere with successful listening. Inadequate listening refers to listening that is plagued by inattention or preoccupation. When listening inadequately, clinicians are preoccupied with their own thoughts and ideas or are overwhelmed by personal needs or emotions (e.g., are too tired to attend, too hungry, too depressed)—states of being that interfere with accurate reception. Evaluative listening is a pitfall that occurs in the processing of the message. It refers to making judgments about what is heard instead of just taking it in objectively and concretely. Evaluative listening not uncommonly leads to giving advice because the therapist has a personal opinion about what is being heard. Filtered or selective listening means that clinicians hear what they expect or want to hear. In this case, therapists make the data fit their expectations. This often occurs if a clinician has preconceived notions about a client that arise from stereotypes, prejudices, and assumptions about individuals or groups of people. Fact-centered listening is not person-centered. It requests a lot of information from the client without attending to the person's true message and without attending to the client's expressed affects and needs (this is experience-distant listening). Rehearsing while listening gets in the way of receiving it because therapists are more preoccupied with what they will need to do or say next to perceive the client's words completely and accurately. This type of pitfall is more common among novice therapists who still have some performance anxiety and rehearse their own responses to statements made by their clients instead of staying with the clients until they have expressed all of their thoughts. Finally, sympathetic listening means that the clinician gets caught up in the content and affect of the client's message and loses the necessary distance to perceive and process covert or latent information. In this case therapists overidentify with clients; they lose professional distance and objectivity and distort the message along with the client.

To make listening an accurate process between client and clinician (experience-near listening), the therapist attends to and processes both overt and covert (or manifest and latent) information. In other words, the therapist not only hears what the client says, but also takes in voice quality, movement and posture, slips of the tongue, moments of unintelligibility (which may communicate emotional difficulty and struggle), and metaphors (Watts, 1996). Listening must be active, not passive. Active listening is marked by grasping the significance or essence of the message (not just the overt content), cutting through unclear messages, distilling and organizing information, and being aware of verbal and nonverbal communication (Watts, 1996). Active listening also means that the clinician listens carefully for the purpose of identifying discrepancies and incongruence. Such incongruence can occur between verbal and nonverbal communication, thoughts and feelings, thoughts and actions, feelings and action, and among feelings, thoughts, and actions (Hutchins & Vaught, 1997).

Responding

The listening process alone is not enough to establish successful communication and to encourage continued self-disclosure by the client. Therapists have to keep the process alive by responding appropriately and regularly, to let their clients know that they are still being listened to and are being heard accurately. A variety of responding skills are available to accomplish this. They range from probing to asking questions to paraphrasing to reflection. The responding skills covered in this section are designed to keep communication going and to encourage self-disclosure; they are not explaining strategies in the sense of attempting to help facilitate insight in the client. These strategies are different and are covered in the relevant section below.

The skills that are needed for adequate responding are encouraging phrases, knowledge of opening questions, restatements, paraphrases, reflections, and summarizations. Examples of each of these microskills are presented in Table 5.1.

TABLE 5.1   Responding Skills to Facilitate Communication and Disclosure

Skill	Definition	Example*
Encouraging	repetition of a word or phrase; nonverbal encouragement to keep talking (head-nodding, leaning in)	"What you have done?"
Questioning	open-ended question encouraging the client to say more and showing the therapist's interest and attention	"What kinds of things go through your mind as you are pacing?"
Restating	repetition of the content of a message using the client's words or phrases	"You are pacing, trying to figure out what's going on with her and what you have done."
Paraphrasing	repetition of the content of a client's message using the therapist's own words	"You are up all night worrying about how she is doing and what you might have done differently to maybe keep this from happening."
Reflecting	rephrasing of a client's message to clarify its affective component or (hidden) essence	"You are worried about your daughter, but also have some sense of responsibility about your role in what is happening between the two of you."
Summarizing	rephrasing and/or restating of several messages to tie them toegether in their meaning or affective content	"You said earlier that your daughter has said that she hates you and that your husband has blamed you for her anger at the two of you. Now you are suggesting that *you* are taking some responsibility for what is happening, questioning what you might have done."

*All examples are based on the following client's verbal cue: "My daughter and I have had a tough relationship all of her life—she's 19 now—but this is the first time that she just decided to leave without talking to me. I've been pacing the last three nights, trying to figure out what's going on with her and what I have done to make this happen."

Encouraging phrases, both verbal and nonverbal, are the simplest means of keeping communication going. They consist of the simple repetition of phrases or words uttered by clients to let them know that more information is desired. Nonverbal encouragers do the same thing but without words. Common nonverbal encouragements include nodding the head, leaning forward, offering tissue, and semiverbals such as "uh-huh."

Opening questions are questions that keep communication going and allow the client to keep self-disclosing. They are to be differentiated from systematic inquiry and from clarifying questions. Systematic inquiry was used in the screening or intake interview. This is a series of questions that explores a topic area in depth. It generally starts with wide-open questions (such as "Tell me about the family you grew up in") and then narrows down as the exploration of given topic area proceeds (e.g., "What was it about your parents' relationship that hinted to you that they were no longer getting along?"). Clarifying questions are designed to create insight and self-awareness and are more complex then either opening questions or systematic inquiries. They are covered in detail below in the Cognitive Self-Awareness section. Opening questions, then, are questions that move the client along within a given topic area while communicating the clinician's interest (Ivey, 1994). Such questions are often very similar in how they are phrased to systematic inquiry questions; it is merely their purpose that sets them apart. In asking questions to keep communication going, the clinician mainly needs to be concerned not to phrase questions as suggestions which give hidden advice or express assumptions about a client (Patterson & Welfel, 1993). Questions to avoid are those that begin with "Don't you think . . . ?" or "Don't you feel . . . ?" because these generally result in hidden advice. Assumptive questions are questions such as "So you have four children? That must be difficult to manage at times?" Suggestive questions are questions such as "Shouldn't you call your sister first?" All of these questions have in common their ability to reflect information about the therapist instead of soliciting information about the client. These questions not only have no way of keeping communication going, but they must be avoided in general—even while engaging in systematic inquiry or clarifying questioning.

Another means of responding that encourages more disclosure is to simply restate or rephrase something the client has already disclosed. Pure restatement is the simple process of repeating back to clients content they have disclosed, using the same words or phrases chosen by the client. Simple restatements can sound much like parroting so are used sparingly. They do have some use, though, if therapists want to emphasize something their clients have said, if the clinicians want to slow their clients down if they are talking too fast or have racing thoughts, if therapists want to clarify a given point for themselves or for their clients, or if clinicians want to encourage their clients to reconsider what they just said either because it was important or because it reflected an irrational belief or distorted thought (Hutchins & Vaught, 1997). More commonly, however, clinicians will use a paraphrase instead. This type of statement also repeats the content of a client's message but does so by rephrasing the essence in the therapist's own words. A rephrase (similar to a restatement) is used to focus the client on a particular element of content or to redirect the client toward content when associated feelings are too premature to be successfully handled by the client at a given time (e.g., when the session is almost over and the clinician is concerned about helping the client get ready to leave; see Cormier & Cormier, 1991).

A reflective statement is one that rephrases the affective or most essential aspect of a client's communication and does so in the therapist's own words. It encourages further and broader self-expression, more intense experience, and important connections between overt and covert communication. Reflective statements also clarify meaning by recognizing and expressing the essence or hidden message revealed by the client. A final means of encouraging responding is called a summarization. The skilled therapist can combine restatements, paraphrases, and/or reflections to delineate several messages delivered by the client and demonstrate how they fit together. Such fitting together may be based on similar contents, similar affective components, or identical or related covert messages.

In the process of restating, paraphrasing, reflecting, and even summarizing messages for clients, it is important that clinicians make their statements brief and to the point. It behooves the therapist to remember that these skills are used to encourage more communication and disclosure on the part of clients; hence, they should not become monologues on the part of the therapists. To be fully successful, these messages are brief, to the point, and pithy. The longer therapists continue to reiterate a certain message, the more likely that both clinicians and clients will overlook the essential point of what the clients wanted to express (Hutchins & Vaught, 1997).

Catalysts That Facilitate Affective Self-Awareness and Internalization

Catalysts that fall into this category go beyond merely keeping communication going and encouraging self-disclosure, though all of them will have that process as an advantage as well. However, their essence is to assist clients in exploring, recognizing, identifying, accepting, and expressing affect and their affective selves. Such affective self-awareness that leads to self-acceptance is greatly conducive to the process of internalization, which is an essential component of a well-working therapy. Internalization as a therapy process will be discussed in detail in a later chapter. Suffice it to say here that internalization is the process through which people develop a personal set of beliefs, ambitions, goals, ideals, and self-perceptions (see Kohut, 1984). It is a process that can include introjection, identification, and modeling. However, it is best enhanced through accurately directed empathic statements by others toward the person, and these lead to the client's improved self-awareness and understanding of emotions and needs. Thus empathy is the central tool in this set of catalysts; in fact, it is perhaps the underlying component of all of the techniques that are discussed in this section and only kept distinct arbitrarily for purposes of discussion.

Catharsis

Although empathy was rightly introduced above as the most central and permeating component in this group of skills, the simplest and most easily explained technique is the process of catharsis. Catharsis is of course not a therapist skill; instead, the clinician must learn how to facilitate catharsis in the client. The skill, in other words, relies on the therapist's ability to help the client experience and ventilate feelings and needs in the therapy setting. The mere experience and subsequent release and expression of emotion is highly therapeutic for many clients despite the fact that it neither necessarily leads to internalization of change nor to insight and growth. Nevertheless, catharsis is often useful in helping clients gain some recognition of the depth and intensity of affect that was formerly held in, repressed, or otherwise kept from emerging uninhibitedly. The therapeutic value of catharsis has been attributed to three factors. First, catharsis acknowledges that the client possesses a strong affective response and this must find expression; second, through expressing the feeling, the client takes responsibility for it; third, expressing affect leads to a new perception of the self and to insight regarding the self within the therapeutic relationship and in the outer world in general (Young & Bemark, 1996).

For catharsis, or ventilation (Corsini & Wedding, 1997), to take place, a client has to feel safe in the therapy environment and has to feel a level of comfort with and acceptance by the clinician. This is so because catharsis does not necessarily result in venting or releasing only positive affects, but also negative ones, and these may appear quite frightening and overwhelming to the client. Indeed, some presenting problems or diagnostic presentations may exist in which catharsis is not necessarily indicated. For example, PTSD clients may best not be encouraged to become affectively aroused early in treatment because their level of arousal may become too intense to be easily tolerated and helpful (Young & Bemark, 1996). Histrionic clients may already be overly emotional, and to encourage catharsis with such clients may be countertherapeutic because it encourages a means of expression that is integral to the client's presenting problem. In other words, as with every strategy in psychotherapy, catharsis must be well-chosen and must be adapted in its use to the specific requirements of each individual client.

Therapists will be able to facilitate catharsis only if they can produce a safe environment for their clients, as has been pointed out elsewhere in this book. However, a safe and predictable environment is only one prerequisite for catharsis to take place; the other is to communicate acceptance and permission. This ability of clinicians rests on their personal willingness to participate in the cathartic process and to allow it without being frightened or overwhelmed by it themselves. Allowing for uninhibited expression of affect is not easy, especially for novice therapists who may themselves not be sure yet whether they will indeed be able to contain a client's emotional state once it is cathartically expressed. Often, novice clinicians unconsciously, and certainly unintentionally, inhibit a client's affective expression or emotional abreaction because of their own uncertainty about what to do once the affect emerges or because of uncertainty whether they will be able to help the client survive and work through the affect. Thus facilitating catharsis does indeed reflect an advanced therapeutic skill that requires some introspection on the part of the clinician. The process of catharsis can further be hindered by clients' tendencies and desires to avoid affective arousal. Only a therapist who is able to help the client maintain arousal safely and to express it productively will be able to make the cathartic process therapeutic and helpful (Young & Bemark, 1996).

For example, one trainee under the supervision of this author was seeing a women who had a great deal of anger and rage that had never been expressed, a fact that was often discussed and analyzed in session. In reviewing supervision tapes it slowly became clear that the therapist often intervened verbally at very critical points in the client's self-disclosure. Had the clinician not intervened, the client would most certainly have expressed this anger and released its grip. In exploring these sections of the tape with the trainee, it became clear that she felt unable to allow the client the necessary catharsis for her angry affects within the session because the trainee herself was unsure of her ability to contain the woman's anger sufficiently thereafter. She was not only afraid of the possible behavioral manifestations of the client's anger but also about her own ability to tolerate the anger and rage should it be expressed against her. Once she realized that it was her own timidity and uncertainty that inhibited the client's self-expression, the therapist learned to allow it. She was also given some information about how to deal with client emotions (see Chapter 7), and this training helped her feel more secure in her own ability to contain and control the affect should the client become overwhelmed and out of control.

Empathy and Understanding

The other essential ingredient mentioned here that assists in the cathartic expression of emotion is clients' perceptions that they are fully accepted by their therapists. This acceptance is integral to an empathic relationship. Empathy cannot exist without acceptance, respect, warmth, and genuineness—the very ingredients of the therapy relationship pronounced by Carl Rogers as essential to and sufficient for client growth and change. Rogers, of course, is often the foremost theorist noted for recognizing empathy as an essential catalyst for treatment, but he has been by no means the only one. The recognition of empathy as central to therapy has been universally accepted by most, if not all, schools of thought; behaviorists pay attention to empathic connections, as do existentialists, psychodynamicists, psychoanalysts, and systems theorists. In fact, some of the most empathic therapists identified through research investigations have been behavioral therapists (Ivey, Ivey, & Simek-Morgan, 1997).

Empathy, as originally defined by Rogers and expanded on by modern writers, is the ability to understand the affective experience of the other person from that person's perspective. It presumes acceptance of the client, though it does not imply accepting the client's behavior in toto. Empathy is not used to excuse unacceptable or dangerous behavior, but merely to accept the person and the person's need to engage in this behavior (Ivey, Ivey, & Simek-Morgan, 1997). The empathic process has been described as cyclical and as consisting of multiple phases or stages (see Barrett-Lennard, 1981; Brems, 1989a, 1993; Egan, 1994; Patterson & Welfel, 1993). This cyclical process begins with self-expression by the client (Brems, 1993), or, if viewed from the clinician's perspective, receiving or perceiving the client's expressed message. It continues through the ability of the clinician to understand and process the message accurately, and it ends with the therapist's assertively feeding the essence of the message back to the client (Egan, 1994). This definition sounds reminiscent of the definition provided above for the process of reflection. There is a critical difference, however. A reflection is merely designed to keep the client exploring and talking; an empathic response (although often sounding like a reflection and being structured like a reflection) is designed to enhance the client's self-awareness and to express understanding of the client by the therapist.

The reception or perception aspect of empathy is greatly dependent on therapists' abilities to hear, see, and sense what their clients are attempting to communicate and their ability to sift through a large set of data to find the essential component or message. The perceptions of therapists need to be unclouded by preconceived notions, and all the cautions provided about the reception process in the Communication section above apply here as well.

The processing or understanding phase of the empathic cycle requires that the therapist make sense of the client's communications. This aspect of empathy is most susceptible to the therapist's theoretical preferences (Patterson & Welfel, 1993). The affects, thoughts, and behaviors expressed by clients will be understood slightly differently depending on school of thought. Cognitive–behaviorists will look for cognitive distortions, irrational beliefs, and automatic thoughts that have been reinforced and developed over a lifetime; humanists will look for evidence that clients are not authentic in their self-expression, that they lack genuineness and congruence, and will seek to understand how these realities came about; self-psychological psychodynamicists may look for expressions of specific needs and how their failure to have been met in childhood has affected current relationships and self-perceptions.

Regardless of the specific content of therapists' understandings of their clients' messages, the next stage or phase of the empathic response must occur to bring closure to the empathy cycle; namely, clinicians must express their understandings (which include acceptance) in a genuine and warm manner back to their clients. This response will have a slightly different content depending on how the therapist derived meaning from the messages (i.e., according to the clinician's theoretical orientation). However, the affective component of the empathic response is the same across all schools of thought: the response must be genuine, warm, respectful, and useful to the client. A response that is cliché, gives advice, parrots, or gives sympathy is clearly an empathic failure (Egan, 1994). Further, at this stage in the therapy, therapists are not interested in providing interpretations but merely in using empathic responses to feed back their understanding and acceptance of clients. This verbalization is designed to draw clients out, to help clients recognize their expressed need, and to become aware of and ultimately accept the emotions that were expressed, a process designed to understand the subjective experience of the client (Strauss, 1996).

An empathic response thus defined reflects caring, clarifies themes, stimulates self-discovery, communicates safety, and provides proof of the expertise of the therapist (Patterson & Welfel, 1993). It helps the client become self-aware and encourages exploration on a deeper emotional level. Empathy is very unlike sympathy, which tends to be designed to squelch feelings by expressing support and the wish for the receiver to get over the expressed emotion (Meier & Davis, 1997). Empathy must also be differentiated from the notion that the therapist somehow magically intuits the client's experience, gets caught up in the client's emotion, provides approval or advice, or attempts to understand how the therapist might feel in the same situation (Rowe & MacIsaac, 1989; Wolf, 1988). Instead, empathy is the prolonged immersion in the client's experience, without getting caught up in it, for the purpose of better understanding the client from that unique perspective. This is a process of data collection that leads to understanding the client (Wolf, 1988) while using the therapist's own affective experience and reaction as a guide (Mahrer, Boulet, & Fairweather, 1994). The idea of empathy as a tool for understanding a client that in turn leads to self-awareness and a sense of being accepted and understood has been most clearly formulated by self psychologist Heinz Kohut (e.g.,

1982, 1984). He has referred to this type of empathy or empathic process as vicarious introspection, which emphasizes that this process is a critical element not only in the therapy relationship but also during healthy development. In fact, Kohut postulates that it is the breakdown in the empathic process between caretaker and child that is the precursor to psychopathology because this hindered development and made it impossible for the child to internalize a healthy, cohesive, strong, and orderly self (Kohut & Wolf, 1978; Kohut, 1984). Vicarious introspection refers to a skill used by therapists to glean an accurate and in-depth understanding of their clients that helps clinicians understand clients from their unique perspectives; that considers their developmental histories, family circumstances, cultural embeddedness, and interpersonal values. This type of empathy does not merely grasp the emotional message of clients and their emotional expression as explained by clients' history, but will instead provide a complete processing of clients' current level of functioning, their expressed and unexpressed needs, their interpersonal adjustment, and their levels of self-development. Vicarious introspection, hence, is a somewhat more complete or comprehensive way of applying empathy than the traditional definition of empathy.

Empathy thus understood affirms, acknowledges, and validates persons, their affects, needs, thoughts, and behaviors in an experience-near manner that acknowledges and considers the here and now, without excusing behaviors or justifying them if they are dangerous or inappropriate (Teyber, 1997). It has as its essence "understanding [that] connotes warmth and a feeling of concern for clients" (Teyber, 1997, p. 41) and is the prerequisite for creating a therapeutic holding environment wherein the therapist is capable of containing the client's distress and need states. Empathy is also essential for attachment to occur and, hence, is needed for establishing a working alliance that helps the client become motivated for treatment. In essence, empathy, according to self-psychological thinkers (i.e., the followers of Heinz Kohut) becomes the cornerstone of therapy, the primary tool through which clinicians come to understand their clients and communicate effectively with them, the tool without which the process of psychotherapy would be doomed to failure, much as its absence during the developmental phase interferes with healthy self-development (Rowe & MacIsaac, 1989; Wolf, 1988). An example of an empathic interchange in a client's tenth session follows. This example relies on the case of Frederick that has been presented in detail in other chapters of this book (e.g., see Intake Report in Chapter 1 and conceptualization in Chapter 4).

> *The client presented to the session very upset and crying. He had just been laid off from work rather unexpectedly and felt completely unable to cope. He had not yet given the news to Sandra and expressed being afraid to do so as this might have further threatened their tenuous hold on their relationship. He also expressed that he had planned not to tell the therapist but that he was so unable to control his emotions on his way to the session that he realized that it would be impossible for him to conceal his perceived failure. He also suggested that maybe therapy was not helping him because he had this strong reaction to being laid off and that he felt that by now he should have learned how to keep his emotions under control. At that point he began to hyperventilate and his sobbing became uncontrollable. The*

therapist intervened by asking him to focus on her and to model his breathing after hers. This intervention was deemed necessary to help the client regain sufficient composure to continue to talk about and express his feelings about the current situation. Once he recovered his breath and was back to crying, not sobbing, the client began to talk about not coming back to therapy and about possibly breaking up his relationship with Sandra. At this point the therapist chose to make the following (empathic) statement:

"Right now therapy is very hard for you, just as hard as being with Sandra. In both cases, you feel so vulnerable, so exposed, so afraid to show who you really are and what you really feel. It's like you have to convince both me and Sandra that you're okay, that you can handle your life just fine and that takes a lot of energy. What you'd really like to do is tell us how overwhelmed you are and how much you want us to take care of you; just take over for you for a while and help you get your life under control again. But you're afraid that if you let us see that part of you, that vulnerable little boy, we might reject you or leave you."

In response, the client once again cried more vehemently. This time, the therapist chose to let him cry without interference as she perceived that the crying was a sign that the client was processing what she had just said; that he was coming to grips with his dependence on women and his need for this dependence and fear of abandonment despite his conscious wish to be independent and detached, as evidenced by his social isolation. The therapist had chosen not to point out that the client was replaying a pattern he had developed in childhood with his depressed and emotionally absent mother whom he perceived as not being able to handle his dependency because of her own emotional needs and whom he perceived as having abandoned him because he had been overly needy. The therapist also did not point out or explain that his social isolation had developed as a protection against these powerful dependency needs emerging. She felt that an explaining strategy was premature at this time because the client had not yet come to accept his contradictory feelings of strong dependence versus his expressed detachment and social isolation. After a few minutes, the client stopped crying on his own and made the following response.

"I think I got all upset about everything on my way over here not so much because I lost my job, but because I was afraid what would happen next. Would you tell that I'm a failure and that I shouldn't overreact so much? Would you finally give up on me?"

Then the client started crying again, but this time he cried not uncontrollably, but sadly and almost as if comforting himself. He also hugged himself and began rocking back and forth, revealing a very young self to the therapist that he had tended to squelch in prior sessions. This confirmed that the therapist's empathic statement had given him permission to accept his strong feelings of dependence and fears of abandonment and showed that he now felt a beginning level of comfort to express them in her presence because she had neither rejected/abandoned him nor told him to keep these feelings and needs tucked away.

This example demonstrates that empathy is a process that generally has its roots in a here and now occurrence between client and therapist but that must be understood by the clinician as of greater significance in the context of the client's entire life history and development. It is not a warm, fuzzy feeling (though conveyed with warmth) but rather an important tool that encourages self-awareness, self-respect, and self-acceptance. Empathy as a process is only possible if empathy exists as a capacity in the clinician. In the German language there is a clear differentiation between empathy, the capacity, and empathy, the process. The former is labeled *Einfuehlung*, and refers to the procedures of understanding outlined above. However, *Einfuehlung* is only possible if the therapist has *Einfuehlungsvermoegen*, the capacity to empathize with the client—that is, the capacity for vicarious introspection that will help the therapist recognize and understand the expressed or unexpressed affects and needs of the client. Only if the capacity of empathy exists can the understanding of the client be fed back to this person in a therapeutic manner.

The example also shows that an empathic response must be clearly differentiated from a therapeutic explanation or interpretation. Its purpose is not to explain despite the fact that understanding and self-awareness are central to its definition. The type of understanding that is being referred to in the context of empathic responding has to do with the clinician conveying understanding of the client and the client's essential and powerful emotions and needs. This is different from conveying an explanation to the client about why these feelings and needs have emerged. In other words, empathy is experience-near; it conveys an important relationship component between clients and therapists that often leads clients to accept their own feelings and needs more completely. The self-acceptance and self-awareness of needs and affects is merely that: recognizing that these needs and emotions exist within the self (when prior to therapy they most likely were repressed, denied, or otherwise kept hidden from the client's conscious recognition and acceptance). The next step, which is insight (i.e., an explanation of *why* they exist), is not part of the empathic, or understanding, process, but rather is within the realm of the strategies of explaining and creating insights, which will be covered below.

It may also be mentioned here that Kohut (1984) did not perceive insight as a necessary component of successful treatment. He believed that empathic understanding and subsequently internalizing self-acceptance and self-structure may be sufficient for some clients to improve to an extent that they can lead happy and fulfilled lives. This is certainly true in the treatment of children, for whom internalization is the more important and growth producing change agent (Brems, 1993).

Affect Identification (Labeling) and Expression

Clearly, the previous section revealed that empathy can be used as a strategy to help clients come to feel and accept their emotions. However, an empathic response is not the only option a clinician has to help clients with affective expression and identification. Many therapy clients are unable to express and identify their feelings for a variety of reasons. It is possible that they were discouraged from the expression of certain affects by caretakers in childhood because of stereotypic reasons (as, for instance, happens to many young boys who are discouraged from expressing pain when hurt); others were punished for expressing certain affects (as, for example, may occur to a young child who expresses aggression or anger); still others may have been socialized never to develop conscious awareness of certain affect states when they had their emotional needs denied and frustrated. These clients present a challenge to the therapist who tries to help them identify and express feelings in the attempt to provide a motivation and catalyst for change. These clients need assistance (and sometimes an empathic response is enough, but not generally) to label their emotions in a very basic way. Several strategies can facilitate this process.

First, clients can be helped to begin to recognize that emotions exist by therapists encouraging them to listen to bodily changes as they have experiences or reactions in the therapy room. For example, a client who just presented the clinician with a scenario that would suggest that the person might have reacted with sadness, but who shows no outward sign of emotion, may be redirected toward exploration of an emotional response by focusing on bodily signs that an emotion has been experienced. Such encouragement may take the following form:

CLIENT: I just found out that my best friend from high school killed herself last week. She and I were so close; we were so much alike. We did lots of things together. Let me tell you what we did when we were at the prom. (*The client starts to launch into one of her common long stories that often detract from the issue at hand.*)

THERAPIST: I wonder if I could ask you a couple of questions before we get into that?

CLIENT: (*nods*)

THERAPIST: How did you react when you heard the news about your best friend's suicide?

CLIENT: I was pretty surprised; I would never have thought that she would do something like that. (*client stops; looks down*)

THERAPIST: What are you feeling right now?

CLIENT: I'm not sure. . . . (*puzzled look*)

THERAPIST: Would you close your eyes for a moment and try to follow my instructions? I think it's important for us to figure out what you are feeling. You seem to have some emotion that you just can't get out right now. . . .

CLIENT: (*closes her eyes*) Okay. . . . (*soft voice*)

THERAPIST: Please pay very close attention to your body right now. Do you feel any physical symptoms—a neck ache maybe, or maybe your eyes are burning; or maybe you have a knot in your stomach? Just focus for a moment. . . .

CLIENT: I'm not sure. (*opens her eyes*)

THERAPIST: Keep your eyes closed. Let's start with your head. Do you feel anything?

CLIENT: No. Well, my neck is kind of tight and my eyes keep watering. . . .

THERAPIST: (*after a careful pause of silence*) Now move down along your body. Any other feelings you can sense?

CLIENT: (after a moment of focusing) Well, my stomach has been upset all day today. I thought maybe I ate something weird, maybe it's something else. . . .

THERAPIST: (pauses and stays silent for a while) Anything else?

CLIENT: (after a pause) No, that's all. . . . *(quiet now and much more in tune with herself)*

THERAPIST: Stay with these bodily feelings for a while and become familiar with them. If you'd like you can tell me more about them or we can just be quiet for a while . . .

CLIENT: (after a several minute pause) Wow, I've never done this before. The more I'm listening to my body, the more I realize how rarely I pay attention to what's going on with me. . . . *(soft, slowed voice; eyes still closed)*

THERAPIST: (remains quiet except for a calm and soft) Yes. . . .

CLIENT: (opens her eyes) What do you think this means—my stiff neck, my eyes, my stomach: what are they trying to tell me?

THERAPIST: I think that's a question you can probably answer for yourself.

CLIENT: Yes, you're right. I guess they are trying to tell me that I'm feeling something about my friend dying?

THERAPIST: What feeling do you think this might be?

CLIENT: Well, I guess sadness—I was so close to her. *(starts crying softly)*

This example shows how even clients who have blocked their emotions successfully for years may be encouraged to recognize feelings. Every human being has a physiological response of some sort when emotionally aroused or stimulated. If therapists can help clients identify that physiological response by drawing attention to their bodily reactions, clients will have valuable lessons about how to begin to identify emotions. In the example, the emotion involved became fairly obvious once the client realized that she indeed had a repressed feeling response to the situation she presented. Sadness is a normal response to a friend's death, and the client was able to give the label for the physiological arousal she felt.

However, this process is not always easy. Sometimes clients who are very new to feeling their emotions consciously not only need to learn to identify that they are feeling at all but may also need to learn to label these feelings. Such clients generally had little guidance during childhood with emotions and their meanings. They learned little about expressing and labeling affect states as a means of diffusing and using it for psychological growth and health. If this is the case, the clinician must be willing to help the client feel and label emotions. Sometimes labeling is also important when clients have adopted all-or-none attitudes about feelings, or when they cannot see that any one affect can manifest at different levels of intensity. This reaction is most common with regard to anger. Clients often believe that anger is inappropriate because when they think of their anger, they associate it with an extreme behavioral response that they perceive as unacceptable. Then, instead of allowing any expression of even mild forms of anger, they deny the entire affect. This inability to differentiate shades of gray also needs to be addressed therapeutically by helping clients recognize new labels that can help them differentiate not just emotions from one another, but also differing levels of intensity of the same emotion. Such a process of identification or labeling of affect (as opposed to merely helping the client recognize that an emotion is present) may occur as follows:

CLIENT: *(talking about his relationship with his wife)* I am not happy with her response to my request because I really wanted her to take some responsibility for why we are having such a hard time with each other right now.

THERAPIST: You say you weren't happy. Can you tell me more about that?

CLIENT: Well, I mean I was upset! *(strong, firm voice; slightly raised; head up and direct eye contact)*

THERAPIST: Just upset?

CLIENT: What are you getting at? Are you saying I was angry? I don't do anger!! My father was vicious when he was angry, and I promised myself I'd never put my wife through what he put my mother and us through!!

THERAPIST: So what is it that you are feeling right now?

CLIENT: Not anger!!

THERAPIST: You can't accept anger as a feeling in yourself. . . . It's just too big and too threatening for you to even consider that that may be what you are feeling!

CLIENT: YES! *(clearly angry about being pushed on this issue)*

THERAPIST: You realize of course that the anger your father had was more than just a little anger. He was in a rage. You have told me how he acted when he hit your mother and when he whipped you with a belt. That was more than anger!

CLIENT: *(puzzled look)* I'm not getting you here. . . .

THERAPIST: Well, there really isn't just one kind of anger. Some anger is incredibly intense and the person gets out of control. I would call that rage. That's what I think your father had. Some anger is pretty mild and the person does very little when he feels it; you might call that frustration or annoyance. You know, like when you told me that your son took your magazine from your bedroom without telling you and you were looking for it, and then you felt sort of miffed—not because he took it, but because he didn't tell you?

CLIENT: That wasn't anger. I told you, I was just a little miffed.

THERAPIST: See, that's what I mean. Being a little miffed is still anger. It's just little anger! You have it in your mind that all anger is like your father's rage, and it just isn't.

CLIENT: I get it—like right now I am "upset" with you because you keep implying that I'm angry. You'd call that being angry—I'd call it "upset" because it makes it easier for me to admit that I'm feeling it.

THERAPIST: Yeah—you don't want to give yourself permission to be angry because anger is this big thing to you; and then what happens is that you downplay your emotions because you find it unacceptable if it even comes close to something you might call anger.

CLIENT: So I'm really mad at Susan, but I don't want to admit it because then I think I might hit her.

THERAPIST: Yes.

CLIENT: But by pretending I'm not mad, I don't work out the problem I have with her because I keep playing it down, and then I keep ignoring what's really going on inside me.

THERAPIST: (*nods*)

This example shows that helping clients differentiate shades of gray in the experience of a single affect both clarifies their experience and gives them permission to be more honest with themselves about what may be occurring. It also demonstrates that understanding the level of intensity of affect will more clearly help clients evaluate their larger (not just affective) response to a situation and will allow them to work on the situation without being distracted or influenced by trying to keep an emotion under wraps. A similar issue may emerge with clients who have mixed feelings. Being capable of reconciling apparently opposed emotions that may occur in the same situation is a developmentally complex emotional task that is not achieved by all adult, let alone adolescent or child, clients (see Brems, 1993). Such blended emotions are often difficult for people to identify and label and leaves them feeling confused and overwhelmed. A clarification exercise similar to the one presented in the anger example can help clients to realize that they may well have two differing emotions in the same situation. For example, it is entirely possible that the client in the above example not only felt anger with his wife, but also felt some sadness because of the troubles they have been having. His word choice of being "upset" might in fact suggest that his anger is not pure but has a component of sadness. This reality can be worked out with the help of the therapist, who may point toward the mixed feelings and the fact that this is a common occurrence.

Another common problem in the client's experience of affect is shown by the highly intellectualized client who talks about feelings all the time, but clearly does not experience them in the moment. This is quite the opposite of the last example dealing with the client's anger, in which the client felt anger but did not want to talk about the affect directly because he felt that just by acknowledging the presence of anger, he would become a bundle of rage. The process referred to here is most commonly observed in highly controlled clients who are somewhat obsessive-compulsive and generally nonemotional in their relationships. They are often very good at talking about emotions, but the therapist will be struck after a few sessions that the client has never truly expressed or experienced an emotion in the therapy room or in the relationship with the clinician. Such clients have to be encouraged to feel their affect, not just to talk about them. The following example demonstrates how this may be accomplished.

CLIENT: I must say that when you just said that about me, I did react with some anger. *(calm, collected voice with little inflection)*

THERAPIST: You did? Tell me more.

CLIENT: Well, you are assuming that I flunked that exam on purpose just because I wanted to hurt my father, and I just don't think that's so.

THERAPIST: So you are angry about my suggesting it?

CLIENT: Yes, I am.

THERAPIST: You know, it is hard for me to believe that. Normally when people are angry, their voice changes and their body tenses up. I don't see any of these reactions in you.

CLIENT: Well, I'm mad.

THERAPIST: Show me!

CLIENT: What are you talking about? *(getting a bit more agitated now)*

THERAPIST: Just that. Show me your anger. We often talk about your feelings, but you know, I have never seen them or felt them.

CLIENT: So? I know I'm mad.

THERAPIST: So show me. *(smiling at the client)*

CLIENT: *(clenches fists)* I am not getting it. What are you talking about? *(raises voice; leans forward)*

THERAPIST: You're still just talking. *(trying to keep the client going)*

CLIENT: Well, I'll show you anger. *(starts yelling)* Who do you think you are, telling me that I'm not feeling anything; you don't know what you're doing. If I'm not feeling, then isn't that your fault? You're supposed to be the expert here!

THERAPIST: Okay! Now—listen to your body for a moment. Look at your hands! *(emphatic voice; leaning forward; very connected with the client)*

CLIENT: *(opens his fists; leans back; looks at the therapist)* Wow—that was something. I could have hit you there. Wow! *(leans back as if in exhaustion)*

THERAPIST: Do you understand the difference now—between talking about anger and feeling it?

CLIENT: (strong, emphatic voice) Oh yeah. Wow, that was something! *(still overwhelmed by the experience)*

Many of the features involved in the above examples are used in therapy in general to encourage clients to become affectively involved in therapeutic work. Most clients (the exception being clients with strong histrionic features) are greatly helped by the expression of affect (see the discussion about catharsis above) and can benefit from having their affective expressions properly and immediately responded to. Clients can benefit from being encouraged to express conflicted feelings; to explore unexpressed, covert, and unverbalized feelings; and to have nonverbal clues to conflicted, incongruous, or unexpressed feelings pointed out to them. Additionally, it is important ultimately (once the client can label and express affects relatively easily in sessions) to help clients identify repetitive affects and primary or underlying affects (Teyber, 1997). Repetitive affects are feelings that are the default (to borrow a computer science term) for the individual (i.e., the client falls back on these when affectively aroused or challenged). For example, some clients may always respond with depression to criticism, regardless of whether the situation justifies such a response or not (i.e., they may respond with sadness even to constructive criticism that was meant to help the client grow and was delivered in a nonthreatening manner).

Primary or underlying affects are emotions covered up by other emotions that are somehow safer or more acceptable to the client. The overt emotion may be referred to as a screen emotion (in the tradition of screen memories, as introduced in the psychoanalytic literature; these refer to memories that cover up other, more important memories that, for whatever reason, are also more threatening). Screen feelings are common phenomena among clients because they have learned through their childhood and confirmed through some of their adult experiences that some affects are far safer to express than others. Rather than not expressing any affect at all, the client thus expresses the safe affect; this reduces some of the emotional arousal, although the true affect may never come to the fore. It is the clinician's responsibility to help a client recognize such a screen affect because it is generally the underlying or primary affect that has the most salience and often holds the key to better understanding and affective self-awareness. Following is an example of a scenario in which client and therapist work on a screen affect.

CLIENT: I just feel so helpless when he asks me what it is I want to do. I tell him, "I don't care," but he keeps bugging me, wanting me to make a decision.

THERAPIST: You feel helpless? Tell me more.

CLIENT: Well, I just feel paralyzed. I don't know whether I should turn left or right. You know, go to the movies or go for a walk. It's like if I pick the wrong one, it's all over!

THERAPIST: If you pick the wrong one, it's all over? What's all over?

CLIENT: He'll just get up and leave; it'll be the last I've seen of him!

THERAPIST: And that would be . . . ?

CLIENT: That would be horrible! Then what would I do? I'd be back to where I was four years ago before we met. I was so alone, so lonely. *(looking weepy)*

THERAPIST: So is it really true that you feel helpless when he asks you to make a decision, or is it not maybe something else, some other feeling?

CLIENT: It seems like I'm helpless. . . . *(looks up questioningly)*

THERAPIST: Okay—what does being helpless mean?

CLIENT: Well, a helpless person doesn't know what to do? *(looks for reassurance)*

THERAPIST: And in that situation you don't know what to do? You don't have a preference?

CLIENT: Oh, I see what you mean. It's like we talked about before. I don't really like these gory movies; I'd much rather go for a walk.

THERAPIST: So it's not that you don't know what you want . . . *(client interrupts)*

CLIENT: Right! It's that I don't want to make the decision because then I'm responsible if it was the wrong decision, and he'll be mad and he'll leave!

THERAPIST: Okay then. So what are you really feeling? It doesn't sound like you're helpless so much as afraid of something.

CLIENT: Yes! *(emphatically)* Yes! I'm afraid he'll leave. *(all the emphasis drains from her voice; lips start to quiver)*

THERAPIST: Tell me. . . . *(softly; leans in a little more; eyes lowered)*

CLIENT: I'm afraid to be alone again—I'm feeling totally alone! Like no one cares and I can't depend on anyone. Lonely, lonely, lonely—empty and alone *(starts to cry; sobs but keeps talking between sobs)* . . . even when I'm with him I'm utterly alone. . . . I can't count on him—he keeps threatening that he's had it, that he'll just get up and walk away. . . . *(cries more now and stops talking)*

To summarize, helping clients label and identify their emotions is an important therapeutic goal that often greatly facilitates affective self-awareness and self-acceptance. Unexpressed affects or emotions often flavor a client's interaction significantly and may distort the client's perception of the world and all others within it. Unidentified affects tend to grow in salience, having an enormous impact on the client's self-perception and sense of self-control. It also takes a lot of energy for clients to remain unaware of affects and to protect themselves from emotions they have not yet learned to deal with because they have remained unexpressed. The next step in the process of affective awareness is to move from affect identification and expression to gaining an understanding of where the affect developed. Hence, identifying sources of affect is another critical strategy with which a therapist must be familiar.

Identification of Sources of Feelings

This catalyst could arguably be called an explaining strategy because it generally does involve some explanation about feelings that may lead to insight. However, it is also a powerfully affective strategy that helps clients gain significant levels of self-awareness in the affective realm and often leads to increased acceptance of strong and chronic affects. Thus it is perhaps best perceived as a bridge between the catalysts that facilitate affective self-awareness and those that encourage cognitive self-awareness.

Identifying the source of feelings is a process though which the therapist assists the client to recognize affects and their origin in the client's history and relationships. Sources of affects can be recent or far removed for the client developmentally. Linking affects to their current sources is often easier and can generally happen earlier in the therapy; linking affects to original or childhood sources is more difficult and requires that the client do some looking back before proceeding and have some understanding of insight-oriented work. As such, perhaps the way to understand this catalyst would be to categorize the process of linking affects to their current sources as self-awareness and categorize the process of linking affects to their original sources as insight-oriented. The actual process, however, is remarkably similar because it involves helping the client recognize that feelings do not develop in a vacuum but are usually a response to environmental or interpersonal circumstances. This recognition helps clients gain a greater sense of control over their affects because they realize that emotions are not simply automatic responses to situations but are often conditioned reactions that can be changed and eliminated.

For therapists to be able to use this catalyst effectively, they clearly must have empathic skills that have helped them recognize the source connections. Obviously, if therapists do not see the connection, they cannot help their clients make one. Making source connections can be strongly influenced by a clinician's theoretical framework. Psychodynamic therapists will look for original sources in the relationship between clients and their caretakers during childhood; they look for those interactions that may have shaped particular affective responses or may have triggered or suppressed certain emotional needs. Cognitive–behaviorists, on the other hand, may look for sources in the client's belief systems, automatic thoughts, and distorted thinking. Behaviorists will consider reinforcement histories across the client's life span and look for patterns reinforcing some affective responses or need states versus extinguishing others. However, all theorists seem to agree that if clients can gain an understanding of why they are reacting emotionally the way they are, they can then choose consciously whether to continue the same affective or need pattern. To reiterate a point made previously, awareness helps clients take control of their emotions and needs—it gives them back some control over their lives and a sense of being more in charge of what to do and how to react.

The strategies a therapist uses to help a client recognize sources of feelings can take many shapes and forms. However, the process always starts with clinicians' empathic awareness that clients' feelings have sources that the clients themselves are unaware of. It then becomes the clinicians' therapeutic task to help their clients gain the same awareness that their therapists have already reached. This is best accomplished by carefully guiding questioning and similar strategies that lead clients to make the connection themselves. If the therapist merely suggests the connection, the client may choose not to accept it; however, if the client can be guided toward making the connection independently, it will have meaning, salience, credibility, and greater power to bring about change. In that sense, the process of connecting feelings to sources is much like an interpretation (see below). However, it always involves a strongly emotionally tinged interchange between client and therapist that revolves around an emotion of the client's in the here and now. This is not always true for other types of interpretation, which may be delivered more cognitively and without direct emotional involvement by the client at that moment. An example of a source–affect connection follows.

CLIENT: I woke up again this morning feeling totally depressed. This just hits me out of the blue.

THERAPIST: Are you still feeling depressed now? You look quite sad. . . .

CLIENT: Yes, I do. I've had no energy all day, and my thoughts kept drifting at work. I feel like I just keep getting sucked into this morass of self-pity and have this drained feeling.

THERAPIST: Your thoughts were drifting. What were they drifting to?

CLIENT: Well, all sorts of things. I think last night I dreamt about my mother again. And today I couldn't get her out of my mind. . . .

THERAPIST: Do you remember your dream?

CLIENT: No, not really; I just have this sense that it was about her.

THERAPIST: And then what were you thinking when you couldn't get her out of your mind today?

CLIENT: I kept remembering how she used to sit and cry at night and how we used to listen to her and feel just horrified!

THERAPIST: We?

CLIENT: Oh, my little sister and I—we shared a bedroom.

THERAPIST: (*nods to indicate "Go on."*)

CLIENT: (*responding to the nonverbal encouragement to go on*) I'm thinking maybe I'm caught up in these memories because I feel just like I thought she would have felt when she cried like that. I feel small and insignificant—just depressed, you know? It's so hard to explain. (*starts to cry*)

THERAPIST: (*soft voice*) That feeling of sadness is just so strong and overwhelming. . . .

CLIENT: (*between quiet sobs*) Yes. . . . I think it's always been there; I've never been happy . . . even as a child.

THERAPIST: It's a very old and familiar feeling!

CLIENT: Yes, and it's so sad—I feel so sorry for myself.

THERAPIST: Like you used to feel for your mother?

CLIENT: Yes. After my dad died it was like she died with him, only she was still alive in her body. And Susi and I couldn't do anything to help her. We were just there, watching her fade away from us—and we were scared sometimes, too, that maybe she would die too and then what would happen to us!

THERAPIST: So that sad feeling you woke up with today is definitely connected to your mom!

CLIENT: Yeah, I guess so. I hadn't thought of it that way, but I think it is. I think she wasn't the only sad one in the house after dad died. Susi and I were sad too, but we were so worried about her that we just sort of kept it all in.

THERAPIST: So that old sadness, why did it come back today?

CLIENT: Yesterday was mom's birthday. She has been dead for four years now, but her birthday is still a tough day for me!

THERAPIST: So in a way there are almost two depressions: there is the depression that's very old and that has to do with your relationship with your mom when you were a little girl, and then there is the new depression that is more of a grieving over her death. But it's hard to keep the two separate.

CLIENT: Yes, they seem to be one and the same. But I think you are right; there is a difference.

THERAPIST: Yes, the new depression is not as disabling as the old depression. You are an adult now, and you have resources you didn't have back then.

CLIENT: Yeah—but by getting the two depressions all caught up in each other, I feel like that little kid again and can't deal with anything.

In this example, identifying the source of the client's feeling was both old and new. One of the sources was recent (the birthday of her deceased mother); the other, more salient source, however, was the affect developed in the relationship with the mother during childhood after the father's death. The client in this example was able to make both connections in the therapy session; she recognized that her depression was both old (i.e., tied to childhood events) and recent (i.e., triggered by a current event). This recognition ultimately helped her realize that although this was an old feeling, she did not have to continue to respond to current unhappy events with severe depression. She realized that although the depression was learned early in childhood, she now had resources as an adult that she had not had available as a child and that she could use these to manage her emotions more successfully in response to current events. However, recognizing both sources remained important throughout her treatment.

Catalysts That Facilitate Cognitive Self-Awareness and Insight

The catalysts in this category are also called explaining strategies (Brems, 1993), and they have as their main purpose creating insight and new learning. They are largely confined to those later phases of the therapy process that are no longer strictly limited to gathering information and empathic understanding. They are not to be confused with either strategies that enhance communication or that create affective self-awareness. They have as their purpose much more than communicating attention and understanding; they help the client explain affects, needs, and behaviors in the here and now and/or in relation to the client's life as a whole. As such, true explaining strategies are used to communicate an understanding of transference or process (i.e., to create insight), as opposed to communicating empathic understanding. Put differently, explaining strategies not only reflect what the therapist observes in the client, but explain it based on the knowledge the clinician has of the client's unique background and history.

There are different depths of explaining strategies. Some of the most basic explaining strategies merely impart new information to clients or may help clients gain a new understanding of their situations, not necessarily based on uniquely personal material. Other strategies in this category are highly idiosyncratic to individual clients and can only work if therapists have vast knowledge about their clients developmental history and self-development. The deeper the explaining strategy is oriented, the more it tends to reflect the therapist's own theoretical orientation. The explaining strategies are listed below in the order of increasing depth and necessity for rapport and understanding. Explaining strategies must always be phrased to match the cognitive capacity and complexity of the client (Ivey, Ivey, & Simek-Morgan, 1997). Because most clients are operating at least at a concrete operational level, but not necessarily any more abstractly than that, the best approach to formulating cognitive strategies is to be concrete. As such, explaining—or insight-creating —strategies need to be clearly formulated while clarifying issues, concrete while being explanatory, and presented without jargon while delivering a new way of looking at things. Further, explaining messages need to be delivered in the most concise and efficient manner, without rambling or lecturing.

Imparting Information

Providing new information or data is appropriate when a client makes a decision, wants to engage in an action, reacts with a feeling, or has a thought about something that appears to be due to the client having faulty, inadequate, or incomplete information; it is also appropriate when having such information may lead the client to make a different response (Cormier & Cormier, 1991). There are at least three ways to impart new information to clients that may help the client gain new perspectives on feelings, beliefs, needs, or behaviors. These can provide information about psychological or developmental processes the client did not have previously, universalize clients' reactions, and reframe their problems.

In providing the client with new information, the therapist merely points out knowledge the client did not previously have but that in and of itself may be successful in changing their interpretation of, reaction to, or behavior in a given situation. Providing new information is a common psychoeducational technique that is used by therapists, especially in group settings. Such psychoeducational information may range from developmental facts about children, to wisdom about parenting interventions, to data about the effects of certain drugs or substances the client is using, to knowledge about the physical effects of a range of behaviors in which the client engages. For example, a therapist may explain to a client that her binging and purging has a variety of effects on her esophageal tissue, her tooth enamel, her normal process of peristalsis, and other physiological processes in her body. Similarly, a clinician may explain to clients who are parents what they can expect from children at various ages to help them understand why different interactions may be necessary with infants, toddlers, young children, and so forth. Therapists may explain to clients that using certain foods can affect their psychological well-being; for example, they can point out that high daily intake of caffeine can result in anxiety-like physiological symptoms. Such basic psychoeducation has a definite place in psychotherapy by creating new insights in the client. On occasion such new knowledge or learning suffices for the client to make some behavioral, cognitive, or affective changes. However, often even enhanced understanding does not translate into behavioral change until the therapist and client have engaged in further therapeutic work. In providing clients with new data, the therapist must take care to do so without condescension, blaming, or arrogance. Instead, the clinician must attempt to present the new knowledge matter-of-factly, respectfully, and in a manner that is well-timed and sequenced. Once the information is provided, the clinician also needs to be sensitive to how the client reacts to the information because the client may well react with some concern or negative affect at the implication that this person has misunderstood or not known certain data until now.

Universalizing certain affects, thoughts, or behaviors is another technique to inform that can at times be successful in creating client change (see Corsini & Wedding, 1997). Universalization refers to the process of giving clients feedback that their responses may not be as unusual or bizarre as the clients may suspect. Clients often come to treatment concerned whether their feelings or reactions are "normal." Helping such clients recognize that their behaviors or reactions fall well within the "normal" or usual range of experiences that other people have to similar circumstances can be a very helpful experience. Having such data at their disposal will help some clients become less concerned over minor problems or painful affects. Overusing universalization strategies must be carefully guarded against. For one thing, it is not always helpful to bring the presence of "others" into the therapy room; some clients do not want to be seen as being like everyone else, but would rather maintain their uniqueness with the therapist. Using this strategy with such clients early in therapy can ruin budding rapport because clients may perceive their therapists as belittling their presenting concerns. Further, the therapist should never claim universalization when it is not true. In other words, if the client presents a reaction that is indeed unusual, the therapist should not attempt to pretend that others may feel the same way; such a therapeutic response would be dishonest and misleading. This may seem like a trite or unnecessary caution, but therapists can indeed be tempted into such concessions by very insecure clients who are looking for reassurance that they are not "crazy" or "strange." Universalization, also referred to as normalization, can be a powerful strategy if used properly; it loses its effectiveness when overused, inappropriately used, or dishonestly used. An example of normalization in a therapy session follows.

CLIENT: I really think I am going crazy. Ever since the rape I have not been able to sleep. I have been totally preoccupied with the rape—I can't think of anything else. Some of my friends have told me I need to stop thinking about it, but I can't. I guess I am just not as resilient as other people; maybe I'm just too sensitive. I wish I could just stop thinking about it and be like other people.

THERAPIST: It is interesting that you compare yourself to others and conclude that you are somehow different or strange because you think they would react differently. If anything, your comparing yourself to others may help you see that your reaction is actually very understandable—in fact, it is common among other women who have been raped.

CLIENT: But my friends are telling me I should just be able to get on with my life and stop thinking about it.

THERAPIST: Yes, I understand. However, have any of these friends ever been raped?

CLIENT: No, they haven't. . . .

THERAPIST: Perhaps it is more helpful to you to compare your reaction to the reaction of other women who have been raped instead of comparing it to the reaction your friends say you should have.

CLIENT: So other rape victims obsess like I do? Do they get scared at night and have nightmares, even though it's been weeks?

THERAPIST: Yes, all of these things are very common.

CLIENT: Wow, I had no idea. So I'm not crazy. . . .

As mentioned above, a third strategy of imparting information is reframing. The reframing technique does not so much impart new information as it does provide a new way of looking at data presented by the client. In essence, it provides new wisdom that can be used to understand a problem or situation differently. Reframing has its origin in systems theory (e.g., Minuchin & Fishman, 1981; Minuchin, Lee, & Simon, 1996) and has also been called relabeling or reformulating. It refers to the therapist's attempt to get the client to see a situation or problem from a new or different perspective that may make the problem more acceptable, solvable, less offensive, or less complicated and that may motivate the client toward a changed mindset and subsequently changed behavior. The process tends to be most helpful if used to remove negative connotations from a situation or behavior or if used to point out overly simplistic interpretations of a situation or response by a client (Cormier & Cormier, 1991; Cormier & Hackney, 1987). Reframing usually introduces a new level of complexity that helps clients perceive the many ways in which behaviors by others may be interpreted; it helps clients learn to attend to different or new situational cues that may enhance their capacity for seeing the best of intentions in others and the fact that the clients themselves may be coping as best as they can. Reframing is often a simple restatement of an idea verbalized by the client (e.g., if clients call themselves "impulsive," therapists may relabel their self-definitions as "spontaneous"). It can also be more complex, as in the example below. However, it can also be achieved more indirectly by asking clients to think of ways in which a situation may be perceived differently, how a behavior may be described otherwise, what a given feeling may signal alternatively, or whether a certain response is the only way of reacting to a given situation. Such leading questions can help clients achieve the necessary cognitive flexibility to reframe occurrences in their lives more independently and globally.

CLIENT: Don't you think that that was a really shitty thing she did to me? I mean, how can she expect me to be grateful that she keeps sticking her nose into my business! She may be my mother but she has no right to keep getting involved!

THERAPIST: So she has done this before then?

CLIENT: Well yeah, she did it last year when I bought my new car—called me three times telling me that she thought I should buy the four-wheel drive because it would serve me better up here, that I'd be wasting money on the convertible.

THERAPIST: When else has she gotten involved?

CLIENT: Well, I just told you—yesterday she called me to tell me that she thought going on this trip right now is a bad idea because Mandy may need braces and we may need the money for that instead. Isn't that my business? Or I guess mine and my wife's business? Why does she keep butting in?

THERAPIST: So she butted in about the trip and the car; what else has she butted in about?

CLIENT: That isn't enough?

THERAPIST: Well, I guess my take on those two situations is that she is worried that you are doing the right thing with your money. I remember you told me she and her family had a terrible time when she grew up making ends meet. I guess to her spending money is serious business and she worries if you understand that the way she does. I see her more as concerned than butting in.

CLIENT: I don't know. She's still butting in.

THERAPIST: Yeah, I sure understand that you see it that way right now; but try to see it from her side: she sees you spending this money, and she never had enough. She's worried that you may end up feeling what she felt when she was your age: always worried about where the next meal would come from. So from her perspective, she's probably not butting in at all. . . .

CLIENT: I guess you're right and all in all she really does stay out of my business; when I compare her to my friends' mothers she is really pretty decent about that kind of thing. It's just when it comes to money, but I guess I could try to see that from her perspective. . . .

This is an example of a fairly complex reframing process that may also have succeeded in enhancing the client's empathic response to others. Often reframing, in its process of helping clients gain a new perspective on a problem, will have the positive side effect of helping them gain a new appreciation for others' feelings and needs, helping them become more empathic and understanding in the process.

Pointing Out Patterns

When pointing out patterns, the therapist ties together multiple messages or contents the client has communicated over time to identify the common thread that ties all of them together. This common thread is then pointed out to clients to help them recognize that apparently disconnected events are actually reflections of a single process or symptoms of a single problem. To be able to point out patterns, therapists have to observe patterns in clients' acting and responding. It requires the clinician to recognize that certain behaviors, needs, affects, desires, and thoughts actually represent repetitions by the client, either in the therapy room or in other settings. Only if clinicians have gained insight into clients' repetitive themes can they help their clients perceive and gain insight into these patterns as well.

At least three types of repetitive themes or patterns clients may manifest (see Teyber, 1997). First, there are relational patterns that are basically interpersonal scenarios that are played over and over again with a variety of people in a variety of contexts. Second, there are rigid cognitive beliefs that underlie and maintain repetitive patterns of behavioral or emotional reactions and that reflect selective and repetitive biases in cognitive processing. Third, there are core affects that are long-standing and recurring, reflecting an affective style that is maintained by the client across situations and contexts, regardless of circumstances. All three types of patterns (relational, cognitive, and affective) can be usefully pointed out to clients to help them recognize that they may respond habitually rather than in a context dependent manner. These patterns lead to almost automatic responding that leaves the client trapped in behaviors and with emotions and thoughts that have long outlived their adaptiveness and usefulness. Once clients are helped to recognize that these patterns can get in the way of more adaptive responses, they may become more motivated for change and growth.

It is also possible that some patterns or responses remain consistent across all three realms of human experience (i.e., across relational, cognitive, and affective realms). For example, clients may show patterns of dependency in relational settings in their strategies of processing cognitive information, or in how they feel about themselves and others. The following example points to such complex patterns and the great importance of a clinician identifying patterns even if they occur cross-modally (i.e., not all in the area of affect or all in the area of cognition, etc.).

CLIENT: I just can't help it—every time I see Jill I just feel sick to my stomach. It's like someone punched me in the solar plexus.

THERAPIST: What do you think that's all about?

CLIENT: Well, I'm not sure—but I know I used to feel like that when my dad and mom were fighting when I was a kid.

THERAPIST: And didn't you say the other day that you have been calling in sick at work a lot recently?

CLIENT: Yes. . . .

THERAPIST: What's been going on at work?

CLIENT: Well, I was given this new assignment, and I am not sure how to go about finishing it. It's making me sick.

THERAPIST: It's making you sick?

CLIENT: Yes.

THERAPIST: Just like Jill "makes you sick"; like your parents' fighting used to "make you sick"; in fact, last time we met, you felt sick in here! Do you remember?

CLIENT: Yes. So?

THERAPIST: Well, I seem to remember that we were talking about some pretty painful things and so I'm wondering if it isn't your general pattern to feel sick when things are too hard to handle; like it gets you away from that for a while because then you focus on feeling sick.

CLIENT: My stomach is hurting right now! Are you saying that pain isn't really real—that I'm making this up?

THERAPIST: No, not at all; what I'm saying is that your body has learned to respond with feeling sick when your mind has to deal with a tough situation—whether it's work, or your marriage, or our relationship, or even your parents' relationship.

CLIENT: Oh—like I'm protecting myself from thinking about these things by getting my mind off of them and onto my feeling sick.

THERAPIST: Exactly!

This example shows how the clinician can point to a pattern that is consistent across a variety of settings (such as work, relationships, and therapy) and with a range of people (e.g., bosses, intimate others, and therapists) and show how such a pattern can serve to hide what is really important for the client to deal with. In this example, the client needed to gain insight in how he used his sick feelings to avoid the more salient aspects of each of these situations and relationships. Only after that insight was gained would he be willing to work on the actual problem, instead of the patterns that covered it up. It is not always the case that the pattern covers up the actual problem. Sometimes, the pattern in itself may present the problem. Even in such a situation, clients' recognitions that they are responding predictably and habitually is needed to motivate change.

Asking Clarifying Questions

As mentioned above, there are several types of questions, one of which is the clarifying question that can be used to lead a client toward insight and cognitive self-awareness (as opposed to employing questions for systematic inquiry and openings that maintain communication and enhance self-disclosure, as covered earlier). Clarifying questions help clients gain better self-understanding by guiding them toward more complex processing of their own thoughts and perceptions and toward answers or insights their therapists have already developed. Clarifying questions can take many different approaches, so it is the process more than the content of these questions that will be demonstrated in the sample below. These types of questions can lead the client toward reframing a problem, toward recognizing a pattern, toward making a self-discovery, or toward solving problems and generating solutions. Essentially, therapists have an idea how they want their clients to go about discovering content and process about themselves, but rather than providing that information to their clients, they choose to lead them to these self-discoveries through targeted questions. It has been commonly argued in the counseling and therapy literature that insights that are discovered by clients themselves—in other words, insights clients own as their own—are more effective in creating actual change. Clarifying questions came about to facilitate this process of self-discovery for and by the clients. The following example demonstrates this process.

CLIENT: I am just totally overwhelmed. I really have no idea what to do!

THERAPIST: Have you ever been in a similar situation?

CLIENT: I don't think I've ever felt this overwhelmed and helpless before!

THERAPIST: How about the not sleeping. Isn't that something that has happened before?

CLIENT: Well, I don't know if it was ever this bad, but I do have trouble with rest when I'm worked up about something. But not like this!

THERAPIST: You've never been this concerned over not sleeping?

CLIENT: I don't know. . . . *(pensive)*

THERAPIST: Think back through your life. Can you think of another time when you didn't sleep, started to have trouble at work, and so on?

CLIENT: A long time ago. Maybe about five years ago, after a harrowing experience with a boyfriend, I had trouble sleeping for many months. Then, from not sleeping at night, I had trouble concentrating during the day and really started screwing up at work and getting mean to some of my friends.

THERAPIST: That is a pretty similar kind of thing, isn't it? This time you are not sleeping, you're having trouble with your boss and you're thinking about breaking up with Jack. . . .

CLIENT: Yeah, that seems to be my pattern. If something goes wrong in my life I start having trouble sleeping—that seems to be the first thing that's affected. But the real problem is that when I don't sleep, I get mean.

THERAPIST: So five years ago, what did you do that worked?

CLIENT: Well, I bought some relaxation tapes and started playing them to myself at night when I went to bed.

THERAPIST: Did that work for you?

CLIENT: At first it didn't; I would ruminate right through all the instructions—couldn't really concentrate on them.

THERAPIST: But later you got it to work for you?

CLIENT: Yeah, I did. And once I started sleeping right again, I also started thinking clearer during the day. Things definitely got better after that.

THERAPIST: What did you do to make it work in the end?

CLIENT: Well, I bought some other tapes that didn't just tell me stuff to do with my muscles but that actually walked me through scenes. I don't quite remember what it was though. . . .

THERAPIST: How did you know to try these different tapes?

CLIENT: Well, I realized that my mind kept wandering with the first tapes, and then I read about these other tapes and I thought maybe that's what I needed.

THERAPIST: Did anyone suggest tapes or help you with picking some out?

CLIENT: No, that was all pretty much my idea. I remembered from somewhere that you can get tapes to relax you, so that made sense to me.

THERAPIST: Why do you think this worked for you?

CLIENT: Well, it calmed me down at night, kept me from going over everything over and over again.

THERAPIST: Have you ever used the tapes again?

CLIENT: Well, I haven't really needed them. . . . Oh, I see; I could use them again NOW.

THERAPIST: Yeah; so I guess you DO know what to do?

CLIENT: Yes, I'll try it. It worked great before, and I actually enjoyed it.

THERAPIST: It's terrific that you can figure these things out for yourself!

CLIENT: Yeah—I guess if I just slow down enough to think about it, I'm not so overwhelmed after all!

In this example the clarifying questions were used first to establish a pattern and then to generate a solution. The therapist recollects that the client had told her during an earlier session of a good solution she had found in a similar situation. The therapist helped the client remember this fact through questions that assisted her to recognize her own problem-solving skills as well as reinforced for her that she was a capable woman who could take care of many of her needs independently. Had the clinician merely reminded the client of the earlier solution, or had she simply told the client to try relaxation and guided imagery tapes to go to sleep, the client may well have resisted the intervention. She may have claimed that her situation was different this time or that she was too overwhelmed to try. By helping the client recognize the similarity between this situation and the earlier one (pointing out patterns through questions), the client owned the solution and could apply it in this circumstance.

Confrontation

Despite the label and colloquial understanding of the term, this catalyst does not imply a harsh challenge or attack on the client. The purpose of this strategy is not to move against the client or to provoke the client, but rather to clarify issues that seem to be contradictory or incongruous. Confrontations are neither aggressive nor hostile but can actually be delivered in a gentle and caring manner (Ivey, Ivey, & Simek-Morgan, 1997). They are used to point out inconsistencies, discrepancies, incongruence, and mixed messages (Cormier & Cormier, 1991; Ivey, 1994) to help the client become aware of them, work through them, and either change them or learn to live with them if they are not under their client's control (i.e., if they involve the incongruence of others). Confrontation is an important therapy ingredient because it tends to move clients forward by giving them new ways of looking at things, awareness of inconsistencies, and the challenge to address these discrepancies by adapting their lifestyles. Without confrontation, therapy would not be as effective in inducing growth, awareness, and change. However, this is not to say that more is better: the client can misperceive too much confrontation as being constantly challenged and put on trial, and the person can respond by increasing defensiveness or guardedness. The key to using confrontation is to apply it when an obvious inconsistency exists and when the therapist–client relationship has matured to a level where the client can tolerate the need to point out incongruence in affect, behaviors, thoughts, or relationships.

Incongruence or discrepancy can manifest in a variety of ways. A client's verbal and nonverbal messages can be out of synchrony, as for example when a client claims not to be angry but has clenched fists, a flushed face, and very tense muscles. Discrepancy can occur between thought or attitude and behavior, as for instance in the case of a client who claims not to be prejudiced and to be open to individual differences, but then discriminates against a coworker who is physically disabled. Clients can display evidence of inconsistencies in beliefs or values, such as believing that everyone but them is allowed to make mistakes (also referred to as having double standards). Incongruence can even occur between two nonverbal expressions, as in clients who laugh and cry at the same time. Finally, content and affect can be out of synchrony with one another, as for example in cases in which clients talk about very sad occurrences in their lives and joke or laugh about them.

As the first step of confrontation, of course, the clinician has to be aware of or detect the incongruence or discrepancy displayed by the client. Then the clinician tries to understand why the incongruence may exist and what may have triggered it in the first place. Once the clinician has processed the discrepancy sufficiently, an outward response to the client may be in order. This outward response includes carefully describing how the therapist has come to see the inconsistency, perhaps by giving an example of it. Phrasing must be done carefully to minimize the client's possible resistance to and defensiveness of the process. Further, the phrasing must not attack or blame the client, but instead it needs to be as supportive and caring as possible. This allows the client to recognize that the clinician is pointing out the discrepancy not as a means of humiliating the client, but as a means of helping the client gain insight into an inconsistency that may be contributing to the person's presenting concern and emotional pain.

Confrontations can be very simple, as for instance in the case in which a therapist merely points out that the client is talking about her mother's death with a very cheerful voice that suggests that she is denying the expression of sadness and grieving that is needed to deal with this event (assuming of course that this is the case and that the client is not genuinely cheerful about the death of the mother). An example of a more complex and involved, yet still very caring, confrontation is presented below.

THERAPIST: You said earlier that you really want to make the relationship with your wife work out?

CLIENT: Yes, I really do!

THERAPIST: And then yesterday when she told you that she needed to talk to you, you said you didn't want to?

CLIENT: Well, as always, she brought that up again while I was watching the game. She always does that. Waits till I'm busy and THEN she suddenly wants to talk. . . . *(client appears angry; face flushed)*

THERAPIST: But you do want to work out the relationship?

CLIENT: Yes, damn it, I do! But she makes it so damn hard for me. She keeps nagging me, yapping at me . . . *(getting agitated)*

THERAPIST: Nagging you, yapping at you? Is that how you see her?

CLIENT: Yea, she really gets to me! I really just need to get away from her!

THERAPIST: So you want to get away from her but at the same time you say you want to make the relationship work?

CLIENT: *(looks up, astonished)* I guess I can't really have it both ways, can I?

THERAPIST: It does seem pretty impossible. . . . Maybe it's that you want to get away from the things you don't like about the relationship but you'd like to salvage the good things.

CLIENT: Yeah, I guess I'm just not sure anymore that the good things will ever come back to THIS relationship. I think maybe we're doomed as a couple. All we've been doing is fighting, fighting, fighting. I don't even know her anymore, don't even remember what I ever liked about her.

THERAPIST: So, do you want to stay in or get out? I guess that's really a central question you have to answer. . . .

CLIENT: Yeah, I can't have both. Maybe that's what's been driving me crazy—the idea that I had to stay when what I really want is to leave. In my family, divorce is just not acceptable. . . . *(From here the client and therapist go on to explore the origin of the client's incongruence between what he said he wanted versus what he behaviorally suggested he may want.)*

This example demonstrates the role of a confrontation: it points out how clients may say in words that they want to do one thing but demonstrate through their behavior that their actual desires may be quite different. This therapist had to recognize the inconsistency between the client's expressed desires (to salvage the relationship) and the client's behavior and the message it communicated (his rejection of his wife's attempts to salvage the relationship) to help the client come to terms with his conflicted emotions. The confrontation that resulted (and was achieved through many clarifying questions) was not an angry attack, but a caring process that was well received by the client. However, not all confrontations go this smoothly or are this well accepted and assimilated by the recipient. Some clients react strongly to a confrontation, no matter how gently delivered, so it is best to refrain from ending a session with this. Not enough time may be left for client and clinician to finish sorting out the message and for the client to resolve and understand it thoroughly in its intended spirit.

Here and Now Process Comments

This catalyst for change and cognitive insight often resembles a confrontation in terms of the process and words it involves. The critical difference, however, is that it is always related to an occurrence that takes place in the therapy room between clinician and client. Process comments by definition have a very strong here and now orientation; they focus on clients as they feel or behave in the relationship with and in the proximity of the therapist. These process comments can be augmented through observations that tie the current relationship between client and therapist to past occurrences in the client's life. This turns the process comment into an interpretation. The latter process will be expanded upon below. The skill referred to here is strictly focused on the therapist's ability to recognize that the client has reacted in a way that is related to the client's relationship to the therapist or therapy in the present moment. No attempt is made yet to interpret the meaning of the here and now process in the context of past events or experiences of the client.

Process comments make the dynamics between client and clinician overt and subject to discussion and expression. The skilled use of this catalyst brings treatment to life because it makes therapy more immediate and enriches the relationship between client and therapist. Process comments provide the client with an opportunity to recognize cognitive, affective, behavioral, or relational patterns and reactions while they occur in an interpersonal context, thus moving therapy from the conceptual and abstract into the concrete and experienced. This here and now orientation helps clients become aware of immediate reactions and needs as well as of the impact they have on others around them. Here and now exploration of the relationship between clients and therapists invites clients to self-explore and to become aware of themselves in relationship to others.

Process comments are excellent to facilitate insight and motivate change and self-recognition (Teyber, 1997). Process comments are most commonly initiated through questions that direct clients' attention to their reactions at this moment (e.g., "What is happening with you right now?"; "What's going on with you [between us] at this very moment?"; "What were you just thinking but decided not to say out loud?"). If questioning is not sufficient to help clients recognize their reactions or responses, therapists may move toward simply pointing out the reactions they observed in the client (e.g., "I noticed that you turned away from me. What do you think that's all about?" or "I can see that you want to say something but instead you seem to try to keep it in"). All of these interventions focus the client on the present and on the relationship or interaction with the clinician. This immediacy can have a tremendous emotional impact on the client and is a most powerful therapeutic tool. An example of a here and now process comment follows.

THERAPIST: Another thing we need to talk about today is the fact that I am going on vacation next month. I will be gone for two weeks between the 15th and the 30th.

CLIENT: (looks up suddenly; then starts trembling, gets tears in her eyes and flushes; her head then is slightly tilted to the side and her eye contact becomes sporadic; client makes no verbal response)

THERAPIST: What are you feeling right now, at this very moment?

CLIENT: I am scared, or at least I feel like I'm scared, but I'm confused too because I don't know why . . .

THERAPIST: You look scared! What is that all about? *(soothing voice)*

CLIENT: I'm not sure. But when you said that you are going on vacation next month I felt this wave of anxiety sweep over me. . . .

THERAPIST: Tell me more about that.

CLIENT: I'm not sure what else to say. I thought I was doing so well. I felt so good today when I came in. I am doing great at work; I am happy with being alone for now . . . and then you said you're leaving and all my old feelings of being scared came back.

THERAPIST: What does that mean to you?

CLIENT: Well, I'm afraid I'm not doing as well as I thought. *(voice quivers, hands tremble)*

THERAPIST: So you're not just scared right now; there is something else!

CLIENT: Yeah—I'm confused *(starts to cry)*

THERAPIST: A lot of old feelings seem to be flooding back. *(quiet voice; less eye contact)*

CLIENT: Can I make it without you? What about the day when you tell me "That's it; we're done." What am I going to do?

THERAPIST: Right now it feels as if all the changes you made are somehow tied to our work together.

CLIENT: To you.

THERAPIST: And yet just last week, in fact, just right until before I told you I was going on vacation, you felt confident that you really changed; *you*, not you in relationship to me!

CLIENT: Yes! *(looks up; grabs a tissue from the box)*

THERAPIST: In fact, you're getting back in touch with those confident feelings right now!

CLIENT: Yes. You're right. It's like for a moment I forgot; I guess what I really still need you for is to remind me sometimes that things really have changed. *(smiles now)*

THERAPIST: So our next step is to figure out how you can remind yourself of that—at least for the two weeks that I'm gone and then, down the line, for good!

CLIENT: I actually think I'll be fine. . . .

This example demonstrates how immediate here and now responses of the client can be used to move the client along into new material and new insight that further augments the therapy. It also shows that much of the processing of the immediate relationship between client and therapist can be achieved through questions that lead the client into certain awareness and recognition. The questions can then be broadened through observations the therapist makes of the client and can be fed back to the client to help clarify the experience. The process comments can then be expanded to lead to interpretations that help the client recognize the pattern of responding; the clinician acts to represent a larger pattern that is lived out with others as well and that can be understood by tying it to affectively significant events in the client's past (Basch, 1980).

Interpretation

Interpretations are the most depth-oriented of the insight-facilitating catalysts. Depth refers to the distance between the explanations based on the client's past relationships or experiences and present affects, thoughts, behaviors, and relational patterns. An interpretation, thus defined, helps clients understand what shaped and still maintains their current self-experience and reactions and does so by making meaningful links between the client's current relational patterns and this person's responses to formative relationships and affectively significant experiences in the past. An interpretation establishes a meaning for a client's reaction or experience and provides a means of explaining why certain affects, cognitions, and behaviors developed. The self-knowledge that results is perceived as a motivator for change, and it serves to enhance self-awareness and understanding (Cormier & Cormier, 1991; Teyber, 1997).

The content of interpretations is highly bound by the theoretical orientation of the therapist; however, all theorists must give explanations of client behavior and thus all theorists use interpretation. A behaviorist can explain a client's experience or response by pointing out reinforcement histories and cause-and-effect relationships. A cognitive behaviorist will attempt to help the client recognize and understand the origins of irrational beliefs or automatic thoughts. A self psychologically oriented psychodynamic therapist helps the client recognize that empathic failures on the part of caretakers in the past resulted in certain vulnerabilities in the client's self-development that have left this person with behavioral patterns and responses that are designed to protect these vulnerabilities. Regardless of the clinicians' theoretical framework, however, three basic implications of interpretation remain the same: (1) current reactions and experiences do not appear out of the blue, but rather are tied to past experiences and social learning histories that greatly affected the client's development, reactions, experiences, or adjustment; (2) clarifying the deeper meaning of a here and now relationship or reaction is helpful to change and self-growth; and (3) explanations are useful only if they are individualized and do not follow a formula.

Because interpretations explain currently manifested affects, thoughts, behaviors, and relationships through past experiences and learning, they are by definition depth-oriented. This depth cannot be tolerated by the client if it is presented by the therapist out of the blue—that is, without preparation and without having established a therapeutic relationship that is stable and trusting. If an interpretation is rendered prematurely or without preparation, the discrepancy between the client's ability to deal with the problem and the therapist's position in understanding and explaining the client's problem may be too large for the client to tolerate or accept (Cormier & Cormier, 1991). An interpretation thus delivered will be perceived by the client as experience-distant and will not have as much impact as an interpretation that is experience-near and understandable by the client (see Kohut, 1984). It is best not to begin the interpretive process in therapy until a firm therapeutic alliance has been established wherein the client has experienced ample understanding by the therapist and until after some of the more basic explaining strategies (outlined above) have been used successfully on several occasions. Like confrontations, interpretations need to be phrased respectfully and gently; they must not be used to blame, attack, humiliate, or deride the client; they need to be phrased to minimize defensiveness and guardedness on the part of the client; and they need to be worded so that the client can perceive them as helpful and positive.

Despite all of these cautions and the belief of some mental health professionals that interpretations should be use sparingly (e.g., Kleinke, 1994), they are actually an excellent means of helping clients achieve better self-awareness and insight and so serve a multitude of purposes. Weiss (1993) points out that interpretations help clients:

- become more self-aware
- see themselves more accurately and positively
- understand their here and now affects, cognitions, behaviors, and relationships in a broader context that ties them to past experiences and events
- better accept their current responses and experiences because they can begin to understand how they developed
- feel reduced anxiety about the self because they provide answers to pressing questions
- feel reduced shame because they begin to understand how certain responses developed
- let go of pathological beliefs because they can recognize their roots
- feel less helpless because by showing how reactions developed, interpretations also imply that these same reactions can hence be changed

Interpretations work only if they have been individualized for each client and express the essence of the entire client. In other words, interpretations are not formulas that can be used equally for all clients (Nichols, 1987); they should not be phrased to fit people in general; they cannot press people into a single mold; and they must not be based on stereotypes, prejudices, or easy assumptions about what "causes" certain behaviors (Ivey, Ivey, & Simek-Morgan, 1997). Instead, interpretations must fit the unique and highly personal, idiosyncratic history and experience of each client. They need to be relevant to and respectful of the person as a whole and should never make the client feel only partially responded to by addressing (explaining) only select parts of the person while ignoring others. Such partial interpretations only make clients wonder whether therapists only accept and understand parts of them instead of feeling wholly and completely understood. Interpretations must be free of jargon; they must be phrased in a way that is easy for the client to understand, and they should be relatively concrete or otherwise match the client's cognitive flexibility and level of abstraction. Given that interpretations make connections between past and present, and hence require some level of objectivity and abstraction, they may not be the best strategy for all clients. For example, with children, interpretations should be used sparingly (see Brems, 1993). An example of an interpretation is provided below. This example continues the theme established in an earlier session with the same client that was presented in the empathy sample used earlier in this chapter.

THERAPIST: You seem taken aback that you are still depending on Sandra so much, despite the fact that you know that she is withdrawing from you. How come you are so surprised by your need for her?

CLIENT: I don't *want* to need anyone. As soon as you rely on someone, they leave you.

THERAPIST: Like your best friend who died and like your mom after she came back from the hospital.

CLIENT: Yes, like mom. She was never the same after she came back. She cried a lot and just wasn't there for us any more. My brothers and I just had to learn to fend for ourselves!

THERAPIST: Because she didn't fend for you anymore? *(to keep the client talking)*

CLIENT: Yes, there was no one else we could rely on; dad wasn't home much, remember? He worked constantly!

THERAPIST: Couldn't count on him either!

CLIENT: Couldn't count on anyone but ourselves.

THERAPIST: And you learned to trust only yourself—not rely on anyone! Interesting, isn't it?

CLIENT: *(looks puzzled)*

THERAPIST: Well, on the one hand, you have developed this pattern of relying only on yourself. On the other hand, you have had some relationships where you came to depend on the other person a lot! There are some interesting patterns of both wanting to be with people and not wanting to be with people.

CLIENT: Yes, I don't have a lot of friends, but once I make them, they really become important to me and then if they threaten to leave, like Sandra is doing now, I flip out, even though what I really tell myself is that I need no one.

THERAPIST: Can you see a parallel between how you feel about people these days and how you related to your mom and dad as a child?

CLIENT: Well, I guess I wanted to be dependent on mom, but I couldn't. . . .

THERAPIST: And not only that, when you did depend on her, you ended up hurt because she wasn't really able to help you and be there for you to the extent that you wanted.

CLIENT: Yes, and so I learned to do things for myself; not even hope any more that she might get better.

THERAPIST: So that pattern, that fear that if you rely on someone, they'll disappear led you to withdraw from people. But that still didn't really take care of what you needed. You really wanted someone to love and to depend on. So being lonely left you depressed.

CLIENT: Yes—and that's where I still am today. Still as sad as when I was as a little boy. . . . *(quiet voice; head down)*

THERAPIST: With glimmers of hope every now and then—like with Jason and Sandra.

CLIENT: Yes, but then I turn them away because I'm ambivalent even then. I think I'm so afraid they'll leave me that I actually turn them off—the very things I do to make sure they'll always be there actually are turning Sandra away from me right now.

THERAPIST: Yeah, you want from Sandra what you needed from your mother. You want her to be there for you, you want to be the center of her universe, you want her to take care of you.

CLIENT: But she doesn't want to be my mother. . . .

THERAPIST: No. . . . *(quiet now, to let the client finish the thought)*

CLIENT: She wants a partner, not a helpless child. . . . *(starts to cry)*

This example of an interpretation demonstrates that interpretations often do not consist of a single sentence or statement, but are actually delivered little by little over the course of a longer intervention. In this example, a lot of interpreting was happening; the therapist provided explanations about the client's dependency needs, his approach–avoidance conflict, and his relationship with his significant other. All the explanations were based in a psychodynamic theoretical orientation, but were notably delivered without jargon. Further, they were given in small amounts and were well-timed to accommodate what the client was able to hear and digest. They were provided caringly and gently; no blaming or stereotyping occurred. The experience was very immediate for the client, and the therapist and client voice and body language were well matched.

SUMMARY AND CONCLUDING THOUGHTS

A variety of treatment catalysts exist that can be used by all therapists, regardless of their theoretical orientations or personality styles. The most important of these were discussed here to give clinicians an idea about how to move therapy along and how to help clients develop affective and cognitive self-awareness. It is certainly true that therapists use many more catalysts besides the ones covered in this chapter; however, many of these basic skills are either theory-specific or less frequently used. Excellent therapy can take place strictly based on the use of the catalysts covered in this chapter, as long as they are embedded in a meaningful therapeutic relationship.

In other words, it must be understood that the use of these catalysts alone does not yet define or round out the therapy experience. The catalysts need to be understood and embedded in the larger context of psychotherapy; they need to be placed into an overall framework of treatment that considers not just intake data, conceptualization, treatment goals, and therapist skills, but also the interpersonal or relational context of therapy itself. The exclusive use of catalysts makes therapy mechanical. Catalysts, and hence therapy, are more effective if they are embedded within an interpersonal matrix of relations that makes the process of therapy experiential. This interpersonal, experiential matrix between client and clinician makes catalysts more effective because it adds an atmosphere to the relationship and work that can contribute to and metabolize the contents and insights brought about by the catalysts. The interpersonal and experiential process of psychotherapy is highly complex, and it will be dealt with in detail in Chapter 6.

6

A FRAMEWORK FOR PROCESS
IN PSYCHOTHERAPY

A child sees a butterfly struggling to get out of its chrysalis. He takes pity on it and uses a penknife to free it. But the butterfly never flies, because nature intended it to develop and strengthen its wings by forcing itself out of the chrysalis. The boy made life too easy for the butterfly; therefore, it never developed.
—STEPHEN R. PEARCE, FLASH OF INSIGHT

Many writers from various schools of thought have come to agree that the most important change agent is the interpersonal relationship and experience that is played out between client and therapist in psychotherapy. The relational experience by the client during the process of psychotherapy may be more helpful to the client than the most sophisticated techniques and detailed explanations about this person's thoughts, affects, behaviors, and relational patterns (Strupp, 1996). It is the collaborative relationship between client and clinician that facilitates change, growth, and healing in the client because it communicates respect, caring, acceptance, and empathy along with important understanding of the client from the client's unique and idiosyncratic personal history. Given the great importance and strong emphasis placed on empathy and understanding in the therapeutic relationship, the relationship between client and clinician and the process that passes between them is central to successful treatment (see Farber, Lippert, & Nevas, 1995). It is the purpose of this chapter to explore the processes that occur between client and therapist as they collaborate to further the client's growth, change, and healing. Focusing on the client–therapist relationship, however, does not imply that therapy is an easy process—either for the therapist or for the client. Therapy can be painful for clients, in fact often *must* be painful for clients as they learn to develop and stretch their wings. It can be stressful for therapists because they must watch their clients suffer and work through difficult situations and issues. Rescuing clients from suffering is not the answer. Allowing clients to master their own suffering instead is the key to a successful therapeutic relationship.

The process of therapy and the relationship between client and clinician are best captured through the discussion of three separate but thoroughly intertwined and circular processes that occur in psychotherapy. Although these processes will be discussed in a linear fashion, it must be made clear to the reader that they rarely occur in a linear manner in the therapy room. It is impossible to reflect in writing the interdependence of these processes: writing is by definition linear, and therapy is by definition circular. Hence, to try to capture therapy process in writing presents a tremendous challenge. Below, three types of processes will be discussed: the relationship or experiential process that occurs between client and therapist to facilitate change, growth, and healing; the interpersonal empathic process that occurs when clients resist and therapists help them recognize and use this resistance therapeutically; and the overall therapy process that manifests as phases in treatment. Each type of process will be discussed individually, but all tend to occur together and circularly. They are intertwined and intimately tied to one another; all are equally important, and the competent clinician is aware of all of them at all times.

To make use of therapy process, each clinician must develop not only the capacity for empathy that was discussed in the previous chapter (i.e., possess *Einfuehlungsvermoegen*), but also an observing ego that helps the clinician observe the interaction with the client as it occurs. Only by being able to be both in the process (being present, real, involved, available, and caring) and yet outside of the process (remaining observing, understanding, and reflecting) can the clinician help the client enhance self-awareness, understanding, acceptance, and knowledge. To summarize what will be presented in detail below, the process of therapy can be understood as follows: clients and clinicians enter into intensely interpersonal and experiential relationships that provide ample opportunity for clients to act out their personalities and self-development in here and now relationships; this relationship at times is challenged through self-protective mechanisms by the client (also called resistance) that are employed to keep the client safe (but stagnated and unchanged); by using both the intense interpersonal process and by successfully understanding and acknowledging a client's self-protective strategies, the therapist facilitates four therapeutic phases occurring that represent the client's movement—through recollection, reconstruction, re-experience, and ultimately resolution or rehabilitation. The discussion and elaboration of this cycle or conceptualization of therapy process (outlined below) represents the essence and purpose of this chapter.

1. processing the relationship through:
   - transference
   - corrective emotional experiences
   - creation of a holding environment
   - projective identification
   - internalization
2. processing treatment challenges (i.e., client self-protection or resistance) through:
   - understanding the purpose of resistance

- reframing resistance as self-protection
- using resistance to therapeutic advantage
3. understanding overall treatment process by recognizing the phases of change:
    - recollection
    - reconstruction
    - re-experience
    - resolution or rehabilitation

PROCESSING THE RELATIONSHIP

For Carl Rogers the central question about how to facilitate change was not "How can I treat, or cure, or change this person?", but rather "How can I provide a relationship which this person may use for his [or her] own personal growth?" (Rogers, 1961, p. 32). This reframing of what creates therapeutic change summarizes perfectly what will be communicated in the following pages about the therapeutic relationship. It emphasizes the experiential components of the relationship between client and therapist that make therapy so real and full of here and now experiences for the client. Other more contemporary thinkers have echoed this understanding of the centrality of the therapeutic experience to the therapeutic process. Wolf (1988) makes the following observation:

> It is not the content of the information conveyed to the patient, not the substance of the interpretations and interventions made, not the correctness of the therapist's conjectures, nor even the therapist's compliance with demands to "mirror" the patient or to be his or her ideal that is pivotal: It is decisive for the progress of the therapeutic endeavor that the patient experience an ambience in which he or she feels respected, accepted, at least a little understood. (p. 100)

This emphasis on the experiential nature of the client–therapist relationship must not be misunderstood as the sympathetic and equal relating of two individuals. As mentioned in several prior chapters, the focus of therapy is and always will be on the client. The therapist does not self-disclose and is never the center of therapy. Clinicians will maintain an emotional distance from their clients that keep them neutral enough to become the target of transferences, projective identifications, and other therapeutic relationship processes. However, this emotional distance is not to be misunderstood as emotional coldness (or even coolness) or lack of emotional involvement. It merely defines the nature of the type of emotional closeness that is created between client and therapist. Specifically, the emotional involvement or experience between clients and therapists comes from therapists' recognition of their clients' needs and affects and therapists' acknowledgment of their own affects and reactions to these disclosures by their clients. The emotional distance that is maintained by therapists refers only to their own emotional state as independent of their clients or the current therapy. In other words, therapists are real people and are emotionally available and accessible to their clients. This emotional accessibility, however, is limited to affective, cognitive, and relational responses by the clinician to the self-expression of and relationship with the client, and this does not include self-disclosure about the therapist's personal life, needs, or emotions (see Kohut, 1984; Wolf, 1988).

The processing of the client–clinician relationship also requires that the therapist have a firm grip on what is contributed to the relationship by the client and what is contributed by the therapist. The issue of countertransference was detailed in the first chapter and is of great relevance here. Countertransferences that are not client-specific will cloud the therapeutic relationship and will make it difficult for client and clinician to tease out what the client needs and wants because the therapist's own needs and wants intrude into the relationship as well. In other words, therapists must be certain that they have a firm awareness of their possible and actual trait-specific, stimulus-specific, and issue-specific countertransference. To reiterate, trait-specific countertransferences are those that introduce therapist issues due to the fact that the therapist has a habit-driven manner of relating to people in all contexts, including the therapy setting (e.g., always responds with irritation to criticism, always has a need to take care of people, is prejudiced about some presenting problems or persons). Stimulus-specific countertransference refers to material that is contributed to the client–clinician relationship due to the therapist's unconscious and immediate reaction to an external stimulus of the client that is independent of the client's treatment needs or transference expressions (e.g., the clinician reacts in a certain way because the client is male and reminds the clinician of a brother). Issue-specific countertransference is the coincidental and unfortunate coming together of therapist and client issues (or transferences) that are incompatible, too similar, or too threatening (e.g., both client and therapist have unresolved childhood histories of client abuse) and results in overidentification and loss of emotional distance (as defined above).

The admonitions about self-awareness of countertransferences are important especially since countertransferences *can* be used therapeutically. As mentioned above and in Chapter 1, client-specific countertransferences are helpful to the processing of the client–therapist relationship because they contribute material that can help both individuals learn about the client's impact on others. Using the therapeutic relationship in such a manner—that is, using it to recognize relational patterns of the client that tend to perpetuate problems—is an accepted and helpful treatment strategy (Teyber, 1997). This process is intimately related to the transference relationship between client and therapist and is thus addressed in that context below. All in all, there are a number of ways through which client and clinician can process their relationship and can learn from what is going on between them in the here and now. The five most important of these exchanges (transference, corrective emotional experience, creation of a holding environment, projective identification, and internalization) will now be addressed.

Using the Transference Relationship

Clients rarely just talk about their problems or concerns when they see a therapist, but rather they also tend to act them out in the therapeutic relationship. They display and express the same behaviors, relational patterns, cognitive styles and interpretations, affective reactions or source feelings, and need states with the therapist that they use with most other human beings and that they learned through human interactions in affectively charged events over their life span (see Brems, 1993; Strupp, 1992; Teyber, 1997). It is likely that clients, through their expression of personal styles, elicit responses from the therapist that are typical of the responses they elicit in other people with whom they interact (Weiss, 1993). The therapist, in other words, is as much a target of ingrained patterns, behaviors, cognitions, and affective responses as anyone else in the client's environment. Similarly, therapists themselves are not the blank screens or neutral persons traditional psychoanalysts had hoped for. Such neutrality is impossible given the reality that therapists are as human as their clients and hence react to human situations and in human interactions. Stated differently, if clinicians accept the ubiquity of clients' transference, clinicians must also accept the ubiquity of their own countertransference (Wolf, 1988). The key to successful treatment is to use this countertransference productively and not to allow it to get in the way of the empathic relationship with the client. This interpersonal cycle of client expression and therapist reaction essentially captures the definition of a transference–countertransference cycle, or transference relationship, between client and clinician.

In the psychoanalytic tradition, transference referred to those needs, feelings, and desires that found expression in the therapy relationship without a reason in the here and now, instead stemming completely from earlier life experiences. Transference, thus defined, viewed the client's responses or expressions as irrelevant to the relationship at hand and interpreted them in the context of previous, usually parental, relationships. Later, and less traditionally, definitions of transference have included all needs and feelings brought to the therapy either by the client or the therapist, regardless of how relevant they are to the here and now relationship between the two (O'Conner, 1991). Such broader conceptualizations have suggested that everyone (client and therapist) is influenced by all earlier life experiences and that therefore all interactions with significant people in a person's life somehow are a function of earlier relationships, and never pure. The contributions that are made in this manner by the client would be labeled transferences; those made by the therapist, countertransferences.

Transference, as it will be defined here, is viewed from a perspective somewhere between these two extremes. It appears unlikely that all interactions between client and therapist reflect their histories more than their present relationship (as O'Connor's definition would suggest); it appears equally unlikely that transference is ever as pure (i.e., unaffected by the therapist) as suggested originally by Freud. Given the intense experiential and relational nature of the therapeutic relationship, it is more likely that a component inherent to the current here and now relationship between client and therapist triggers old feelings and needs related to past relationships. Put differently, the transference relationship between client and therapist is not seen as completely independent of what the therapist brings to treatment, a definition of transference that deviates from the traditional, or pure, models. Instead, the definition of the transference relationship proposed here suggests that this relationship is always affected by both the client's transference and the therapist's countertransference. This definition of transference is entirely compatible with Gill's (1982) conceptualization of transference as the patient's experience of the relationship with the therapist and Wolf's (1988) definition of countertransference as the therapist's experience of the relationship with the client. Both experiences are subjective and flavored by each individual's history, background, and current affective and need states. Hence, the client–therapist relationship is an intersubjective relationship that reflects both the client's and therapist's reality (see Atwood & Stolorow, 1984: Natterson, 1991). It is through this relationship to which both client and therapist contribute knowledge and wisdom that they arrive jointly at a higher and more accurate understanding of the client (who despite this definition always remains the sole focus of therapy).

Therapists contribute to the transference relationship in at least three ways. First, they contribute through overt and intentional behaviors—that is, by using the treatment catalysts that were detailed in the prior chapter. Although these catalysts do not create specific reactions in the client, they facilitate a relationship and environment in which previously existing affects, behaviors, relational patterns, thoughts, and needs can be reactivated, as well as freely expressed and understood. Second, the therapist inadvertently contributes characteristics that may further stimulate or hinder a client's self-expression. These inadvertent contributions are generally secondary to personality style, personal feelings, beliefs, and affects; they are truly in the spirit of trait-specific, stimulus-specific, and issue-specific countertransferences, as defined above. Third, the clinician contributes to the transference relationship through client-specific countertransference that is used for therapeutic purposes. Most of these contributions will be flavored by the therapist's reality and life experience—by virtue of being human, the clinician is not and cannot be a neutral and blank slate (Natterson, 1991).

Clients contribute to the transference relationship with clinicians because they are not blank slates either, but rather (like the clinicians) the product of intense past experiences that have helped shape the persons. Clients have grown up in unique environments with very individualized interpersonal relationships that influenced self-development in a manner that defines how they react emotionally, cognitively, behaviorally, and in relationships. These patterns are not only relied on in day-to-day relationships, but are also stimulated and expressed in the context of psychotherapy. Therapists who are self-aware (and either contribute only client-specific countertransferences to the therapy relationship or are capable of recognizing how their other countertransferences have affected the relationship) facilitate activating and expressing client needs and reactions. This aware therapist does not alter the client's reactions in the sense of producing needs or affects that would not otherwise be expressed by the client. However, this therapist is aware that these affects and needs, however grounded in past relationships, were currently stimulated through the here and now relationship with the clinician. By inspecting the intersubjective transference relationship that transpires between client and therapist at that moment, the therapist can then gain further insight into the client's development, environment, needs, and directions for change.

This understanding of transference can accommodate various theoretical frameworks, because it neither implies the specific content of the client's expressions nor the therapist's means of understanding or interpreting (explaining) them. For example, a cognitive behaviorist will focus on clients' cognitions (content) and will try to understand their current manifestation by inspecting clients' and their experiences in the here and now relationship (understanding) as well as gleaning insight into their development through learning histories in clients' lives (interpretation or explanation). A humanist will focus on clients' feelings and self-expressions (content) and will look for meaning in the here and now relationship (understanding) while also searching for their origins in a family environment that provided varying levels of acceptance, genuineness, warmth, and empathy (interpretation). A family systems theorist will explore relational patterns and behaviors (content) and will attempt to recognize the ways they are activated or stimulated in the here and now relationship (understanding); trace their origins to family interactions; and pay attention to issues such as inappropriate boundaries, triangulation, and so forth (interpretation).

Regardless of how the transferential feelings, cognitions, relational patterns, and behaviors are understood and explained, the fact remains that they are present in the client–therapist relationship and that they present the therapist with the unique opportunity to work on these expressions and responses concretely in the therapy relationship (i.e., experientially and intersubjectively in the here and now), despite the fact that their origins were in a different setting. This reality facilitates an experiential process that is less abstract than the original use of transference in that it explores previously established patterns in here and now circumstances instead of abstractly discussing them only in the context of prior relationships. Without such an intersubjective transferential relationship, the process of understanding clients and/or explaining their experiences would be reduced to "an empty shell of intellectualizations" (Wolf, 1988, p. 136) because it is the presence of a true empathic connection in the here and now between client and therapist that makes the therapeutic process both experiential and meaningful. Understanding and explanations provided within the transference relationship are more experience-near and, hence, have more impact on the client than interpretations about the client in relationships in the distant (or even not so distant) past (Gill, 1982).

How the therapist deals with the client's reenactment of prior relationships (from the distant and not so distant past) or reactivation of previously developed affects and needs in the current relationship critically determines whether the transference–countertransference cycle will be therapeutically helpful, hurtful, or useless. The optimal therapeutic response involves several actions and processes:

- Therapists must understand and recognize that an intersubjective transference relationship has been established between them and their clients in the here and now.
- Therapists have to gain an understanding of the intersubjective transference relationship in terms of what it communicates about the content of their clients' needs, affects, cognitions, behaviors, and relational patterns.

- Therapists have to gain an understanding of the intersubjective transference relationship in terms of what it communicates about clients' needs, affects, cognitions, behaviors, and relational patterns in relation to the therapist—that is, what transpired between clients and therapists that activated or motivated clients' expression and experience.
- Therapists have to gain an understanding of the intersubjective transference relationship in terms of what it communicates about clients' affects, cognitions, behaviors, and relational patterns and their etiology in relationships in clients' pasts.
- Therapists have to be able to tease out their own countertransference and must recognize when the responses they have are idiosyncratic to themselves, as opposed to client-specific.
- Therapists help clients recognize and understand how their transference (i.e., emotions, needs, thoughts, behaviors, and relational patterns) manifest in their relationships with therapists.
- Therapists help clients see how they play out their transference with others in their environments.
- Therapists may (or may not) assist clients in linking the current transference relationship patterns (with the therapist and with current others) to their origins in relationships of the client with significant others in the past.
- Therapists avoid getting drawn into the transference and thus become able to provide accepting responses that are different from what clients expect in the here and now and/or have experienced in the past.
- Therapists assist clients with exploring alternate responses to current relationships that are independent of the need states created in past relationships.

The therapist who is successful in taking all of these steps in dealing with a client's transference (i.e., the client's experience of the therapeutic relationship) will be successful in providing the kind of therapeutic environment that helps the client feel understood and accepted. This will ultimately help clients gain a better understanding of their needs and experiences in a current and lifelong interpersonal context. The sense of being understood and accepted by the clinician is a new and different emotional experience for the client that can induce and facilitate change in and of itself. The experience of such a corrective emotional experience is an important relationship component that deserves discussion in its own right.

Providing a Corrective Emotional Experience

Credit for the label "corrective emotional experience" goes to Alexander and French (1946), two neo-Freudian psychoanalysts. They (like Fromm-Reichmann [1950], who pointed out that intensive psychotherapy needs to provide an experience, not just an explanation) recognized that insight did not suffice to create change, but that instead an interpersonal experience had to be part of analysis for it to be effective. The client has to be able to experience a relationship in which certain feared or anticipated consequences and painful outcomes do not occur, resulting in an experience that is surprising, influential, and corrective for the client. Alexander (1961) believed that therapists' responses had to be different from how clients' parents would have responded to them, and he saw making this distinction as the foremost responsibility of the clinician. In striving to maintain this distinction, Alexander suggested, the therapist may have to consciously play a role that is designed specifically for that purpose. Although the idea of the corrective emotional experience has survived new generations of therapists since Alexander's writing (while having been attacked by traditional thinkers), his concept of playing a role with the client for the sole purpose of being different has been eclipsed since then.

The concept of the corrective emotional experience led Rogers (1961) to believe that the essential ingredients in psychotherapy and the motivators for change were genuineness, acceptance, empathy, and unconditional regard, interpersonal experiences rare in the general life experiences of most clients. The concept of the corrective emotional experience led Kohut (1982, 1984) to conclude that empathic understanding of the client and its communication to the client were more important change agents than insight-oriented explanations. Overall, when the need for the corrective emotional experience was recognized, this contributed to the great emphasis on safe therapy settings and establishing trusting and accepting therapeutic rapport, emphasizing processing of the therapeutic relationship in the here and now, and gave importance to the idea that the therapist should respond to the client in a manner that is unexpected, yet genuine (i.e., not role played), and hence more forceful and salient. All of these ideas in turn (i.e., Rogers's emphasis on unconditional regard, Kohut's recognition of the centrality of empathy and understanding, the general emphasis on safety, here and now process, and unexpected genuine therapist reactions) facilitate a change in the experience of interpersonal process and in the self-perception of the client.

What does it mean to provide a corrective emotional experience? Clients expect their therapists to respond to them in the same way others have responded to them throughout their lives. They fully expect that whatever interpersonal experiences, needs, and conflicts they have had in the past, they will recapitulate again with the clinician. Clients' behaviors, affects, and cognitions while with the therapist remain the same as they were in most other relationships. If clients have a generally dependent style, they will express these dependency needs with the clinician. If clients are generally aggressive or demanding, they will show these relational patterns with the therapist; depressed clients will manifest their depression in therapy just as anxious clients will evidence their anxiety. The recapitulation of relational patterns, behaviors, affects, and cognitions is not a conscious attempt on the client's part but is truly the power of transference—that is, the power of prior learning in past relationships that is reactivated or stimulated in the here and now relationship with the clinician. If therapists succeed in providing healing responses to these transferential manifestations of client experience, they have succeeded in providing corrective emotional experiences for these clients (Teyber, 1997).

Examples of such healing responses are at least twofold. First, there are responses that are different from what the client is attempting to elicit from the therapist (whether consciously or unconsciously). A client who has a tendency to challenge others, attempting to make them feel inferior or inadequate, who tries to be in control and to usurp leadership must not be allowed to assume the power in the therapeutic relationship. Instead, with such a client (who has developed a relational style of moving against people), the therapist would respond by assertively maintaining the boundaries of therapy, prohibiting the client from lateness, nonpayment of fees, or complete control over the content covered in treatment sessions. Conversely, if clients manifest styles that elicit approval, acceptance, and kindness, who attempt to be perfect clients for the therapist, these may need to be challenged to explore what fears underlie their nonassertiveness. In other words, the unexpected response is highly idiosyncratic to each client's presentation and demands that the therapist has a firm understanding of the client's general interpersonal style and expectations. Such an understanding comes from a thorough conceptualization that is etiologically based and keeps the therapist aware of the style of the client as well as its origin (as was discussed in Chapter 4 in great detail).

In providing such an unexpected response, however, the therapist must continually attend to the therapeutic relationship and ascertain that an empathic bond remains between client and therapist that is accepting of the client's needs. In other words, providing the unexpected response is not to be misunderstood with depriving clients of what they really need. It is based instead on the assumption that the responses clients elicit from their environment are familiar responses clients have come to expect, but in actuality these are perceived as nonempathic or even traumatic. Thus providing an unexpected response actually means being empathically aware that clients need different responses from the environment than they normally elicit. Simply the presence of empathy, acceptance, genuine concern, and caring in the therapeutic relationship often provides such a corrective emotional experience for the client (Donner, 1991). Most clients arrive in therapy with or because of a history of minor or major traumatic interactions with significant others in their past and current environment. The therapeutic relationship is very different from these prior experiences with interpersonal relationships. Therapists strive to be empathically attuned, to accept their clients, and to communicate to clients that they are understood. This process in and of itself is emotionally different from most other relationships clients have experienced, thus providing incidental corrective emotional experiences. Therapy constructed on a basis of empathy and understanding offers the client a different type of relational and self-experience and so provides an alternative model for relating and experiencing a healthy self in relationships.

Second, there are responses that are healing because of acknowledged errors by therapists that have resulted in recapitulation of the client's earlier experiences and that caused a subsequent rupture in the empathic relationship. This rupture, however, can be recognized by therapists by being aware of clients' responses and allowing them to be healed through clinicians' acknowledgment of (or apology for) the empathic failure from the client's perspective. This empathic rupture, though distressing for clients temporarily, is healing over the long run if they are recognized by clinicians and processed with their clients (Donner, 1991; Kohut, 1984). Their healing power comes from two sources. First, these ruptures challenge clients to begin to provide for their own needs and to take responsibility for their own affects (much as children learn to take care of themselves through being challenged to do so by their parents' occasional mistakes). Second, and more importantly for providing a corrective emotional experience, the acknowledgment of such ruptures (i.e., the therapists' mistakes) leads to an acknowledgment of clients' need for particular responses from their therapists. Therapists not only acknowledge that their clients are in need of these responses or experiences, but they fully accept their clients' need. It is through accepting their clients' need for particular responses by their therapists that makes therapists different from the clients' parents who failed to acknowledge their children's needs in these earlier relationships, perhaps humiliating or shaming clients for having this. Further, therapists' willingness and genuine attempts to understand their clients' reactions to the therapists' (less than optimal) responses are likely to be perceived as unexpected and healing. For most clients, empathic failures by others in a relationship with these clients were met by these failing others by using defensiveness, blame, or belittling of clients for needing particular responses from these persons. Therapists, in accepting their clients' perceptions of their responses as inadequate or nonempathic, further provide healing reactions that acknowledge the validity and reality of their clients' experiences and reality.

A corrective emotional experience can thus be generically defined as an experience wherein the therapist, against the client's expectations, accepts the client's reality without moral overtones of right and wrong, and accepts and acknowledges the client's needs completely. The corrective emotional experience essentially demands the therapist can recognize, understand, and acknowledge (though not gratify) what Kohut would refer to as the mirroring and idealization needs of the client (see Kohut 1984; Wolf, 1988). Simply put, mirroring needs of clients refer to their needs to be affirmed and valued, whereas idealization needs refer to their needs to be supported and strengthened. A therapist who provides a corrective emotional experience or optimal therapeutic response remains emotionally connected to the client by accepting the client's needs for affirmation and for strength and support. The acceptance of these needs ultimately guides the client through the crisis and facilitates continued emotional expression that leads to catharsis and all its associated benefits, including self-awareness.

It is the experience of being fully accepted that results in the corrective emotional experience for the client; in other words, a corrective emotional experience is not the gratification but the acceptance, understanding, and acknowledgment of the client's needs (Kohut, 1984; Rowe & MacIsaac, 1989). Clinicians, unlike earlier relationship partners (whether parents or significant others) do not disavow or judge their clients' reality and emotional needs or expressions. Instead, they honor their clients' deeply felt yearning for understanding and acknowledgment of their mirroring and idealization needs (Wolf, 1988). This process, here defined as a corrective emotional experience, has also been referred to as "optimal responsiveness" (Bacal, 1985, p. 202), a label that (though more descriptive and, hence, preferable) has, unfortunately, not yet replaced the label "corrective emotional experience."

Creating a Holding Environment

If the corrective emotional experience demanded an unexpected accepting response from the therapist, the creation of a holding environment demands a response by which the client feels supported and can glean strength. As is true for normal human development, clients need both the experience of a corrective emotional experience and a holding environment; the former attends to the client's needs for understanding and acceptance, and the latter to the needs for strength and guidance through relationships with idealized others (Kohut, 1984). Bowlby (1988) similarly applied the concept of a holding environment to normal human development and psychotherapy. Bowlby suggested that both the human child and the human adult in therapy must experience a relationship in which the person's emotions, needs, and distress are safely contained throughout the relationship. That the essential need for a sense of being embedded within a human matrix satisfies a child's and client's fundamental human needs has been confirmed in the developmental literature (Brems, 1997; Stern, 1985). Studies point toward the necessity of having affirming and supportive adults in the child's environment for their healthy development to take place. The first theorist to write about the holding environment was Winnicott (1958b), who described it as the environment created for infants by their mothers, who contain and experience the infant. Winnicott suggested that the self of the infant starts out unintegrated and diffuse and has to be strengthened and consolidated through interactions with a primary caretaker. Mothers who can help infants organize their self-expressions thus help them develop self-integration. "An infant who has had no one person to gather his bits together starts with a handicap in his own self-integrating task" (Winnicott, 1958a, p. 150). Just as the mother needs to provide a holding environment for the infant, the therapist is perceived by Winnicott as having to provide a holding environment for the client that reflects reliability, attentiveness, responsiveness, memory, and continuity across time—all of which ultimately serve to help the client integrate a healthy self (Winnicott, 1965).

A stable and supportive holding environment is suggested as a prerequisite to therapeutic change, growth, and healing. This presumes the presence of a therapist who is capable of helping the client recognize that both client and therapist can survive and deal with even the most powerful of client affects, that the therapist will not abandon the client regardless of the relational patterns or burdens contributed by the client, and that the therapist has the necessary strength and emotional stamina to keep the client safe, protected, and supported, while the therapist remains strong, firm, and caring (Teyber, 1997). Providing a holding environment does not imply that the therapist takes care of the client's needs for support and guidance, just as a corrective emotional experience did not imply that the clinician would gratify the client's needs. In the corrective emotional experience, the clinician accepted and acknowledged the reality of the client's needs without challenging their developmental appropriateness or moral correctness. In a holding environment, the therapist similarly recognizes the client's distress but does not attempt to reduce it. Instead, the therapist helps the client recognize the distress and the client's ability to tolerate it, survive it, and ultimately solve it. Clients learn to tolerate their distress in the holding environment through the presence of their therapists who are calm and confident and who do not share their clients' emotional panic. Clients learn that they can survive their emotional distress by being encouraged by the therapist to experience this distress in the clinician's presence and in the holding environment that provides a structure that makes such experience less overwhelming or frightening. Finally, clinicians assist their clients with resolving this distress by helping them recognize its original source. In other words, the provision of a holding environment is a three-phase process: holding the distress or emotion with the client without diffusing it; allowing the client to feel the entire emotion and thus recognize that it is survivable (assisting with emotional regulation as needed); and understanding the emotional distress in the here and now relationship, as well as explaining it from a past relationship perspective.

The skills that are necessary for facilitating a holding environment have been covered previously. First, the therapist has to be *empathically attuned* to see that the client has an emotion and has to feel self-confident enough not to squelch that emotion in the client but to allow for its *catharsis*. Second, therapists have to be able to tolerate their clients' affects and have to be able to help their clients feel safe with these affects by understanding that affective regulation can be achieved, if necessary, through the therapist's ability to help the client stop crying, reduce anger, eliminate panic, and so forth (as will be described in the next chapter). In this process, therapists also help clients survive the emotional arousal by helping them begin to *identify affect, label it, and express it* in healthy ways. Third, therapists have to be able to help their clients *connect affect to its sources*, both in their here and now relationships and in past relationships. Through this process, the therapist provides an environment that holds the client's affective arousal and distress—which makes it sufficiently tolerable for the client to experience it fully—recognizes that it is not as devastating and destructive as feared, and understands its meaning in the here and now as well as from a historical perspective.

The clinician can get in the way of creating a holding environment by making a variety of mistakes that essentially interfere with the full expression and resolution of the client's affective arousal or distress. These mistakes have been previously summarized by Teyber (1997, p. 144) and are repeated here. Clinicians interfere with the creation of a holding environment in response to clients' affective arousal or distress if they feel compelled:

- to interpret what the feelings mean and intellectually distance themselves
- to become directive and tell the client what to do
- to become anxious and change the topic
- to fall silent and withdraw emotionally
- to self-disclose or move into their own feelings
- to reassure the client and explain that everything will be all right
- to diminish the client by trying to rescue the person
- to overidentify with the client and insist that the client prematurely make some decision or take some action to manage the feeling

This listing of therapist mistakes that interfere with the creation of a holding environment is an excellent means of demonstrating what not to do. These also have clear implications for the types of behaviors that will help the therapist create a holding environment. Clinicians who want to create a holding environment for their clients to express, explore, survive, and come to accept their affects and needs must be able to do the following: provide a conducive structure, express specific therapeutic traits, and exercise accepting and supportive therapy skills. (All of these have been covered in detail elsewhere in this book.) These skills are summarized here, in the (approximate) order in which they will occur if a therapist attempts to create a holding environment. Most importantly, it must be noted that generally to facilitate expression is first, then to facilitate the client's recognition that the experience is survivable, and concluded by accepting the experience by processing its meaning and origins. To achieve these goals, the therapist:

- must be emotionally connected to the client and have developed an intersubjective relationship
- must communicate acceptance, interest, and empathy, both verbally and nonverbally
- must know how to elicit affect and catharsis
- must be able to accept and affirm the client's affective experience
- must know how to help the client learn to identify, label, and express emotion
- must know how to help clients recognize variations on affects and shades of gray in the affective experience and expression
- must feel confident in one's own ability to tolerate intense client affect
- must not be overwhelmed or threatened by a client's affect
- must communicate one's own ability not to be hurt, burdened, or overwhelmed by the client's affect
- must feel confident in one's own ability to help clients get affect under control if necessary
- must be able to put limits on the client's behavior, if necessary, to provide a safe environment
- must accept the client's experience as real and must not judge the client's experience or its expression
- must recognize, understand, and (if appropriate) communicate the meaning of the affect in the here and now
- must help the client accept the subjective reality of the experience
- must, after appropriate expression and survival, help the client recognize the immediate and/or past sources of strong affect and distress

Creating a holding environment is an essential process skill that again focuses on the here and now experience of the client in relationship to the therapist. The experiences stimulated that need to be contained and held for the client during this process are most likely to arise out of an interaction between client and therapist, but generally are linked to an experience in the client's life. However, the experience, survival, and acceptance of the affects and needs are of foremost importance. Accepting these needs and affects, in addition to holding or containing them with the client, can be greatly facilitating. In other words, a holding environment is not something that occurs in isolation but most generally is superimposed on a transference relationship or a corrective emotional experience. Creating a holding environment is not the only way through which therapists can help their clients begin to deal with apparently overwhelming affects and needs. The process of projective identification serves a similar purpose of containing and processing affect in the therapist–client relationship, so deserves some attention.

Understanding Projective Identification

The direct or verbal expression of affect is perhaps the most difficult form of self-expression for many clients. Thus it is useful for the therapist to be aware of a way of understanding and processing a client's affects without the need for a verbal exchange between clinician and client. Projective identification is one such nonverbal method or therapeutic technique. Melanie Klein (1955) first described projective identification as a defense mechanism. She described it as a process wherein an individual splits off negative aspects of the self and projects them onto another person in an attempt to control this person and get the person to act in accordance with the projector's own needs. Bion (1959) viewed projective identification as a normal developmental process used by young children to explore strong affects while these emotions are safely contained within another person. This process involves projection and reintrojection of strong affects so that there is no threat to the developing self or personality. This definition of projective identification implies that it is an interpersonal process, or a mode of interaction, that is relevant in everyone's development—as well as in the developmental setting of psychotherapies, individual or otherwise.

Bion's understanding of the interpersonal nature of the projective identification process is most closely related to the view of a more contemporary writer, Ogden (1982). Ogden views projective identification as serving four functions: as a defense mechanism, a mode of communication, a means of object relatedness, and as a pathway to psychological change. He indicates that, as a defense mechanism, projective identification helps individuals rid themselves of undesirable or frightening affects (Klein's definition); as a mode of communication, it helps individuals feel understood by others by imbuing them with their own feelings; as a way of relating to others, it constitutes a relatively safe way of being with others; and finally, as a pathway of psychological change, it makes difficult feelings that had been projected, available to the individual in altered (i.e., less threatening or frightening) form for reintrojection. It is this latter view of projective identification that makes the concept most relevant to the therapeutic process (Brems, 1989b).

As a therapeutic catalyst or technique, projective identification consists of three stages. First, the client projects an unacceptable or frightening affect, need, or aspect of self onto the therapist to calm and soothe the person and to keep the disturbing experience from the person's conscious awareness. Second, the projection of the client is recognized by the therapist with acceptance and understanding, who metabolizes or alters it in some fashion to make the affect or experience acceptable to the client. The therapist offers empathic understanding of the client to help the client recognize the projected experience and to help the client explore feelings in the relationship. The clinician's acceptance of the projected affect or experience is communicated nonverbally. Metabolizing the affect or experience allows therapists to recognize that the affects they are experiencing with the client have originated from the client, are overwhelming or otherwise unacceptable to the client, and must be made less frightening (more acceptable) before the client can identify with and own them. Third, once thus altered or metabolized, clients identify these affects as their own so they will be reintegrated into their experience of self. This process of reintrojection is a critical component of projective identification, because without the introjection, no change in the client will have occurred.

Without reintrojection, the projective identification would merely have served as a defense against the affect, which was successfully concealed from the client's self by projecting (or rejecting) it. Without the metabolism of the projected affect by the therapist, reintrojection would not be possible in a therapeutic way, because the unaltered affect would remain unacceptable or overwhelming to the client, could not be reintegrated into the client's conscious concept of self, and would continue to be rejected by the client. However, if the therapist is successful in recognizing, accepting, and altering the affect, it will become acceptable to the client and can be incorporated successfully into the client's healthy self.

Although this process sounds somewhat technical and abstract, it is actually a very experience-near procedure because it presumes an experientially-based relationship involving client and therapist. It is this very involvement, however, that occasionally causes the cycle to derail and to end unsuccessfully. Namely, if therapists receive the affect or experience but do not recognize it as a client's, but rather perceive it as their own, a projective counteridentification is set in motion. In this scenario, the therapist will feel equally overwhelmed or disturbed by the affect or need, cannot contain or alter it, and the therapeutic cycle cannot be closed. For instance, if a client is utterly confused about life and the direction this person wants to choose for life, it can and does occur that the therapist takes on some of the client's projected confusion, only to begin to feel disoriented and ambivalent about the client's treatment. For example, one supervisee began to avoid talking about a particular client's case. When the supervisor addressed this avoidance, she confessed that she felt very confused and unclear about her treatment goals with this individual. Her therapy had been unfocused and no themes had begun to emerge across sessions. After some exploration with the supervisor, this therapist came to realize that much of her confusion had originated from her client's utter inability to give any focus to his life. When she recognized that the confusion she experienced was not entirely her own, she was able to formulate clearer treatment goals, and was able to begin to direct the sessions. In turn, her client began to model the supervisee's sense of direction and structure (to reintroject the altered affect), and began to develop some focus of his own.

Projective counteridentification, as described in this example, is most likely to occur around affects therapists themselves have not mastered completely. Thus a novice therapist, who has not worked with very many clients and feels somewhat anxious in sessions, will be particularly vulnerable to projections of anxiety. However, any client affect, need, or experience can lead to a projective counteridentification if therapists are either unaware of the emotions within themselves, have strong personal reactions or proneness for that particular affect, and are unaware that they are identifying and accepting the client's affect. This is yet again a reason why therapists must be self-aware and knowledgeable of their own unresolved conflicts or vulnerabilities about self. Lack of affective or experiential self-awareness on the part of the therapist is the relationship component that is most likely to get in the way of a successfully resolved and therapeutically useful projective identification.

An example of a successful projective identification was noted in the treatment of a young woman who had come to therapy because of approach–avoidance conflicts to intimate relationships and frequent narcissistic rages that interfered with all her relationships. This client had a long history of having had humiliating interactions with her stepfather, who chronically ridiculed her and embarrassed her in front of others. This client presented for therapy with intense feelings of anger and rage that often threatened to spin out of control. By providing a firm holding environment, the therapist was ultimately able to help the client recognize that the rage was not the source affect, but rather a screen affect for intense shame. This shame, however, was not an acceptable affect for the client because it greatly threatened her self-experience of being worthwhile and good enough. Not surprisingly, it was the client's shame that became the focus of a projective identification. In one session the therapist noted that she had begun to feel unsure of her interventions and to wonder about the effectiveness of treatment with this client. She recognized doubts about her efficacy and skill as a therapist with this particular client and felt somewhat humiliated at her perceived failure. Because these feelings were very incongruent with her usual self-experience in relationships with her clients and because she was by then well aware of the client's source feeling of shame, she began to wonder about a projective identification. Once she had conceptualized her own affect and experience as such, she was able to reorient herself and to regain awareness that the interventions with her client were appropriate, felt more confident and strengthened about having chosen correct treatment strategies, and was able to withstand the client's narcissistic rages against her that questioned her ability as a therapist. The stronger the therapist became in warding off feelings of shame, and the firmer she became in recognizing that her interventions were indeed good enough, the calmer the client became. Ultimately, the client stopped raging against and humiliating the therapist and moved toward exploring her own feelings of shame in the relationship to her stepfather.

This cycle of interaction suggests that once the therapist recognized the client's shame and made it more manageable by accepting the affect as part of the client without allowing it to spin out of control by becoming overwhelmed by the affect herself, the client was able to take on the modulated affect and could begin to deal with it in its less intense form. Had the therapist reacted with a projective counter-identification, she would have continued to doubt her own skills, would have felt shame at her inability to intervene properly with the client, and would have made it impossible for the client to deal with her (now even less controllable) feelings of shame (and the screen feeling of rage). Instead, the therapist recognized the origins of the strong affect in the client, and was able to accept the affect and to tolerate it in its milder form. The clinician made attitudinal changes that rendered the affect manageable and tolerable to herself and to her client. Once the affect was thus metabolized, the client could recognize it in its milder form as tolerable, could reidentify with it, and could reintroject it into her own repertoire of self-experiences in the milder, more tolerable form, then was able to process her shame directly.

The change in affect that occurs through projective identification is created entirely through nonverbal interpersonal processes that never have to be discussed or interpreted. It also relies heavily on the process of internalization which in itself is an important relationship component of the overall therapy process. Specifically, the ultimate incorporation of the modified affect into the client's self-experience requires that the client be capable of both identification and introjection as skills or developmental tasks that are the foundation of the process of internalization (Rowe & MacIsaac, 1989). Both greatly facilitate therapeutic change without requiring insight. Internalization occurs in all therapies, regardless of the client's age, but it is particularly helpful in treating children or highly emotionally underdeveloped adults. The same is true of projective identification (see Brems, 1989b, 1993).

Facilitating Internalization

As mentioned previously, insight is no longer perceived as the exclusive or necessary answer to therapeutic change. The experiential nature of the relationship has been assumed to involve the power to create growth, change, and healing in the client. The usefulness of experiences within the therapeutic relationship is perhaps best exemplified through the process of internalization, which by definition is relational, experiential, and healing. Internalization is the process of helping a client own certain beliefs, feelings, needs, behaviors, values, and relational patterns through the use of imitation, identification, modeling, and similar healthy developmental and interpersonal occurrences. Internalization is a process through which clients make the positive aspects of the therapeutic relationship part of themselves, a development which in turn reduces symptoms (Harrist, Quintana, Strupp, & Henry, 1994), thereby supporting internalization as an important change agent in psychotherapy.

Internalization is a developmental process that begins at birth and functions to help children develop a cohesive, orderly, and vigorous self through interactions with caretakers and significant others in their environment. Almost from the moment of birth, children observe their environments very curiously and intently (Stern, 1985), learning much of what they will come to know during their lifetimes through imitation and modeling after their significant others and by internalizing certain beliefs and experiences that arise in these relationships with early caretakers. There are two major components of a child's self that are developed through the process of internalization as it begins early in life. First, the child has to internalize the mirroring function of the self. This has to do with the acquisition of self-esteem, self-affirmation, self-acceptance, and realistic self-appraisal; and second, the child has to internalize the idealizing function of the self, which has to do with developing a direction in life, values, strong perception of self, and the ability to cope (the interested reader is referred to Kohut [1984] for more detailed information about these functions of the self).

In early developmental stages, internalization of self-affirmation (or mirroring) and strength (or idealization) is achieved through the healthy interaction with empathically attuned caretakers. These caretakers affirm their children's needs and affects, help their children believe in their own basic goodness, and allow their children to glean strength, support, and guidance by interacting with the caretaker. If children's environments are essentially consistent in providing for these particular developmental needs, the children will internalize selves that can take on these functions in the absence of a caring and empathic adult, essentially accepting the role of caretaker for themselves (though the need for affirming and strengthening others is never completely outlived; Kohut, 1984; Wolf, 1988). Occasional failures on the part of the caretaker to provide the needed self-affirmation and strengthening are necessary and unavoidable developmental processes that enhance the internalization process. Specifically, the child learns to take on the functions served by the caretakers when they fail to provide this function that they offered so consistently before. These optimal empathic failures or frustrations challenge children to begin to rely on their own (internalized) resources to take over the affirming or strengthening responses previously provided by the caretaker.

The issue is one of balance: empathic failures are optimal and allow for internalization of healthy self structure if they are occasional and embedded in an interpersonal matrix that overall is adequate and consistent at meeting or gratifying most of the child's needs. Non-optimal failures, that is, failures that children do not easily overcome, occur when the child's environment never meets the child's needs and no healthy modeling of self-affirmation or self-strengthening takes place. In such a depriving, nonempathic environment, the children never internalize the capacity for self-affirmation and self-soothing because these functions were never provided to or modeled for them. The internalization process can also be interfered with if the environment is overavailable—that is, if there are never any failures on the part of the caretakers to meet the child's needs for self-affirmation and strengthening and parents always responded immediately and completely. Children in such environments would never be challenged to internalize these self functions and would for the rest of their lives depend on others to meet their needs. Internalized self-affirmation and self-soothing behaviors thus depend on the overall embeddedness in an interpersonal matrix that provides for most children's basic needs while occasionally leaving them to fend for themselves. It is during the occasional empathic failures that children learn to internalize skills and to begin to fend for themselves, psychologically speaking (Kohut, 1984; Rowe & MacIsaac, 1989; Wolf, 1988).

If clients did not internalize the mirroring (i.e., self-affirmation) and idealization (i.e., self-soothing) capabilities or aspects of the self in their relationships with significant others in their lives during childhood (either due to the inability of caretakers to respond empathically or due to the absence of optimal empathic failures), clients will develop a vulnerable sense of self that is unable to function independently and in a healthy manner. It is this very person who is most likely to become a client in psychotherapy. The failed process of internalizing may then need to be restimulated in the therapeutic relationship with the clinician and can be used to help the client complete the development of the self that was left incomplete in childhood and that led to the person's basic vulnerabilities. This rekindling of the normal developmental process can occur in two ways: it can happen incidentally through internalizations of modeled behaviors and expressions evidenced by the therapist in the therapeutic relationship (Bacal, 1985), or it can happen through the transference relationship between client and therapist that is empathically attuned but occasionally disrupted through optimal empathic failures (Kohut, 1984; Wolf, 1988).

With regard to the former process, interactions with the therapist can assist the client to internalize adequate self-affirming and self-soothing functions; these strengthen the client in many ways without the need for insight or explaining. Clients can glean self-esteem and strength merely from the empathy and acceptance around the interaction with their clinicians, in much the same way as infants or children in a healthy interpersonal environment will learn to meet their own needs by modeling after, imitating, and internalizing their parents' responses, values, and so forth. This process of internalization is more or less incidental to the work with clients because it takes place nonverbally and preverbally, it does not rely on cognitive insights, and yet it builds the basis for a strong, goal-directed and confident self. This type of internalization is best understood as the client's incidental modeling after the clinician. This is neither encouraged nor discouraged by the clinician, but this happens incidentally due to the experiential nature of their relationship. It is synonymous with similar concepts proposed by social learning theory (Bandura, 1969; Johnson, 1994). This process of internalization, however, demonstrates why therapists must carefully explore their own values and beliefs and must be aware of how they inadvertently communicate these values to their clients. If the research is correct that internalization takes place primarily through identification, modeling, and imitation, then therapists must remain ever aware that everything they do and say in a session with a client may end up becoming part of the client's own repertoire of beliefs, values, and experiences. This places some responsibility on the clinician to model appropriate and healthy values and self-experiences.

The internalization process that is based on an empathic break in the therapist–client relationship is an equally unplanned process between client and therapist. This must be recognized and then used strategically by the therapist when it counteracts the client's movement toward healthy development of self. This process relies heavily on the desire for an empathic relationship with the client and must occur within a relationship that is based upon acceptance, genuine concern, and caring (Donner, 1991). It is unavoidable that therapists will occasionally fail the client and will not adequately understand and reflect back the client's self-expressions during treatment. Just as the empathic failures in a developing child's life can be either helpful or hurtful, these empathic breaks in the therapeutic relationship can be to the client's advantage if they occur spontaneoulsy to be processed with the client. This working through process was already alluded to earlier in the context of the corrective emotional experience. In that context, the corrective aspect of having a therapist recognize, affirm, and accept a client's needs was discussed along with the need for apologies by the therapist who misunderstood or failed to accept a need expressed by the client. The emotional aspect of this occurrence is indeed a corrective emotional experience. There is, however, another process that goes on at this same time that is called a transmuting internalization.

The transmuting internalization is equivalent to the process of developmental internalization when a parent fails to meet a child's basic need for affirmation or soothing. It is because the parents failed in responding empathically that the children are challenged to internalize those functions and to become capable of meeting their own personal needs without the consistent presence of the caretaker. The empathic break in the therapeutic relationship is an imitation of this developmental process. In the therapeutic relationship, the therapist—while not gratifying the client's needs for affirmation and soothing (as a parent would in normal development)—always accepts and confirms that this need exists in the client; as such, this helps the client accept and meet this need through the relationship with the clinician. An empathic break occurs when the therapist is unaware of such an expression of need or fails to accept it. In such an instance, the client is challenged to take the role of the therapist and to provide acceptance and understanding for the emerging need alone or without the therapist's help, at least for a while. This is the same challenge that is met and mastered by the child during healthy development. It challenges clients to internalize the self-affirming and self-soothing functions that they did not internalize during childhood (due to the unresponsive environment provided by the caretakers at that time) and to move toward relative independence from their therapists. This internalization ultimately leads clients toward self-acceptance and understanding as well as enhanced self-efficacy regarding the ability to meet their own needs for self-affirmation (mirroring) and self-soothing (idealization; Kohut, 1984; Wolf, 1988).

Concluding Thoughts about the Relationship Process in Psychotherapy

The preceding discussion hopefully clarified the complex interactions that occur overtly and covertly at all times between a therapist and client. These relationship patterns or experiential aspects of the therapeutic relationship cannot be overstated; they must be attended to by all clinicians and must be processed carefully either by the therapist independently or by therapist and client together. The relationship in psychotherapy presents unique challenges and invaluable opportunities for change, growth, and healing—and more than likely is even more complex than we can even now only begin to fathom. The intersubjectivity between client and therapist is so unique and so idiosyncratic that one can easily say that no two therapy experiences are ever the same. With each new client, even experienced therapists must start to pay attention to their own relationship reactions and experiences all over again. Each new client can stimulate a new set of personal reactions (affect, thoughts, needs, behaviors, and relational patterns) in the therapist. Self-awareness, a recognition of process, an understanding of developmental needs and stages, and the empathic attunement to the client's reality and phenomenology of the self are crucial aspects of the therapy and carry with them tremendous responsibility and opportunity.

PROCESSING TREATMENT CHALLENGES

Webster's dictionary defines resistance as "a force that opposes or retards motion," where motion in the therapeutic context may be understood as change, growth, or healing. This definition suggests that something in therapy is getting in the way of forward movement; however, it does not specify from where this force is emanating. According to this understanding, therapy can contain several possible sources of resistance: from the client, the therapist, and the environment (Cormier & Cormier, 1991). This definition of resistance differs significantly from the traditional definition that saw the source of resistance as emanating from clients and their ambivalence about change. Namely, Freud viewed resistance as a means of protecting the client's mental apparatus against allowing awareness of anxiety-provoking unconscious processes or contents. Because this understanding of resistance presumed the ubiquity of client resistance, a major portion of analysis was devoted to helping clients recognize, understand, and overcome their resistance. Resistance and its interpretations were used to help clients gain better insights into their conscious personality dynamics and conflicts, and were perceived as unavoidable aspects of treatment. This definition of resistance has come under severe attack by some clinicians and writers who understood it to mean that therapists do not look at themselves when growth or change in the therapy relationship has been impeded, but instead used the concept of resistance to explain these failures.

For example, Lazarus and Fay (1982) expressed the belief that resistance "is probably the most elaborate rationalization that therapists employ to explain their treatment failures" (p. 115). Similarly, Szasz (1973) claimed that resistance is simply therapists' disapproval of clients who talk about what they want to talk about instead of talking about what their therapists want to talk about. Turkat and Meyer (1992) defined resistance as any behavior that is antitherapeutic. It appears that these writers have missed the point of both the traditional and more contemporary definitions of resistance but merely point to how the concept was misused. Blaming the concept for being misused by some clinicians can lead a theory to be prematurely or irrationally rejected although it is both useful and can be productively applied. Given the resistance expressed in the literature to the concept of resistance, it appears important first to define it from a contemporary perspective, then to discuss how and why it may manifest, and then to review how it can be dealt with to render it therapeutically useful.

Definition of Resistance

Resistance, as defined here, neither blames the client for treatment failures nor makes the client responsible for therapist failures. It is neither perceived as antitherapeutic, nor as an impediment to growth, change, and healing. Instead, resistance is viewed in the spirit of Kohut's (1984) understanding of it. This redefines resistance as a self-protective mechanism employed by clients to keep themselves safe from attacks (invasion or destruction) to their vulnerable selves. Behavior that may traditionally be labeled as resistance (see Signs and Symptoms below), is better understood as "activity motivated by fear of injury to the self and designed to protect the self's structure and boundaries" (Wolf, 1988, p. 136). Inherent in this definition of resistance is the fact that it can take many shapes and forms and can be motivated by several possible reasons. Thus resistance as self-protection is best defined through how it manifests (signs and symptoms) and according to its reasons (purposes and sources).

Signs and Symptoms of Resistance

Self-protection can manifest in a variety of ways in the therapy process, and every clinician needs to be aware of the signs and symptoms to be able to recognize when clients feel threatened or attacked and perceive the need to protect themselves. Being able to read the signs and symptoms of resistance helps the therapist recognize the client's vulnerability and will put the therapist on notice to consider having to intervene therapeutically to help the client move forward. Signs and symptoms are also helpful if used to remind therapists to look at their own behavior with their clients and its possible interference with therapeutic progress. A thorough discussion of what to do when the signs and symptoms of resistance emerge is provided below.

Pipes and Davenport (1990) have summarized the signs and symptoms of resistance or self-protection into three overall categories: disarming behavior, innocuous behavior, and provocative behavior. Disarming behavior is understood as any action on the part of the client that keeps the therapist preoccupied and distracted from more important issues at hand. They include actions such as praising the therapist, asking the therapist personal questions, or engaging in many safe personal disclosures so that little or no attention is paid to more important therapeutic contents and processes. Innocuous behaviors are actions that are not overtly challenging to either therapist or therapy process but hinder the unfolding of therapeutic work nevertheless. For example, such clients may display passive or helpless behavior, may remain silent much of the time, or may recount events without emotional involvement or investment. Provocative behavior is openly resistant behavior and is the most easily recognized form of client resistance. It consists of actions such as challenging the therapist, making sexualized comments or behaving seductively toward the therapist, missing sessions, failing to come on time, and similar conduct. The grouping of signs and symptoms into these three categories is helpful because is focuses the clinician's attention on the fact that a client's self-protective behavior is not always easily recognized simply because it is not always overtly directed against the therapist or therapy. Instead, resistance can be expressed subtly and through behavior that, on the surface, appears like compliance.

Following is a list of possible client behaviors that can reflect resistance or attempts at self-protection. This list is by no means complete but gives clinicians an idea of the kinds of behaviors they may need to look for to become aware of the hesitation a client may experience toward treatment. This list is based on a number of therapy resources, including Cormier and Cormier (1991), Egan (1994), Morrison (1995a), Pipes and Davenport (1990), Teyber (1997), and others.

- tardiness for sessions
- no-shows for sessions
- cancellations or rescheduling of sessions
- refusal to pay or forgetting to bring payment
- requests for special favors (e.g., lower fees, shorter sessions, flexible schedules)
- sabotages to treatment (e.g., bringing an infant to session, scheduling important work meetings right after session)
- prolonged silence in sessions
- brief answers or refusal of answers
- evasiveness in response to particular questions to topic areas
- changes of subject for no obvious reason
- pauses or hesitation before answering questions
- diversionary tactics (e.g., telling jokes, asking personal questions, requesting to use the rest room)
- talk only about "safe" issues
- work that is less hard than the therapist's
- contradictions in information provided
- claims of forgetfulness or poor memory (in the absence of physical/neurological evidence or reason)
- omission of critical information about self or history
- involuntary behaviors suggesting boredom, agitation, or other forms of discomfort (e.g., yawning, flushing, psychomotor agitation)
- voluntary behaviors suggesting discomfort (e.g., repeatedly looking at the time, poor eye contact, squirming)
- inability or unwillingness to decide on therapy goals
- failure to take responsibility for own behavior
- sexual or seductive behavior toward the therapist
- challenges to the therapist (e.g., blaming, questioning competence)
- attention distracted away from important contents (e.g., personal questions for the therapist, rambling, talking about others and not self)
- exaggerations (e.g., of own accomplishments, or other's actions)

This list could probably be twice as long and still not be complete because symptoms of resistance and self-protection are as diverse and unique as all other aspects of any given client's behavior. The list is provided as a means of getting therapists to think about how people manifest their discomfort or ambivalence about a process that many, on a conscious level, have actually initiated voluntarily. Thus any behavior clients express that appears to be designed to protect themselves from further (and painful) self-exploration, hinder change, slow down growth, or interfere with healing can be understood as a self-protective mechanism. These can be approached as resistance and as part and parcel of the therapeutic process. For therapists to be able to recognize self-protective mechanisms and to make use of them therapeutically and helpfully, they have to learn the purposes or sources of resistance. These sources or purposes are highly idiosyncratic to each client and are as diverse as the manifestations of resistance; however, they are general information.

Purposes and Sources of Resistance

Resistance can be understood from numerous perspectives. Psychoanalytic thinkers perceive resistance as a process through which the client keeps anxiety-provoking materials from conscious awareness (based on Freud's writings). Social learning theorists suggest that resistance is an expression of fear of consequences of changed behavior (Meier & Davis, 1993). Existential theorists propose that change threatens the "self-and-world" structures clients have come to rely on to create meaning and to understand the world and themselves (Bugental & Bugental, 1996). Behaviorists understand resistance as the response to inadequate reinforcement for change (Harris, 1996). Interpersonal theorists believe that clients resist by blocking self-disclosure until they feel safe in the therapist relationship (Teyber, 1997). Obviously, these theoretical beliefs will guide a clinician's understanding of the sources and purposes of self-protective mechanisms or resistance. Nevertheless, a generic discussion will be attempted here that may fit several theoretical frameworks or may be acceptable to more than one school of thought.

Resistance can occur when clients play out familiar relational patterns that they developed over the years to keep themselves safe in relationships (Teyber, 1997). Such behavior patterns may reflect approach–avoidance conflicts or other forms of ambivalence in relationships. Given the strong experiential and relationship focus of psychotherapy, it is not surprising that clients with such relational patterns will have difficulty with treatment and will evidence some signs and symptoms of resistance. Their general ambivalence and fear of relationships interferes with the therapists' need to establish a therapeutic relationship; this interference is not based on clients' active attempt to undermine therapy or be antitherapeutic, but rather must be understood from their idiosyncratic history and the role that behavior has played in the original environment. Such resistance is best understood as clients' attempts to keep themselves safe in the therapeutic relationship through the only means they know.

Resistance can occur when a client's defenses begin to break down and the person becomes vulnerable to those source feelings that are frightening and overwhelming (Kohut, 1984). When clients begin to recognize the affects they feared (such as shame, rage, anxiety, panic, emptiness, deep depression), they may mobilize old patterns of functioning that had a prior history of keeping these affects under wraps. In this case, resistance is truly a self-protection against painful affects emerging that the client did not anticipate as part of therapy. Thus even though clients may have originally been motivated for treatment, they may now hesitate due to their perceived (and real) vulnerability as therapy reaches a level that becomes more painful to them than their self-experience before therapy began.

Resistance can also occur later in treatment as the client is beginning to make behavior changes outside of the therapy room (Teyber, 1997). Such behavior changes may threaten current or past relationships outside of treatment, leading clients to fear the loss of significant others in their lives. Clients—when confronted with the reality that their own change (even if it was clearly for the better due to improved affect and clearer thinking) may interfere with their relationships—often try to protect themselves from these losses through changed attitudes about therapy. Often clients at this stage of resistance fear the loss of approval from parents, the affection of friends, or the intimacy with significant others.

In all three of these examples of complex motivators of resistance, the common theme remains self-protection. Clients protect themselves, as best they know how, from consequences, affects, behaviors, thoughts, or relational patterns that have become threatening to their self-integrity or self-experience in relationships with others. Most other reasons for resistance that have been addressed in the therapy literature will fit under this common theme. These reasons include, but may not be limited to, the following possibilities (based on Egan, 1994; Kohut, 1994; Morrison, 1995a; Patterson & Welfel, 1993; Teyber 1997; Wolf, 1988):

- fear of exploring painful past
- fear of painful needs re-emerging
- fear of regression
- fear of abandonment by significant others in the present
- embarrassment or stigma about being in therapy
- shame over having a problem that the client cannot solve independently
- guilt over asking for help
- apprehension about the difficult task of going through therapy
- fear of change and its consequences
- fear of criticism
- anxiety over others' reactions about the client's choice for therapy
- fear of losing control over emotions, thoughts, behaviors, and relationships
- fear of intensity
- fear of a general loss of control over one's own life
- fear of disorganization or loss of sense of self
- inability or reluctance to build trusting relationships
- testing a therapist's persistence and caring
- recapitulating a transference relationship

In reading over these possible sources of resistance, it is striking that all involve a component of painful affect (shame, fear, embarrassment, loss of control). It is critical that therapists become sensitive to the fact that this is the essence of true resistance: clients are fearful, not obstinate; they are replaying old patterns, expressing old affects, and using old cognitions to process a current relationship. The only means of self-protection they perceive is to use these protective strategies they have developed (and that once were adaptive) and have used for many years. If thus understood, resistance can no longer be perceived as something the client does that is antitherapeutic, willfully negative, or by design counterproductive. Instead, resistance is then viewed as a safeguard and as evidence of the great vulnerability the client perceives in the therapy setting.

That these safeguards or protective mechanisms are mobilized in the present therapy relationship also implies that the therapist may contribute to the client's perceived vulnerability (Wolf, 1988). As such, one source of resistance can always arise from the therapist who may be inappropriately attuned or responsive to a client or who may otherwise stimulate the client's self-protective mechanisms (Harris, 1996). As such, therapists must always consider the following possibilities when clients fail to make movement in therapy or show evidence of significant efforts at self-protection:

- the therapist is disavowing or discouraging a client's affect
- the therapist is holding the client back due to a countertransference reaction
- the therapist is not empathically attuned to the client
- the therapist makes stereotypic or prejudicial assumptions about the client
- the therapist has engaged in unethical behavior with the client (e.g., dual relationships)
- the therapist is not sufficiently skilled in the use of therapeutic catalysts
- the therapist is unaware of therapy process
- the therapist is unable to form a therapeutic relationship
- the therapist fails to process the experiential, intersubjective relationship with the client

The perusal of these therapist factors clearly suggests that the source of the resistance is not always the client, but can also be the therapist. Careful introspection is necessary for a therapist to respond adequately and appropriately to a client's expressed self-protection and resistance. To summarize, the purpose of resistance is always a client's self-protection in response to a perceived threat to the self that results in the experience of vulnerability. The source of this perceived vulnerability, however, can emanate from the client or from the therapist. As such, resistance is always something that the client contributes to treatment (i.e., it is the client's self-protective behavior that is being addressed and processed in therapy) but stimulating it can be the responsibility of the client *or* the therapist. Stated differently, resistance is a client (not therapist) behavior, but the source of resistance arises in the relationship, is experientially based, and hence is as intersubjective and jointly contributed as all other processes in the therapy relationship. This conceptualization of resistance has clear implications for intervention (i.e., for how to deal with resistance) because the source of the resistance may be as important in that process as its purpose.

Dealing with Resistance as a Helpful Therapeutic Process

Given the understanding of resistance as self-protection, it is most important that the therapist does not falsely challenge or attempt to eliminate the defense. If clients feel sufficiently vulnerable in the therapy relationship to use self-protective mechanisms to keep themselves safe, it is not a good idea to strip them of these defenses and leave them even more vulnerable and exposed. As such, clinicians have advised that it is best to respect resistance, to understand it, and only then to explore it (Meier & Davis, 1993). It may be helpful to slow down the therapy process because the clinician may be pushing too hard or too fast for the client to be comfortable. Slowing down the process allows the client to develop trust and safety before delving into particularly painful content and affect (Wolf, 1988). Further, because change is never easy, it is helpful for clinicians to empathize with any ambivalence clients have about change (Harris, 1996). Additionally, given that the therapist can be the source of resistance, it is good standard practice to explore the therapist's own contribution to the client's signs and symptoms of resistance and to assess whether these self-protection needs could have been avoided through a behavior change by the therapist that would have been more therapeutic (Morrison, 1995a). This latter caution is not to suggest that therapists change their behavior if it was therapeutic but difficult for their clients. In other words, sometimes therapists have to intervene in a manner that is painful or anxiety-provoking for the client; clients do not always leave sessions feeling better than they did when they arrived. Therapy work is difficult and challenging. Thus therapists should not change their behavior because their clients react with painful emotions if the therapists' behavior was therapeutic and well-chosen. Therapists' behavior as source of resistance is only changed if it is therapeutically inappropriate (i.e., was listed above as a possible source of resistance).

Once therapists have explored these basic possibilities of overcoming or dealing with resistance (i.e., have looked at and adjusted their own contributions, have assessed the appropriateness of slowing down the process to allow the client to build more trust and safety) and have decided that these approaches do not suffice to deal with the self-protective process set in motion by their clients, they will move toward more active attempts at dealing with clients' resistance. The first step in this process is to acknowledge the presence of clients' needs for self-protection and to accept their right to slow down the therapy process through the use of these strategies. Part of this acceptance is an educational response that helps clients recognize that most clients struggle with some ambivalence about treatment and that some resistance to change is normal and common. It can be very helpful for the client to hear it acknowledged that resistance is an important part of stabilizing one's life and of keeping in charge or control over events (Harris, 1996)

If an important aspect of clients' resistance is the issue of trust and safety in the therapy relationship, it is helpful to encourage these clients to talk about their conflicted feelings about therapy and about the relationship with their therapists. If this exploration of the therapeutic relationship reveals a mismatch between client and therapist, resistance is sometimes best overcome through switching therapists. Of course, this should not be the standard answer to client resistance, but it must be acknowledged that sometimes a particular client and therapist simply do not work well together, for whatever reasons. To try to force either individual to persevere in working with the other would be wasteful and unnecessarily painful for the client (and perhaps even for the clinician). An intervention at this stage might best be introduced with a statement such as "I noticed that after I said . . . you grew quiet, and since then you haven't really said much more about yourself. I wondered what happened." or "I noticed that you were a few minutes late the last three times we have met. I wonder if something is going on between us or in here that we need to talk about." Such statements give clients permission to talk about their withdrawal and give the clear message that clients are not being blamed but are certainly encouraged to talk about their reactions or experiences. If clients remain reluctant to talk about the process or relationship, they need to be gently encouraged to do so.

If this process is not sufficient in itself to resolve the client's fear, ambivalence, or other vulnerability, the clinician initiates a joint exploration of the purpose of the resistance with the client. In this process, client and therapist take a look at the fact that the resistance is a coping mechanism that was developed by the client some time ago and that may have outlived it usefulness. In that context, the adaptive value of the protective mechanism is explored, and the client's associated ambivalent feelings about change or therapy are addressed. This exploration is not meant to talk the client out of the resistance. Quite to the contrary, it acknowledges the client's need for it (Bugental & Bugental, 1996) and provides acceptance and understanding. Challenging the resistance is a mistake that only leads to more resistance because it means asking clients to let go of the only behaviors that they have in their repertoire of skills that they perceive as able to keep them safe. Asking clients to relinquish their resistance would thus mean stripping them of the only defense they have to keep themselves protected (Brems, 1993; Bugental & Bugental, 1996). Relinquishing resistance or protective strategies will occur naturally as treatment progresses and as the client internalizes strength and learns new coping strategies. As such, the need to explore self-protection that takes place at this level of intervention is one that delves into the reason for the resistance (i.e., the fear that underlies it), not the content (see also Teyber, 1997). In other words, therapists do not challenge clients by forcing them to confront their feared affects or needs, but do help clients process their fears of the affect and clients' needs to protect themselves from it. An example of a therapist and client processing a self-protective strategy follows:

THERAPIST: I noticed that the last couple of times we met, and then again today, that you were late for your session. I wonder if something happened between us that we need to talk about?

CLIENT: No, not really.

THERAPIST: Okay. I just wanted to let you know that if you ever do feel uncomfortable or reluctant about something, we can talk about that. It is very normal for people in therapy to feel ambivalent sometimes or to feel cautious about bringing something up with their therapist that was maybe upsetting to them.

CLIENT: Okay. But it's really just that I have been having car trouble and it's been a bad coincidence that I've been late for my session. . . .

THERAPIST: Okay; well, I just want you to know you can talk to me if something goes wrong between us or if you feel uncomfortable about something in here. All right?

CLIENT: All right.

THERAPIST: What have you been thinking about this week?

(The therapist provides an educational response and then decides not to challenge the client further, merely making a closing comment to move ahead with other things.)

(next session, client is late again)

THERAPIST: Remember last week, I mentioned your being late and wondered if something about our work was maybe a bit difficult for you, right?

CLIENT: Yes?

THERAPIST: Well, I'm noticing that you are late again today and I wonder if you're maybe having a hard time letting me know what's going on between you and me? Did something happen that is hard for you to talk about?

CLIENT: No—not really.

THERAPIST: If there were, would you be able to tell me?

CLIENT: I'm not sure. . . .

THERAPIST: What might get in the way of you telling me?

CLIENT: Well, I'm not sure if I could tell you if I thought you didn't understand something I said.

THERAPIST: What would be hard about telling me that maybe I didn't respond to you quite right?

CLIENT: Well, you might get upset and that would be scary for me.

THERAPIST: What needs to happen between the two of us so that that would be less scary, so that you can feel safer with me?

CLIENT: I'm not sure. I'm reluctant to tell people if they do something wrong or if I don't like something they did. . . .

THERAPIST: Tell me more about that. What's hard about it?

(The client and therapist move on to talk about the purpose of the client's resistance without delving into the content; i.e., they do not touch on the actual behavior in which the clinician engaged that was hurtful to the client and resulted in her self-protective response. However, they are processing this issue indirectly by exploring what purpose her avoidant behavior serves, not just in therapy but in general. This exploration will be therapeutically valuable and could only arise out of the recognition that the client had withdrawn from the clinician.)

(next session; client is on time)

THERAPIST: What have you been thinking about this week?

CLIENT: Well, I've thought some more about how I can't tell people what I really think, especially if they did something to hurt or upset me. I guess I have felt that way with you too—maybe it's just that I am not sure that you will still like me and want to work with me if I confront you like that?

THERAPIST: It's tough for you to trust that I'll stick with you no matter what happens.

CLIENT: Yes, so many people in my life have come and gone! I just don't trust that you'll really be there for me when I need you.

(The client and therapist are now beginning to get to the core of the client's relationship problems, and this was facilitated by processing the client's resistant behavior. Also note that the client, once the resistance was acknowledged and processed more persistently, began coming on time.)

This example demonstrates that even dealing with a client's resistance is an interpersonal process that needs to be engaged in carefully and respectfully. The client is not asked to give up her resistance (i.e., is not told "You have to be on time next week"; "You have to tell me if I did something wrong," or "You have to share all your thoughts and fears with me") but is merely encouraged to take a look at the purpose of her resistance ("Is something going on between us?", "Is there something you are afraid might happen if you . . ."). She is also not forced into processing the resistance until the therapist is certain that she has understood the meaning or purpose of the resistance. It was for that reason that the discussion was brief the first time the therapist raised the issue but persistent the second time. Further, the example demonstrates that the processing that does take place centers on the client's reluctance or on her need for the self-protective mechanism, not on the content that is feared. Such respectful exploration of clients' resistance or needs for self-protection often leads to major therapeutic breakthroughs because it communicates to clients that their therapists understand and accept clients' need to keep themselves safe for now, and they allow clients to explore why they need to keep themselves safe. Once clients' needs for self-protection have been processed, the resistance will often resolve naturally and painlessly for clients (as shown in the example when the client initiated the topic of trust with the clinician and arrived on time for her next session).

PHASES OF PROCESS IN THERAPY

The processing of the therapeutic relationship and of a client's self-protective strategies in that relationship occurs throughout therapy. It waxes and wanes in importance, depending on the stage or phase of therapy that has been reached with a client. In fact, the phase of treatment often carries with it strong implications about what catalysts to use at any given time and how thoroughly to explore the process in the here and now. Therapy has been consistently conceptualized in the literature as consisting of three stages: beginning, middle, and end. These stages have specific purposes and serve to clarify for client and therapist that their relationship will change over time (see Alexander, 1994). As such, the beginning stage of therapy has been identified as the time period when client and therapist get to know each other, learn the rules of treatment, collect data, and build rapport. The middle stage of therapy is identified with working through, and represents the bulk of the therapeutic work the client and therapist engage in together. The end phase of therapy is preoccupied with termination issues as client and therapist recognize that goals have been achieved.

Superimposed on these concrete stages of therapy are four phases of processing, each of which can occur in any of the three stages but that tends to be most pronounced in the first or second. These four processes are recollection, reconstruction, re-experience, and resolution or rehabilitation. The recollection phase of process overlaps to a significant degree with the beginning stage of therapy, but does not necessarily end there. Recollection can occur during any stage of therapy. Reconstruction occasionally begins during the beginning stage of therapy, but more commonly and pervasively occurs in the middle stage. Re-experience never occurs in the beginning stages of therapy, but is generally limited to the middle stage of therapy, though it may at times occur with lesser intensity during the end phase of treatment. Resolution or rehabilitation occurs most intensely in the middle stage, but may well continue into the final stages of treatment. This is particularly true with multiple presenting problems, the resolution of which may occur at differing intervals.

Each phase has implications for therapist behavior and can be useful in making some predictions about client behavior. It is also important to note that a client can have completed different phases of a therapeutic treatment plan with regard to their different goals or problems. As such, a client may have reached the resolution phase with regard to one presenting concern while still being stuck at the recollection or reconstruction stage with another. The recognition of where in the process the client is with regard to a given problem, concern, or issue helps the therapist respond appropriately to explorations of that particular content. It prevents premature interpretations in areas where the client has not yet reached a thorough level of self-understanding as well as overly superficial processing in areas where the client has achieved greater self-awareness and acceptance. Thus familiarity with the phases of process helps the therapist decide how and when to intervene. It guides catalyst selection and decision-making about which types of therapy and relationship processes to emphasize or facilitate. For example, in earlier phases, the therapist may emphasize a corrective emotional experience or holding environment, whereas in later phases using resistance processing or exploring transference is more strongly indicated. Each phase of therapy will be discussed below. An overview of the phases and their associated client variables, catalyst selections and emphases, and process priorities is provided in Table 6.1.

Recollection

In the recollection phase, clients share current data, recollections of past events, and information about themselves that is requested by the therapist. Although the recollection process begins during the intake, it is by no means completed during that stage of therapy. Recollection represents a relatively matter-of-fact presentation of data, much of which is recalled by clients on request by therapists. In fact, although therapists explain during the intake why they require these data, clients may oftentimes not be entirely clear why the therapists are asking for all of this information. Nevertheless, most clients easily comply with the recollection aspect of therapy, because it is generally not very threatening to them. Recalling events or presenting current data is relatively free of affect and hence is not too difficult for

TABLE 6.1   The Phases of Therapy Process

Phase/Stage	Client's Experience and Actions	Client's Level of Understanding	Catalysts Used by Therapist	Therapy Processes Emphasized
Recollection (mainly beginning)	providing information sharing memories disclosing on request	no conscious tie to presenting problem or etiology	attending, listening, responding (open questions) catharsis	holding environment incidental corrective emotional experience
Reconstruction (mainly middle)	affective involvement in memory and information sharing spontaneous self-disclosure	still no direct tie to etiology, though affect is recognized as out of proportion	attending, listening, responding catharsis empathy and understanding identifying/labeling affect imparting information asking clarifying questions	corrective emotional experience holding environment beginning transference resistance processing
Re-Experience (mainly middle)	affective expression in the here and now with recollection of past events spontaneous self-disclosure spontaneous linking/insight beginning self-awareness beginning self-acceptance	beginning recognition of a tie between current issues and past events	all catalysts: emphasis on advanced affective self-awareness techniques emphasis on cognitive self-awareness techniques, especially process comments and explaining strategies	transference corrective emotional experience holding environment projective identification beginning internalization resistance processing
Resolution/Rehabilitation (middle and end)	self-affirmation self-soothing skill development problem resolution	tie forms between presenting problem and other issues/etiology insight and self-understanding	all catalysts: emphasis on advanced explaining techniques some advanced affective awareness catalysts used	transference resistance processing internalization insight termination

clients. Clients, in other words, do not necessarily make a conscious connection between the data that are being talked about and the presenting problems that brought them to treatment.

In this phase of therapy, clinicians mainly attend to their communication skills by using catalysts such as attending, listening, and responding. They will use many open questions to facilitate clients' self-disclosures because much of their clients' sharing is done not spontaneously, but rather on request by their therapists. This phase of treatment can be cathartic for the client should some emotion regarding events in the here and now occur. However, any affective work or experience that emerges during this phase is less likely to be oriented toward gaining self-awareness because it represents the client's current affective state that may have been part of the reason for presentation to treatment. Cognitive awareness catalysts are not appropriate at this phase of treatment, and neither are advanced affective self-awareness techniques. The therapist provides a holding environment in which clients can feel comfortable with their level of self-disclosure, and this holding environment may provide occasional, yet incidental (i.e., not planned), corrective emotional experiences. Little relationship processing takes place at this time, because the client and therapist are still building rapport and determining whether they will engage in therapeutic work together. Once the client begins to connect with the therapist and begins to move beyond simple recollection of events, the next phase of therapy has been initiated. This may occur uniformly across all presenting problems the client is dealing with, or it may occur selectively. It is possible that a client begins to become affectively involved in therapeutic work around certain issues while still avoiding others. In that case, the client has moved on to reconstruction for some issues, but remains in the recollection phase with others. Therapists must be cognizant of the differences in their clients' experiences across topic areas to ascertain whether they will respond most empathically to the client. The following is a transcript that is typical of a client–therapist interaction in the recollection phase of treatment. It follows the same case of a depressed male client that was presented in prior chapters. In this transcript, the client and therapist are working on data collection around the client's relationship with various family members over the years.

CLIENT: Well, my mother had to be in the hospital for quite a few weeks at that time. I think she may have been hospitalized even longer than she was when I was a little kid, and she got so depressed.

THERAPIST: But you don't remember just how long she was there?

CLIENT: No, I didn't live at home anymore by that time. I was living in Arizona, and I really did not keep in touch much with my family. I guess once I moved I sort of became less and less a part of the family. . . .

THERAPIST: Less so than before?

CLIENT: Yeah—we were never really close, as I said before. But once I moved out it was like I didn't exist for them anymore. Even my oldest brother and I lost touch, and we had been the closest before I moved.

THERAPIST: You didn't talk to him much anymore after moving?

CLIENT: No, we called each other on birthdays—the first couple of years we talked on Christmas and maybe occasionally if something special happened to one of us. But that faded out over the years too. And now he is dead. That is still hard to believe!

THERAPIST: How about with your other siblings? How did your relationships change over time with them?

CLIENT: Well, I was never particularly close to my oldest sister. She moved out early and had kids of her own. I think she was really unhappy at home, and she wanted nothing to do with us after she first got married. My mother was very upset about this.

THERAPIST: How about you?

CLIENT: It didn't really matter much to me because I never had much to do with her before that. Plus my oldest brother was still around for me then, so he was really the one I would have missed if he had moved out.

THERAPIST: You really were close. . . .

CLIENT: Yes, I miss him; strange, isn't it? All these years I never called or talked to him and I didn't miss him. I guess I knew he was there and that was enough. Now he's gone and now I suddenly realize that I loved him—*(voice drops; lips quiver)* now that it's too late. . . . *(cries quietly)*

THERAPIST: *(silent; allows for the grief to emerge)*

CLIENT: *(After almost two minutes the client looks up and grabs for a tissue.)* I guess I need to learn something from this. That's why I called—really—and came here. I don't want to die with a lot of regret about relationships I never had

THERAPIST: Yes, you want to take a look at what you can and need to change in your life.

CLIENT: Yes! Like with Sandra—we used to be so good together. But now I feel her slipping away from me. I couldn't handle losing her—she means too much to me.

THERAPIST: Tell me about your relationship with Sandra.

CLIENT: Well, I don't know where to start? *(looks questioningly)*

THERAPIST: Well, let's see. How about we go in chronological order. How and when did you meet?

This excerpt of an early session outlines how, during recollection, current affect may emerge and is dealt with through acknowledgment and acceptance. However, it also demonstrates how data collection keeps the work focused and goal-directed in a way that keeps the client safe from premature painful reconstruction or re-experience. Instead, the therapist pursued with the client the details of his life and allowed for spontaneous disclosure when it happened, but was more likely to encourage disclosure using open questions. That a holding environment was clearly provided was shown when the client felt safe enough to mourn his brother's suicide and cathartically express grief. Detailed reconstruction, however, either of current or past painful events was neither initiated nor encouraged at this time because the therapeutic relationship had not yet matured to a level at which the therapist knew the client felt safe with more intense emotional involvement. Should he have expressed intense and prolonged painful affect spontaneously, and expressed trust and safety with the therapist spontaneously as well, client and therapist would have moved into the reconstruction phase of process.

Reconstruction

In the reconstruction phase, the client begins to tie affect to the recalled events or the current data that are being shared. This affective involvement presumes a certain level of trust between client and therapist; hence, reconstruction generally signals that therapist and client have moved beyond the beginning stages of therapy. Most generally, once clients have moved into reconstruction even in just a single content area that is being dealt with in therapy, they have left the beginning stages of treatment and have entered the middle stage, a stage that presumes their rapport and commitment to therapy. Thus moving on to reconstruction tends to be a good sign that the client has begun to work in therapy and is a good prognostic indicator for consistency in appointments.

In the reconstruction phase, the client not only recollects events or shares information about current events, but becomes affectively involved in this recollection and recounting. This affective involvement means that the client will experience feelings that were related to past events at that time and will recognize affects about current events that until that time may have been relatively hidden or unconscious. This often makes the reconstruction phase difficult and startling for clients because they may not have expected to feel emotional about some of the material that they are now talking about. Clients are not yet clear about cause-and-effect ties between events and emotions and may be somewhat startled by their emotional responsiveness and reactions. For example, clients may become tearful and sad while recounting childhood events without fully recognizing the relevance of a given event to their current situation. Clients will realize that certain childhood events are somehow of significance because they have this unexpected emotional response to the situation. It is not uncommon for clients to cover the same topical ground that they covered during recollection; the primary difference in the recounting of these events is that they are now involved affectively, whereas before they merely recalled events without the emotional response. Further, the client's disclosures are now spontaneously and intrinsically motivated. The therapist's use of questions during this phase decreases significantly as the client begins to have an internal motivation for sharing.

Differentiating between recollection and reconstruction is important and relatively easy. If clients are affectively involved with the material that is being shared, have made emotional connections with their therapists, and are beginning to disclose spontaneously, they have moved into reconstruction. It is possible for clients to skip the recollection phase altogether for some events, especially if they have had prior therapy or are in a state of crisis. Differentiating between recollection and reconstruction is important, because the catalysts on which the therapist will rely to keep therapy going will be somewhat different. Clinicians continue to use all of their communication skills to facilitate catharsis. However, most importantly, they now add empathic understanding responses to their repertoire of reaction. Some basic identification and labeling of affect is also useful for clients who may become overwhelmed or bogged down by emotions that appear unfamiliar or frightening. Imparting information can be helpful most particularly for normalizing some of the client's therapy experiences as well as in reframing and providing psychoeducational information. The therapist can begin to ask clarifying questions during the reconstruction phase, but will in all likelihood not use any more advanced insight-creating strategies. The prime function of this phase is for clients to become more affectively aware and vulnerable, a state of being and experience that is motivating for change and growth.

Empathic understanding is perhaps the most crucial of catalysts in this phase of treatment. In other words, therapists intervene with great empathic concern and then communicate to their clients that they both understand and accept the affects and needs that are beginning to emerge in the therapy setting. This empathic response is critical because clients themselves are somewhat startled and overwhelmed by their emerging needs and affects. Having the experience of being accepted for or in spite of these strong reactions is often extremely important to successfully negotiating this phase of treatment. If interpretation were to begin at this phase, the client would most likely shut down and withdraw from treatment. This is so because interpretations at this phase would be experience-distant and would be perceived by the client as contrived and confrontational. Self-acceptance and understanding must precede insight, and self-understanding only begins to emerge during reconstruction. The empathic skills of the therapist will be critical to helping clients develop the beginning self-acceptance that ushers in the re-experience phase.

Common therapeutic processes that begin to emerge in this phase of treatment are the client's continued and even stronger need for a holding environment and the opportunity for corrective emotional experiences. Toward the end of the reconstruction phase, and often ushering in the re-experience phase, clients will begin to develop certain transference themes, and therapists will begin to have their first insights of countertransferences they may be developing with clients. Some resistance is likely to develop at this phase of therapy because a client begins to feel more vulnerable; this vulnerability will stimulate the client's prior means of self-protection and may result in some reconstruction work being closed down. Thus it is not surprising to have some movement back and forth between recollection and reconstruction. However, if this vacillation occurs, therapists must respond to their clients as if they were in the reconstruction phase, even if clients regress to purely recollecting what has occurred. This response by the therapist includes the need to process resistance and it helps the client begin to recognize that therapy is different from other interpersonal relationships. It is in this context as well that corrective emotional experiences become particularly likely and important. As the relationship between client and therapist grows in importance and impact, the client cautiously begins to enter the re-experience phase. This shift in experience on the part of the client is most easily recognized by a shift to the importance of the relationship between client and therapist in the here and now. The client will begin to make comments or will begin to show clear reactions to the therapist's interventions and comments. Once clients begin to form transference relationships with their therapists, the therapists must recognize that they have moved on to the re-experience phase of treatment. Following is a transcript that is typical of a client–therapist interaction in the reconstruction phase of treatment. This one follows the same case of the depressed male client that was presented in prior chapters and earlier in this section. This excerpt focuses on an exchange that happened around the fifth week of treatment and that signaled that the client had moved firmly into reconstruction.

CLIENT: Sandy was very upset with me again today. I am such an idiot! *(forceful voice)* I did it again! She told me that she was going to dinner with a friend of hers, and I just left the room—didn't even look at her, didn't say a word. Can you believe it? I am so stupid! Of course, you can believe it. You've heard this from me every week. You probably think it too!

THERAPIST: Think what?

CLIENT: That I'm stupid. Why am I getting so upset that she wants to have friends besides me? Why can't I just accept that I'm not enough for her! I guess I really want her world to revolve around me!

THERAPIST: You'd like to be the center of her universe. . . .

CLIENT: Yes! *(slumps down; voice lowers)* Why? Why do I need her so much? She doesn't need me. . . . *(starts to weep)*

THERAPIST: It is very sad for you to feel like you need her more than she needs you. . . .

CLIENT: Yes, I want her to love me as much as I love her. I do love her, you know. So much that is hurts. *(very quietly)*

THERAPIST: Like it hurts right now. . . .

CLIENT: Yes. *(cries more openly now)*

This excerpt demonstrates the amount of spontaneous disclosure that occurs in the reconstruction phase. The client chose to talk about a painful situation involving his significant other. He made this choice knowing that it would be a painful matter to talk about, and he took this risk knowing that his strong feeling would be safe with the therapist. He relied on the holding environment to help him process and express his affect, and he was encouraged to do so by the therapist's empathic interventions. The interchange, despite its depth of affect and a clear connection between therapist and client, was a reconstruction, not a re-experience. The client made no attempt to understand his affect, but merely noted that he was overwhelmed by it and that he did not understand it. The therapist also chose not to move to a process or catalyst that would go beyond affective awareness; she noted that not enough work had been achieved in treatment so far to make more advanced interventions appropriate. She chose instead to respond with empathy and understanding for his affective experience and indicated by her empathic response her acceptance of his experience although she was not agreeing with his own assessment that he was overreacting. This intervention was chosen to help the client recognize his affect as valid with the intention of leading to an acceptance and a sense of feeling affirmed and understood. It should also be noted that in this excerpt, a hint of a beginning transference emerged as well. Specifically, the client expressed his concern that the therapist may think him "an idiot." However, this possible transference was very tentative and hence was not responded to directly. It did suggest, however, that the client would be able to move deeper into treatment, getting ready for the re-experience phase.

Re-Experience

The re-experience phase of treatment is marked by expressions of needs and affects in the here and now that are both relevant to the current relationship with the therapist and to past events and affectively charged past relationships. Clients are beginning to grasp the fact that their current reactions are somehow tied to their past experiences and are now becoming aware of some of the deeper meanings of their reactions in the therapy room and with the therapist. Present psychological and emotional states are related to past ones that may have contributed to current issues or presenting problems at least at an affective level. In other words, clients begin to realize that there is a tie between their emotions and needs in the here and now and old emotions and needs that developed in past relationships. These clients may not yet understand the specifics of these ties but are certainly aware that neither experience exists in a vacuum. One way clients are beginning to recognize the tie of here and now events to past events is by recognizing that current relationship issues with the therapist often lead to recollections about past events that triggered similar affects or needs. Clients are also becoming more aware of overreactions or strong need states in the present and the likelihood that such responses that are apparently out of proportion indicate that the current situation is triggering old emotions.

Given the spontaneous linking that is possible at this phase of treatment, it is not surprising that at this time the full arsenal of catalysts is used by the clinician. Client and therapist begin to work on tracing affects and needs to their sources, are beginning to explore patterns in the client's experience, are confronting incongruence and inconsistencies in the client's life, and are beginning to use explaining strategies to help the client recognize the sources of these current thoughts, feelings, behaviors, and relational patterns. It is less common to use more basic microskills, and the therapist is able to begin to use silence as a successful intervention tool. The transference relationship is fully developed at this time and considerable experiential processing of this relationship takes place. Process comments in the here and now about the transference relationship help point out patterns and critical links. All this work is thoroughly embedded in the interpersonal matrix of empathic concern and therapeutic rapport established during prior phases of therapy. Providing a firm and consistent holding environment and corrective emotional experiences becomes critical to the success of treatment. Resistance is processed as it emerges. Projective identification may be encountered and must be recognized, metabolized, and used to therapeutic advantage. The work the client and therapist are doing together to help the client become more affectively self-aware and self-accepting as well as more cognitively self-aware and able to cope leads to internalizations of skills by the client. The therapist's occasional empathic failures, embedded into corrective emotional experiences, facilitate this process of internalization and begin to help the client move toward the resolution or rehabilitation stages of process.

Re-experience is easily differentiated from reconstruction because it always involves a strong interpersonal experiential component in the relationship between the client and therapist. When the client is affectively aroused, the therapist feels fully connected to the client and the client feels fully understood and supported by the clinician. In the reconstruction stage, clients may sometimes feel alone in their feelings or needs because the therapist has not yet taken on the salient role in their lives that they will have during re-experience. Similarly, therapists may sometimes express these feelings on the outside during reconstruction, when the client is doing cathartic work. However, in the re-experience phase, the client and therapist are fully connected and emotionally bonded. This does not mean that the therapist will no longer make mistakes or fail the client occasionally. It merely means that if ruptures take place in the empathic relationship between the client and therapist during this phase of treatment, both the client and therapist will be keenly aware of them. It is critical at that time for the therapist to use corrective emotional experiences to allow the client to internalize emotion as well as to grow.

Luborsky (1984, p. 22) writes of the therapy process,

> The reexperiencing with the therapist in the here-and-now of the conflictual relationship problems gives the patients the most impetus toward meaningful insight and permits greater freedom to change. Past relationships gain in meaning when they are related to current ones. Keeping the relevance of the present in sight is one way for the therapist to insure that the insight is emotionally meaningful and not just intellectual.

It is this experience-nearness that is the critical component of this phase of treatment. Without it, therapy remains sterile and unsuccessful because it would have less emotional impact and meaning for the client. If client and therapist can successfully negotiate their transference relationship during the re-experience phase of treatment, the client will slip into the resolution phase almost automatically and unrecognizably. The boundary between re-experience and resolution or rehabilitation is, not surprisingly, very fluid and it is often hard to differentiate exactly when the client has moved out of re-experience and into resolution. However, this differentiation is not as critical as the movement between the other phases because the therapist's behavior can remain essentially the same across these two phases of treatment. Recognizing that a client has resolved an issue is most important in the sense that termination must be thought about once a client has reached the resolution for all or most of the presenting problems and has reached a level of rehabilitation of the self that enables this person's functioning to become healthier. Following is a transcript that is typical of a client–therapist interaction in the re-experience phase of treatment. It shows the same case of a depressed male client that was presented in prior chapters and earlier in this chapter. This interaction between client and therapist occurred around the twentieth session, by which time the client had firmly moved into the re-experience phase of treatment.

CLIENT: And so I think you can understand why I had to get so depressed! I just couldn't feel good about myself at that moment because I was weak—a wimp, like always. I try to be so strong, like I need no one. But then when it comes right down to it, I really need someone to take care of me!

THERAPIST: Yes, you feel that way with Sandra, you feel that way in here sometimes too, and I would guess that you felt that way with your mom?

CLIENT: Probably so. I hadn't really thought of it that way; I don't know if I can remember that far back. It strikes me as true, though. *(pensive)* But! I do know that when I felt like you didn't think I was tough enough to handle Sandra leaving for her trip this time, I felt pretty bad. *(stops himself)*

THERAPIST: Tell me more about that. *(calm, soothing voice)*

CLIENT: Well, it's important what you think about me. It's like with Sandra. I need her but I'm afraid to tell her because if I tell her how much I need her then I feel so vulnerable. Like she's going to leave me right there and then because she doesn't want to have to take care of me!

THERAPIST: And it feels that way with me sometimes?

CLIENT: Yeah; sometimes I'm afraid to tell just how much I need these sessions. Sometimes I can't wait for Thursday to get here to tell you about me and my week. The thought of you not being here is terrifying! *(slightly anxious, agitated)*

THERAPIST: That though is as bad as the thought of Sandra never coming back!

CLIENT: Yes. *(calms down; clearly felt understood)*

THERAPIST: What do you think is so frightening about the thought of either me not being here for you or of Sandra leaving?

CLIENT: I depend on you, I depend on you both. Like I never was able to depend on anyone in my life! Not even Jason!

THERAPIST: Not even your own mom!

CLIENT: *(looks up; then looks away and starts to sob)* That's it, isn't it? I'm still that scared little boy who is afraid that his mom is gonna leave again and that this time she'll never come back. *(cries)*

THERAPIST: *(long silence to allow for the affect to unfold)*

This excerpt demonstrates the emotional connectedness, transference relationship, and processing of events in the here and now that take place during re-experience. Client and therapist were firmly connected and in tune; the therapist was aware of and facilitated the client's experience in the therapy relationship while simultaneously tying this experience to the relationship with his significant other. The therapist communicated complete acceptance and understanding and thus provided the client with a corrective emotional experience: she did not judge him or humiliate him for his dependency needs. As the client moved toward generalizing his pattern of relating to others (bringing his best friend into the equation), the therapist decided that it was safe to make an interpretation that tied the current affect of the client to his relationship with his mother. The client clearly felt understood and perceived this interpretation as experience-near and relevant. His acceptance and elaboration of the explanation—and his ability to accept his own affects in the context of the therapeutic relationship and the holding environment that was provided—suggested that he was coming to some resolution with this aspect of his self-experience, perhaps getting ready to take a step toward rehabilitating his self-experience.

Resolution

Resolution and rehabilitation refer to resolving the presenting problems and rehabilitating the client's self-experience. Resolution implies that clients have worked through their presenting problems and have reached most, if not all, of their stated therapy goals. Further, they experience their Selves as more cohesive, vigorous, orderly, and conclusively healthier than before. They have developed (internalized) self-affirmation and self-soothing skills that were not present to the same degree before treatment. The client's self-experience, in other words, shifts significantly during the rehabilitation phase of treatment. Whereas it is generally the therapist who recognizes shifts between phases before, the shift between re-experience and resolution may be noticed by the client before it is noticed by the therapist. Clients often become aware of their greater inner strength and improved coping skills, feel more comfortable with their experiences in and out of the therapy room, and take charge of their lives both in and out of session.

For the therapist, the resolution phase is often somewhat anticlimactic because the most intense therapy work is carried out in the re-experience phase. Occasionally, therapists may not recognize the resolution phase until they notice that they are working less hard and using more silence, and that their clients are giving signals that they may be ready to end therapy. A sure sign that clients have reached rehabilitation is when they begin to do the therapists' work for them (e.g., by asking questions and providing their own answers). Clients' needs in the therapeutic relationship will either vanish or change in quality and quantity, and clients will function much more independently. A certain level of emotional detachment may be notable as the client moves away from the therapist during this phase to make more important attachments outside the therapy room. The intensity of the therapeutic relationship decreases and both client and therapist will be less intensely focused during and after their work together in each session.

The resolution phase overlaps to some degree with the end stage of therapy and often signals that termination needs to be initiated. Termination is a complex therapeutic process between client and therapist in itself and is therefore discussed separately in Chapter 8. Suffice it to say here that reaching resolution and rehabilitation clearly suggests to both client and therapist that their relationship as it has existed so far is drawing to a close and that both need to prepare for saying goodbye. Some assessment of treatment goals may need to be completed to reassure both client and therapist that they have indeed reached the goals they had set for themselves. This assessment will be done in the context of termination and review of therapy progress hence will be discussed in Chapter 8.

Resolution and rehabilitation clearly imply that a major shift has taken place in the client's self-experience and that treatment goals have been achieved. For most clients, this means that they have internalized new skills and self-perceptions. It may also imply that they have gained new insights. However, often clients are not able to verbalize the many insights they gained in therapy; instead, they speak of their shift in self-experience and of greater self-awareness and acceptance. If a client cannot recapitulate the many brilliant explanations offered by the therapist (and the client) over the many weeks or months of treatment, this does not mean that therapy was not successful. It is the internalization of change that signals rehabilitation, not the cognitive ability to retrace every insightful step that was taken in the process. With some clients, insight may never be verbalized; instead, these clients merely verbalize that they feel different than they did before treatment. Such a reality is particularly common with children and does not signal failure, but rather success of therapy. Following is a transcript that is typical of a client–therapist interaction in the rehabilitation phase of treatment, showing the same case of a depressed male client that was presented in prior chapters and above. This excerpt is from around the thirtieth session and reflects that the client has internalized much strength and the ability to affirm his own sense of goodness. He demonstrates self-acceptance as well as self-understanding and has clearly come to terms with, if not eliminated, his dependency needs.

CLIENT: And then I told Sandra that I was okay—that she didn't have to worry about me. She is still a little freaked out every time she has to travel because of my suicidal stuff when she had to leave last year. You remember that, don't you? *(smiles)*

THERAPIST: *(smiles back)* Yes; you've come a long way since then!

CLIENT: I don't even feel like the same person anymore. I mean, I can understand how it all happened. But I still look back sometimes and think "Wow, I was so needy." I mean, I realize that I still depend on Sandra a lot—and on you, too—but I don't need her as much as I used to, you know? I can survive without her and before that I was never sure about that. The funny thing is that now that I know I can survive without her, I'm not as afraid anymore that she'll actually leave. I mean, it would still hurt. But it wouldn't kill me! Maybe that's why things are going better between her and me—I can let her go and so she wants to stay. Does that make sense?

THERAPIST: It sure does. How about in our relationship—do you feel the same way?

CLIENT: (looks puzzled)

THERAPIST: That you don't really need me anymore?

CLIENT: Oh—I don't know about that! *(gets a little agitated)* I haven't even thought about that!

THERAPIST: Well, maybe it's something to start thinking about.

CLIENT: Wow! I guess you're right. I have started to figure a lot of things out for myself.

(The client goes on to recite examples of how he has been able to take care of himself.)

This excerpt demonstrates how the client in the resolution phase has internalized strength and self-confidence and begins to recognize a shift in his relationships with others. He recognized this shift in his relationship with his significant other first, but then this understanding is redirected to look at his therapeutic relationship as well. Although a bit startled by this at first, he clearly and quickly recognized that he had indeed made a lot of changes and felt strong and capable in his own right. Given the centrality of his dependency needs in his original presentation for treatment, this interaction suggested to the therapist that the time for termination was indeed drawing near.

Concluding Thoughts about the Phases of the Therapy Process

Understanding how clients move through therapy helps therapists conceptualize their responses in a meaningful and planned manner. Being aware of the subtle differences between recollection, reconstruction, and re-experience helps the therapist prevent premature interpretations and at the same time avoids overly inhibited interventions when the client is clearly ready for more advanced therapeutic work. It must be stressed again that these phases are not orderly linear processes. Instead, they are merely a framework for the therapeutic work with clients. Some clients may skip some of these phases altogether. Some clients may persevere in one phase for a very long time before moving to the next, whereas other clients may move through some phases very quickly. Much of clients' movement is highly idiosyncratically determined by their presenting problems as well as the history or etiology of these. Further, it must be kept in mind that the movement through these phases is not necessarily parallel for all of the client's issues. A client may have resolved one issue completely while still struggling in the reconstruction or re-experience phase with another. Therapists must be aware of these differences in their interventions to tailor the therapeutic approach to their clients as much as possible.

Having a framework of phases is helpful in guiding therapists through the many complex relationship issues that emerge with clients. They can help anchor the therapists as they provide them with a framework for responding to and understanding what is happening. Awareness of the therapy phases helps therapists focus their interventions and attend to the necessary therapeutic processes that can serve to facilitate their clients' journeys. Especially for relatively inexperienced therapists, having such a framework or anchor can be a very stabilizing experience that helps them feel more confident and in charge of the sessions with the client. It also keeps inexperienced therapists from moving too fast with clients who need a little bit more time to move through the early phases of treatment. Nothing is worse than an overly eager therapist who attempts to make interpretations and insight-oriented interventions with a client who is still grappling with reconstructing affective experience. Having an awareness of phases will help therapists rein themselves in when necessary.

SUMMARY AND CONCLUDING THOUGHTS

Psychotherapy is a complex endeavor that is a cognitive and emotional challenge for the therapist. The better prepared the clinician is with regard to understanding what to expect and to conceptualizing how to relate to a client, the more likely the clinician will approach treatment in a relaxed and confident manner. In the same way that clients need to learn self-affirmation and self-soothing in their general lives, new or inexperienced therapists need to learn to self-affirm their strategy choices and intervention selections. Similarly, they must feel strong and capable of setting a therapy course that will be most beneficial for clients. As such, the therapist needs to be capable of being goal-directed, yet flexible; insightful, yet experiential; and focused, yet empathic.

Recognizing the strong experiential component of therapy and being prepared to process relationships, resistances, and other treatment challenges readies therapists for assisting clients with navigating their way through the four phases of therapy process. It also readies the therapist and client for the time when they must part ways, helping both deal fully and in a more healthy way for the termination process. Although the information that was presented in this book up to this point may suffice to commence psychotherapy, there are several additional cautions, skills, and strategies that can be used by clinicians to enhance, speed up, or otherwise support the therapeutic process. Cautions about and possible solutions to common treatment challenges will be covered in Chapter 7.

7

PRAGMATIC ISSUES RELATED TO PROCESS IN PSYCHOTHERAPY

*If I ignore the emotional plea and respond only to the words,
I will not be communicating with you, there will not be
a flow of understanding between us, I will not be feeling
you and so I will be frustrated and you will be also.*
—*HUGH PRATHER*, NOTES TO MYSELF

The information presented so far has perhaps provided the reader with a solid background in assessing, planning for, and facilitating the process of psychotherapy. However necessary this knowledge is, it is not sufficient to prepare a new or inexperienced therapist for work with clients. Instead, this clinician must also have pondered a number of questions about pragmatic issues in psychotherapy and must be prepared for some of the more unusual or less common challenges presented by clients on a regular basis. Although the solutions to these potential rough spots in therapy are implied in the process discussion that has already taken place in earlier chapters, it was deemed helpful to mention them separately and in their own right in this chapter for the novice clinician or the more casual reader. This list of suggestions or guidelines included here must not imply that readers would not or could not already have ascertained these answers on their own, but it does help them double check whether they have understood the spirit of the foregoing discussions and whether they can apply it in actual pragmatic situations that frequently occur with clients. Further, it must be noted that all the guidelines and suggestions provided in this chapter are somewhat subjective and are certainly not to be understood as the only ways of dealing with the questions or challenges posed. Instead, they represent only one way of dealing with these situations—a way that is considered compatible with the process concerns that have formed the foundation of the philosophy of therapy expressed in this book and that are used to guide the type of clinical and supervisory work on which it is based. Finally, in using the suggestions offered here, the reader must continue to keep in mind that in most interactions with clients around challenging situations, it is critical to evaluate the client's needs and the therapist's beliefs before reacting. Only if therapists can move beyond focusing on the overt actions of clients and truly try to understand the affects and needs that motivate them, will they learn to respond "correctly." The three process-related pragmatic issues that will be addressed in this chapter are:

- common questions pondered by therapists as they embark on therapeutic work with clients
- common challenges presented by clients in the therapy room through behavioral or relational patterns
- common intense affects expressed by clients in the course of psychotherapy and their management by the therapist

Common therapist questions revolve around issues or concerns that tend to be unclear or poorly defined in the mind of the novice or inexperienced therapist, but that are frequently observed as decisions made on the spot by the experienced therapist while with the client. Being prepared for these issues as they emerge helps the clinician react more gracefully and appropriately. The most common client challenges that will be addressed are forms of resistance, self-protection, symptoms, or mere relational patterns of the client in the here and now relationship with the therapist. Their exact classification is not as important in this chapter as the fact that all of them reflect situations that are common enough to be experienced by all therapists at some point in their careers and challenging enough to tax their patience or creativity. Common affects addressed in this chapter are intense emotions such as panic attacks, uncontrollable crying, and similar feelings of being out of control that emerge in therapy and that need to be managed by the therapist to keep the client safe.

The solutions and actions suggested here in response to common questions, challenges, and affects are most important for novice clinicians who have not yet worked out their own therapeutic styles and manner of confronting difficult therapeutic situations to follow very closely. More seasoned clinicians can afford to deviate from the suggested solutions on occasion because they have developed sufficient judgment about when an exception to the rule is appropriate and superior to the generic approach. Less experienced therapists should stick to the solutions suggested here to gain an appreciation of how clients react when therapists intervene in tough situations. Novice clinicians do not yet have the knowledge to identify when a client's situation manifests the exception to the rule; in all likelihood, less damage is done in a tough situation if—when in doubt—the clinician follows the suggestions provided here. It is critical to note, however, that none of these challenges has a single and unquestioningly correct or true way in which to respond; the suggestions offered here are merely an outgrowth of clinical experiences collected over years of doing and supervising therapy that have worked more often than not and that apply in most general cases. Beginning therapists should follow the format presented here in detail. Experienced therapists will learn to present the essence of the following suggestions (with appropriate modifications when indicated) more briefly and more idiosyncratically, and in a manner tailored to their own way of doing therapy.

COMMON QUESTIONS

Common questions that are posed to therapists, but that are often not covered in traditional psychotherapy texts, range from how to open a session to how to deal with between-session phone calls to whether to use strategies that involve homework or bibliotherapy. The questions that are posed and answered below by no means are meant to represent all the possible questions that a new or inexperienced therapist may need to ponder; they merely represent the most common questions I have encountered with my supervisees and in my readings. The answers to these questions are suggested as frameworks or guidelines, not as the final word on any one of them. They were arrived at through clinical experience as well as theoretical or philosophical beliefs about therapy. All answers are given to provide the most therapeutic response to the client from a perspective consistent with the philosophy and process understanding expressed in the book so far. As therapists encounter difficult questions or situations in therapy for which they do not have a ready answer and which are not covered here, the issue of what is therapeutic is the best guide to answering the question. All therapists have the answers to difficult questions within themselves; they merely need to ask how these situations need to be handled to result in the most therapeutic responses for their clients. The solutions suggested below will effectively model such problem-solving treatments and will help readers develop their own answers to these same questions or to similar questions that are not covered here.

Opening Questions and Closing Comments

A common concern therapists have is how to open each session with the client. Innumerable approaches to this question are available, and some possibilities are shared here. These possibilities are presented mainly as suggestions that give the reader some idea about how to make decisions about opening questions. They are based upon three guidelines that can be used to ponder the appropriateness of any potential opening question. First of all, opening questions should have a therapeutic purpose. They should not be random acts by the therapist, but should be well thought out to have a therapeutic meaning for each individual client. Second, opening questions are initiators of therapy, not social interaction; hence, they need to be phrased not just for a therapeutic purpose but also in a way to begin the therapeutic process immediately on entering the session. Third, opening questions need to be flexible enough to be individualized to render them optimally appropriate for a given client.

Opening sessions in a way that meets all three criteria can be done by using one of three fairly standard questions, depending on the dynamics of the client: (1) "How have you been feeling this week (or since our last session)"; (2) "What have you been thinking this week (or since our last session)"; or (3) "What have you been doing this week (or since our last session)"? These questions meet the criterion of therapeutic purpose. Each client presents with a primary problem that manifests in the areas of affect, thoughts, or behaviors. Depending on where therapists perceive the primary deficit to be, they want to place the therapeutic focus of their sessions with the client on that area of functioning as soon as the opening questions. As such, if the therapist is primarily concerned with a client's emotional well-being and wants therapy to focus on the client's affective state, the first question would be used. If a client's primary presenting problem is in the area of unusual or problematic cognitions and the therapist wants to work on these thinking patterns with the client, the second questions would be chosen to set both client and therapist on the right path. If the client's behaviors or relational patterns are the primary topic of therapy, the third questions would be chosen. As such, these opening questions have the purpose of directing client and therapist toward the most important topic of the therapeutic interaction.

These questions also meet the second criterion of not making therapy a social interaction. Inappropriate openers would be such questions as "How are you?", "How have you been?", "How's it been going this week?", "What's up?", and so forth, which are social questions that generally lead to superficial answers. The phrasing of the opening questions suggested here, on the other hand, is clearly different from what the client would be asked in social or casual contexts. The questions also meet the individualization criterion in that the most appropriate question is chosen for each client, given the client's presenting concerns or therapeutic issues that are being worked on at a given time. Further, the therapist can rotate the three questions with the same client over time as needed and as is appropriate for the therapeutic context of prior sessions or topics that are being explored.

Another question, or range of questions, that meets the three criteria of being therapeutic, nonsocial, and individualized is that which requests the client to reflect on the prior session. This can be accomplished through such questions as "What stayed with you from the last time we met?", "What did you think/feel/do about what we talked about last week?", "Of all the things we talked about last time, what left the most lasting impression on you?" Questions such as these start a therapy session right away by asking clients to tie their initial responses in the new session to content covered in the prior session. Such a question is never mistaken as social chitchat because it clearly orients the new session toward therapeutic content and emphasizes that both client and therapist are present to work on specific issues. Finally, the question can be individualized to the client by adding content the therapist remembers if the client fails to respond immediately or by adding content the therapist deems most important. For example, any of these questions can be individualized by stating them as follows: "Last week we talked about a number of things. The two that seemed most important to me were . . . and . . . What was it that left the most lasting impression on you?"

Other common opening questions include, but may not be limited to, such questions as "What would you like to work on today?", "Where would you like to start?", "Have you been thinking about our last session?", "Let's start with where we ended last week." Each of these questions has some advantages and some disadvantages. The clinician should approach each of these questions by checking it against the three guidelines provided above. For example, "What would you like to work on today?" clearly meets criterion two, which requires a nonsocial opener. However, using this question with all clients means that it is never individualized to a given client's needs. Additionally, it may not be a therapeutic question for all clients. Some clients may need for the therapist to be in charge of early sessions by guiding the client toward what therapeutic work is about. For such a client being put in charge of what to talk about or work on may not be therapeutic. Furthermore, some clients may not want to work at all and, if given the opportunity to choose the topic of work (as opposed to being directed to processing their feelings, thoughts, or actions), may choose to go with safe material.

A final option for opening sessions is silence. This works very well with clients who are therapeutically skilled or have been in therapy for a while and are aware of the demands of the situations. With these clients, it is sufficient to sit down and look at them to let them know that the therapist is ready to work. Silence is a wonderful opener when used with clients who can deal with it, but it can be extremely anxiety-provoking for clients who are new to therapy, not therapeutically inclined, or anxious to begin with. Thus if silence is chosen, it needs to be chosen wisely and needs to be used only if therapeutic for the client. The suggested opening questions can be combined with silence over the course of a single client's therapy. It is possible that early in treatment one of the three opening questions is most appropriate. The therapist may then shift to another question as treatment proceeds. Finally, the therapist may decide to allow the client to choose the opening of the session by using silence.

Closing comments refer to the final words therapists say to their clients as they get ready to leave the room. Again, many options exist, ranging from a simple "good-bye" to a more complex response. The preferred comment suggested here is one of caring that shows continuity across sessions. Specifically, a simple "See you next week; same time, same place. Take care." is a parting comment that reaffirms the standing appointment and the therapist's availability, as well as the continuity not just across time ("same time"), but also across space ("same place"). It also expresses the therapist's ongoing caring for the client ("take care").

Starting and Ending Individual Sessions

In traditional psychotherapy (as described in this book), a therapist usually frames a structure for the therapy that is presented during intake (or screening; see Chapter 1). This structure usually contains some guidelines about starting and ending sessions. Most commonly, sessions are scheduled for 45 or 50 minutes at the same time every week. Sessions always begin on time (even if the client arrives early) and always end on time. Questions arise most frequently when the client is late for a session. Should the client still be given the 45- or 50-minute session or only the remainder of the time that is left in the scheduled session? Should the client be seen at all? The answer suggested here is that the client be given the time that remains in the session, as long as enough time is left to do therapeutic work. It is best to stick to the time delimiters that were agreed on to begin with and to end the session at the agreed upon time regardless of the client's arrival time. As such, if the client arrives 10 minutes late for a 50-minute session, the client will have only 40 minutes of time with the therapist. This structure appears important because it provides both client and therapist with clear boundaries and limits that protect their psychological needs. If a therapist has scheduled another client, it would be very stressful to run overtime with a prior client because of the person's tardiness for a session. This stress would be acted out by the therapist at some point and a client would suffer. Similarly, clients may have other business after the end of the session, and running overtime with the therapy session may cause them stress and tension and make them less emotionally available in session.

If a client is very late for a session, the clinician may decide to skip a scheduled session with the client altogether. This is a decision all clinicians have to make for themselves. This decision should be based on considerations about how much time is needed with the client to provide a truly therapeutic service. If a therapeutic intervention can be accomplished in ten minutes, then a client may be seen even if the person is so late as to only leave 10 minutes in the session; if, on the other hand, therapists believe that they need at least 30 minutes with a client to get therapeutic work done, the session should be canceled if the client arrives more than 20 minutes late. If this occurs, the therapist may choose to take the client aside to the scheduled room to explain that insufficient time is left in the session to accomplish anything and that the therapist fears that if the client and therapist begin work together that day, they may open up issues for which there is not enough time to finish, making the client leave the session vulnerable or in crisis. The client and therapist then agree to meet again during their next regularly scheduled session. Alternatively, it is possible for therapists to explain this rule up front to their clients (e.g., during the intake) and then not be available to meet with clients if they arrive more than 20 minutes late.

Each therapist needs to make a decision about how to deal with these situations and needs to have a procedure in place when this becomes a reality. Trying to make such a decision when the event occurs leads to countertransferential decisions instead of healthy treatment-based decisions. Finally, therapists must also be aware that chronic lateness may need to be processed as a resistance issue (see the resistance example in Chapter 6). In addition to pondering the issue of a client being late for sessions, therapists must also ponder the issue of their own timeliness. Lateness by the therapist is incompatible with the values expressed in the therapeutic process, as defined in this book. Thus the best solution to this problem is not to allow it to happen. Life is not always ideal, however, and the occasion may arise when a therapist runs late (e.g., due to a crisis situation with a prior client that had to be resolved before the clinician could move on to the next session).

If the clinician is late, it is best to attempt to notify the client of this necessity rather than expecting the client to sit in the waiting room wondering. The therapist may notify the receptionist (if available) or briefly leave the situation that is causing the lateness to let the client know that the therapist will meet with the client as soon as possible. Once in session, therapists must immediately acknowledge their lateness to clients and must check in with clients to explore and address their reaction to the therapists' lateness. Lateness on the part of the therapist needs to be processed as an optimal empathic failure (see corrective emotional experience in Chapter 6) and generally carries with it an apology to the client. Fee payment may need to be adjusted if the therapist is very late. In most instances, client and therapist will still end at the regular time even if it was the therapist who was late, unless both client and therapist can agree freely and without constraints that they can meet for the full 45 or 50 minutes. Such an agreement is only possible if both client and therapist are free beyond the regularly scheduled time so that neither has to be nervous about being late or missing yet another appointment. If such an agreement is made, it must be clear to both client and therapist that it is an extraordinary arrangement and will not be engaged in on a regular basis.

Ending on time is important in all circumstances, whether related to the issue of lateness or not. Sometimes clients present very salient or crisis-related information at the end of a session in the clear (though generally unconscious) attempt to extend their time with the therapist. Such attempts by the client should not be responded to. Instead, sessions must end on time to communicate the therapist's clear boundaries and self-care skills. The therapist who runs overtime with a client fails to communicate strength and self-confidence. Such a therapist may be perceived as easily controlled or manipulated, and the client may perceive such loss of boundaries as permission to test other limits. Not running overtime helps put both client and therapist at ease because both know the parameters of the session and do not have to worry about their schedules after the session. It is very stressful for clients to think that their sessions may be open-ended because they may plan their lives around schedules.

The same is, of course, true for the therapist. Running overtime hardly ever communicates greater caring or concern (a common misconception) but instead suggests that the therapist has problems with setting limits or has a countertransference reaction with a client. One supervisee who ran chronically late with clients finally realized through some supervisory guidance that she did this because she had the firmly held belief that she was not a good enough therapist. Offering her clients an extra 5 to 10 minutes free at the end of each session was her way of affirming to herself that she was at least caring and generous. She failed to recognize that this behavior did not communicate this same message to her clients and that it resulted in poorer self-care for her when she had no time for herself between client sessions. Once she processed her countertransference of never being good enough, she was able to end on time and she became much more relaxed and available to her clients.

No-Shows and Cancellations

No-shows and cancellations are dealt with on a slightly more individualized basis, depending primarily on the type of relationship that has already been established with a given client. If clients fail to show for a first appointment, they may need to receive a call from the therapist to assess whether they have simply forgotten the appointment. If this is the case, the appointment is quickly rescheduled over the telephone (without engaging in a lengthy interaction with the client over the phone). If the same clients again fail to show for a second (i.e., rescheduled) appointment, no phone call is initiated, but clients instead receive friendly letters asking them to contact the clinic or therapist when they decide that they would like to begin to receive regular therapy services.

No-shows by established clients are somewhat more difficult to deal with and, to a large extent, depend on the history that has been established with a given client. If a client has never missed an appointment and suddenly fails to show for a session, more than likely the therapist will feel some concern about the client, given this unusual occurrence. Thus the therapist may choose to call the client during the scheduled time (for which the client is currently absent) to check that the client is safe and to reaffirm the next standing appointment. In most instances, the therapist and client would thus skip an appointment rather than reschedule it (the exception being a crisis that precipitated the missed appointment that needs to be dealt with swiftly). If clients who fail to show have had several standing appointments for which they did show, and then began to skip appointments, a phone call would be made only after the first appointment was missed in such a manner. If the client returns for an appointment, then skips, and so forth (i.e., establishes a less than regular pattern of attendance), this issue must be raised as a resistance issue in therapy. In all likelihood, a limit will need to be set on the no-show behavior because it interferes with therapy as well as with the therapist's livelihood. Assertiveness by the therapist about having a predictable schedule is important and needs to be presented to the client in terms of the therapeutic value of regular appointments for the client. Therapy cannot progress well if regularity is sacrificed for convenience in scheduling. Only through regular contacts can the transference relationship be maintained to a therapeutic degree.

Emphasis on regular attendance is also the guiding principle that determines how to deal with cancellation. Every client will need to cancel at one time or another. Though unfortunate, even clinicians may need to cancel appointments at times (e.g., due to illness, emergencies, or vacation schedules). Such occasional cancellations need not be overinterpreted. However, if a client begins to cancel frequently and appears to cancel with minimal notification time, this may present a pattern of resistance that needs to be addressed therapeutically by the therapist with the client during a regular session. Further, each clinician needs to have a rule about payment for missed sessions. The common rule of thumb appears to be to charge for sessions that are regularly scheduled and for which the client fails to show or gives less than a 24-hour notification of cancellation. Collection of fees for the missed session will take place during the next regularly scheduled time with the client.

If the therapist has to cancel the session, the client needs to be given as much prior notice as is therapeutic and feasible. Vacation schedules are generally set far in advance and, hence, can be discussed with the client with at least a month's notice. This provides sufficient time to process the client's reaction to the therapist's absence and to address any important therapeutic or relationship issues that emerge in this context. Illness, on the other hand, generally occurs more abruptly, so little prior warning may be possible. Such cancellations need to be processed with the client in the next scheduled session. With some clients such missed sessions may need to be processed as empathic failures on the part of the therapist; with more mature clients a simple apology and very brief explanation may suffice. It is probably not necessary to point out that clients are never charged for sessions canceled by the therapist.

Fee Payment

Two primary options are possible about when to accept payment for services: before the session begins or after the session ends. Several good reasons exist why accepting payment before the session begins may be the more optimal approach to this issue. Therapy sessions are not always easy for clients, and it can occur with some regularity that clients leave sessions feeling vulnerable, anxious, stressed, or otherwise affectively challenged. It is much easier for this client to be able to walk away from the session without having to deal with money matters at that time. Collecting fees before the session starts also ensures that the client cannot artificially extend the session around fee payment. Further, if the client fails to bring payment, this issue can then be discussed and processed in the session, as opposed to having to be dealt with outside of the session or during the session in the upcoming week.

Occasionally, therapists will arrange payment plans with clients or accept third-party payment. If this is the case, guidelines about this procedure need to be spelled out clearly. Both client and therapist need to be clear about when payment is required and how it is to be rendered. In this case, the main issue is to ascertain that the client feels the burden of responsibility for payment for services even if the therapist accepts a payment plan or third-party copayment. In other words, the client must be clear that the service rendered by the therapist is a valuable service that must be reimbursed in the most timely manner possible. If the client is seen under a managed care plan that requires a copayment from the client, the collection of the copayment should be handled in the same manner as all other fee payment. The client then needs to be made aware of the procedure the clinician follows to collect reimbursement from the managed care company (also refer back to Chapter 1 for a discussion of this issue). Should a third-party payor refuse payment, clients need to be aware that it will be their responsibility to make payment. These issues need to be clearly spelled out in the informed consent form and discussed with the client before initiating regular services (i.e., are best dealt with in the intake or first session with the client). Enforcing the guidelines agreed on will then need to be taken up during therapy and, as such, these will need to be carefully fitted into the therapy process. Refusal or lateness of payment may become a therapeutic issue that can be processed as resistance to therapy.

Some therapists and many mental health clinics operate on sliding fee scales. If this is the case, a fee needs to be agreed on before regular therapy services begin. If a client's financial situation changes during treatment, fees may need to be adjusted up or down. It is rare that therapists provide services that are completely free; more likely, they will negotiate a very low fee even for pro bono services. The literature has suggested that some fee payment is necessary so that clients understand and perceive therapy as an important component of their lives to which they need to make a firm commitment. Further, fee payment clarifies that the service provided by the therapist is valuable. Negotiating fees that are too low or setting fees at zero may inadvertently send a wrong message to the client. Instead of communicating caring and concern, it may communicate that the therapeutic service is not important or not valuable. Most clients are able to render some minimal payment for services, and this minimal amount must be negotiated and then must be both charged and collected regularly and without apologies.

Adhering to fee payment agreements appears to be particularly difficult for novice therapists who either still feel unsure about their ability or have the false idealistic belief that giving therapy away for free is a humane or right thing to do. These clinicians need to realize that even with their relative newness to therapy, they provide a valuable service. Further, they must understand that not collecting fees will undermine the therapist's authority, expertness, and trustworthiness in the eyes of the client. Finally, setting fees unusually low may also be a sign of other countertransferences that have nothing to do with the therapist's newness to therapy. Instead, this can occur even among seasoned clinicians. Thus if therapists note that they have agreed to an unusual fee schedule with clients, they need to evaluate whether this agreement was reached due to therapeutic reasons or due to countertransference reasons (e.g., attraction to a client, caretaking response, savior fantasies).

Phone Contacts

Therapists need to make their own decisions about how to handle phone contacts with clients, whether these contacts are therapist- or client-initiated. Most therapists rarely call their clients between sessions. In fact, the only times therapists tend to call clients are if the client has failed to show for a standing appointment that had been kept on a regular basis for some time (see above) or if the therapist needs to inform the client of a sudden need for cancellation or rescheduling. Usually, most phone contacts between client and therapist are client-initiated. If the client's phone contact is about a cancellation or a need to reschedule a session, it is, of course, extremely appropriate and can be dealt with quickly and easily. If the client calls to extend time with the therapist outside of sessions, however, firm limits will need to be set with the client lest the client and therapist develop an unhealthy alliance. As a rule of thumb, no therapeutic work is done over the phone between sessions. If clients call with an emergency, they should be encouraged to schedule an appointment with the clinician, if at all possible (no clinician will, of course, turn away a client who appears imminently suicidal or homicidal—every rule has its exceptions). Some therapists or clinics include a clause in their informed consent that clients will be charged for phone contacts that extend beyond a given number of minutes (most commonly 10 minutes). Two primary cautions about phone contacts between sessions concern where the therapeutic work is done and the need to establish firm and therapeutic boundaries. Regarding the first, in most circumstances it is more appropriate to keep therapeutic contacts between client and therapist limited to face-to-face contacts during regularly scheduled sessions. The second caution has to do with clients exploiting a therapist's willingness to have phone contact between sessions in an attempt to change the nature of the therapeutic relationship.

Related to phone calls with clients, though somewhat separate, is the issue of unlisted phone numbers for therapists. It is a good idea for mental health professionals to keep unlisted phone numbers to prevent clients from intruding into their private lives. Therapists must maintain clear boundaries between their work and private lives to prevent burnout and to take care of their own mental health needs. Making sure that clients cannot intrude on clinicians at home is one boundary that is very helpful in this regard. In addition to keeping phone numbers unlisted, therapists also need to be aware that should they ever make phone calls to clients from home, caller identification services are now available in most communities. Through caller identification, the party called can see the phone number of the caller on a digital display on the phone. Thus if therapists call their clients, they should assume that the clients have caller identification. This means one of three things: the therapist needs to be willing for the client to learn of the clinician's home phone number (not recommended), the clinician should never call from home (the best and easiest solution, because it also keeps work and private lives separate), or the therapist needs to have the phone line blocked from participating in caller identification. The latter is possible on a permanent or call-by-call basis and can be negotiated with the phone company that provides the caller identification service in the community.

Food and Drink in Sessions

Food and drink greatly distract from therapeutic work and are also strongly associated with social interaction. Friends and acquaintances eat together; family members join each other for meals. A therapeutic relationship needs to be set apart from social and familial interactions and, hence, food or drink is rarely appropriate in sessions, especially among novice clinicians who are still struggling to set and maintain appropriate therapeutic boundaries. Food or drink is also an excellent means for clients to distract themselves from therapeutic work or difficult affects. Clients can delay responses by taking a bite or a drink; clients can redirect anxiety or other affects by slurping on a soda or sipping on coffee. As a general rule of thumb, given the social connotations and affect-reducing properties of food and drink, they have no appropriate role in therapy. Certainly, a therapist would never eat or drink in clients' presence, if at all possible.

Are there exceptions to this rule? Perhaps. With some child clients, sharing food can be therapeutic (e.g., see Brems, 1993); however, if sharing food is considered, therapists must be clear that they permit this interaction for therapeutic, not social, reasons. It is also generally only used to celebrate special occasions or to make a therapeutic point; as such, sharing food may occur once in a client's entire course of treatment, but never on a regular basis. Other therapeutic exceptions can be made on a case-by-case basis, especially by more seasoned clinicians who are clear about when food is used therapeutically versus socially. For example, with adults as well as children, excessive shyness or embarrassment can initially be soothed by a relaxing cup of tea. If food or drink comes to be used as avoidance by either client or therapist, however, this must then be processed like any other therapeutic issue. Certainly, when deep emotional work is done, even a cup of coffee or tea would be out of place. However, after a particularly exhausting experience or catharsis, a cup of water or tea may help ground and stabilize certain clients sufficiently to help them leave the session intact. Finally, water may also be appropriate if there is a medical reason. If a therapist or client has a cold that results in frequent coughing that can only be alleviated with a drink, a cup of water in the therapy room may be appropriate. To reiterate, if a clearly defined therapeutic (or compelling medical) reason is available, food or drink may be used on a specific occasion; however, overall food or drink seldom has a place in psychotherapy. This is particularly true for inexperienced clinicians.

Also relevant to the discussion of food and drink is the issue of smoking. Smoking, more than any other behavior, can serve as an anxiety reducer and distraction for the client and should never be permitted. Smoking by the therapist is equally distracting and interferes with the type of empathic relationship that is deemed crucial to successful psychotherapy. Because of the unique relationship of therapy, it can never be assumed that a client's permission for the therapist to smoke is truly informed consent. Further, the profound health concerns of smoke in a closed room must be considered and must never be imposed on clients, even if they agree to the therapist's smoking or if they also smoke. Given these considerations, there appear to be no exceptions to the no smoking rule in therapy.

Homework

Although an integral and automatic part of some types of therapy, the issue of homework deserves some consideration before being used with a given client. Homework is not always a good idea, despite the fact that it is widely (and successfully) used by a variety of therapists. The potential drawbacks of homework need to be carefully weighed before a therapist decides to use this strategy. Most importantly, homework must not lead to shame, guilt, or fear on the part of clients should they fail at their assignments or should they not complete them. Additionally, homework needs to have a clear therapeutic purpose that cannot be achieved through in-session work. Finally, homework may need to be avoided with certain types of clients who may misunderstand or misuse it given their particular type of pathology or presenting problem.

One potential drawback of assigning homework to clients is the possibility that they are unable to complete it and then feel shame or guilt about their noncompliance with the therapist. These affects may then lead the client to avoid the therapy altogether, leading to no-shows or defensiveness with and apologies to the therapist. Either situation tends to be countertherapeutic. Homework in such instances can backfire because it does not meet its intended purpose, but rather can lead to side effects that actually hinder treatment. Given the potential drawbacks (i.e., guilt or shame about failure; defensiveness associated with not completing it), homework should only be assigned if the therapist is convinced of its therapeutic necessity and nature. Homework must have a clearly defined purpose; otherwise, the risks associated with it will not make it worthwhile. Assigning busywork that has no therapeutic value is counterproductive and in the long run will lead the client to noncompliance as well as to questions about the entire therapeutic process. If homework is assigned, the clinician must discuss with the client the therapeutic value of and reasoning behind the assignment and must also address the issue of possible noncompliance. Alternatively, therapists may phrase assignments that clients are expected to work on or complete at home in terms of options or opportunities, not homework. They would stress that the clients have the option to comply or not to comply depending on their preferences and state of mind. Leaving homework optional will eliminate the shame and guilt associated with noncompliance. Further, if a therapist chooses to assign or suggest homework, it is critical that this homework be appropriate to the client's current state of mind and abilities. Assigning homework that is too difficult will lead to failure and will reinforce low self-esteem, poor self-efficacy, and self-doubt. Assigning homework that makes the client vulnerable to failure or to actions that may be painful or overwhelming will threaten the therapeutic relationship because the client will lose faith in the therapist's ability to keep the client safe. It will also cast doubt on therapists' expertise because they have clearly misjudged the usefulness, helpfulness, and safety of the assignment for the client.

If homework is considered, the therapist must first decide whether the assignment will be countertherapeutic given the client's presenting problem. For example, assigning a behavioral logging exercise to an obsessive–compulsive client will most likely backfire because the client may pursue such an assignment with the same inflexibility and perfectionism as other life tasks. The assignment in this case will reinforce the client's problematic behavior patterns. Similarly, asking histrionic clients to journal their emotional ups and downs would unnecessarily place emphasis on a way of being that is already out of balance or consistently overused. As such, a therapist must have a clear reason for the assignment, must be certain that it will not interact with the client's presenting problem in a manner that produces a vicious cycle or reinforces less than healthy behaviors or experiences, and must ascertain that noncompliance will not lead to guilt or shame.

If homework is assigned, the therapist then also needs to remember to follow up on the assignment. Assigning homework and then not checking with clients suggests to them that these tasks were not especially important to begin with. If they engaged in the tasks, clients may feel as though they wasted their time, and this may lead to anger; if clients did not engage in the tasks, they may breathe a sigh of relief because the therapists did not catch them being noncompliant. However, this will only delay clients' guilt reactions because they may once again worry about their therapists' reactions during the subsequent week. Thus if homework was assigned, it is important for therapists to remember and follow up. Time will need to be taken in each session to process these assignments and how they went for the clients. This underscores the great importance of the therapeutic value of the assignment. Not only will clients spend valuable time on the tasks outside of session, but therapists and clients will spend even more time processing the assignments in sessions.

The easiest way to avoid these problems is by not assigning tasks to be completed outside of the session as "homework." If a therapist believes in the value of getting the client to work on therapeutic issues between sessions, such work may be framed in other ways that do not suggest that a given task is intended as a homework assignment. The therapist can make suggestions about possibilities of things that a client might do between sessions without requesting that the client comply or carry them out. For example, a therapist may say something to the effect of, "Some people have found it helpful to track their feelings and how they change or fluctuate across the days and weeks by keeping sort of a feelings journal. Have you ever tried that?" If the client shows interest, client and therapist can explore further how such a journal may be kept. The therapist does not assign journaling to the client but rather leaves it up to the client to make a decision about whether this may be a helpful task. This approach to homework has the added advantage that the therapist does not have to (though still may choose to) remember during subsequent sessions to check with the client about whether the client did the assignment, because no assignment was given. In all likelihood, if clients chose to try the task, they will let the therapist know and the therapist can then process how this experience went for the client and whether the client perceived it as helpful or insight-producing.

To summarize, homework has potential drawbacks that can interfere with the therapeutic relationship and process. Its risks need to be carefully weighed against its benefits; if the assignment can be made in a way other than a straight suggestion of doing homework, this approach is preferable. If therapists are in doubt about the therapeutic value of particular tasks, they should refrain from assigning them. If therapists worry about remembering to check with their clients about compliance, they should not make the assignments; if therapists wonder if noncompliance will get in the way of the therapeutic relationship, no assignments should be made. Finally, therapists must weigh the possibility that homework assignment may suggest something about the nature of the client–therapist relationship that is more educational than therapeutic. Homework or assignments are most commonly associated with educational settings, and unless clients are very clear about psychotherapy and its unique nature and implications for the therapist–client relationship, assigning homework can get in the way of forming a therapeutic alliance. In such cases, therapists may want to refrain from homework assignments until much later in therapy when clients have a clear understanding of the nature of therapy and have developed clearly therapeutic rapport with the clinician.

In closing, it must be emphasized one more time that there are types of therapy that rely on homework and that integrate assignments into their particular way of doing therapy. These types of therapy are often more psychoeducational in nature, and within their framework homework can be appropriate and safe. However, the model of therapy presented here appears somewhat incompatible with the *routine* assignment of homework.

Bibliotherapy and Workbooks

In recent years a plethora of therapy-related workbooks have hit the bookstores, with the suggestion that clients can work through their presenting problems with a self-help approach. Many of these workbooks have also found their way into the therapy room, with some therapists choosing to work through these workbooks with their clients. A number of concerns arise about this approach to therapeutic work. For one thing, what makes therapy unique is the special relationship between client and therapist that cannot be found in any other interpersonal context in a client's life. Working through a workbook with a client, however, tends to get in the way of establishing such a unique experiential, client-focused relationship in the here and now. Instead, the therapy becomes focused on the workbook and the agenda prescribed by it. It is no longer the client who chooses the topic or agenda for each session, and it is no longer the therapist who steers and guides the process in a therapeutic direction. Instead, the work revolves around a predetermined schedule of events. Such an approach to therapy appears counterproductive because it is in direct juxtaposition to the usual therapeutic values endorsed by process-oriented clinicians. Namely, this process is not flexible, not client-oriented, not focused in the here and now, not experiential, and not tailored to the idiosyncrasies and needs of each individual client.

Furthermore, workbooks expose clients to certain materials according to a schedule that was decided on by a person who is not part of the therapeutic process (i.e., the workbook author). Thus it is sometimes possible for clients to be overwhelmed by the material in the workbook because they may not have been ready to deal with a particular issue when it comes up in the book. The gravest such concern exists for the area of workbooks that deal with sexual abuse histories. Clients generally need to approach this issue slowly and cautiously, and many clients have completely different schedules than others. Their needs and affects emerge idiosyncratically, based on their particular sets of self-protective mechanisms that have been developed over time. Workbooks throw caution aside and expose clients to material whether they are ready for it or not. As such, workbooks can be less than safe. Workbooks also tempt a client to read them between sessions, which again may result in premature exposure to or processing of information that may be too overwhelming for the client. Painful affects may be stimulated too early or outside the presence of the therapist (i.e., outside the context of a holding environment or corrective emotional experience) who (or which) could otherwise keep the client safe by slowing down or speeding up the therapy process as needed for each individual client.

Bibliotherapy has the same potential drawbacks, and it appears somewhat unnecessary to differentiate between workbooks and other types of self-help books that have come to accompany some therapeutic work. The concerns expressed above are not meant to discourage therapists from buying books that can accompany therapy or from perusing and buying workbooks that can guide therapeutic treatment. These cautions merely suggest that these books be read by the therapist alone outside of the sessions with the client. They may guide the therapist on a certain path with a client, but they should not rule the therapeutic process through their presence in the room or through the client's awareness of their existence. In other words, the way to use workbooks and still do the type of process-oriented, experiential psychotherapy promoted by this book is for the therapist to buy the books or workbooks and read them thoroughly. The therapist can learn from these workbooks what has worked for other clients, and may glean from them some useful exercises to engage in with the client *during* sessions. However, only the therapist would be exposed to the workbook and aware of its existence. Clients never know which resources their therapists have used to prepare themselves for the therapeutic work with the client. Instead, clients are free to develop relationships with their therapists that are unencumbered by agendas imposed by a third person who is not part of the therapeutic process. Such use of workbooks is responsible and safe for individual clients and is often extremely helpful for inexperienced or novice clinicians who are still struggling with the direction to take with clients. It prevents the problem of prematurely exposing clients to material that they are not yet ready to confront. Further, it maintains the experiential focus of psychotherapy and allows for flexibility, here and now processing, and idiosyncratic (or individualized) treatment.

Clients Outside of Sessions

Running into clients outside of their sessions is a reality that can hardly be avoided in any community but which becomes particularly important if the clinician works in a small town, village, or rural area. Most professional guidelines for mental health professionals clearly state that dual relationships with clients are unacceptable. Regulating dual relationships is deemed important to ensure that therapists remain objective in their interactions with clients (which having a personal relationship may prevent) and to assure that clinicians do not exploit their clients (e.g., for sexual favors, needed professional or technical services, or business opportunities; Swenson, 1997). The stipulation against dual relationships includes not only a prohibition against clearly exploitative relationships with clients, but also against interacting with clients socially or through other avenues outside of therapy, lest clinicians lose their objectivity about the work with clients. Further, ethical guidelines require that therapists maintain clients' confidentiality and privacy in all settings. Thus acknowledging clients in any form, but in particular as their clients, in any setting outside of therapy is clearly unethical. These two ethical guidelines have very pragmatic implications. The fact that chance meetings with clients outside of sessions can and do happen (especially in small communities) suggests that this issue needs to be discussed with clients early on in therapy so that the individual knows what to expect if the encounter occurs. This discussion would raise the points shared below.

First, if a therapist sees a client in public, the best course of action is not to acknowledge the client unless the client approaches the clinician first. Even if the client approaches the clinician, however, the clinician needs to keep the interaction with the client to a minimum and must never delve into therapy-related topics. If the client insists on introducing the therapist to a significant other or a friend who is with the client at the time of the chance meeting, the therapist can accept the introduction but will not engage in an extended conversation with the client and this person's companion. Although this may seem rude or unfriendly behavior, it is the most ethical approach to preventing a dual relationship from forming and to maintaining the client's confidentiality. As mentioned above, it is best to warn clients early in treatment about the privacy and dual relationship requirements that are part of therapy so that clients know why their therapists react as they do when they happen to meet in public. Even with this explanation before the fact, the therapist must remember to follow up on chance meetings outside of session the next time client and therapist meet for their regular appointment. Follow-up is important because the therapist does take such a distant stance with the client in public. This stance and its reasons need to be processed and discussed with clients to remind them of the ethical obligations that the therapist has to meet. The therapist should follow up on chance meetings even if the client did not acknowledge the therapist and the two never interacted whatsoever. In this circumstance, clinicians should bring up that they saw clients and remind the clients that when this happens they will not acknowledge them first. This mention of the meeting is important to remind clients of their confidentiality rights and to prevent clients from misinterpreting therapists' behavior.

More difficult are chance meetings that involve a service or social interaction that is unavoidable. This may occur if a client and therapist living in the same community find out they have been appointed to the same committee or invited to the same party; if a therapist seeks a service and only at the moment of requesting it realizes that the client is the person providing it (e.g., having a prescription called into a pharmacy by a physician and when picking it up being served by the client); or if the therapist attends a public function and realizes the client is present as well. All situations like this certainly need to be processed with the client during the next appointment, much in the same way as chance meetings. However, the therapist may occasionally need to take action beyond simply discussing the event with the client during the next appointment. For example, if clinicians are appointed to committees on which their clients serve, they may need to turn down these appointments; if they find themselves seated next to clients at public events, they may need to switch seats; if they use service providers who employ these clients, they may need to switch to different providers. The latter is easy if the therapist lives in a large enough community and can choose among a group of service providers. Yet there are very small rural towns where such options may not exist. If the client is the only mechanic in town and the clinician's car breaks down, interacting with the client outside of session is unavoidable. If this is the case, processing the interaction in a session is essential. The issues of privacy, confidentiality, and dual relationships need to be revisited, and the client needs to be assured that the therapist is capable of maintaining professional boundaries. All interactions around the service delivery are kept to a minimum, and client and therapist will attempt to refrain from the usual social interchange that may normally surround such a service. Further, the therapist needs to be sure that the relationship with the client does not become exploitative in any way (e.g., by accepting or expecting services for free or ahead of others on a waiting list, etc.). All of this needs to be processed with the client in the session to prevent the client from perceiving the therapist as rude or aloof outside of the session.

COMMON CHALLENGES

Given the reality that most clients have some ambivalence about therapy and change, it is not surprising that they may engage in behaviors that can threaten or distract from the therapeutic relationship and process. If the therapist is prepared for these behaviors and challenges, they can be used to therapeutic advantage and may barely disrupt the therapeutic process. However, if the therapist is caught unaware by such challenges, they may easily derail the therapeutic process or interfere with forming or maintaining the therapeutic relationship. Being prepared for possible challenges is hence a critical piece of learning about the therapy process. Some of the most common challenges are presented here, though in all likelihood many others exist. However, even being exposed to the potential problems dealt with here will give the therapist an idea about how difficult interactions can be handled successfully, nondefensively, and therapeutically.

Personal Questions

Although personal questions are most likely to occur early on in treatment, they can occur at any point in time, perhaps most commonly during difficult moments in the therapy. Personal questions can range from simple requests for information to intrusive inquiries into the therapist's personal life. A few personal questions are appropriate to the therapeutic process and should be answered. Most, however, have a different purpose and should not be answered but should be processed instead in the context of their meaning to the therapeutic work being done. Despite this rule of thumb about not answering personal questions, occasions may arise when these rules can be broken, if answering a particular question appears essential to maintaining therapeutic rapport.

Personal questions that are appropriate and can be answered are questions that reflect good consumerism on the part of the client. Such questions most commonly have to do with a therapist's credentials, experience, and theoretical orientation. Such questions can be answered matter-of-factly, directly, and nondefensively. Therapists most vulnerable to mishandling these requests for information by clients are novice therapists who have some doubts about their abilities or are not yet satisfactorily credentialed from their own perspective. It is very important for these therapists to be honest in their responses to the client's questions and to remain nondefensive. No therapists must justify their backgrounds in response to these questions; they merely have to state their credentials and experiences, then allow the client to decide whether the answers meet the client's expectations, needs, and approval. It does happen on occasion that even these innocuous questions about credentials have a hidden agenda or underlying purpose. If this is the case, the client will in all likelihood not be satisfied with this simple response by the therapist but will continue to challenge the therapist in other ways. This is a suggestion or hint for the therapist that even this line of questions by the client may need to be dealt with like other personal questions (see below).

Personal questions that are not related to credentials, experience, or theoretical orientation but are more personal in nature are, as a general rule of thumb, not answered by the therapist. Instead, the clinician will acknowledge the client's curiosity, may validate that this curiosity is natural and common, and then will return the focus of the session to the client. If this simple approach suffices to return therapy to its intended purpose (i.e., returns the attention to the client's life), no further intervention may be necessary. However, at times clients are quite persistent in their inquiries and are not easily redirected in their focus. If this is the case, client and therapist need to look at the purpose or underlying need that fuels the client's questions. The therapist will then respond to the underlying concern but will still not answer the personal questions. For example, a client may ask whether a clinician has children. If the therapist is unable to redirect the focus by simply acknowledging the client's curiosity, the therapist will need to try to find out why the client is asking this question at this time. This sounds more difficult than it really is, because most personal questions arise in a broader therapeutic context that generally guides the therapist toward an understanding of why the question emerged at this point in time. Returning to the example, the therapist may note that one client had been talking about her own children and her self-doubts regarding parenting. The clinician may deduce that the client is really asking about the therapist's expertise in the area of parenting. A response would therefore be directed toward this presumed purpose that guided the question and may be something like, "You are wondering whether I will understand the complexity of issues involved in parenting three children." If the client acknowledges this as the truth, therapy can now continue by considering the client's concerns about the therapist's understanding and expertise. The latter issue may re-emerge again and again and will possibly need to be dealt with further. However, the question was clearly not about whether the therapist had children, but about the therapist's ability to understand the client—it is this topic that will be dealt with in the therapy. Other common questions for the therapist include questions about shared experiences, familiarity with certain issues or topics, and intrusions into the therapist's private life. All of these questions can be handled in the same manner as the sample question above.

Only in the rarest of instances will clinicians decide that they must answer personal questions lest therapeutic rapport become derailed or stymied. One example of such an instance was my experience with a gay client whose therapy became stagnant after she questioned my sexual orientation. This request was addressed first merely by acknowledging her curiosity, then through processing the purpose behind the question and the client's needs that had motivated it. The client stated adamantly that in her gay community the belief was strong that a client needed to know the sexual orientation of the therapist to be able to trust the therapist fully. For this client, not knowing the sexual orientation of the therapist was perceived as equivalent to not knowing whether the therapist has a master's or doctorate degree. A delayed answer to this question resulted in a significant decrease in trust and openness on the part of the client toward me as her therapist, and the delayed response was perceived by her as rejecting her and her very reasonable request. The issue finally came to closure in therapy when the client's partner also decided to begin therapy and chose a clinician based on that clinician's professed sexual orientation (the partner's therapist was openly gay and worked primarily within the gay community). I then chose to disclose that I was not gay but felt strongly grounded in and familiar with the gay community and its values. I observed that withholding this information was affecting the quality of therapeutic work and I could no longer prevent the focus of therapy from being on me rather than on the client. Instead, by refusing to answer the question, I had become the intense focus of treatment, and the client perceived me as being secretive and withholding. Once I had answered the client's question, therapy almost immediately resumed. The client had never questioned my ability to work with her (whether I was likely to be gay or not), but merely needed to know. I learned that the question needed to be answered by the fact that the client requested no additional personal information from me in the future.

This example hopefully clarifies that self-disclosures in response to personal questions by clients are generally not made and, if they are made, are kept to a minimum and must serve a therapeutic purpose. The decision to disclose is never made lightly or quickly but must reflect careful consideration by the therapist. The example was also chosen to show how at times not answering a question very matter-of-factly (after redirecting or exploring its purpose were attempted thoroughly but unsuccessfully) can restore trust and confidence in the therapist. The example was *not* chosen to demonstrate that self-disclosure can facilitate the therapeutic process. Most commonly, it does not do so because it places the therapist in a role that is social and equal—relationship dimensions that are not truly part of the type of psychotherapy outlined here. One way to assess whether a personal question was answered and whether such a response was appropriate and therapeutic is the future behavior of the client. If the client moves on to therapeutic work, the decision was probably correct. If the client moves on to ask further personal questions, the decision was probably incorrect and future personal questions should not be answered.

Questions about Other Clients

Questions about other clients are generally easily dealt with and tend to fall into one of three broad categories. Sometimes clients are curious about someone they meet or see in the waiting area, either while waiting for or leaving their sessions. They may inquire about these clients and their identities or presenting problems out of curiosity or interest in these particular persons. Such questions, however innocuous, must never be answered. This refusal to answer is easily dealt with by reminding clients of the confidential nature of the therapeutic relationship and the fact that the same right to privacy would be extended to them should someone else express interest about them.

Occasionally, clients will ask questions about other clients not because they have seen them in the waiting area but because they know them socially and have heard from them that they are indeed seeing the same therapist. In such cases, therapists must remember that they cannot even acknowledge knowing these other clients, much less provide information about whether they are truly seeing these clients, and even much less how therapy is progressing with another person. Reminding the client of confidentiality and privacy usually suffices to redirect the client's focus and attention. In both of these instances, maintaining confidentiality and offering reminders about client privacy are also essential because both communicate to the client the therapist's ability to guarantee these ethical requirements to the client as well. After all, if the therapist were to answer these questions for the client, the client could thereafter never be certain that such confidential material would not be discussed similarly with another client. Occasionally, a client's request for information about another client is used as a test of the therapist's ability to maintain the professional boundaries of confidentially and privacy, especially if the client does indeed know another client socially or personally who is being seen by the same therapist.

A third type of question about other clients has less to do with the other clients than it has to do with the therapist. In essence, these questions are hidden personal questions about the therapist and are often motivated by a need on the part of the querying client. Such questions include inquiries about how many clients the therapist sees in any one week, if other clients have the same problems as the current client, if the therapist has favorite clients, if the clinician is successful in the work with other clients, and so forth. These questions clearly have a completely different purpose than the other two types of client questions. They are generally questions about the therapist. The first example ("How many other clients do you see each week besides me?") may be an inquiry about the therapist's ability to track and respond appropriately to the current client given the therapist's large case load. Clients may really be asking if they are special enough to the therapist to be responded to individually and carefully. The second example ("Do other clients have the same problems?") can have two possible meanings. Clients may be seeking normalizing responses that confirm that they are not strange or crazy but that other people have similar problems or concerns. Alternatively, a client may be asking if the therapist has the necessary skills to treat the client by having gained experience with other clients having the same presenting problems. As was the case with personal questions, this type of questioning about other clients needs to be processed in the context of the underlying purpose or meaning of the question instead of being answered directly.

Complaints about Another Therapist

Complaints about other therapists can be grouped most simplistically into two categories. First, there are complaints that are genuine—the client truly was poorly treated by another clinician and has a legitimate concern or grievance. Second, clients present with a relational pattern that interferes with the therapist easily establishing therapeutic relationships and they misrepresent the therapist's actions according to an established pathological or unhealthy response. The therapist's response to complaints about another clinician thus can be made only after exploring whether the complaint is genuine or a function of the client's pathology. Clearly, a therapist will respond differently to clients with genuine concerns than to clients who are merely manifesting their general relational style. However, it is always a good idea to talk to prior therapists (with appropriate releases of information, of course) regardless of whether a client complains about the prior therapist and regardless of whether a complaint, if present, is legitimate.

If the concern of the client is genuine, and if the therapist becomes privy to a violation of a prior client–therapist relationship, the therapist's role in dealing with this information is somewhat more complex, because therapeutic, professional, ethical, and legal issues may be involved. If a genuine breach of ethics or professionalism is uncovered through the client's complaints about another clinician, the therapist is faced with a difficult situation. The therapist faces an ethical obligation to intervene, not only with the client, but with the alleged perpetrator in the attempt to prevent the same behavior from occurring again with future clients. The first step of intervention is to talk with the client about options the person has in this situation. The client has the right to confront the prior therapist and to take the necessary legal steps to report the violation of the therapeutic trust to the relevant licensing board or professional organization (see below). Discussing these options with the client is often quite therapeutic because it returns a level of control to the individual, who can take steps to recover from the trauma experience resulting from the inappropriate treatment by another provider. Options to be discussed with the client do not differ significantly from the steps (outlined below) that need to be taken by the therapist when the client chooses not to take these steps directly.

The next step in dealing with a legitimate complaint involves contacting alleged perpetrators to talk to them about the alleged behavior in the attempt to reach an informal resolution to the problem (Swenson, 1997). To assure that the clinician is not charged with a breach of confidentiality by the client, it is required by law and/or professional ethics in most situations to approach the accused colleague only after having secured a release of information from the client making the complaint. This release would spell out which information needs to be conveyed to the colleague in the attempt to resolve the complaint informally. Legal opinions appear to vary somewhat in regard to the therapist's duties to approach the colleague if the client refuses to provide a release of information. Swenson (1997) implies in his writings that the therapist has an absolute duty to approach the accused colleague regardless of release of information. While doing so, clinicians must take all necessary precautions to maintain the confidentiality of their sources (i.e., of the client making the complaint); however, in a given situation this may be exceedingly difficult. Not surprisingly other sources (R. Slizs, 1997, personal communication) maintain that an approach should *only* be made with a signed release of information. Slizs, attorney for the State of Alaska and investigator for the Board of Examiners of Psychologists and Psychological Associates, offered the legal opinion that a clinician who does not act on a complaint about another provider because the client refused to sign a release of information will, in all likelihood, not be prosecuted for complicity should the accused colleague later become the target of formal ethics charges. This is clearly a gray area where legal opinions vary. The easiest approach to this dilemma is to receive a release of information from the client; if this is not possible, the therapist should carefully chart in the client's record that this refusal was made and that it prevented the clinician from intervening. If the conduct of the other professional was highly dangerous, however, the clinician may need to intervene even in the absence of a signed release of information. If this step is necessitated, it may be best for the practitioner to seek confidential counsel from the local licensing board before taking action.

If resolution is not possible at the informal level (i.e., through resolving the issue with the provider directly), most professional guidelines (e.g., American Psychological Association, 1992) suggest that the next step of intervention occur through institutional channels. If the provider works at an agency, this would mean contacting the person's superior or the agency's grievance council, all the while fully protecting the confidentiality of the client. If the provider is a private practitioner, this may mean reporting these actions to the ethics board of the professional group or to the licensing board that regulates the provider's license or certification (see below).

If the action by the prior therapist was a major offense or if the informal or institutional-level resolution of minor offenses was not possible, the current therapist is required to report the colleague to the ethics committee of the professional organization to which the alleged perpetrator belongs. If the alleged perpetrator holds no such membership, the report must be made to the licensing board or governmental agency that regulates the provider's profession. If the matter is very serious, it will be the professional group or licensing board that will take the complaint to the legal system (Swenson, 1997). It is also the professional group or governmental agency that must see to the fact that the alleged perpetrator will be guaranteed due process in all investigation and decision making that will occur. Although therapists have an ethical obligation to pursue the matter themselves outside of therapy, they may also see fit to talk with the client about the client's options to take action with regard to the improper conduct of the other professional. The client may need to be given information about the inappropriateness of the prior therapist's behavior and avenues for reporting such unethical behavior to the appropriate professional organization or the licensing or credentialing board. Providing clients with such information may help empower them to take charge of their lives and to overcome their sense of victimization through action on their own behalf. Further, in any case of violation of ethics or traumatization (mild to severe) of the client in a prior therapeutic relationship, the therapist needs to consider how this behavior has affected the client's mental health and must integrate dealing with this victimization of the client in the current treatment.

If the complaint about a prior therapist was legitimate and involved significant traumatization of the current client, the issue, of course, also has to be addressed therapeutically. Exact intervention is beyond the scope of this discussion because it involves specific interactions that go beyond the general therapy situations attended to here. However, resources are available for clinicians that outline how to deal with clients who have been traumatized (in particular through sexual relationships or abuse) by other therapists (Pope, 1990a, 1990b, 1994). The sequelae of abuse of a client by a therapist have been likened to the effects of sexual abuse or rape, and treatment with such clients proceeds very similarly to therapy with clients of that specific presentation (Sonne & Pope, 1991). Therapists who encounter a client who has been maltreated by a prior mental health care provider must avoid several specific, relatively common reactions. Specifically, current therapists must beware not to express disbelief in the client's report, not to revictimize or blame the client, to control the expression of feelings of ambivalence toward the client, and not to fail to report the prior provider. Further, they must involve clients in their own recovery by empowering them to take action against the previous provider independently, and they need to avoid feelings of collective guilt for the experience of the client that may allow the client retribution (Sonne & Pope, 1991). Instead, clients who have been traumatized by a prior clinician must be treated with respect and caring that help the client recognize that the current provider is different from the therapist who engaged in inappropriate behavior during the client's prior treatment. The client must be provided with the opportunity to work through the experience of maltreatment by a trusted care provider and must be allowed to progress through stages of adjustment to this realization. Careful attention must be paid to allow these clients to proceed at their own pace of building trust with the new provider and not to push them into self-disclosures for which they are not ready. In other words, many treatment issues similar to those of clients suffering from complex post-traumatic stress reactions to other forms or abuse by a trusted other (e.g., childhood abuse; Herman, 1992a, 1992b) will emerge in the treatment of clients who have been abused by prior therapists. Thus therapists who encounter such clients in therapy (and many will, because 50% of surveyed practicing psychologists report having encountered at least one client who had been victimized by a prior mental health care provider; Pope & Vetter, 1991) may benefit from perusing the literature on treating complex PTSD victims (e.g., Dolan, 1991; Gil, 1988; Lebowitz, Harvey, & Herman, 1993).

If the complaint about a prior provider is a function of the client's pathology, the therapist may need to remember foremost that however the therapist handles the client's complaint may lead to either strengthening or rupturing the current relationship. Should a rupture occur, the therapist will most likely become the target of very similar complaints on the part of the client to another therapist. Clients who complain about previous providers often also intend to give a veiled message that they are not convinced the current provider will be able to help them. Thus complaints about prior therapists are often a challenge to the current therapist to approach the client differently lest they become a similar target of complaints. Remembering this, therapists must be careful not to condemn their colleagues who in all likelihood are being misportrayed by the client. In such an event, it is best to work toward strengthening the relationship with the client, not risking a rupture in and loss of the therapeutic relationship that would merely result in perpetuating the client's pathology and would not be helpful to the client.

Such a strengthening response may most likely be achieved through a concerned approach to the client's complaints that does not side with any one party. As such, the therapist will listen attentively, will not argue with the client's perception of reality, but will also not agree with the client's perspective or reinforce the client's unhealthy way of relating. The complaints will be dealt with much in the same way as complaints by the client about any other person in the client's interpersonal world and will be processed as yet another relationship in which the client has experienced difficulties. In other words, such complaints will not be reacted to in any special way; they will merely become embedded in the overall treatment approach with this particular client.

Sexual Advances and Seductiveness

Sexual relationships may not be the only dual relationships clients attempt to establish with their therapists; however, they are certainly the most potentially damaging and destructive. All dual relationships must be avoided with clients, and therapists must learn to resist offers of social or other interactions with clients to make sure that treatment remains nonexploitative and objective. Sexual advances and seductive behaviors are only the extreme end of the continuum of dual relationships, but they serve well as an example of how to deal with suggestions for inappropriate dual relationships by clients toward clinicians.

For some clients, seductive behavior is a normal pattern of relating that they have developed over a lifetime of experiences in interpersonal contexts. Most seductive behavior can be viewed from that perspective and hence can be understood as being transferential in nature. Remembering this may help tempted therapists recognize that they are not truly the target of admiration, but rather are only convenient objects in the client's environment with whom to act out ingrained behavior patterns. The most important caution that must be heeded at all times and in all circumstances is that the therapist must neither give in to a client's sexual advances directly (by establishing a sexual relationship) nor indirectly (by allowing a mutually sexualized or seductive relational pattern with the client). The therapist must draw and maintain firm, professional boundaries and must not respond to the sexual advances of the client. Instead, the client's sexualized behavior must be understood from its etiological or historical perspective and must be dealt with like any other relational pattern or resistance that emerges in treatment with a client.

That is, therapists must empathize with the client's need for the behavioral pattern, must communicate that they understand the client's needs and accept them and their developmental relevance, but not gratify these needs. Instead, they will help the client understand how and why the behavior developed, what function it has served and continues to serve, and what consequences it may have for the client and the client's relationships. This process, while presented here in very few sentences, may well require many months of therapeutic work. Through these months of work, clinicians consistently set firm boundaries with the client around the behavior, do not waver in their commitment to prevent a dual relationship with the client, and never become seductive or sexual in their own reactions to the client.

Maintaining firm and clear therapeutic boundaries may never be more important than with clients who have a relational pattern that involves poor boundaries, as is often the case with clients who behave seductively or in a sexualized manner. Thus being clear about all of the questions and implementing all of the solutions outlined in the previous section of this chapter is particularly important with seductive clients.

Intoxicated Clients

If a client arrives for therapy under the influence of alcohol or other drugs, it is best to reschedule the session. A necessary precondition for therapy is that both client and therapist are of clear mind and can process information optimally and efficiently. Clients who are under the influence of chemicals will not have the cognitive wherewithal to benefit from treatment. This needs to be explained to them and the appointment needs to be rescheduled. Some clinicians include a statement in their informed consent or discuss in the screening or intake session that they will refuse services to clients who are clearly under the influence of mind-altering substances. If this was done, then clients merely need to be reminded at the time of the event that no services can be provided given their state of intoxication. If the client is clearly impaired, the therapist who has wisely chosen to reschedule the client's session now has some responsibility about the client's behavior outside of the therapy room after the client leaves the premises. Given this responsibility, it is crucial to explore how clients transported themselves to the session. If they are driving under the influence and plan to leave by car as well, the therapist will need to intervene. Specifically, clients now represent a potential danger to self and others because they are planning to operate vehicles while clearly cognitively impaired and functioning under poor judgment. Therapists will need to persuade these clients to make alternative arrangements for transportation, such as phoning friends or family members to pick them up or ordering taxis that will take clients home. If clients refuse such intervention, they need to be warned that given the therapist's legal and ethical obligations to protect and warn, the clinician will need to notify the police of any client's intent to drive under the influence. Clearly, this situation has the potential to become a major interference in the therapeutic relationship, but therapists must react responsibly and within the parameters of the law. Despite these potential difficulties, they nevertheless will want to avoid seeing their clients in altered states of consciousness.

Mandated Clients

Some clients present to treatment not by their own choice but because of external pressures that force them into therapy. Such clients may be referred by child protection agencies that have clarified for them that unless they seek therapeutic services, intervention by the agency may be more severe and intrusive. Alternatively, such clients may be mandated into treatment and may not be given a choice at all. They have to appear for treatment or suffer a variety of consequences (e.g., incarceration, the removal of a child, the termination of employment). Such mandates may be made by the courts, child protection agencies, or employers. Finally, clients may be pressured into treatment by spouses, family members, or significant others who have given them some type of ultimatum. What all of these clients have in common is an external, rather than internal, motivator for treatment that, in all likelihood, serves to intensify the natural ambivalence most clients feel about entering psychotherapy. These clients would often rather not talk about themselves, often do not trust the therapist's motives, and may take a hostile stance toward treatment (Patterson & Welfel, 1993). To these clients, therapy does not feel like an act of freedom, but rather an act of coercion, so "accepting the reluctant client involves accepting the client's reluctance as part of the agenda" for therapy (Patterson & Welfel, 1993, p. 207).

Dealing with mandated clients usually presents a significant challenge, especially in the early stages of treatment, while clients decide on their levels of commitment to therapeutic work. With some mandated clients, therapy may never be possible. However, there are a few interventions the therapist can use to attempt to pull the client into the therapeutic work and process. First of all, the therapist must acknowledge to clients that it is their right not to want to be in the therapy or not to want to talk about themselves. The client's reluctance and affect around being in therapy needs to be addressed in a caring and concerned manner that communicates to the client that the therapist is not colluding with the external pressure point that has forced or coerced the client into treatment. The client's reluctance and emotions can be put into a larger context of the client's general experience of life and thus can represent a point of empathic entry into a more positive relationship with the client. Much of this early therapeutic work can center around the client's feelings about being forced into therapy, and the therapist can attempt to join with the client around recognizing and acknowledging the client's tough situation of being asked to perform a task that is not intrinsically motivated.

Additionally, or alternatively, the clinician can attempt to shift the therapeutic focus to an area that may be intrinsically motivating for the client. Clinicians may indicate to clients that they understand that the clients were referred for a particular reason but that there may be an agenda that might be of some importance to them and that this agenda can be integrated into the current therapeutic work. In other words, the therapist may work toward identifying a presenting problem that is genuinely bothersome to the client, not the referring agent, thus making the therapeutic content one of relevance and interest to the client. If this route is chosen, both client and therapist must acknowledge that they may also have to work on the specific referral requests by the mandating agency. However, at least the client will have some input into the agenda and may perceive more control over what initially appeared to be an entirely externally controlled situation.

COMMON INTENSE AFFECTS

The very nature of the therapeutic model presented here suggests that there will be times when clients will feel very intensely during their sessions. The intensity of affect is not in itself a dangerous thing during which the therapist must intervene.

Most of the time, even the most intense affects are successfully resolved using the usual therapeutic tools, processes, and catalysts that have already been discussed in detail (e.g., catharsis, corrective emotional experience, holding environment). However, occasionally it is necessary for a therapist to intervene with a particularly intense affect. For example, if clients are experiencing intense emotions over which they appear to be losing control toward the end of a session, a therapist may have to intervene to help the client get ready to leave. Another example that requires the intervention of the clinician is the client who has an affective experience that is so severe as to result in a dangerous situation either for the client or the therapist (e.g., hyperventilation during a panic attack; the potential for acting out aggression during an intense spell of anger). In such situations, the clinician needs to know what to do to restore a sense of safety to the therapy session. As mentioned in Chapter 6, one important aspect of providing a holding environment is the clinician's capacity to contain the client's affect if it threatens to be overwhelming. The following helpful hints about how to deal with intense affects when they need to be managed will help the therapist develop the necessary skills to contain such client affects.

Dealing with Loss of Control over Emotions

Though seemingly out of control, strong affective experiences generally cannot last forever; in fact, these usually cannot even last for a whole session. Thus depending on the amount of time left in a session, the first approach to apparent emotional loss of control is to let it play out as long as this does not appear to be destructive to the client. The catharsis that comes from allowing the emotion to flow freely for a while is often extremely helpful for the client as long as the affect is one that is not accompanied by highly uncomfortable physical feelings or by dangerous behavior. For example, once it is out of control, anger must be gotten under control if the client appears to be on the verge of violent action; a panic attack must be controlled lest the client hyperventilate or experience other severe physical consequences.

If the emotion is one for which catharsis is appropriate (e.g., anxiety not of panic proportions, depression or sadness, frustration), this is the first choice. The intensity displayed by the client will decrease on its own once the affect has been given free range for a while. If the length of time elapsed becomes too long (either because the session is almost over or because either client or therapist becomes too uncomfortable), the clinician can begin to take steps to calm the affect. This can be done by asking the client to begin to focus on the therapist (e.g., "I need you to: look at me; look up; catch my eyes; look at my hand . . ."). Any behavior connected to the affect needs to be stopped (e.g., "I want you to stop pacing now; please sit back down" or "I need for you to stop bouncing your leg and picking on your hair" or "Please stop wringing your hands now."). Therapists lower their voices significantly and speak much more slowly than usual, but with emphasis. Once clients have stopped the associated behavior and have begun to focus on the clinician, they are asked to pattern their breathing after the therapist's (e.g., "Let's get your breathing back to normal. Follow my lead. Slowly breathe in . . . *[clinician takes a long, calm breath]*, and out . . . *[clinician releases the breath forcefully]*, in . . . , and out . . .). This breathing exercise is continued until the client becomes calmer. During the entire time, therapists must be aware of their body language, which must express confidence, calmness, and collectedness. This is one time when therapists definitely do not want to mirror clients' body language. All demeanor on the clinicians' part must exude relaxation and calm. For clients who lose control over their emotions on a regular basis, it may be important to develop a structured and predictable sequence of interventions for dealing with these situations. Not only will this help clients begin to be aware of how to regain control over affects with the therapist's help during sessions, but they may also be able to begin using some of the same, regularly rehearsed strategies outside of the session.

Dealing with Uncontrollable Crying

If the uncontrollable affect includes uncontrollable crying and this crying needs to be stopped (again, it is best to allow appropriate catharsis first, which may be sufficient to stop the crying by itself), a few additional strategies are available. First, handing clients a box of tissues is usually a nonverbal signal that it is time for them to pull themselves together. Once clients have been given the message to alter their behaviors and have begun to focus on the therapists, clinicians ask clients to look directly into their eyes while talking calmly to them (e.g., "I am going to help you stop crying now so that we have enough time to talk about what happened before you have to leave today. I need you to look into my eyes—look directly into my eyes."). Once clients are able to maintain firm eye contact, the same breathing exercise mentioned above needs to be initiated. Clinicians should encourage their clients to blow their noses to clear their heads. The reason for firm eye contact is simple: it is physiologically difficult (if not impossible) to cry and focus one's vision at the same time. Thus if clients are asked to focus on therapists' eyes, crying will automatically stop in most cases. Occasional clients will respond to increased eye contact with more intense experience of affect. If a clinician encounters such a client, eye contact may not be the best method to stop the client from crying. However, in most cases eye contact is incompatible with crying. Clients can be taught this trick for home use as well—they can simply look at and focus on their own eyes in a mirror and can thus get crying under some control. If the breathing exercise can be used in addition, calming will ensue.

Dealing with Strong Anxiety Reactions and Panic

A strong anxiety reaction or panic attack needs to be controlled much sooner than the type of emotion referred to above because it often is self-perpetuating. Highly anxious or panicked clients have physiological responses that further frighten them and often serve to increase the panic. Thus early intervention is definitely indicated in these cases. The actual intervention is not very different from that outlined above. However, it is even more important that the therapist appear in control and be capable of setting firm limits (e.g., "I have to stop you from . . . NOW." or "You need to stop talking about . . . now." or "We need to move on NOW to thinking about how to get you ready to leave today."). Therapists must use their voice and body language to underline the command nature of this direction, providing verbal and physical structure (e.g., handing the client a tissue box; taking away the pillow the client may be beating; stopping the client from twirling the hair, perhaps by physically moving and then holding onto the client's hand). The clinician's voice must be firm but caring, as well as calm and controlled. Once the structure has been set, clients are asked to find a focal point and to place their attention on it. Once clients have established eye contact with the focal point (e.g., a picture in the therapy room), they are asked to describe it (e.g., "I need you to look at . . . right there across from you. Okay, now tell me what you see. Describe it in detail."). This simple task serves to shift clients' focus of attention away from the distressing thoughts that fuel the anxiety or panic. All the while, therapists also need to pay attention to clients' breathing. If the client is hyperventilating, intervention is imminently important. This can be accomplished through the same breathing exercise outlined above, in which clients are asked to model their breathing frequency and intensity after that of the therapists'. In extreme cases, therapists may need to ask clients to breathe into a paper bag or through a straw (or to engage in any similar strategy that prevents taking in too much breath too quickly, termed *overbreathing*). As was explained with regard to intervening with other affects that are out of control, it is important to slow all interactions with clients to a calm level. This is accomplished by using a lower and slower voice. All the while, clinicians also give reassurance about the safety of the room and setting, doing so with firmness and calm. If clients are still panicking, it is often helpful to ask them to pick up a pillow and hug it tightly to their bodies. This action helps reestablish some body boundaries and may help with any beginning symptoms of depersonalization.

Any and all of these strategies can be combined in any order depending on what the clinician believes is most likely to work. If the client is hyperventilating, the first step of intervention would be the breathing exercise; if the client appears to have a sense of loss of boundaries and self, the pillow intervention is best (if no pillow is available in the room, clients can hug their purses or bags; or as a last resort, can hug themselves firmly around the torso). If the client appears extremely cognitively preoccupied, the focal point exercise is best. Combining strategies can be easily accomplished as well, in that the client can hug a pillow, do slow breathing, and focus on a specified object (including the therapist's eyes) all at the same time, while the therapist calmly talks about the safety of the room and the setting. Certainly, whenever anxiety is high, the client may need special help with transitions of any sort, including beginning and ending sessions or changing topics within sessions. Specific instructions, more time, clear directions, and similar structuring events may assist such clients to move more successfully through the treatment process even while highly anxious or agitated.

Dealing with Thought Racing and Pressured Speech

If the primary problem appears to be that the client's thoughts are racing out of control, resulting in pressured speech, the therapist again intervenes with calming strategies that can include the breathing exercise outlined above. The clinician begins by asking the client to stop talking altogether and to begin breathing and relaxing. These clients are asked to model their breathing after the therapist's and to be completely quiet (i.e., nonverbal) during this exercise. The simple breathing can be kept up for some time if the clinician believes that it is sufficient in slowing down the client's thought process. If the client's thoughts appear to continue to race (as perhaps suggested by a difficulty in slowing down the breathing or fidgety psychomotor behavior), the focal point exercise introduced above should be added. It should distract the client's focus of attention away from the racing thoughts. This client may need some assistance in this case because thoughts may be more preoccupied than in the simply anxious client. If this is the case, the therapist may need to do some modeling of description (e.g., "Okay—what do you see? I see a brown picture frame—do you see it? Okay . . . what shape does it have? . . . Yes, that's how I see it; it's almost square. . . . What else?"). Overall the focus is on helping clients stop thinking about the obsessive thoughts to slow their cognitive processing and to model calmness and relaxation through calm breathing, controlled body language, low and slow voice, and firm directions about what they need to do next. The focal attention exercise is generally extremely helpful with these clients.

Dealing with Depersonalization and Dissociation

These reactions are often closely tied to anxiety and a loss of sense of personal boundaries. Hence, the same techniques that have been outlined so far (for emotional control, for anxiety and panic, and for racing thoughts and pressured speech) may all apply to some extent. The breathing exercise may be the most important and effective exercise because depersonalization can be due to overbreathing (Bellak & Siegel, 1983) or taking in too little breath (by holding one's breath or other irregular breathing), termed *underbreathing;* in the latter the client breathes so little that this person falls into a trance state to avoid difficult feelings (Linda Olson-Webber, August 14, 1997, personal communication). In severe cases of overbreathing, asking the client to breathe into a paper bag may be helpful. The pillow hugging exercise is very useful in that it provides the client with some definite body boundaries. If the hugging is not enough in itself, the therapist can ask the client to explain what it feels like to hug the pillow and focus on establishing body boundaries (e.g., "Tell me how the pillow feels. Is it soft? Hard?" and "On which parts of your body can you feel the pillow? Your arms. Where else?" and "Tell me how your stomach feels with the pillow pressing on it." or "Squeeze the pillow a little tighter. What changes can you feel? Where can you feel the additional pressure in your body? In your arm muscles? On your stomach?"). Also saying the client's name can often be helpful, and beginning all verbalizations by repeating the client's name is good routine practice.

For clients prone to dissociation (i.e., clients traumatized as children or adults by events such as chronic and inconsistent abuse, combat, natural disasters, and so forth; Pope & Brown, 1996), the therapist must learn to pace sessions carefully and must prepare signals for the client to become alert and return to the safety of an unaltered state of consciousness. Dissociation-prone clients need help in recognizing the feelings and thoughts they might have that signal the onset of a dissociative experience so that they may learn to prevent the episode from occurring, both in and out of sessions (Sanderson, 1996). Carefully pacing clinical material is critical to avoid retrieval of painful memories that come too quickly and painfully and trigger a dissociative episode. As explained by Gil (1988), it is most helpful to determine when dissociation occurs (i.e., in what setting or under what circumstances), its precipitants (i.e., the specific events that lead to the flight response), and the emotions associated with it. Further, the client must be helped to understand the dissociation as an adaptive strategy developed for purposes of psychic or emotional survival. Once these issues have been clarified, the client can be taught alternative strategies of coping or defense under circumstances that tend to trigger a dissociative response (e.g., relaxation exercises, activities for purposes of distraction, conversations with supportive others, and so forth). If dissociation occurs during a session nevertheless, the clinician needs to be prepared to assist the client in regaining a normal alert state of consciousness. This eventuality is best prepared for by developing a bridge between the dissociative, trauma-related state of consciousness and the present, or nondissociative state of consciousness (Dolan, 1991). One such bridge is the symbol for the present, wherein the client is asked to identify an item in the client's possession that can be used as a reminder of the here and now. Should a dissociative event threaten or occur, the symbol of the present can be used by client and therapist to bring the client back to a normal waking state (Dolan, 1996). A similar bridge, also recommended by Dolan (1996), is the first session formula task in which clients are asked to make a list of events or activities that are currently ongoing in their lives to which they have strong positive commitments. The list is used during dissociative periods to remind clients of current resources that were not available at the times in their lives when the dissociative defense was developed. A third bridging or grounding technique developed by Dolan (1991, 1996) is the older, wiser self. This technique involves seeking advise from an older, wiser version of the client's self during stressful periods that, when invoked, will prevent a dissociative episode. This older, wiser self is described to the client as follows (Dolan, 1996, p. 406):

> Imagine that you have grown to be a healthy, wise, nurturing, old woman (or man) and you are looking back in this time in your life in which you were integrating, processing, and overcoming the effects of the past experience of sexual abuse [or other traumatic event]. What do you think this wonderful, old, nurturing, wiser you would suggest to you to help you get through this current phase of your life? What would this person tell you to remember? What would the person suggest that would be most helpful in helping you heal from the past? What would the person say to comfort you? And does this woman (or man) have any advice about how therapy could be most helpful and useful?

All of these centering or grounding techniques can be use to return the client to the here and now. More explicit techniques that involve imagery have also been described (e.g., Sanderson, 1996). These grounding techniques encourage clients to imagine themselves as trees with strong root systems that are anchored in safe settings and are indestructible even by the most powerful forces. Such visualization exercises can help the client regain equilibrium after a dissociative episode, as well as being useful in preventing dissociation during stressful periods (Sanderson, 1996).

Dealing with Psychotic Breaks, Hallucinations, and Delusions

The key to successful intervention with a client who is experiencing a psychotic break is to reestablish psychological contact with the person. Therapists should frequently and calmly use clients' names to get their attention. They must respond with calmness to clients' hallucinations or delusions to make psychological contact and must not get caught up in the psychotic content of the delusions or hallucinations about which clients are talking. It is best to respond to delusions and hallucinations by listening and taking the person seriously without encouraging the psychotic content. Delusions should not be challenged, but rather the therapist needs to focus on giving the client a sense of being understood. It is very likely that clients are used to experiencing ridicule, challenge, and harassment when voicing delusional thinking or while talking about specific hallucinations, and it is important to provide them with alternative experiences. Understanding and accepting attitudes by therapists are extremely helpful in these instances and greatly facilitate psychological contact.

The second goal is to reestablish contact with reality. This is accomplished not by challenging the delusional content of clients' verbalizations or by challenging the reality of their perceptions, but rather by redirecting clients toward other here and now concerns (e.g., "I understand what you are saying. Tell me, how did you deal with your son when you heard this voice telling you to kill yourself?" and then "And what do you do to get your son to daycare on time when this happens?" and similar interventions to get clients refocused on real, but related problems). It is also important to explore and then allay any fears stemming from the hallucinations or delusions by asserting clinicians' awareness of reality (e.g., "I understand your fear, but please let me assure you that I can guarantee you that Satan is not in this room with us."). If there is a kernel of truth to a client's delusion (and there usually is), it is important to find it and to respond to it (e.g., "I believe that you have been followed, especially that one time you told me about when . . . Can you tell me more about THAT incident?").

While reestablishing psychological contact and some degree of touch with reality, therapists must remain calm and focused themselves, being careful not to become frightened of clients and not to be persuaded to reinforce clients' delusions. It is always possible for therapists to express their understanding of why clients may have these thoughts without suggesting that the therapists believe them as well. It is also always possible to acknowledge that clients are hearing or seeing things that are distressing, while reinforcing that others do not hear or see these same things. It is also important to maintain an empathic stance that provides understanding and guidance. In other words, it is not enough to keep clients happy by giving emotional support; it also important to set firm limits on clients' behavior to ensure their and the clinicians' safety (e.g., "I need you to do ABC before we can go on" or "I understand you feel . . . ; however, right now we need to do . . . to keep you safe"). A final note is necessary here: despite their portrayal in the media to the contrary, psychotic individuals are not dangerous and not usually aggressive. They certainly can be aggressive (especially if their delusions involve paranoia and clients experience the need to defend themselves from threats). However, more often than not, aggression is not something the clinician has to fear from the psychotic client. It is much more important to get the client reoriented than to worry about the physical safety of the therapist. Obviously, if the client cannot be reoriented, the in-session intervention may need to end with institutionalizing the client. The client should generally not leave the clinician's office while flagrantly psychotic.

Dealing with Anger and Hostility

If the therapist is faced with an angry, agitated, or hostile client, the primary concern becomes diffusing the affect and maintaining behavioral safety for client and therapist. It is best not to challenge the accuracy or truthfulness of an agitatedly angry client, and this is true ever more so as the levels of anger and agitation increase. Instead, the therapist should acknowledge the client's feeling and validate it (e.g., "I certainly understand that you are very angry right now. And I can certainly see why. After all, what happened to you when . . . was very upsetting."). It is important to remain calm and not to get defensive, even if the client's affect and behavior become a personal attack against the therapist (e.g., "And it's all your fault. If you were a better therapist you would have helped . . . by now."). In other words, it is very important not to get caught up in the client's affect. If, for example, clients accuse their therapists of various transgressions or misdeeds, clinicians best do not defend themselves but rather acknowledge the clients' experience (NOT: "I think you are wrong there. I really have been doing my best, but you have not been following the advice or recommendations I have made." And NOT "If you had listened, you would know that that is not what I said. What I really said was . . ."; instead, say "I understand that you feel as though I have let you down. Please tell me what I could have done differently to help you better." or "I really appreciate that you are disappointed in therapy. We have not progressed as much as you wanted." or "I am sorry that you heard me as so critical of you. How could I have said things differently that would not have been so hard for you to hear?").

Although acknowledging clients' feelings and validating their right to these, therapists must still insist on basic safety rules. In other words, clients may get as angry as they want, but they do not have permission to act out this anger physically in aggressive or hostile ways. Behavioral boundaries on the client's actions have to be very clear (e.g., yelling is fine, so is hitting a pillow—but acting out physically against the therapist or breaking therapy room furniture is not). The therapist may choose to avoid too much direct eye contact if the client's affect escalates and should generally not touch the agitated client. Providing extra interpersonal space can also be helpful. Especially when dealing with angry affect that appears to have the potential to be acted out, the therapist must remember the caution never to be a hero. If the client becomes too agitated or openly aggressive, it may be time to end the session or to call for help. It is generally relatively clear to a therapist when a situation reaches a danger zone of potential physical aggression. The clinician will begin to feel unsafe and will sense a loss of control on the client's part that involves not merely affective but behavioral control. The strength of a client's voice in itself is generally not the best predictor. Better predictors are a client's eyes and physical movements. Specific physical symptoms that signal increasingly angry affect are things like muscle twitching or restlessness, movement and pacing, pantomimed aggression (such as pounding, choking someone, beating), stares or lack of eye contact, shallow breathing, a quivering or loud voice, clenched fists, and angry words. When the therapist begins to notice these symptoms, diffusing the affect quickly is important or the session may need to be discontinued. This can be communicated to the client directly because it may often serve to diffuse the behavioral reaction (e.g., "Unless you can calm down a little bit, we will not be able to keep working today."). Similarly, if the therapist feels the need to end the session or call in a helper, an explanation needs to be given (e.g., "I believe we are no longer safe in this room because I am sensing that you are about to blow up. Let's stop for today and continue our work next session" or "Let's stop for a moment and call in one of my colleagues to get this person's perspective on this issue").

If the clinician has a client who regularly gets extremely angry, it is a good idea to plan ahead and have supervision and consultation available. If the therapist is lucky enough to have videotaping facilities or one-way mirrors, it is best to have a colleague watching the session. Thus if the clinician misjudges the intensity of the client's affect and behavior, help is immediately available. If this route is chosen, the clinician needs to make sure that the observer does not overreact. For example, once I was with a habitually aggressive and angry client whom I had been seeing for some weeks. I never arranged for an observer, but I always made sure to only schedule this client when other staff were available so that if I should need help I could call for it. Over the course of the session, the client became extremely agitated and began screaming at a pretty good volume. I did not feel threatened at all and viewed the behavior as appropriate and cathartic. A colleague, however, literally burst into the room (he was so worried he did not even knock) to make sure we were safe. This was quite a disruption to treatment at the moment (though relatively easily mended once explained to the client from the colleague's perspective). Thus if clinicians see aggressive clients, they must make some provisions for observers and may want to agree on some (nonverbal) sign that signals the observer to intervene. If nothing else, knowing that backup help is available will help therapists feel less nervous and concerned, making them more emotionally accessible and available to clients.

SUMMARY AND CONCLUDING THOUGHTS

This chapter outlined possible means to manage difficult situations that can arise in the context of psychotherapy. It addressed some of the more common questions raised by therapists as well as the most common challenges presented by clients.

All guidelines and suggestions made in this chapter are identified as somewhat subjective solutions that may not represent the best or only way for all clinicians to deal with any of the sample situations. Instead, the solutions provided here reflect my way of dealing with tough situations given the philosophical beliefs and understanding of therapeutic process endorsed in these pages. All therapists will need to think about the questions and challenges posed in this chapter as well as their preferred responses to them and use the suggestions here as mere guidelines or bases for thought. The guiding principle underlying the search for solutions and approaches is that there is an optimally therapeutic response for each client from the clinician's perspective. This optimally therapeutic response has to be consistent with the general philosophical foundation that guides the clinician's therapeutic work and the appropriateness of the response given the therapist's overall approach to therapy process.

DOCUMENTATION AND RECORD-KEEPING

As mentioned in several prior chapters, therapists have an ethical obligation to keep records of their work with clients. Such record-keeping facilitates transfer in case of client–therapist mismatches or other circumstances that require that the client shift work to another care provider. The type of documentation that is most helpful for recording treatment process or progress is referred to as a progress note. In other words, therapists do not prepare full-length reports for each session they have with a client, but do prepare a brief document that outlines the most essential information about it. Progress notes must be written after each contact with the client, including between-session phone contacts. The ideal progress note addresses the following issues (cf., Meier & Davis, 1993; Parsons, 1986; Seligman, 1996):

Presentation

1. client-related observations and information:
   - objective, observable client behavior
   - presentation and mental status of the client
   - new data relevant to the client's history
   - life changes related by the client
   - changes in condition or status of the client as compared to prior sessions
   - client's movement or progress toward treatment goals

Process

2. session and process-related information and observations
   - content and themes of the session
   - interventions and response or effectiveness thereof
3. here and now process as related to process outside the therapy context

Interpretation

4. therapist understanding of the process as it unfolded
5. therapist reactions to and impressions about the session

Plan

6. evaluation of selected strategies
7. plans for the next session

A sample of a progress note follows to give the reader a concept of the brevity and contents of such a note. A progress note, by definition, places its emphasis on client progress (i.e., changes and plans). Some clinicians choose to write process notes that tend to be slightly lengthier and somewhat more subjective than progress notes. In this day and age of litigation, progress notes appear to have become the preferred mode of recording session occurrences. They are briefer, more objective, and less involved. Most progress notes are no more than a half to a full page of typed notes. The exception to this rule of thumb is recording sessions that involved a crisis. Such sessions are recorded in more detail and often are much lengthier and more specific.

Sample Progress Note

Client Name: Frederick X. _____   Clinician: Chris Brems _____

Date of Session: 24 January 1995; 2:00 P.M.   Session Number: 13 _____

Payment Made: $60 (receipt provided)   Next Session: 31 January 1995 _____

Presentation: The client arrived five minutes early and appeared eager to work. He appeared to be in better spirits than last w‹ k and reported a significant decrease in depressive symptoms. He had several positive experiences at work this week that shored up his self-esteem and improved his sense of self-efficacy. He believes that these events precipitated his currently improved mood. Client also indicated that he thought the work that was done in the last session had helped him recognize some dependent behavior patterns at work that were less than optimal and that the positive responses by his boss this week were a direct result of several changes the client had made in his behavior after the last session. Namely, he had been more assertive about doing his job in a particular way that is more in line with his personality style, rather than trying to please his boss by trying to imitate his behavior. He not only felt better about himself doing his work this way, but he also experienced more success.

Process: In relating this information to the clinician, the client checked with her several times about whether she perceived the situation in the same way as he did. When this pattern of requesting affirmation was pointed out, he talked about it as being a common interactional style that he had maintained all of his life. Although this was not news (i.e., had been a topic in sessions before), it appeared to be more meaningful to and understood by the client today. He spontaneously linked his need to please the clinician to his dependency on her and his fear that she may abandon him if he wasn't a good enough client. This pattern was explored further both in the context of the therapeutic relationship and the context of other relationships (e.g., with boss and significant other).

Interpretation: The client appears to continue to make improvements and is moving into a more insightful processing of the relationship with the therapist and with others in this environment. He is responding well to explaining strategies and appears less dependent on affirmative and supportive response, being able to sustain criticism and challenge much better than before, both inside and outside of session. However, this change still appears to be subtle and he still comes across as vulnerable and somewhat emotionally needy and frightened.

Plan: Therapy appears to be on the right track and will continue to pursue his relational patterns (particularly his dependency needs and abandonment fears) in the attempt to help him internalize the necessary self-structure that will help him become less dependent and freer in interpersonal relationships.

8

TERMINATION OF THERAPY

Das Ende eines Dinges, in der Anfang eines anderen.
(The ending of one thing, is the beginning of another)
—GERMAN PROVERB

Perhaps one of the most unfortunate word choices mental health professionals have made is the choice of the label "termination" to describe ending a therapeutic relationship. The colloquial use of the word termination has become associated with many less than positive connotations, often implying notions of death and threats to life. It is important to overcome these connotations of the label to ensure that successful terminations can be initiated with clients. Termination of a therapeutic relationship is a desirable and necessary outcome of every therapy, and there is almost general consensus among mental health professionals that termination is not only one of the most important treatment goals but is actually worked toward from the very beginning of treatment (Freud, 1937; Goldberg, 1975; Kramer, 1990). As Teyber (1997, p. 319) notes, "Therapists often underestimate how powerful an experience termination is for clients. It holds the potential either to undo or to confirm and extend the changes that have come about in therapy. Thus therapists must be prepared to utilize the further potential for change that becomes available as therapists and clients prepare to end their relationship." Careful preparation for termination is essential to ensure that the experience will be helpful, not traumatic or negative. Successful treatment "leads to termination, not as trauma, but as another step forward in client growth" (Pate, 1982, p. 188). Successful termination provides the client with yet another experience that encourages growth, change, and healing and that provides the therapist with an opportunity to create yet another corrective emotional experience for the client. No doubt, termination has its sad moments; but, all in all, it should not be a sad, but rather a bittersweet, event. The fact that clients are ready for termination means that they have accomplished change and healing and these are happy feelings for both client and therapist. However, knowing that the relationship between client and therapist is over can bring some sad moments. Good termination will have components of both happiness and sadness, with the participants mourning the loss of the relationship while realizing that the process is actually healthy, necessary, and positive. If a termination is well done, the joyful feelings will be more powerful than the sad feelings; both client and therapist will focus on the positive aspects leading to the ending of the relationship and will recognize that, despite the fact that they are saying goodbye, both will have lasting memories of their work together. The end of the relationship may have come. However, contrary to common client fears, ending the therapeutic relationship does not mean that changes that the client has made and progress that the client has achieved will be reversed. Instead, internalization that has taken place over the course of treatment is such that both client and therapist will leave the relationship forever altered. Certainly, terminating therapy is no guarantee that clients will never return to treatment or even that they will never be unhappy again. Quite to the contrary. The goal of therapy is healthier functioning; such change neither implies interminable happiness nor lack of need for assistance in the future. In fact, often clients who have had very successful therapies return for treatment again and again because they realize that therapy is a helpful process that can speed up change and healing in a variety of circumstances.

It is helpful here to differentiate two distinct types of psychotherapy termination: natural and unnatural (or premature) endings. The former category is more likely to fall in the bittersweet category because it implies that, at least for the moment, the therapeutic work is done and client and therapist can rejoice in their accomplishments. The latter category is more likely to have negative feelings associated with it and, hence, often must be handled even more carefully than a natural termination (Kramer, 1990). However, the particular strategies that are used to bring closure to a client's case are largely the same, regardless of whether termination is premature or natural. It is the purpose of this chapter to provide a framework for psychotherapy termination that is positive, comprehensive, and useful for client and therapist alike.

It must be noted that within the two larger categories of types of termination (i.e., natural versus unnatural or premature), there are additional subtypes (summarized in Figure 8.1). In the category of natural terminations, the process of ending may be initiated by the client or by the therapist; in the category of unnatural terminations, the process of ending may be initiated by the client, the therapist, or an external force over which neither client nor therapist has control. Client-initiated premature (unnatural or imposed) terminations can fall into two categories: voluntary or involuntary. One example of voluntary client-initiated premature terminations is the client who is satisfied with the progress made to date, even though this progress is not in line with treatment goals and even though the therapist may not agree that the client is ready to end therapeutic work. Involuntary client-initiated premature termination may be due to family pressure on the client to quit or due to a family move to another city. Premature terminations initiated by therapists may also be voluntary or involuntary. Voluntary termination of this type includes events such as a therapist's decision that a client has derived maximal benefit from treatment, despite the fact that not all treatment goals have been reached; decisions that

Natural Terminations

- Therapist initiated with client agreeing
- Client initiated with therapist agreeing

Premature Terminations

- Therapist initiated
  voluntary (e.g., no more benefits to be derived; referral necessary due to limited expertise)
  involuntary (e.g., end of a training period; job change; retirement)
- Client initiated
  voluntary (e.g., satisfied with progress made; does not find therapy helpful)
  involuntary (e.g., moving due to a job change; family move; family pressure to quit)
- Externally imposed (e.g., clinic closure; loss of insurance benefits)

FIGURE 8.1   Types of Terminations

the current therapist may not be the best clinician for the client; or decisions that recognize that the client is in need of services that the current therapist cannot provide (e.g., for lack of equipment). Involuntary therapist-initiated terminations may include events such as the end of a training period for the therapist, a job move by the therapist, or retirement. Finally, an example of an externally imposed termination may be the closing of the clinic where the client was seen or of insurance benefit limitations being reached. In each case, termination will be handled slightly differently but will still be within the general natural termination framework that will be presented below. In other words, whether a termination is natural or premature will result in some differences in terms of what a clinician needs to attend to; however, in terms of the overall strategy, there are many similarities. The general guidelines for termination will be discussed in the section on Natural Termination. The special issues that must be addressed in the various forms of premature terminations are then added in the section on Premature Termination.

NATURAL TERMINATIONS

The most desirable treatment outcome in psychotherapy is the termination agreed on that is initiated either by the client or the therapist because treatment goals have been achieved. In such a case, termination is truly the kind of bittersweet event mentioned above. Such a natural termination can be a great asset to treatment. It reinforces the gains made by the client and once again provides the client with a valuable corrective emotional experience. It is important that therapists learn to recognize when a termination is appropriate and that, once they have decided that termination is in order, they know how to facilitate this process to maximize its benefits for the client. A therapist must know the reasons for natural termination, must be able to recognize the clues offered by the client that a termination is indicated, must know the guidelines that surround a natural termination, and must be knowledgeable of the type of client and therapist behaviors that can be expected as termination progresses. A minimum of four aspects have to be present for a natural termination to be possible. Clients must have achieved therapy goals, must have generalized some learning, must feel ready to end, and must feel that the therapeutic relationship has reached closure (Kleinke, 1994). It is the responsibility of the therapist to ascertain that these preconditions exist.

Reasons for Natural Termination

The reasons for termination are fairly straightforward conceptually, and must be measured carefully to be successfully recognized. Even Freud (1937) suggested that therapy should come to a close when several conditions are met. Specifically, therapy ends when clients have resolved the symptoms that were presented for treatment, when some level of insight has been achieved, when clients have improved their coping skills to prevent future symptoms, and when clients would not make significant additional gains by remaining in psychotherapy. Most contemporary writers agree that the overwhelming reason for a natural termination is that clients have achieved their treatment goals, have obtained from therapy whatever it was that they sought to accomplish, and have generalized these changes to the world outside of the therapy room (see Cormier & Hackney, 1987; Hutchins & Vaught, 1997; Patterson & Welfel, 1993). Other writers suggest that reasons for termination may not merely mean goals are achieved in and out of therapy, but also show an increase in the client's capacity for enjoyment, enhanced self-acceptance, a more completely integrated sense of self, an improved sense of humor, and heightened acceptance of others (Kohut, 1984). Further, changes in the client, whether due to achieving treatment goals or from other improvements, need to be verified through multiple sources. This task is best accomplished by checking therapists' impressions regarding goal achievement with clients themselves and with significant others in clients' lives (via client report; Teyber, 1997). Additionally, if it is the client who reports changes, the therapist needs to verify these reported improvements through changes in the therapeutic relationship.

How goal achievement is measured varies from therapist to therapist, but this must be given careful consideration and may depend to some extent on the theoretical orientation of the clinician and the clarity with which goals and objectives were defined in treatment. Some therapists develop rigorous and measurable goals, whereas others set goals that are less easily objectively quantifiable. As suggested in Chapter 4, it is best to set at least some goals that are quantifiable to make them amenable to objective measurement that can help assess whether the time has come for termination. Such measurement can be very formal or somewhat informal, again largely depending on the preferences of the therapist. For example, some clinicians may set a goal of decreasing depression and choose to measure such decreases by repeatedly administering a depression scale. Others may assess a decrease in depression through talking with the client and assessing appetite and sleep patterns, changes in interest, and self-reported mood. Yet others may be satisfied with observations of the client during sessions that suggest an enhanced client mood. To provide another example, some clinicians may assess decreases in anxiety by formally and repeatedly administering anxiety inventories; others may talk to clients about manifestations of anxiety in day-to-day life to assess whether changes have occurred; yet others may observe clients for obvious signs of anxiety in sessions, such as counting how often clients twirl their hair, bounce their legs, wring their hands, and so forth, to show progress in decreasing such anxiety-related behaviors over time. However assessment of change or improvement is conducted, it must be done consciously and with purpose and must be documented in the client's file. If observation is chosen as the primary means of assessing change, it is also important to check with the client to verify the impressions of the clinician.

Although ending treatment is predicated on achieving treatment goals and other desirable changes in the client and they are the best indicators for when the time has come to end treatment, they are not the only signs or signals a therapist can rely on to suggest termination to a client. Clients themselves may decide to suggest termination with the clinician when they feel satisfied with the perceived improvement in themselves as persons and in their general thoughts, feelings, behaviors, and interactions. Some clients, however, may not have the courage to bring up the idea of termination with the therapist because the therapeutic relationship is cherished and important to them, and they may not want to face the idea of ending this enjoyable interaction. In fact, at the point of significant improvement, therapy becomes less difficult for the client and old resistances and ambivalences vanish, which leaves the client enjoying the process perhaps more than ever. It is not up to the client to recognize when termination must be initiated—it is strictly the responsibility of the therapist to recognize when the time has come after which therapy will no longer offer the client significant gains. Some therapists resist termination themselves; this issue is of sufficient importance to be dealt with separately in the section below. Often when clients improve, they give inadvertent signals to the clinician that they are ready to end treatment, even long before they can or are willing to verbalize this recognition. A good therapist will recognize these signs and signals and will use them as motivators to broach the topic of ending therapy.

Signs and Signals of Readiness for Natural Termination

Clients can give a variety of signals to their clinicians that they are ready to end treatment; learning these signals will help therapists prevent unnecessarily prolonged therapy. Some of these signs may occur even before the therapist has identified the reasons for termination outlined above. In this case, the therapist may have to analyze such signals and to decide whether they are occurring because of resistance or other nontherapeutic reasons, or because the reasons for ending have been reached but were overlooked by the therapist. It is indeed not uncommon for a therapist to rationalize the need to continue therapy, even after presenting problems have been resolved, under the guise of working on underlying problems or personality restructuring. Such continued work may indeed be justified in some cases; however, if signals arise from the client that indicate that it is time to end, therapists may need to explore their own countertransferences about why continuation is deemed important.

Clients who are ready for termination have increasingly less to talk about in therapy; they indicate less need for feedback from the therapist and begin to treat the therapist more as an equal than an expert. Not surprisingly, they are less affected by mistakes or reactions from the therapist because clients have now internalized a stronger sense of self-confidence and self-efficacy and begin to measure themselves and their own behavior less by how others react to it than by how they themselves perceive it. Clients become more capable of accepting the therapist's own fallibility and can begin to accept the therapist as a human being with faults and shortcomings, without this fact diminishing the therapist's value in the clients' eyes (Wolf, 1988). Additionally, the therapist will perceive that the client feels better, responds more adaptively in and out of sessions, and demonstrates new skills. Clients at this stage in treatment often begin to relate stories of how others are giving them feedback that they appear different somehow, and they begin to bring stories into the therapy about how they are surprised at their own ability to handle formerly difficult situations with more equanimity and ease (Teyber, 1997). Clients who are close to termination also begin to discuss their futures more often than their pasts; they begin to spend more and more time talking about issues that concern this future that are not directly relevant to topics that had so far preoccupied treatment (Brems, 1993). Clients may also begin to engage in new behaviors in the therapy room. For example, they may suddenly choose to sit in a different chair; they may rearrange a display or clutter on a table in the therapy room; or they may make comments about furnishings and decorations they never seemed to notice before. Clients begin to take in their environment more completely and begin to comment on it. There may also be new behaviors related to treatment that occur outside of the therapy room. As such, clients may suddenly be late for sessions when this never occurred before; clients may begin to cancel sessions occasionally; or they may "forget" to come to their regularly scheduled sessions (Brems, 1993).

All of these signs obviously may also communicate resistance to treatment. However, their context, timing, and novelty usually help the therapist recognize them for what they are. In other words, if a client had been in treatment for only a brief period of time, had not yet shown a significant attachment to the therapist or the therapy process, and has started running out of things to say, this client's behavior could be confidently interpreted as resistance (or self-protection; see Chapter 6). However, if the same behavior occurred in a client who had been in treatment for several months, had built a meaningful relationship with the therapist, had repeatedly evidenced a belief in the importance of the therapy, and had made notable strides in treatment, it could be interpreted confidently as a termination signal. None of these signals is foolproof; none can be used in isolation. It is best to view each in its context, to look for additional signals, and to explore whether the reasons for termination are obvious as well. If all of these factors are answered affirmatively, it is time to consider termination.

Signs that it is time to end therapy can emanate not only from the client, but also from the therapist. Signals experienced by the therapist are quite varied in nature, but are always related to the relationship that has been established with the client. An important signal is given when therapists begin to note that they are growing increasingly fond of the client, have fewer and fewer ambiguous feelings about them, and consider the client increasingly interesting. The therapist develops high hopes for the client's achievement and health outside of the therapy room but feels less responsible for making these things happen. The therapist feels less burdened by the work with the client, less protective, and less in need to provide continuous support. In other words, the client is perceived as more capable, stronger, and more of an equal partner in the therapeutic relationship. Thus when termination is near, therapists may note that they have to work less hard in sessions and perhaps are even bored on occasion by the work that is being done. If therapists ever find themselves feeling less responsible—for example, justifying lateness or cancellations—it may well be time to reiterate the client's treatment goals and assess whether the reasons for a natural termination have been reached. If this is indeed the case, the therapist must begin to prepare for the termination process. This preparation is essential and cannot be skipped lest the best therapy suddenly go awry in the end.

General Procedural Guidelines for Successful Natural Termination

Good termination procedure is essential to maintaining therapeutic gains (Fair & Bressler, 1992). Failing to follow a clear process for termination may recapitulate a client's old conflicts about ending relationships and may recreate a therapeutic ending that is as painful and unsuccessful as endings experienced in prior relationships. In fact, Teyber (1997) suggests that the lack of proper termination procedure is the most common reason for unsuccessful treatment. A good termination process has several components and a clear time line developed by the therapist (perhaps in consultation with the client), and it is openly addressed and discussed with the client. Termination is a process that needs to be dealt with openly, talked about freely, and discussed often. Only if it is dealt with directly and matter-of-factly, as a valuable and important aspect of therapy, will the client come to value the ending process and understand it as a meaningful and useful component of treatment (Teyber, 1997). Termination is easiest if the client perceives it as desirable (Kramer, 1990) and the therapist agrees.

The process of terminating therapy always starts with the therapist's recognition that the client has met (or is close to meeting) the reasons for ending therapy (i.e., has achieved treatment goals and/or has made and generalized other desirable changes) and that both client and therapist are beginning to give signals that suggest that a new level has been reached in the therapeutic relationship. Once clinicians understand this, they need to begin to plan for termination by preparing themselves for the ending. Such preparation first and foremost consists of a review of any possible countertransferences they may bring to the ending process. Only when therapists are aware of their possible interfering contributions to the termination process are they ready to initiate the procedure. Countertransference in the termination process is often best recognized through feelings of resistance to the process in the clinician. Just as clients resist ending therapy by bargaining with the clinician for an extension, so therapists may resist termination with all or certain clients. The motivation to resist ending therapy is often similar for clients and therapists. Specifically, just as clients react to the suggestion of termination out of old fears of loss and abandonment, fears of losing ground won in therapy after the relationship ends, or fear of having to cope with difficult life situations alone from then on, therapists may have fears that are stimulated by the termination process. Common fears that fuel a clinician's resistance include, but may not be limited to, fears of loss and abandonment, fears of being perceived as rejecting or abandoning, fears that the client may relapse without weekly therapeutic support, fears of not having been a good enough therapist, guilt over perceived abandonment, and fears of imperfect performance (Cormier & Hackney, 1987; Patterson & Welfel, 1993; Teyber, 1997). Therapists must be aware of potential countertransferences that get in the way of a healthy ending for the therapeutic relationship and must themselves work on learning to let go and learning to trust their professional judgment about the readiness of a client to end treatment. Only then will the clinician be able to help the client end the therapeutic relationship healthily and usefully. Another possible countertransference that appears to emerge among clinicians in private practice is hesitating to let go of clients who are well-paying and/or have good insurance benefits. It is tempting to allow therapy to be interminable with such clients, especially if the clients themselves express little motivation to end. However, therapists must keep in mind that therapy has to end when the reasons for termination have been met; to keep clients in treatment beyond a time when they derive clear benefits from it is not only nontherapeutic but also unethical and unprofessional (American Psychological Association, 1992).

The best way to begin termination is to bring it up with the client on a relatively informal level when it appears most relevant given the topic at hand. As such, termination is best broached with the client when evidence emerges in the session that ending therapy is indicated, such as evidence of significant improvement or the emergence of signs and signals. For example, if clients come into their sessions repeatedly late or if clients suddenly sit in the chair formerly reserved for the therapist, this can be pointed out to the client. It must be noted that at this stage of therapy, interpretations can be made easily as treatment is almost complete and it stands to reason that by now clients are thoroughly familiar with interpretations and the issues surrounding them, have developed the necessary emotional health to "survive" them, and are sufficiently secure in the therapeutic relationship that they can tolerate them. Thus signs and signals of termination can be addressed freely with clients because the presumption at this time in treatment clearly is that the client is relatively healthy and ready to function independently. Nevertheless, clients do not always react positively to the suggestion that therapy needs to come to an end. Therefore, in making interpretations about signs and signals it is still best to proceed with normal therapeutic caution, by first allowing the client to make the interpretation an experience-near one. To return to the second example above, if a client suddenly takes over the therapist's chair, the following interaction may take place as a means of exploring the possibility of termination.

THERAPIST: I noticed you are sitting in my chair today.

CLIENT: Oh, am I? . . . I didn't notice. *(smiles)*

THERAPIST: You didn't notice . . . (also smiles, acknowledging nonverbally that both client and therapist are fully aware of the fact that the client _did_ notice)

CLIENT: Well, I guess I did notice. (grins)

THERAPIST: What's that all about?

CLIENT: What do you mean?

THERAPIST: Well, by now you know that I really believe that most behaviors have a meaning and that you are probably trying to tell me something here.

CLIENT: Well, I'm not sure I planned it. But when I walked in today, I just felt like I belonged in your seat.

THERAPIST: You belonged in my seat?

CLIENT: Yeah—I'm not sure why. . . .

THERAPIST: Almost like you're saying—hey, I can do that job!

CLIENT: Do your job?

THERAPIST: Yeah—do my job; you know, do for yourself what maybe I have been doing with or for you all these weeks.

CLIENT: Hm, I have noticed that more and more often I catch myself thinking "What would Chris say to me now?"—and then I know what I need or want to do. It's like you don't have to be present anymore to actually help me out.

THERAPIST: Like you're doing my job. (smiles)

CLIENT: Yeah—I guess you're right. I'm doing your job and I'm doing pretty well with it.

THERAPIST: Yes, I have noticed that you are doing all kinds of things these days that were very tough for you when we first started working together. Have you noticed this?

CLIENT: Yes. (and goes on to explain how she too has noticed change)

This interaction demonstrates how clinicians get their clients ready to recognize that their behaviors communicate something about themselves that suggest that they are making significant strides and changes—in fact, changes that may be significant enough to begin to talk about termination. Once the changes have been processed by client and clinician, the exchange that began in the example above may then continue as follows, to introduce the idea of ending.

THERAPIST: So with all these things that you see as changed, what do you think this may mean about our relationship and your therapy?

CLIENT: Well, you really helped me and therapy really is good for me—and that even though I really wasn't sure if I wanted this when I first started!

THERAPIST: And what do you think it means for our relationship and therapy in the future?

CLIENT: Oh, I see what you're after: in the future. . . . Hm, I guess you mean what do we work on now. It's like we've run out of important things that need to be talked about.

THERAPIST: Yeah—I wonder if we need to start talking about ending.

CLIENT: Oh—well now, that's a scary thought.

THERAPIST: I'm not talking about quitting today or even next week or even next month. I'm just talking about starting to consider ending our work together and whether you're ready for that and if so, when and how.

CLIENT: I don't know if I'm ready. . . .

THERAPIST: Okay—well, why don't we talk about that a bit.

From here the clinician and the client need to explore whether the therapist has read the signals correctly and whether the client has really reached a point in therapy where continued treatment will not result in significant additional changes and most or all treatment goals have been met. The therapist never makes the presumption from an isolated event that termination is definitely indicated; instead, the topic is broached and then assessment and planning begins. If the assessment reveals that client and therapist indeed agree that the client has improved and changed sufficiently to warrant ending treatment, they will then begin to plan the process of termination that will culminate in the event of actually saying good-bye.

The next step in the process of termination is setting a firm ending date. Setting a date for the final session is important to reduce anxiety for both client and therapist (Teyber, 1997) and to keep bargaining by the client about an extension of time with the therapist to a minimum (Brems, 1993). The timing of the date for a final session depends on how much time the therapist believes the client needs to gain closure in the therapeutic relationship—a time frame that will be dictated somewhat by the theoretical orientation and therapy model to which the therapist adheres. Clearly, in a short-term approach to therapy, such an end date may be reached rather quickly; in long-term therapies, such an end date may be several weeks away. Lamb (1985) suggests a model in which termination takes place over a seven-week period. In this model then, the ending date would be set for seven weeks after the therapist and client have decided to end treatment. Whatever model clinicians choose, they must discuss their rationale for setting an end date to let their clients know what will happen over that time period of work. In other words, it is helpful at this time to explain to the client what the termination process is like and what the client can expect. Issues of relapse, review, and planning are addressed and explained to the client in a manner that provides an overview of the remaining weeks of treatment (Brems, 1993; Teyber, 1997). Such an explanation may take the following form:

THERAPIST: So, now that we have decided that it is time to end therapy, we need to set a date for our final session and talk a little bit about what you can expect from the few weeks of work that we have left together. I would like to give us plenty of time to get some closure on our work and relationship, and to me that means allowing us about six or seven more sessions before we quit meeting. That would mean our last session would be on April 19. How does that sound to you?

CLIENT: Soon!

THERAPIST: Yeah, we'll be pretty busy during those six sessions after this one.

CLIENT: What if I'm not ready to leave then? Can we go on?

THERAPIST: I picked six more sessions after today because I am very certain that we can get everything done that we need to do before then. We've already decided that you're ready to stop because things have improved for you. So, you will be ready by then.

CLIENT: Are you sure? It feels like that will be pretty soon.

THERAPIST: I am sure.

CLIENT: Okay.

THERAPIST: What we'll do with the six sessions we have left is review the work we've done, take another look at how things have changed for you, explore a little bit what else is left to do for you in the future, and talk about how you feel about quitting. You and I have become very important to each other over the last nine months, and we need time to say good-bye and to let each other know how we feel about saying good-bye. So that, in a nutshell, is our agenda for the next six weeks. Is there anything you want to add to the list?

CLIENT: I don't think so. Can I add stuff if I think of it?

THERAPIST: Of course. Just like always—you'll still be in charge of deciding what we talk about. I'll just remind us every week how many sessions we have left and remind us to talk about ending at least a little bit each time. The last week or two that's probably all we'll talk about. And the last session we'll reserve to say good-bye to each other.

CLIENT: That sounds good.

THERAPIST: Let me say just one more thing. Sometimes when we start talking about quitting, people go home and then they suddenly get depressed again, or anxious, or whatever it was that they came to therapy for. That's a natural thing and it doesn't mean that you're back to where you were when we started. It's quite a different story, especially now that you have the skills to deal with these old feelings. But if that happens, let me know and we'll talk about it. Also don't let it scare you. You're not losing ground—you're just reacting to ending therapy and that's to be expected and natural.

Once an end date has been agreed upon by the client and therapist and they have discussed what will happen in the remaining weeks of therapy, it is the responsibility of the therapist to track the time that is left for therapeutic work and to remind the client each week how many sessions remain (Lamb, 1985; Teyber, 1997). These weekly reminders ensure that neither client nor therapist deny that the termination is impending and that both begin to deal with the reality of having to say good-bye to what has come to be a gratifying and enjoyable interaction for both. Early on, the therapist may choose merely to remind the client of the ending date and the number of sessions remaining. However, as the actual final session approaches, the therapist must become increasingly insistent upon processing the impending termination with the client. A good rule of thumb is to reserve at least the final three sessions for thorough discussion of termination, with the very last session being reserved for saying good-bye and gaining relationship closure. Discussions of terminating revolve around four topics or issues: they will address the changes the client has achieved, with a thorough look at how these have manifested in the client's life outside the therapy room; they will explore the shifts that have taken place in the therapeutic relationship, with an attempt to help the client gain an understanding of what this means about the evolution of the client's growth and healing, including in future relationships; it will explore what the client can expect after ending therapy with regard to future symptoms and relationships and must address the idea of future therapy; and it will allow the client to express affects as they emerge throughout the termination process (Lamb, 1985; Patterson & Welfel, 1993; Teyber, 1997).

The discussion of changes in clients is important because it validates clients' experience that something about themselves is different. It is also often a beautiful reminder for clients that things really have changed. Change occurs over the course of a relatively long-term intervention (ranging from several months to several years), and clients sometimes lose track of just how much they have improved. They have forgotten the pain they felt when they first entered therapy; they have suppressed memories of irrational thoughts they may have had; they have lost all recollection of old behavior patterns and relationship patterns that used to create problems or pain for them. The therapist reminds clients of how they presented for treatment and of the characteristics that marked their behavior, affect, thoughts, and interactions. In so doing, the therapist also helps clients compare and contrast their state of well-being at the beginning of therapy and at the current time. The discussion of change will remind clients of the long journey they have made and will give them a new appreciation of how much change they are capable. This is not only a validating experience (Cormier & Hackney, 1987) but also an encouraging activity, because it suggests to clients that they can continue to change and grow beyond the confines of the therapy room.

The review of the client–therapist relationship is helpful because it provides a model for a successful relationship that can be used by clients in the future. It also is useful in bringing closure to this relationship and in helping clients have the experience of ending a relationship positively, painlessly, and with integrity (Teyber, 1997). In the process of recapitulating the means of moving the therapeutic relationship forward, clients are allowed to express feelings about their therapists and the fact that these relationships are ending. Their therapists acknowledge the great importance of therapeutic relationships to the changes their clients have experienced and may share personal feelings about the ending process, being somewhat more self-disclosing about their emotional reactions to clients than at earlier times in treatment. It is helpful for clients to see that therapists also have affective responses to ending, that clients are special to them, and that termination evokes a similar reaction in therapists. Therapists can share their ambivalences about ending therapy with their clients and about the fact that they must experience a loss as well. This process of self-disclosure is not to be overdone, of course; clients should not feel guilty for making their therapists feel bad about losing the therapeutic relationship. After all, then the relationship would no longer be therapeutic; instead, therapists engage in termination self-disclosure to let clients see their human side and to model for clients that endings are best accomplished by sharing emotions and reactions openly and freely. This process models that losing relationships is difficult and must be acknowledged lest the loss fester and result in excessive and unrecognized pain. In other words, therapists' self-disclosures serve the function of modeling a successful farewell.

Discussion of the therapeutic relationship also includes recapturing how the relationship between client and therapist evolved over time. Clinicians remind their clients of their journeys from distrust to trust, from ambivalence to commitment, from feeling like strangers to feeling close, from not knowing what to expect to having developed clear communication and a common language. The evolution of the relationship is explored to help the client recognize that all relationships evolve and change over time and that it takes two active and conscious participants to make a relationship work. Recapturing the relationship has a strong flavor of reminiscing, of realizing what the two people in the therapeutic relationship have accomplished together, and how they have experienced each other (Patterson & Welfel, 1994). They will use a lot of phrases such as, "Remember when . . .", "I can still recall when . . .", "Can you recollect how we . . .", "Compare then and now . . .", and so forth. Client and therapist will thoroughly commemorate the relationship they developed over time and will thus gain closure with one another. An acknowledgment of the close connection they have, and that breaking this connection is painful, will run throughout this discourse, while also acknowledging a joyful meaning of the good-bye.

The discussion of the future is designed to help clients recognize that having completed therapy for now does not mean that they will never need therapy again or will never be unhappy again. Instead, clinicians and clients will work together on helping clients recognize that they will have painful and irrational thoughts again in the future; they will use this opportunity to help clients recognize that now, however, they have skills to cope with such events. Talking about the future also helps clients realize that therapy is a process that can be used over and over again—that is, that the client can return to therapy should the need for this arise in the future. This opening of the door to future treatment is deemed important but should never be used to avoid saying a firm and final good-bye. In other words, clients can be encouraged to avail themselves of therapy in the future, but not with the suggestion that they can or must always return to see the same therapist again. The door is open to further therapy, not to the therapist per se. This caution is made to prevent a watering down of the process of saying good-bye. If clients are allowed the false perception that therapy is not really over, but just put on hold for now, she or he may not gain the type of closure that is desirable in the termination process. The client needs to learn how to end relationships successfully; leaving the door open to *this* therapist and no other prevents this learning from being complete (see Brems, 1993).

Throughout the process of ending therapy, the client is allowed to express affects and is helped to see these affects in the context of termination. Much mourning or grieving the loss of the relationship will take place at this time, and many clients go through a process that parallels the mourning process of having lost a loved one (either to death or for other reasons). Thus it is not surprising that many of the reactions the client will experience parallel the process of dealing with death and dying outlined by Kuebler-Ross (1971, 1975). This conceptualization of the affective response to termination by the client will be discussed in detail in the Stages of Termination section below. Understanding the stage model of client reactions that will be outlined below will help the clinician respond more appropriately and therapeutically to the client as termination progresses. Such therapeutic responding, in turn, will ascertain that neither therapist nor client overreact to affects potentially revealed by the client and will prevent inappropriate revisions of termination time lines, as well as excessive countertransference reactions on the part of the therapist.

Once client and therapist have progressed through the few sessions preceding the very last session of a client's treatment, they are ready to say good-bye. Most, if not all, of the processing that has been discussed so far takes place in the few sessions before the final session; the final session is reserved for saying good-bye and allowing the client to recapitulate any of the most important contents or affects. The final session may be one session when the meeting between client and therapist violates the timing boundary: when the good-byes are complete, the therapist may decide to end the session, even if a few minutes are left. Trying to fill the prescribed 45 or 50 minutes when closure has been gained and good-byes have been said makes for an awkward ending. It is easier to allow the session to flow naturally and to end when closure has been reached. This is no license, however, to run overtime. Clients may not be available to spend more time, and if they suddenly have to leave before closure has been gained, the whole termination process is called into question. Saying good-bye means both client and therapist share their feelings about ending, probably verbalizing yet again the bittersweet nature of the event. Therapists will recapitulate that they feel sad about losing the client, but happy that losing clients means that they have improved and are more content with life. Clients are similarly encouraged to share their feelings and to review whatever they deem important. A therapist's closure will include all of the thoughts provided below. Although the following statement is written as a cohesive monologue, this is of course not how these thoughts would be shared with the client. Instead, the thoughts contained in the statement would be shared with the client over the entire course of the final session, because they fit in with the work the client is doing. The statement is provided to give the reader an idea of the content that needs to be covered by the therapist to gain closure with the client and to model how the relationship needs to be ended and acknowledged.

Thoughts Shared by the Therapist with the Client over the Course of the Final Session

We have come a long way together in these last 11 months. I have learned a lot about you and have appreciated that you have allowed me into your life. We started out with you not being sure if you could trust me, and I am grateful that a point came when you decided I was trustworthy and you began to open up to me. Once you trusted me and shared yourself with me, we accomplished a lot. Life is so different for you now: when I look at you now as compared to 11 months ago, I see a person who moved from being shy and nonassertive to one who knows what she needs and can ask for it without guilt or shame; I see a person who felt sad and lonely much of the time and now feels content and even happy at times; I see a person who used to keep herself at a distance from other people for fear of being judged and rejected and who now is able to form and keep relationships successfully. I have admired your stamina throughout this process because I know it wasn't always easy for you. I feel privileged that you allowed me into your life and that you shared your journey from this person 11 months ago to this person who sits before me today. I have enjoyed our work together. I have been sad with you, and I have been happy with you; I have worried with you, and I have felt able to keep you safe. You have been very important to me, and the work with you has left me changed too. I am happy today that you are ready to leave, but I am sad that we have to say good-bye. It's kind of bittersweet for me: I am sad to see you go, but I am so happy that you are ready to go. I will miss you, and you will always be in my mind. I will never forget our work together.

The final session allows the therapist to thank the client and often results in the client thanking the therapist. Such appreciation can be accepted graciously and with a reminder that the work was shared by client and therapist and that neither could have worked in a vacuum. Clients will be reminded that they will always carry a memory of their work with the therapist and that, in this sense, the ending of therapy is not final; instead, the gains made in therapy will be forever the clients', and they will always have a recollection of the important work and changes that took place. Such a reminder of the permanence of therapeutic work—so beautifully acknowledged by Milton Erikson's statement to his clients, "My voice will go with you"—provides a softening in the harshness of the final parting.

Stages of Client Reactions during Natural Termination

As client and therapist progress through the termination of their relationship, several predictable behaviors or affects may emerge in the client. These behaviors and affects are best understood in the context of how human beings tend to deal with loss. One framework that has been developed for exploring and understanding people's reactions to loss uses the stages of adaptation to death and dying outlined by Kuebler-Ross (1971, 1975). Kuebler-Ross observed in her work with terminally ill patients and their families that patients and family members passed through distinct phases of affect in the process of adapting to the thought of the death or loss of a loved one. Specifically, persons facing death or the loss of a loved one tended to respond with initial denial, followed by anger, that tended to progress to the attempt to bargain with a higher power to prevent the loss, in turn followed by depression when this bargaining did not result in a change of the situation, and finally resulted in accepting the inevitability of the situation. Although these stages tend to occur most commonly in this order, Kuebler-Ross conceded that for some individuals stages overlap, may be skipped, or may occur in a different order. However, overwhelming evidence showed that this stage model could describe the affects and behaviors often noted in dying patients and their family members.

Although Kuebler-Ross developed these stages or reactions specifically with death and dying in mind, they can be applied to numerous situations involving significant losses in people's lives. The loss of a friend can be equally tragic and can result in the same sequence of feelings and behaviors, whether the friend is lost to death, to a geographic relocation, or to some other ending. Thus in further discussing clients' termination behaviors and affects, Kuebler-Ross's stage theory will be applied as a framework for the conceptual understanding of what is occurring between client and clinician in the termination phase of therapy. As is true in the original theory, the stages may occur in any order. Furthermore, some clients may skip a particular stage or may go through more than one stage at once; however, all clients end at the stage of acceptance, provided termination as the therapist has planned does succeed. For ease of presentation, Kuebler-Ross's (1971) original stage order is maintained in the following discussion and in the overview of the stages in Table 8.1 as it applies to terminating treatment.

Denial

Clients' first introduction of termination is not uncommonly met with the same type of denial encountered in family members when a patient is dying or when a person is facing death. In an attempt to deny the inevitable ending of their special relationship, the client may ignore the therapist when the subject is broached or may make light of the subject in such a manner as to deny the potential impact of the ending of their relationship. This denial is one of the major reasons why the topic of termination needs to be introduced with sufficient advance warning. It may then be reintroduced repeatedly, with each repetition making the client's willingness to deny it is coming more difficult. Sometimes, the client's denial is so pronounced that special care may need to be taken to ascertain that the client has heard the therapist and has registered the meaning of the message. For instance, one client—on being asked how long he thought he would keep coming to see the therapist—indicated that he believed therapy would last forever. The therapist proceeded to explain the realistic time limits of treatment and tried to negotiate an ending time with the client. The client did not let the therapist finish talking but began talking over her, telling about a recent stressful event in his life. He raised his voice sufficiently to drown out the therapist and ignored her efforts to regain control quite effectively. The clinician decided to interpret his behavior for him, explaining that she understood his wish to continue forever. She understood that it was difficult and sad for him to imagine not

TABLE 8.1   Stages of Termination

Stage	Client Behaviors and Affects	Therapist Reactions
Denial	ignores the therapist's attempts to talk about ending therapy avoids the topic of ending represses the information pretends not to have heard the therapist	works to get the client's attention brings up the topic repeatedly discusses the topic until convinced that the client has heard it
Anger	behaves aggressively talks about aggressive, seemingly unrelated events blames the therapist behaves with anger or hostility toward the clinician	recognizes client's affect and behavior in the context of ending interprets client's behavior/affect helps client express anger and frustration
Bargaining	reports return of symptoms reports appearance of new problems openly tries to negotiate an extension of therapy finds reasons not to end therapy	recognizes old symptoms and new problems in the context of ending interprets client's symptoms holds firmly to the original ending date
Depression	expresses sadness over the loss of the relationship may evidence mild symptoms of depression fears loss of therapeutic progress without the therapist grieves the loss of the relationship and the therapy process	recognizes depressive symptoms in the context of ending interprets client's symptoms expresses own feeling of loss and sadness models grieving process for client acknowledges and validates affect
Acceptance	accepts the inevitability of ending reviews therapy process reviews and recognizes own progress makes plans for the future says farewell to the therapist has bittersweet feelings	models acceptance helps review the therapy process helps review client's progress models leave-taking delights in client's progress shares own feelings

to come back to see her. The client did lower his voice and end his monologue at this time but never acknowledged the message of the clinician during this session. His denial made it extremely important for the therapist to continue bringing up the topic in ensuing sessions. The client finally conceded that he understood he needed to end therapy, but also explained that it was not time for him to do so because he had started feeling panicky again at work. The return of presenting symptoms signaled to the therapist that the client now indeed had received the message of having to terminate. Moving on to a later stage in the process of adjusting to ending, he was now bargaining for an extension of the therapy experience through relapse.

Sometimes denial is veiled well under a cover of easy acceptance. This form of denial may be operating when a client denies the potential impact of ending and responds without affect to the discussion of termination. For instance, one client, when presented with ending the therapy relationship, indicated that she of course had thought of the fact that therapy needed to end and that she was prepared to face this termination when it came. She showed no significant affect or concern, and her willingness signaled the therapist to proceed to set a date with the client. Because she accepted the date easily, the therapist assumed that he did not need to remind her carefully; he then failed to bring up termination during several subsequent sessions. Finally, in the last month of treatment, he reminded her that only four sessions were left remaining for the two of them to say good-bye. The client feigned shock and surprise, indicating that she had no idea that treatment needed to be ended. When the therapist reminded her of their prior conversation, she denied any recollection of it, and even when shown progress notes from that session insisted that the therapist may have meant to bring the issue up to her but failed to do so. She then proceeded to get angry, signaling that she had moved on to the next stage of dealing with her impending loss.

Anger

Denial is most commonly, but certainly not always, followed by anger, as in the second example above. Anger can be expressed by the client in a number of ways and needs to be understood in the context of ending, rather than as a re-emergence of original anger and hostility. The better prepared the therapist is for the client's anger, the easier it will be for the therapist to refrain from personalizing this anger and from feeling guilty about abandoning the client. Guilt feelings for the therapist are a possible occurrence at this time because the client's anger often will target the therapist for destroying a beautiful relationship, the client for feeling rejection or abandonment, and the therapist for being the harbinger of unnecessary and unfeeling news. The clinician must refrain from letting only anger become the focus of the interpretation and instead must interpret the client's anger in the context of ending; this keeps firmly in mind that the client is angry not at the therapist for bearing bad news, but with the process of having to end. It is also important to realize that the anger may not be expressed immediately after termination is discussed, but it may become an issue later in the same session, or in a subsequent session.

For instance, on discussing termination with one female client, she proceeded to cooperate in setting a date and was able to express her agreement with the therapist that she had indeed improved significantly. When the topic felt settled to both client and clinician for the time being, the woman turned to a usual discussion of her relationship with her mother. However, her voice and the content of presentation had an unusual flavor during this session and became increasingly aggressive and hostile. Soon she related an event between herself and her mother that had occurred some time ago and had previously been processed completely in one session. This event, a particularly vicious argument that almost began a physical fight between the women, had been the motivator for the client to seek treatment. The client explained that she felt this event was a harbinger of things to come in relationships with other women and indicated that it was impossible to trust women because they were competitive and rejecting. The therapist clearly understood the client's message as an angry reaction to the idea of termination. Through the client's fear of ending the relationship with the therapist, some of her old (and worked through) abandonment issues resurfaced temporarily, resulting in anger and hostility. This hostility was pointed at the mother directly, and at the therapist indirectly, through her expression that all women were rejecting. Because the therapist was female, this was clearly a message directed toward her as well. The therapist allowed the client her anger and did not attempt to intervene. She decided instead to wait and see whether the woman would be able to resolve her anger on her own, which she indeed was able to do in her next session. Only after having evidence that the client felt less angry and had resolved some of her feelings of rejection and abandonment did the therapist introduce the idea that some of her strong feelings may have been related to ending treatment. The woman then began to cry and revealed that she was very afraid of saying good-bye; she feared that she would once again feel as poorly about herself as she had when treatment began. She had moved to a more advanced stage in the termination process and was beginning to experience depression and was mourning the loss of the relationship.

Bargaining

Often, when faced with the inevitability of ending despite having expressed anger about it, clients make a final attempt to change the situation by bargaining. Bargaining is either directed toward never ending therapy, or toward at least extending it for a while. Whereas dying patients are reported to do much of their bargaining with a higher power in the attempt to extend their lives, clients bargain with the therapist to stay in therapy just a little bit longer. Bargaining is not necessarily a conscious endeavor, though it may be. Conscious bargaining may be reflected in the client's attempt to negotiate a later ending date or in promises to make certain changes a therapist may have implied as desirable in exchange for additional sessions. However, unconscious bargaining is much more common. As symptoms return or new problems emerge, they represent a client's attempt to bargain for extra therapy time. After all, from the client's perspective, if one stated therapy goal was for the client to stop having panic attacks, the return of such severe anxiety may result in renewed efforts on the therapist's part, which may in turn lead to postponing the termination date. Or if a client indeed improved in all areas targeted by treatment, perhaps the development of a new problem, such as feeling mildly suicidal, may lead the clinician to continue treatment a while longer.

Return of symptoms and sudden new problems after having negotiated an ending date must be understood in the context of bargaining and cannot be accommodated. Instead, the therapist needs to help the client understand what is occurring and to point out that a hope that has to do with extending treatment is connected with the problem emerging. It is critical not to extend the termination date at this time, but rather to stress to clients that they will indeed be ready to end when the agreed on time comes, regardless of the current crisis. Predicting a possible relapse to a client as the termination process is initiated (see the sample dialogue above) is often helpful in negotiating this stage of termination reactions. If clinicians have warned their clients that old problems may re-emerge, they can now use these predictions to point out to clients how predictable the termination process is and how knowledgeable they as clinicians are about their clients. The fact that clinicians have been able to predict clients' reactions lends credence and expertise to their ability to decide that this is indeed the right time to end therapy.

Depression

Depression is also a common affect expressed by clients in the ending phase. It can range from rather severe dysphoria with decreased psychomotor movement, self-disparaging comments, slight insomnia, or temporary loss of appetite, to relative mild feelings of sadness. Fortunately, the latter is much more common than the former in natural terminations (though this is not necessarily the case in forced terminations). The need to express sadness about ending the relationship with the therapist is often a most important component of working through termination. It helps clients express their attachments to their therapists and their sadness of loss. The healthy aspect of this expression is that it usually leads to a recognition of the positive features of the relationship that will not be lost even after termination, thus leading to acceptance—in fact, to a joyous and proud ending to treatment. Sadness is also often felt by the therapist, so this stage is accepted as an appropriate time for self-disclosure even among therapists who do not usually do so. Clinicians may share with their clients that they also feel sad about not seeing the clients any longer, and then proceed to model for them that this sadness can be part of saying good-bye without overshadowing the positive implications of therapy.

For instance, in the example of the woman who related anger at her mother and distrust of all women to terminating therapy, her anger eventually gave way to sadness. This sadness did not just grieve the loss of the therapist, but also expressed her fear that losing the therapist implied losing her progress in treatment to date. Addressing the fear of losing ground is an important feature in the depression phase of adjusting to loss. The therapist must help the client recognize that progress is independent of continued meetings and will be maintained even without weekly sessions. Generally, if the client was indeed ready for a natural termination, sufficient self-esteem has been internalized by this time in treatment that the client will be able to recognize the therapist's message. The stage of depression is therefore critical to helping clients not only recognize their sadness about, yet also the survivability of, loss and the continuity of change and general strengthening of the self after treatment.

Acceptance

Once the client has understood the inevitability of ending, has expressed anger about it, has attempted to bargain an extension, and has expressed sadness over the loss, accepting the termination usually follows naturally. By progressing through the prior stages, the client has explored all possibilities to extend treatment and has processed all important feelings connected with the loss of the therapy relationship. Client and clinician have come to the realization that there is continuity in the change that has occurred, that the client has been strengthened and is capable of saying good-bye in a productive way. Having dealt with these possibilities and affects, client and therapist are now ready to explore the positives of their relationship and work together up to this point, and to move to an acceptance that is full of joy and pride, despite the sadness over the loss of the weekly meetings. The phase of acceptance, in other words, is the phase in which client and therapist do most of their personal termination work. As mentioned previously, this work involves reviewing treatment progress together, exploring the changes the client has made, taking a look at the specialness of the therapeutic relationship, and becoming aware of the positive implications ending therapy has for the client. Both acknowledge the importance of the relationship, and both may choose to reveal that they will always keep alive a memory of the other person, even if they should never see one another again. Exchanging a gift, or sharing a closing ritual, can symbolize the two people's acceptance that their relationship in its present form has come to an end.

PREMATURE TERMINATIONS

The strongest negative reactions tend to occur when a termination is premature. Both client and therapist are more likely to feel negative consequences from premature endings, with clients feeling more anger, sadness, or rejection, and therapists being more likely to experience countertransference reactions such as guilt, shame, or self-doubt (Teyber, 1997). These potential negative reactions to both client- and therapist-initiated unnatural terminations, however, are not a given. Even a premature termination can be handled positively and helpfully for both client and therapist, regardless of whether it was imposed externally or was initiated by the therapist or the client. To ensure the success of an imposed termination, it is best to follow as many of the general guidelines for successful natural termination as possible. Plenty of time needs to be reserved even for premature terminations and a processing of important content messages needs to take place. Client and therapist need to share their feelings about ending work together and need to achieve a sense of closure with regard to their therapeutic relationship. The process of termination must not be underestimated or undervalued even in these negative circumstances, and careful attention needs to be paid to client and therapist reactions both in and out of session. Awareness of countertransferences must be heightened in these situations, as must awareness of a client's potential negative emotions in response to leaving treatment. Although all premature terminations must be dealt with thoughtfully and carefully, they are dealt with slightly differently and different cautions apply, depending on the exact circumstances of the termination. Most concretely, client-initiated versus therapist-initiated treatment discontinuations must be differentiated.

Client-Initiated Premature Termination

If clients want to terminate therapy and the therapists disagree with their clients' judgments, it is still best to go along with clients' decisions because it is rarely helpful to try to talk clients out of them (Kramer, 1990). Trying to convince clients to remain in treatment against their wishes generally serves to alienate clients further and may work against the therapists. Instead, it is best to empathize with clients' perceptions that therapy needs to end and to find out why clients perceive the situation the way they do. One important exploration consists of finding out whether clients initiate the termination voluntarily or involuntarily. Stated differently, therapists must find out if clients want to end treatment (e.g., because they are not satisfied with the progress being made, not comfortable with their therapists, or expected something different from therapy), or if they have to end therapy (e.g., because of life circumstances that dictate this, such as a job move or family pressures). To be able to gather this information, therapists must clearly meet clients' requests for ending treatment nondefensively and openly. Resistance on the part of therapists will only result in clients being affirmed in their opinion that therapy must end and so it backfires. If clients bring up ending treatment, therapists best react by indicating interest in their clients' perceptions that it is time to end and allow them to express why they have this need. Once therapists have ascertained whether their clients want to leave or have to leave (voluntary versus involuntary termination), they can begin the proper termination procedures, so they need to keep in mind certain cautions that go along with each type of ending.

If clients want to leave therapy, it is most important that therapists not get caught up in countertransference feelings of self-blame, self-doubt, feelings of being rejected, or a sense of having to defend themselves against the actions of their clients. This is, of course, particularly true if clients verbalize that at least one of the reasons for termination has to do with their clinicians. It is important to remember that clients endow clinicians with character traits that may or may not be present. It is also important to realize that personal or temperament differences can truly get in the way of a therapeutic relationship, and discrepancies in values can get in the way of building trust. Clients must never be questioned in their choices, if discomfort with clinicians is expressed in a respectful and clear manner. It is also a good idea to reflect on clients' perceptions of their therapists that may have led to the decision to quit therapy as a way to decide whether this was an idiosyncratic reaction or a reaction that other clients may have had or will have in response to themselves as therapists. A client-initiated termination wherein the client verbalizes certain traits, attributes, values, beliefs, or characteristics of the therapist as a reason for ending treatment is a good motivator for self-exploration. This self-exploration, however, is done during the clinician's private (or own therapy) time, not in the presence of the client. The main issue to keep in mind in the presence of clients is to remain nondefensive, to empathize with clients' perceptions, and to allow clients to process their feelings about therapy and about themselves as therapists openly and freely, though within respectful limits. No therapist has to endure vicious attacks by clients or tolerate unfounded slander. Once the client's reasoning behind ending therapy at this time and with this clinician has been processed, the clinician needs to explore whether the client is interested in a referral. If this is the case, the therapist can help the client transfer to a new clinician. Because referrals are a common process in premature terminations, they will be discussed separately below.

If clients want to leave therapy because the process is not what they expected, their expectations need to be explored to assess whether they were realistic. If they were realistic in the sense that they can be met by another type of clinician, this must be acknowledged; if they are unrealistic (for example, the client expected a fast and easy "miracle cure"), then this reality must be shared with clients. This sharing is not to convince clients to remain in treatment, but to help them recognize the true nature of therapy so that they may make more informed choices about psychological treatment in the future. If warranted, a referral is recommended and a transfer process is initiated.

If clients want to end because they are satisfied with their progress in therapy thus far, a relatively natural termination process can be initiated as long as clients are willing to commit to at least three or four more sessions with the clinician. In this process, greater emphasis may be placed on setting future goals and on helping clients understand the therapist's perspective on their needs for therapy in the future. Such future treatment planning must be done respectfully and without suggesting that clients have not made good progress already. In other words, although this planning is important, it must not detract from rejoicing in the progress that has already been made.

If the client does not want to but has to end therapy for external reasons, countertransferences by the therapist are less likely to occur. The therapist may not need to search for personal reasons why the client is quitting and may be less likely to feel shame, self-blame, or guilt over having failed the client. However, the therapist may still have some sense of abandonment or loss and, most importantly, may begin to feel very protective of the client who is clearly not ready to end but has to succumb to external pressure to leave. The most destructive countertransference in this instance may occur if the therapist is angry at the external forces that pushed the client out of treatment. This anger must not be communicated (either actively and openly or passive aggressively and indirectly) to the client. This is true particularly if the pressure to end comes from family members. Clients probably have some anger themselves, and if their therapists also express anger at the family member pressuring them, this may place undue pressure on their clients, though they are clearly not yet capable of sufficient self-assertion to place their own needs ahead of those of the other person. In fact, processing client feelings is critical in this circumstance. No doubt, clients who are forced externally to end treatment have strong emotional reactions to a premature termination being imposed. They may be angry at the pressuring family member, feel guilty toward the therapist, feel angry at an employer who is forcing a job move, and be frightened about life without therapy. Clinicians must be extremely attuned to these potential reactions in their clients and must help them deal with these emotions and fears thoroughly and positively. In the case of an involuntary termination of this sort, the most natural termination process possible needs to be initiated. In most such cases, it is possible to spend at least three to four more sessions with clients to allow them to process feelings about the termination and to explore progress made so far, as well as to acknowledge that work is left to be done. The therapeutic relationship can be observed as well and closure on it gained that will help the client reconcile future relationships more positively and usefully. Leaving an open door is most appropriate in this type of termination; both client and therapist are very clearly aware that the client is not ready to end treatment and could still do excellent therapeutic work with the same clinician or another one. If the termination is imposed by a move, some clients may wish to continue treatment in their new communities. In these instances, therapists can help clients with referrals.

To summarize, client-initiated terminations pose several difficulties for the therapist because they tend to elicit relatively strong countertransferences of various types. Clinicians must work diligently outside of the session to keep these countertransferences under control and not to allow them to intrude into treatment in an unhealthy manner. Similarly, clients often have a variety of negative affects (ranging from anger to guilt to sadness) and must receive an opportunity to vent these feelings in the caring and empathic presence of the clinician. In all circumstances, the clinician must listen carefully and thoughtfully and must respond respectfully and with acceptance. Attention must be paid to the need for referrals, and, if appropriate, a referral process has to be initiated. Further, natural termination procedures should be followed to whatever extent possible to give client and therapist as much time as possible to reconcile their relationship and the ending thereof. As a rule of thumb, it is best not to challenge the client's opinion about ending at this time; however, at the same time, the therapist may not want to agree too eagerly with the client and needs to express the opinion that termination is indeed premature. In all circumstances, clinicians serve their client best by insisting on at least one, but preferably two to four, more sessions to bring treatment and the therapeutic relationship to a close.

Therapist-Initiated Premature Termination

Fair and Bressler (1992) have argued that therapist-initiated terminations can be harmful to clients and leave the person feeling worse than before treatment. Given these circumstances, some clinicians argue that more care has to be taken with therapist-initiated imposed termination than with any other type. Clients who are told by their clinician that therapy must end although it is not complete can have a variety of negative affects, ranging from feeling betrayed to feeling rejected and abandoned. They can respond with anger, depression, panic, and rage. Similarly, even though the clinician initiates the termination, there may be negative affective responses to the process—ranging from guilt, sadness, mourning, and helplessness to rivalry with the next provider. Awareness of potential affective reactions by both client and therapist is critical to making therapist-initiated terminations the least potentially harmful and most potentially useful. As with client-initiated terminations, some differences in the process exist secondary to whether the termination is initiated voluntarily or involuntarily.

If therapists decide that treatment must end despite not being complete because of some reason or another in the client–therapist relationship or the therapeutic process (e.g., the clinician is not experienced enough to deal with the client; the clinician is close friends with a friend or family member of the client but did not find this out until late in therapy; the clinician believes that the client is not currently benefiting from treatment), they must proceed with caution to inform the client of this decision. Ample time needs to be reserved to bring treatment to a close: the client must never be dismissed from therapy in a single session. If this type of termination is requested, therapists must thoroughly and respectfully explain to the client why this conclusion was reached. The explanation must not be blaming of the client (even if the therapist is annoyed with the client at the person's lack of progress); instead, therapists must take responsibility for the actions they choose to take. Keeping countertransference under check in such situations is critical. Reserving enough time to engage in a process that is as close to a natural termination process is optimal. Following is an example of a therapist's explanation of a premature termination by the therapist's choice.

THERAPIST: We need to talk about something today that's been nagging in my mind for a couple of weeks. I have given this a lot of thought and have come to the conclusion that I am not the best therapist for you at this time. I know we have been working together for six weeks now, and we have already done quite a bit of work. However, there are some things you are dealing with and that you need to work on that I cannot help you with. I believe it would be best if we started talking about transferring you to another clinician.

CLIENT: *(interrupts)* But I like coming here and I'm feeling better already!

THERAPIST: Yes, I know you enjoy coming here, but therapy isn't really just about enjoying yourself; it's also hard work that leads to a goal that you set yourself that may not always be easy to get to. I am not the right person to help you do that right now.

CLIENT: Why not?

THERAPIST: Well, it occurs to me that one thing you need to do is to work on your cocaine use. Over the last three weeks it has become clearer and clearer to me that you are using cocaine quite often and in greater quantities than we had initially talked about. That concerns me deeply. It is my belief that the best way to deal with this is to refer you to someone who knows how to treat substance abuse. You see, I know very little about that; that was not really part of my training, and I have not had a lot of clients who used cocaine—and I've never had a client who used it as regularly as you.

CLIENT: I don't use it that much either. *(gets defensive)*

THERAPIST: I don't mean to criticize what you are doing. I am trying to let you know that I am concerned. When you were here last week, it was clear that you were high and I didn't know what to do about that. You need a therapist who knows what to do when that happens. This transfer is about me not being able to help you, not about you being a bad client or a bad person.

CLIENT: Yeah—like I believe that. You think I'm a crack head and you want to get rid of me.

THERAPIST: I understand your feelings about me; I'm sending you off to start all over again with someone new after we have already invested so much time in this. I just don't feel it would be right for me to try to help you when the help you need is clearly outside of my area of expertise. I would like to help you find a therapist who is trained in this. I am not talking about you and me never meeting again after today. In fact, I'd like to meet with you a couple more times so we can talk about the work we have done together and about how both you and I feel about not being able to continue work together. In the meantime, we can look for a new therapist for you together. And then, when we're ready to say our good-byes, you can start immediately with a new person.

CLIENT: But I don't want to start all over *(starts to cry)*; I trust you.

THERAPIST: Yes, I know you do, and I really appreciate that. And I don't want to abuse your trust. I don't want to pretend I can help when I can't.

This interaction only shows the explanation phase of this termination; it would then be followed by a discussion of how treatment will be brought to a close and that at least two to four sessions will be needed to process what has happened in treatment so far, how the therapeutic relationship developed (or failed to develop), and what the client may expect from the next therapy experience. This discussion over the remaining few sessions would be brought to a close by the therapist making appropriate referrals and ascertaining that a new support network is waiting for the client when they end their work together. The sample also demonstrates that terminating therapy is often a difficult process that is met with resistance by the client. The clinician must refrain from becoming defensive or guilty and must maintain an empathic stance that reflects that the decision reached was made out of concern for the client. Therapists, once they have reached the conclusion that therapy must be ended, must not second-guess themselves due to the client's responses or reassurances of the value of treatment or respect for the therapist so far. The therapist made a careful decision, and deciding differently at this time would in all likelihood reflect a countertransference reaction that may not be in the best interests of the client. Although a clinician may have doubts about the appropriateness of a termination, the clinician does not bring it up with the client; once it is brought up, the therapist is convinced it is necessary.

In cases of involuntary therapist-initiated terminations, clinicians must give ample prior warning. Generally, such involuntary terminations are predictable far in advance, because they are usually due to clinicians' training periods ending or their retirement, both of which are usually known to the clinician far in advance. If clinicians already know that they have a limited time period left to work with a client when treatment commences, this needs to be discussed up front. Some clients may not choose to remain with a clinician who is only available for a certain period of time that may or may not be long enough to complete treatment. Giving clients warnings about the availabile hours of the clinician before they start treatment is an important component of ethical treatment and informed consent. If the issue of an involuntary termination emerges during the course of therapy (e.g., due to a sudden decision to make a job move or due to being expelled from a training program unexpectedly), therapists need to warn their clients as soon as they find out that they may not be able to remain with the clients to the end of treatment. Such ample prior warning greatly facilitates the possibility of reaching as natural of a termination process as possible. The number of sessions remaining must be calculated, and client and clinician together may decide to revise treatment goals for the remaining time period to make the most of it. They will then continue to work until it is time to begin the termination process. This procedure will be identical to the natural termination process, with the exception that more emphasis will be placed on processing what needs to happen for the client in therapy in the future and on making appropriate referrals (transfers). In these types of terminations, it is particularly important to allow clients to express their feelings fully and openly about ending treatment early. The therapist must be able to tolerate anger from the client and, at the same time, must not be overcome by guilt and shame. Therapists can certainly acknowledge that they have failed the client by leaving them early, but there is no reason to wallow in guilt or shame with the client. If done properly, remaining sessions can be used effectively and efficiently; if prepared carefully, the termination can be graceful and positive.

In summary, therapist-initiated terminations pose special problems for clients and clinicians because they have the potential to evoke a large amount of negative affect in both. The clinician must have good control over any countertransference feelings and must be open to the client's reactions to the news about ending earlier than expected. The clinician must strive to make the termination process as natural as possible by leaving ample time and going through the usual procedures as much as possible. This natural termination is accompanied by careful and thorough referral planning that allows the client to make a transfer to a new clinician in the easiest manner possible. Transfers within a clinic may be preferable, but they are not absolute requirements. Finally, if therapist-initiated terminations are predictable from the beginning of a client's treatment, the clinician has an ethical and professional obligation to warn the client of this (Fair & Bressler, 1992). Such a warning also greatly reduces the amount of negative affect involved in such a termination, because both partners in the therapeutic relationship are aware of its special limitations from the beginning of treatment.

Making Referrals due to Premature Termination

There are a number of things a therapist can do to make referrals easier and more successful. First of all, clinicians must never hesitate to make referrals when therapy has ended prematurely. Some clinicians feel hesitant about referrals, especially if the termination was initiated by the client. Such hesitation is often the result of a therapist's defensive reaction and is not therapeutic for the client. Clinicians may refrain from making referrals because they are certain that no other therapist can help this client; because they want to believe that because they were unsuccessful with the client, everyone else will be; because they justify in their own minds that they would rather not wish a given client on a colleague; because they believe no other therapist will be good enough for a certain client; or because they do not want to take the time to find an appropriate clinician for the person. If clinicians have these hesitations about making referrals, they need to take some time to ponder why they are resisting being helpful to and facilitative for the client. Not all therapeutic relationships work out; clients do not deserve to be punished for this fact. Certainly, some clients may truly be difficult and perhaps even not treatable; but is it really up to a single clinician to make this decision? Thus the first step in making successful referrals is to decide to *make* them.

Once the decision to prompt a referral has been made, the clinician must do so in a professional manner that maximizes the potential for success. It is important to know the referral target—if not personally then through the recommendation of a trusted professional. If a therapist needs to make a referral within the community, this personal or indirect knowledge is generally no problem. Most clinicians have some contact with colleagues and are well aware of who provides what types of services to whom. However, if a referral needs to be made long-distance, such knowledge may be more difficult to obtain. Most professional organizations now have referral information networks anyone can access. For example, in the United States, each state has a psychological association that can be contacted to receive information about providers in the state. Thus some phone calling or browsing on the Internet may be necessary, but much information is available that facilitates referrals. The clinician must know the following information about the referral target: educational credentials, licensure or certification credentials, fees and related financial information, contact numbers, and whether the person has confirmed ethical charges (information obtainable from state licensing boards).

Beyond knowing the referral target, the responsible referring clinician also obtains releases of information from the client for ease of communication with the new clinician. Such communication reduces duplication of services and can move along the client's treatment at a faster pace than if the new provider has to start from the beginning. Obtaining a release of information is, of course, dependent upon the collaboration and agreement of the client; if the client does not agree to sign such a form, the therapist has no permission to communicate with the new provider. Further, at times releases are impossible to complete because the client may not know before the last session who the new provider will be. It behooves the referring clinician to impress on the client that it will be helpful to encourage the next provider to request records from the referring provider to prevent duplication of services. However, by then this process is under the complete control of the client and the referring therapist no longer has permission to contact the new provider.

If the client does sign a release of information, the referring therapist must make contact with the new provider and must release all records that the release of information specified as to be shared. Responses to releases of information need to be fast and appropriate. It is totally unacceptable to make the referral target wait for several weeks before records are mailed or phone calls are returned. After all, it is early in treatment with the new provider that these records will be most helpful. In releasing records, care must be taken only to release information the client requested to be released. If the client specifies that only written documentation may be released, the therapist is not at liberty to talk to the next provider. If the client agreed only to the release of intake reports, the clinician is not allowed to release termination reports, even if these are deemed more helpful to the treatment of the client.

Once the decision has been made to make a referral, a referral source has been identified, and the issue of releasing information has been addressed with the client, the therapist needs to prepare the client for the transfer. The specifics of this process will depend somewhat on the client and on the therapist's preferences. However, a few issues may be addressed with all clients. First, clients need to be prepared that, in all likelihood, even with the release of information, they will probably be required to reengage in a screening and intake process with the new clinician. Second, clients need to be informed that they have the right to reject the referral target if they do not find this person acceptable. Often clients have the misconception that because a referral was initiated by a trusted clinician, the referral is absolute and that they have to remain with the new provider, even if they have a problem with the person. It is a consumer issue to let clients know that they have the right to evaluate the new clinician in the same way they had the right to evaluate the current clinician for acceptability of joint therapeutic work. Third, the client needs to be allowed to ask questions about the new provider, and these questions need to be answered within the same general guidelines as questions about the current provider. In other words, although it is perfectly acceptable to answer questions of professional relevance about the next clinician (i.e., credentials, education, type of clientele), it is not proper to reveal personal information about the colleague (e.g., marital status, children, car). Fourth, clients need to be encouraged to verbalize any feelings or fears they may have about the referral process, and these concerns need to be addressed directly and clearly.

Once the referral has been made and termination has been completed, the relationship between the referring clinician and the client ends. The client is now in the hands of the next therapist, and the referring clinician becomes a figure in the client's past. The clinician must not hold on to the client, but has to make a clean break. Holding on to the client by overlapping treatment with the new clinician is not helpful to the client because it tends to dilute the newly emerging relationship between the next clinician and the client. It also undoes the finality of the termination. In other words, referrals are final and, once made, remove the client from the original therapist's care. Because it is not advisable for clients to have more than one therapist at a time, this means not accepting the client back for treatment as long as the client remains with another clinician.

SUMMARY AND CONCLUDING THOUGHTS

Termination represents the final interaction between client and therapist and, as such, plays a powerful role in therapy. A well-executed termination will leave client and therapist feeling good about the entire treatment process, whereas a poorly performed termination has the potential to undo good therapeutic work. Given this reality, clinicians must give considerable thought to the termination process to proceed carefully, thoughtfully, respectfully, empathically, and slowly. Giving enough time to the termination is perhaps one of the most important ingredients of a successful termination, especially a successful premature termination. Termination is a predominantly joyous event, if natural—a predominantly sad event, if premature. By its nature, therapy is designed to help people deal not only with joyous, but also with sad occurrences; this alone suggests that no termination, regardless of the circumstances, ever has to be a disaster.

Termination in natural circumstances is celebration, a rejoicing in a great accomplishment. It is important to take sufficient time to allow for such celebration. Termination when imposed can be a sad or frightening event. It is important to allow ample time to let these affects subside to a tolerable level for both client and clinician. In both cases, however, termination ushers in a new beginning—the beginning of a life without therapy and improved mental and emotional health, or the beginning of another therapeutic relationship. If the client is ready for this new beginning, both termination and therapy have succeeded. If the process through which the client was readied for this new beginning was well-conducted, this person has learned a valuable tool of having practiced a manner of saying good-bye that is healthy, growth-producing, and productive. Because life is full of good-byes, the benefits of healthy and therapeutic good-byes modeled through a successful termination cannot be underestimated. In other words, every moment in therapy is equally important—from the first moment of meeting to the last moment of parting. The ending of treatment is indeed as important as its beginning.

DOCUMENTATION AND RECORD-KEEPING

When therapy ends, the work that was accomplished together must be documented in the client's file for future reference. This is, of course, particularly important if therapy was incomplete and another professional will begin work with the client in another course of treatment. The commonly agreed upon document that is used to chronicle treatment process and progress is a termination report (Cormier & Hackney, 1987). This report is a thorough reconstruction of the therapy process, along with a detailed outline of the client's history. It incorporates all information contained in the intake report and includes any new details about the client's life that were uncovered over the course of treatment. Additionally, the termination report outlines what happened in the therapeutic relationship and clarifies whether goals were met, and if so, how. It also indicates whether work is left to be done, and if so, what. The following list contains pieces of data that are commonly included in the termination report (at a minimum):

1. date started and ended (number of sessions)
2. presenting problem
3. client data (history—see intake report outline)
4. case conceptualization
5. goals and objectives for therapy
6. therapy process
   - interventions used
   - effectiveness of interventions

7. client's reactions within the therapeutic relationship over time
8. progress made and goals achieved
9. future needs and recommendations

The termination report needs to be completed in a timely manner so as to be available to the next clinician who may work with the client at a future date. It can, of course, only be shared with appropriate releases of information. It must be written with the same cautions and guidelines in mind that are necessary for all client documentation discussed in detail in earlier chapters. As a professional document, it needs to be concise but detailed, and precise but nonjudgmental. A sample of a partial termination report follows, written for the same client for whom other data were presented in prior chapters (e.g., intake report in Chapter 2; genogram in Chapter 3; conceptualization in Chapter 4). This partial report reflects only the treatment process, relationship, progress, and recommendation sections of the report because the client data (history), case conceptualization, and goals and objective sections are virtually identical in nature to the examples provided throughout prior chapters of this book.

Sample of a Partial Termination Report

Client Name: Frederick X.   Clinician: Chris Brems

Date of Birth: 23 June 1957   Intake Date: 1 September 1994

Fee Arranged (see fee schedule): $60   Termination Date: 12 December 1995

Total Number of Sessions: 62   Cancellations/No-Shows: 2 / 0

Therapy Process

The recollection phase of this client's therapy lasted approximately 10 weeks, and even after that time memories and new material continued to emerge almost until the end of treatment. The client began to express emotion (through reconstruction) relatively early on in therapy, in approximately week five, but then had difficulty making the leap to a re-experience more oriented in the here and now. He remained somewhat detached from the therapist for the first three months of treatment, reflecting his strong ambivalence about relationships in general—and close relationships in particular—especially given his difficulties with trusting others fully. The recollection and reconstruction phases of therapy were difficult for this client, who had become accustomed to repressing all thoughts of his family of origin because these were painful for him and often stimulated strong latent dependency needs.

When recollection proved highly anxiety-provoking for the client and intensified his depressive affect (as well as associated symptoms, such as sleeplessness), relaxation strategies were initiated in this early phase of treatment to provide some immediate symptom relief. Deep breathing and progressive muscle tension relaxation exercises were combined to develop deep relaxation skills. Three practice sessions (of 20 minutes each) were incorporated into therapy sessions 5, 6, and 7; in therapy session 8, a tape of the relaxation exercise was made and the client continued to practice this technique at home (i.e., this was moved out of the therapy session context). The client continued to use the relaxation tape for several weeks on a regular basis and is currently using it as needed during times of increased stress. During these early phases of treatment no attempt at interpretation was made; the emphasis remained squarely on empathic interventions that communicated acceptance and understanding of the client's frame of mind or state of being and perceptions of the world around him.

Because reconstruction was sometimes difficult for this client (who did not easily express emotion freely), once a basic (rudimentary) trusting relationship had been developed, self-exploratory guided imagery was added to help him gain further affective awareness of himself and his emotional needs. This guided imagery consisted of themes that encouraged the client to look at his level of self-development and interpersonal needs in the context of a safe and nurturing environment. He responded well to this technique, and it assisted in moving him into a consistent and strong transferential therapeutic relationship with the clinician. As the client began to re-experience his painful affects and needs in the therapeutic relationship, he became strongly aware of his sense of helplessness and hopelessness. During a period of absence from his significant other, he developed suicidal ideation and became a mild suicide risk. Management of this suicidal crisis ultimately served to accelerate his treatment because it came to represent a turning point in the client's life. The suicidal crisis had given concrete evidence of his strong dependency needs on others and initiated self-reflection on the client's part to pinpoint the origin of this strong emotional neediness. He remained mildly suicidal for approximately one month and has not experienced renewed suicidal ideation since that time. Throughout the suicidal crisis, strong emphasis was placed on providing a holding environment in which the client could feel safe and protected without being encouraged to become overly dependent on the therapist. In other words, hospitalization or increased numbers of sessions were not offered as on option for this client because they were felt to be counterproductive to his need to establish a stronger sense of self-reliance and self-efficacy. Instead, focus was placed on cognitive restructuring that assisted him in recognizing the difference between his current self and the young vulnerable self that was present during his mother's and father's emotional absence in childhood.

After the suicidal crisis had been resolved successfully, the client responded well to the exploration of sources of affect and to explanations of current concerns and manifestations of painful emotional and unmet needs. A true shift gradually began to take place in his self-experience as he became stronger and more able to tolerate interpretations and other cognitive interventions that challenged his perceptions of the world and of others. During this phase of therapy, while the client re-experienced emotional needs in the here and now relationship with the clinician (as well as outside of therapy with his significant other), he began to journal (with the encouragement of the therapist). He found this technique very helpful in making connections between here and now occurrences (both in and outside the therapy room) and experiences from his childhood, as well perceptions he had formed earlier in his life that now emerged as clearly less rational and adaptive than he had assumed them to be. The journal also served as a transitional object the client used to bridge the gap between particularly difficult therapy sessions.

As therapy progressed through these stages, the client's depressive symptoms began to ameliorate and ultimately disappeared almost entirely. He remains somewhat vulnerable to depressive mood at this time, but has coping skills that help him understand and accept these periods of dysthymia. The severe symptoms of depression, however, are resolved, as are his interpersonal difficulties and unrealistic world views and expectations. As these changes occurred, the client became aware that he was becoming increasingly independent of the therapy process and recognized that he would be able to relinquish the therapeutic relationship in the near future. Termination was initiated and six sessions were planned for the termination process. The client never was angry about having to end the therapeutic relationship but did grieve the loss in depth with some increase in depressive symptoms for a period of time. He bargained for an extension of treatment when his significant other had to leave town for a business trip two weeks before therapy was to end, but he understood and accepted that the termination date was not adjusted at that time. He accepted the ending of therapy and rejoiced in his progress, recognizing that he had not only resolved his presenting concerns, but he had also internalized strengths as a person that he would never have deemed possible.

Therapeutic Relationship

The therapeutic relationship with this client went through an intense testing phase that was needed by the client before he could begin to trust the therapist and relate to her consistently and predictably. Throughout the recollection and reconstruction phase, the client challenged (though passively) the therapist's ability to keep him safe, to help him manage his emotional pain, and to understand the depth of his suffering. Her consistent presence and nondefensive manner, even when under attack, ultimately helped the client trust that she would at least be physically available to him, as promised. Ultimately, relationship testing gave way to prolonged periods of trust that were disrupted by briefer and briefer periods of withdrawal and rejection of the therapist by the client. His approach–avoidance and occasional rage with the therapist were understood to be his pattern of dealing with fears of rejection and abandonment in the therapeutic relationship and were not challenged or criticized. Instead, the client was given permission and received understanding for the fact that he had to protect himself from perceived threats to his self by the therapist.

Following the shift to a strong transferential therapeutic relationship after the suicidal crisis, the client became more secure in treatment and was able to relinquish much of his resistance. Nevertheless, throughout the first few months of the re-experience phase of treatment, the client remained extremely vulnerable to actual and perceived failures on the part of the therapist to understand him and be available to him. For example, when the therapist had to leave town abruptly due to a family emergency, the client became extremely enraged and accused her of not caring for him. This rupture was ultimately used to his therapeutic advantage when it helped him recognize the strength of dependency he tended to develop in relationships. Other therapeutic ruptures occurred in the client's perception (e.g., the therapist's minimal lack of attunement during periods of intense self-pity) and were used to facilitate internalization of skills and abilities that helped develop the client's underdeveloped sense of self. It was through the ruptures that he ultimately came to rely on himself to provide nurturance and soothing in the absence of others. As the client grew stronger in his relationship with the clinician, he also began to note shifts in his relationships outside of therapy. The most profound early changes occurred in his relationships at work, where he became more assertive and self-confident; such behaviors resulted in increased success in the workplace, a reality that was very reinforcing to the changes he was beginning to make. His change in relating to others also made itself felt strongly, though later in treatment, in his relationship with his significant other, who initially was somewhat threatened by his self-assertion but then came to appreciate it.

Therapeutic Progress and Goals Achieved
Through the use of the therapeutic relationship and processing the interpersonal needs between client and therapist, client and significant other, and client and work colleagues, the client was ultimately able to establish a clearer sense of self and a more accurate perception of his world. He began to be capable of self-nurturance, and he internalized a realistic sense of self-esteem, self-confidence, and self-reliance. He became capable of appraising situations and himself realistically, and this strongly assisted in his process of setting life goals and deciding on a life direction. As he internalized these mirroring skills, he also began to recognize coping resources within himself that decreased his dependence on others. As he became more self-reliant and able to deal with stressful circumstances in his life independently, he could relinquish his strong emotional dependency on his significant other (which improved their relationship) and was able to come to understand his parents more accurately and forgivingly. He reestablished some family-of-origin ties to begin to build a new and healthier history of his life, and he was able to do so without unrealistic expectations for his family members. He became increasingly capable of tolerating perceived failures on the part of others, being able to recognize, understand, and accept his significant other's needs for independence, space, and other relationships. When he was able to rely more on himself and less on others, his relationships actually began to deepen, and he built more external supports than he had ever had before. His friendship network, although still limited at this time, has begun to grow and to include a few good acquaintances on whom he can rely for some assistance and social interaction. As mentioned above, his depressive symptomatology has been resolved, with the exception of some vulnerability to mild dysthymia during periods of intense stress.

Future Recommendations
A few issues that had been discussed with the client at the outset of therapy have remained unexplored. These issues were discussed with the client during the reso-

lution phase of therapy as unfinished business that he may consider pursuing on his own. A list of these issues follows in the form of future recommendations:

1. Despite several recommendations, the client never obtained a physical exam or nutritional consultation. On termination, it was emphasized to him that follow-up with relevant health professionals would still be helpful, if not for psychotherapeutic, then for medical reasons.
2. The client is exercising more frequently than before therapy but still has no consistent exercise regimen. Given his continued vulnerability to some dysthymic symptoms during stress, a recommendation for a more concrete and consistent exercise program was made.
3. At this time, the client felt quite ebullient about his progress in therapy and indicated his delight at never having to be in therapy again. A reality check helped him recognize that no therapy is ever complete and that there may be future periods of stress or vulnerability during which he may want to consider outside assistance. It was pointed out that this process would not have to jeopardize his newly developed sense of independence and self-reliance.
4. The client was reminded of the relaxation tape, the guided imagery exercises, and the process of journaling as supportive strategies he can continue to rely on during times of stress or painful occurrences.
5. The continued development of an even stronger support system was mentioned as an issue that the client may need to revisit occasionally, given his remaining tendency toward isolation and overly strong self-reliance.

REFERENCES

Alarcon, R. D., & Foulks, E. F. (1995). Personality disorders and culture: Contemporary clinical views (Part A). *Cultural Diversity and Mental Health, 1,* 3–17.

Alexander, F. (1961). *The scope of psychoanalysis.* New York: Basic Books.

Alexander, F., & French, T. M. (1946). *Psychoanalytic therapy: Principles and application.* New York: Ronald Press.

Alexander, T. (1994). The process of psychotherapy: An essential element. *Psychotherapy, 31,* 309–317.

Allen, J. P., & Columbus, M. (1995). *Assessing alcohol problems: A guide for clinicians and researchers.* Bethesda, MD: National Institute on Alcohol Abuse and Alcoholism.

American Counseling Association. (1995). *ACA code of ethics and standards of practice.* Alexandria, VA: Author.

American Psychiatric Association. (1980). *Diagnostic and statistical manual of mental disorders* (3rd ed.). Washington, DC: Author.

American Psychiatric Association. (1994). *Diagnostic and statistical manual of mental disorders* (4th ed.). Washington, DC: Author.

American Psychological Association. (1987). Resolutions approved by the National Conference on Graduate Education in Psychology. *American Psychologist, 42,* 1070–1084.

American Psychological Association. (1992). Ethical principles of psychologists and code of conduct. *American Psychologist, 42,* 1597–1611.

American Psychological Association. (1993). Record keeping guidelines. *American Psychologist, 48,* 984–986.

Anderson, B. S. (1996). *The counselor and the law* (4th ed.). Alexandria, VA: American Counseling Association.

Anderson, S. K., & Kitchener, K. S. (1996). Nonromantic, nonsexual posttherapy relationships between psychologists and former clients: An exploratory study of critical incidents. *Professional Psychology: Research and Practice, 27,* 59–66.

Arthur, G. L., & Swanson, C. D. (1993). *Confidentiality and privileged communication.* Alexandria, VA: American Counseling Association.

Atwood, G., & Stolorow, R. (1984). *Structures of subjectivity.* Hillsdale, NJ: Analytic Press.

Bacal, H. (1985). Optimal responsiveness and therapeutic process. In A. Goldberg (Ed.), *Progress in self psychology* (pp. 202–227). New York: Guilford Press.

Bandura, A. (1969). *Principles of behavior modification.* New York: Holt, Rinehart & Winston.

Barrett-Lennard, G. (1981). The empathy cycle: Refinement of a nuclear concept. *Journal of Counseling Psychology, 28,* 91–100.

Basch, M. F. (1980). *Doing psychotherapy.* New York: Basic Books.

Baumrind, D. (1971). Harmonious parents and their preschool children. *Developmental Psychology, 4,* 99–102.

Baumrind, D. (1973). The development of instrumental competence through socialization. In

A. D. Pick (Ed.), *Minnesota Symposia on Child Psychology* (Vol. 7, pp. 3–46). Minneapolis: University of Minnesota Press.

Baumrind, D. (1983). Familial antecedents of social competence in young children. *Psychological Bulletin, 94,* 132–142.

Bavolek, S. J. (1984). *Handbook for the Adult–Adolescent Parenting Inventory (AAPI).* Eau Claire, WI: Family Development Resources.

Beck, J. S. (1995). *Cognitive therapy: Basics and beyond.* New York: Guilford.

Becker, W. C. (1971). *Parents are teachers: A child management program.* Champaign, IL: Research Press.

Bellak, A. S., Herson, M., & Kazdin, A. E. (1990). *International handbook of behavior modification and therapy.* New York: Plenum Press.

Bellak, L., & Siegel, H. (1983). *Brief and emergency psychotherapy.* Larchmont, NY: C.P.S.

Berman, P. S. (1997). *Case conceptualization and treatment planning: Exercises for integrating theory and clinical practice.* Thousand Oaks, CA: Sage.

Bernstein, I., & Glenn, J. (1988). The child and adolescent analyst's emotional reactions to his patients and their parents. *International Review of Psycho-Analysis, 15,* 225–241.

Beutler, L. E., & Berren, M. R. (1995). *Integrative assessment of adult personality.* New York: Guilford.

Beutler, L. E., Clarkin, J., Crago, M., & Bergen, J. (1991). Client–therapist matching. In C. R. Snyder & D. R. Forsyth (Eds.), Handbook of social and clinical psychology (pp. 699–716). New York: Pergamon.

Bion, W. R. (1959). Attacks on linking. *International Journal of Psychoanalysis, 40,* 308–315.

Blackstone, P. (1991). *Things they never told me in therapy school.* Kingston, WA: Port Gamble Press.

Blaine, J. D., Horton, A. M., & Towle, L. H. (Eds.) (1995). *Diagnosis and severity of drug abuse and drug dependence.* Rockville, MD: National Institute on Drug Abuse.

Blazer, D. G., Kessler, R. C., McGonagle, K. A., & Swartz, M. S. (1994). The prevalence and distribution of major depression in a national community sample: The national comorbidity survey. *American Journal of Psychiatry, 151,* 979–986.

Block, J. H. (1965). *The child rearing practices report.* Berkeley: Institute of Human Development, University of California at Berkeley.

Booth, T., & Booth, W. (1994). *Parenting under pressure: Mothers and fathers with learning difficulties.* Bristol, PA: Open University Press.

Bowen, M. (1978). *Family therapy in clinical practice.* New York: Jason Aronson.

Bowlby, J. (1988). *A secure base.* New York: Basic Books.

Boylan, J. C., Malley, P. B., & Scott, J. (1995). *Practicum and internship: Textbook for counseling and psychotherapy.* Bristol, PA: Accelerated Development.

Brems, C. (1989a). Dimensionality of empathy and its correlates. *Journal of Psychology, 123,* 329–337.

Brems, C. (1989b). Projective identification as a self psychological change agent in the psychotherapy of a child. *American Journal of Psychotherapy, 43,* 598–607.

Brems, C. (1990). *Manual for a self-psychologically oriented parent education program.* Anchorage, AK: University of Alaska Anchorage Psychological Services Center.

Brems, C. (1993). *A comprehensive guide to child psychotherapy.* Boston: Allyn and Bacon.

Brems, C. (1994). *The child therapist: Personal traits and markers of effectiveness.* Boston: Allyn and Bacon.

Brems, C. (1997). Implications of Daniel Stern's model of self development for child psychotherapy. *Journal of Psychological Practice, 3,* 141–159.

Brems, C., Baldwin, M., & Baxter, S. (1993). Empirical evaluation of a self-psychologically oriented parent education program. *Family Relations, 42,* 26–30.

Brems, C., & Johnson, M. E. (1997). Co-occurrence of substance use and other psychiatric disorder: Research and clinical implications. *Professional Psychology: Research and Practice, 28,* 437–447.

Brooks, J. B. (1994). *Parenting in the 90s.* Mountain View, CA: Mayfield.

Brooks, J. B. (1996). *The process of parenting* (4th ed.). Mountain View, CA: Mayfield.

Brown, T. A., & Barlow. D. H. (1992). Comorbidity among anxiety disorders: Implications for treatment and DSM-IV. *Journal of Consulting and Clinical Psychology, 60,* 835–844.

Bugental, J. F. T., & Bugental, E. K. (1996). Resistance to and fear of change. In *Hatherleigh guide to psychotherapy* (pp. 33–46). New York: Hatherleigh.

Canter, M. B., Bennett, B. E., Jones, S. E., & Nagy, T. F. (1994). *Ethics for psychologists: A commentary on the APA ethics code.* Washington, DC: American Psychological Association.

Carey, K. B., & Teitelbaum, L. M. (1996). Goals and methods of alcohol assessment. *Professional Psychology: Research and Practice, 27,* 460–466.

Castillo, R. J. (1997). *Culture and mental illness: A client-centered approach.* Pacific Grove, CA: Brooks/Cole.

Chambless, D. G., Babich, K., Cris-Christoph, P., Frank, E., Gilson, M., Montgomery, R., Rich, R., Steinberg, J., & Weinberger, J. (1993). Task force on promotions and dissemination of psychological procedures. *Report adopted by the APA Division 12 Board,* 1–17.

Chambless, D. G., Sanderson, W. C., Shuham, V., Bennet-Johnson, S., Pope, K. S., Cris-Christoph, P., Baker, M., Johnson, B., Woody, S. R., Sue, S., Beutler, L., Williams, D. A., & McCurry, S. (1996). An update on empirically validated therapies. *The Clinical Psychologist, 49,* 5–22.

Choca, J. P. (1988). *Manual for clinical psychology trainees* (2nd ed.). New York: Brunner/Mazel.

Chrzanowski, G. (1989). The significance of the analyst's individual personality in the therapeutic relationship. *Journal of the American Academy of Psychoanalysis, 17,* 597–608.

Chung, C. (1990). Psychotherapist and expansion of awareness. *Psychotherapy and Psychosomatics, 53,* 28–32.

Connors, G. (1995). Screening for alcohol problems. In J. P. Allen & M. Columbus (Eds.), *Assessing alcohol problems: A guide for clinicians and researchers* (pp. 17–30). Bethesda, MD: National Institute on Alcohol Abuse and Alcoholism.

Corey, G., Corey, M. S., & Callanan, P. (1988). *Issues and ethics in the helping professions* (3rd ed.). Pacific Grove, CA: Brooks/Cole.

Cormier, W. H., & Cormier, L. S. (1991) *Interviewing strategies for helpers* (3rd ed.). Pacific Grove, CA: Brooks/Cole.

Cormier, L. S., & Hackney, H. (1987). *The professional counselor: A process guide to helping.* Englewood Cliffs, NJ: Prentice Hall.

Cornelius, J., Salloum, I., Mezzich, J., Cornelius, M. D., Fabrega, H., Ehler, J. G., Ulrich, R. F., Thase, M. E., & Mann, J. J. (1995). Disproportionate suicidality in patients with comorbid major depression and alcoholism. *American Journal of Psychiatry, 152,* 358–364.

Corsini, R. J., & Wedding, D. (1997). *Current psychotherapies* (5th ed.). Itasca, IL: Peacock.

Crawford, R. L. (1994). *Avoiding counselor malpractice.* Alexandria, VA: American Counseling Association.

Cromwell, R., & Snyder, S. (1993). *Schizophrenia: Origins, processes, treatment, and outcomes.* New York: Oxford University Press.

Cuellar, I., Harris, I. C., & Jasso, R. (1980). An acculturation scale for Mexican American normal and clinical populations. *Hispanic Journal of Behavioral Science, 2,* 199–217.

D'Andrea, M., & Daniels, J. (1991). Exploring the different levels of multicultural counseling training in counselor education. *Journal of Counseling and Development, 70,* 78–85.

D'Andrea, M., Daniels, J., & Heck, R. (1991). Evaluating the impact of multicultural counseling training. *Journal of Counseling and Development, 70,* 143–150.

Dana, R. H. (1993). *Multicultural assessment perspectives for professional psychology.* Boston: Allyn and Bacon.

Darling, N., & Steinberg, L. (1993). Parenting style as context: An integrative model. *Psychological Bulletin, 113,* 487–496.

Department of Health and Human Services (1993). *Maternal substance use assessment methods reference manual.* Rockville, MD: Author.

Dietzel, L. A. (1995). *Parenting with respect and peacefulness.* Lancaster, PA: Starburst.

Dillard, J. M. (1983). *Multicultural counseling: Toward ethnic and cultural relevance in human encounters.* Chicago: Nelson-Hall.

Dinkmeyer, D., & McKay, G. D. (1976). *The parent's handbook.* Circle Pines, MN: American Guidance Service.

Dolan, Y. M. (1991). *Resolving sexual abuse: Solution-focused therapy and Ericksonian hypnosis for adult survivors.* New York: W. W. Norton.

Dolan, Y. M. (1996). An Ericksonian perspective on the treatment of sexual abuse. In J. K. Zeig (Ed.), *Ericksonian methods: The essence of the story* (pp. 395–414). New York: Brunner/Mazel.

Donner, S. (1991). The treatment process. In H. Jackson (Ed.), *Using self psychology in psychotherapy* (pp. 51–71). Northvale, NJ: Jason Aronson.

Dreikurs, R., & Grey, L. (1968). *A new approach to discipline.* New York: Hawthorne Books.

Dreikurs, R., & Soltz, V. (1964). *Children: The challenge.* New York: Hawthorne Books.

Eells, T. D. (1997). *Handbook of psychotherapy case formulation.* New York: Guilford.

Egan, G. (1994). *The skilled helper* (5th ed.). Pacific Grove, CA: Brooks/Cole.

Elkind, D. (1995). *Ties that stress: The new family imbalance.* Cambridge, MA: Harvard University Press.

Ellis, A., & Dryden, W. (1987). *The practice of rational–emotive therapy (RET).* New York: Springer.

Evans, D. R., Hearn, M. T., Uhlemann, M. R., & Ivey, A. E. (1993). *Essential interviewing: A programmed approach to effective communication* (4th ed.). Pacific Grove, CA: Brooks/Cole.

Fabrega, H. (1992). The role of culture in a theory of psychiatric illness. *Social Science and Medicine, 35,* 91–103.

Fair, S. M., & Bressler, J. M. (1992). Therapist-initiated termination of psychotherapy. *The Clinical Supervisor, 10,* 171–185.

Farber, B. A., Lippert, R. A., & Nevas, D. B. (1995). The therapist as attachment figure. *Psychotherapy, 32,* 204–212.

Frankl, V. E. (1969). *The will to meaning: Foundations and applications of logotherapy.* New York: World.

Freud, A. (1946). *The ego and the mechanism of defense.* New York: International Universities.

Freud, S. S. (1937). Psychoanalysis terminable and interminable. *International Journal of Psychoanalysis, 18,* 373–405.

Fromm-Reichmann, F. (1950). *Principles of intensive psychotherapy.* Chicago: University of Chicago Press.

Gelso, C. J., & Fretz, B. R. (1992). *Counseling psychology.* New York: Harcourt Brace Jovanovich.

Gendlin, E. T. (1981). *Focusing.* New York: Bantam.

Gerard, A. B. (1994). *Parent–Child Relationship Inventory (PCRI): Manual.* Los Angeles: Western Psychological Services.

Gibbs, J. T., & Huang, L. N. (Eds.). (1989). *Children of color: Psychological interventions with minority youth.* San Francisco: Jossey-Bass.

Gibran, K., & Haskell, M. (1975). *I care about your happiness: Quotations from the love letters of Kahlil Gibran and Mary Haskell.* Boulder, CO: Blue Mountain Arts.

Gil, E. (1988). *Outgrowing the pain: A book for and about adults abused as children.* New York: Dell.

Gill, M. (1982). *Analysis of transference (Vol. I).* New York: International Universities.

Giordano, P. J. (1997). Establishing rapport and developing interview skills. In J. R. Matthews & C. E. Walker (Eds.), *Basic skills and professional issues in clinician psychology.* Boston: Allyn and Bacon.

Goldberg, C. (1975). Termination—A meaningful pseudodilemma in psychotherapy. *Psychotherapy: Theory, Research, and Practice, 12,* 341–343.

Gordon, T. (1970). *PET: Parent effectiveness training.* New York: Wyden.

Gordon, T., & Sands, J. (1978). *P.E.T. in action.* New York: Bantam.

Greenberg, L. S. (1994). *Process experiential psychotherapy.* Washington, DC: American Psychological Association.

Gutheil, T. G. (1980). Paranoia and progress notes: A guide to forensically informed psychiatric recordkeeping. *Hospital and Community Psychiatry, 31,* 479–482.

Haley, J. (1980). *Leaving home: The therapy of disturbed young people.* New York: McGraw Hill.

Harris, G. A. (1996). Dealing with difficult clients. In *Hatherleigh guide to psychotherapy* (pp. 47–62). New York: Hatherleigh.

Harrist, R. S., Quintana, S. M., Strupp, H. H., & Henry, W. P. (1994). Internalization of interpersonal process in time-limited dynamic psychotherapy. *Psychotherapy, 33,* 49–57.

Hazler, R. J., & Kottler, J. A. (1994). *The emerging professional counselor: Student dreams to professional realities.* Alexandria, VA: American Counseling Association.

Hedlund, J. L., & Vieweg, B. W. (1984). The Michigan Alcoholism Screening Test (MAST): A comprehensive review. *Journal of Operational Psychiatry, 15,* 55–64.

Helmchen, H. (1991). The impact of diagnostic systems on treatment planning. *Integrative Psychiatry, 7,* 16–20.

Helzer, J. E., & Przybeck, T. R. (1988). The co-occurrence of alcoholism with other psychiatric disorders in the general population and its impact on treatment. *Journal of Studies on Alcohol, 49,* 219–224.

Herlihy, B., & Corey, G. (1992). *Dual relationships in counseling.* Alexandria, VA: American Counseling Association.

Herlihy, B., & Corey, G. (1996). *ACA ethical standards casebook* (5th ed.). Alexandria, VA: American Counseling Association.

Herlihy, B., & Corey, G. (1997). *Boundary issues in counseling: Multiple roles and responsibilities.* Alexandria, VA: American Counseling Association.

Herman, J. L. (1992a). Complex PTSD: A syndrome in survivors of prolonged and repeated trauma. *Journal of Traumatic Stress, 5,* 377–391.

Herman, J. L. (1992b). *Trauma and recovery.* New York: Basic Books.

Hershenson, D. B., Power, P. W., & Seligman, L. (1989). Mental health counseling theory: Present status and future prospects. *Journal of Mental Health Counseling, 11,* 44–69.

Hohenshil, T. H. (1994). DSM-IV: What's new. *Journal of Counseling and Development, 73,* 105–107.

Holmquist, R., & Armelius, B. A. (1996). The patient's contribution to the therapist's countertransference feelings. *Journal of Nervous and Mental Disease, 184,* 660–666.

Hood, A. B., & Johnson, R. W. (1997). *Assessment in counseling: A guide to the use of psychological assessment procedures.* Alexandria, VA: American Counseling Association.

Hutchins, D. E., & Vaught, C. C. (1997). *Helping relationships and strategies* (3rd ed.). Pacific Grove, CA: Brooks/Cole.

Iijima Hall, C. C. (1997). Cultural malpractice: The growing obsolescence of psychology with the changing U.S. population. *American Psychologist, 52,* 642–651.

Ivey, A. E. (1994). *Intentional interviewing and counseling.* Pacific Grove, CA: Brooks/Cole.

Ivey, A. E. (1995). Psychotherapy as liberation: Toward specific skills and strategies in multicultural counseling and therapy. In J. G. Ponterotto, J. M. Casas, L. A. Suzuki, & C. M. Alexander (1995). *Handbook of multicultural counseling* (pp. 53–72). Thousand Oaks, CA: Sage.

Ivey, A. E., Ivey, M. B., & Simek-Morgan, L. (1997). *Counseling and psychotherapy: A multicultural perspective* (4th ed.). Boston: Allyn and Bacon.

Johnson, F. (1993). *Dependency and Japanese socialization.* New York: New York University Press.

Johnson, M. E. (1993). A culturally sensitive approach to child psychotherapy. In C. Brems, *Comprehensive guide to child psychotherapy* (pp. 68–94). Boston: Allyn and Bacon.

Johnson, M. E. (1994). Modeling theories. In *Magill's survey of social sciences: Psychology.* Pasadena, CA: Salem Press.

Johnson, M. E., Brems, C., & Fortman, J. (1993). *Between two people: Exercises toward intimacy.* Alexandria, VA: American Counseling Association.

Kamphaus, R. W., & Frick, P. J. (1996). *Clinical assessment of child and adolescent personality and behavior.* Boston: Allyn and Bacon.

Karoly, P. (1993). Goal systems: An organizing framework for clinician assessment and treatment planning. *Psychological Assessment, 5,* 273–280.

Keinan, G., Almagor, M., & Ben-Porath, Y. S. (1989). A reevaluation of the relationship between psychotherapeutic orientation and perceived personality characteristics. *Psychotherapy, 26,* 218–226.

Kessler, R. C. (1994). The national comorbidity survey: Preliminary results and future directions. *International Journal of Methods in Psychiatric Research, 5,* 139–151.

Kessler, R. C., McGonagle, K. A., Zhao, S., Nelson, C. B., Hughes, M., Eshleman, S., Wittchen, H. U., & Kendler, K. S. (1994). Lifetime and 12-month prevalence of the DSM-III-R psychiatric disorders in the United States. *Archives of General Psychiatry, 51,* 8–19.

Kessler, R. C., Sonnega, A., Bromet, E., Hughes, M., & Nelson, C. B. (1995). Posttraumatic stress disorder in the national comorbidity survey. *Archives of General Psychiatry, 52,* 1048–1060.

Kirk, S. A., & Kutchins, H. (1992). *The selling of the DSM-IV: The rhetoric of science in psychiatry.* Hawthorne, NY: Aldine De Gruyter.

Kitchens, J. M. (1994). Does this patient have an alcohol problem? *Journal of the American Medical Association, 272,* 1782–1787.

Klein, D. F., & Rowland, L. P. (1996). *Current psychotherapeutic drugs.* New York: Brunner/Mazel.

Klein, M. (1955). On identification. In M. Klein (Ed.), *Envy and gratitude and other works, 1946–1963* (pp. 141–175). New York: Delacorte Press/Seymour Laurence.

Kleinke, C. L. (1994). *Common principles of psychotherapy.* Pacific Grove, CA: Brooks/Cole.

Klonoff, E. A., & Landrine, H. (1997). *Preventing misdiagnosis of women: A guide to physical disorders that have psychiatric symptoms.* Thousand Oaks, CA: Sage.

Knobel, M. (1990). Significance and importance of the psychotherapist's personality and experience. *Psychotherapy and Psychosomatics, 53,* 58–63.

Kohatsu, E. L., & Richardson, T. Q. (1996). Racial and ethnic identity assessment. In L. A. Suzuki, P. J. Meller, & J. G. Ponterotto (Eds.). *Handbook of multicultural assessment* (pp. 611–650). New York: Jossey-Bass.

Kohut, H. (1982). Introspection, empathy, and the semi-circle of mental health. *International Journal of Psychoanalysis, 63,* 359–407.

Kohut, H. (1984). *How does analysis cure?* Chicago: International Universities.

Kohut, H., & Wolf, E. (1978). Disorders of the self and their treatment. *International Journal of Psychoanalysis, 59,* 413–425.

Kolevzon, M. S., Sowers-Hoag, K., & Hoffman, C. (1989). Selecting a family therapy model: The role of personality attributes in eclectic practice. *Journal of Marital and Family Therapy, 15,* 249–257.

Kottler, J. A., & Brown, R. W. (1992). *Introduction to therapeutic counseling* (2nd ed.). Pacific Grove, CA: Brooks/Cole.

Kottler, L. A. (1997). *Finding your way as a counselor.* Alexandria, VA: American Counseling Association.

Kramer, S. A. (1990). *Positive endings in psychotherapy.* San Francisco: Jossey-Bass.

Krumboltz, J. D., & Krumboltz, H. B. (1972). *Changing children's behavior.* Englewood Cliffs, NJ: Prentice-Hall.

Kuebler-Ross, E. (1971). The five stages of dying. *Encyclopedia Science Supplement* (pp. 92–97). New York: Grolier.

Kuebler-Ross, E. (1975). *Death: The final stage of growth.* Englewood Cliffs, NJ: Prentice Hall.

LaFramboise, T. D., Coleman, H. L., & Hernandez, A. (1991). Development and factor structure of the Cross-Cultural Counseling Inventory—Revised. *Professional Psychology: Research and Practice, 22,* 380–388.

Lamb, D. H. (1985). A timeframe model of termination in psychotherapy. *Psychotherapy, 22,* 604–609.

Laughlin, H. P. (1983). *The ego and its defenses* (rev. ed.). New York: Jason Aronson.

Lauver, P., & Harvey, D. R. (1997). *The practical counselor: Elements of helping.* Pacific Grove, CA: Brooks/Cole.

Lazarus, A. A. (1981). *The practice of multimodal therapy.* New York: McGraw Hill.

Lazarus, A. A., & Fay, A. (1982). Resistance or rationalization: A cognitive–behavioral perspective. In P. L. Wachtel (Ed.), *Resistance* (pp. 115–132). New York: Plenum Press.

Lebowitz, L., Harvey, M. R., & Herman, J. L. (1993). A stage-by-dimension model of recovery from sexual trauma. *Journal of Interpersonal Violence, 8,* 378–391.

Lemma, A. (1996). *Introduction to psychopathology.* Thousand Oaks, CA: Sage.

Levine, R. E., & Gaw, A. C. (1995). Culture-bound syndromes. *The Psychiatric Clinics of North America, 18,* 523–536.

Lewis, J. A., Dana, R. Q., & Blevins, G. A. (1988). *Substance abuse counseling: An individualized approach.* Pacific Grove, CA: Brooks/Cole.

Lewis, K. N., & Walsh, W. B. (1980). Effects of value-communication style and similarity of values on counselor evaluation. *Journal of Counseling Psychology, 27,* 305–314.

Litten, R. Z., & Allen, J. P. (1992). *Measuring alcohol consumption.* Totowa, NJ: Humana Press.

Luborsky, L. (1984). *Principles of psychoanalytic psychotherapy: A manual for supportive/expressive treatment.* New York: Basic Books.

Mahrer, A. R. (1989). *Dreamwork in psychotherapy and self-change.* New York: W. W. Norton.

Mahrer, A. R., Boulet, D. B., & Fairweather, D. R. (1994). Beyond empathy: Advances in the clinical theory and methods of empathy. *Clinical Psychology Review, 14,* 183–198.

Makover, R. B. (1992). Training psychotherapists in hierarchical treatment planning. *Journal of Psychotherapy Practice and Research, 1,* 337–350.

Mash, E. J., & Barkley, R. A. (1996). *Child psychopathology.* New York: Guilford.

Matsumoto, D. (1994a). *People: Psychology from a changing perspective.* Pacific Grove, CA: Brooks/Cole.

Matsumoto, D. (1994b). *Cultural influences on research methods and statistics.* Pacific Grove, CA: Brooks/Cole.

McGoldrick, M., & Gerson, R. (1985). *Genograms in family assessment.* New York: W. W. Norton.

McLellen, A. T., Luborsky, L., Cacciola, J., Griffith, J., Evans, F., Barr, H. L., & O'Brien, C. P. (1985). New data from the Addiction Severity Index: Reliability and validity in three centers. *Journal of Nervous and Mental Disease, 173,* 412–423.

Meier, S., & Davis, S. R (1997). *The elements of counseling* (3rd ed.). Pacific Grove, CA: Brooks/Cole.

Meyer, R. G., & Deitsch, S. E. (1996). *The clinician's handbook: Integrated diagnostics, assessment, and intervention in adult and adolescent psychopathology.* Boston: Allyn and Bacon.

Mezzich, J. E., Kleinman, A., Fabrega, H., & Parron, D. L. (1996). *Culture and psychiatric diagnosis: A DSM-IV perspective.* Washington, DC: American Psychiatric Press.

Miller, G. A. (1985). *The Substance Abuse Subtle Screening Inventory: Manual.* Spencer, IN: Spencer Evening World.

Milliones, J. (1980). Construction of a black consciousness measure: Psychotherapeutic implications. *Psychotherapy: Theory, Research and Practice, 17,* 175–182.

Minuchin, S., & Fishman, H. C. (1981). *Family therapy techniques.* Cambridge, MA: Harvard University Press.

Minuchin, S., Lee, W., & Simon, G. M. (1996). *Mastering family therapy.* New York: Wiley.

Morrison, J. (1995a). *The first interview: Revised for DSM-IV.* New York: Guilford.

Morrison, J. (1995b). *DSM-IV made easy.* New York: Guilford.

Nagel, K. L., & Jones, K. H. (1992). Sociological factors in the development of eating disorders. *Adolescence, 27,* 107–113.

Namyniuk, L. (1996, November). *Cultural considerations in substance abuse treatment.* Paper presented at the 3rd Biennial Conference of the Alaska Psychological Association: Unraveling the Thread of Substance Use in Psychological Disorder, Anchorage, AK.

Namyniuk, L., Brems, C., & Clarson, S. (1997). Dena A Coy: A model program for the treatment of pregnant substance-abusing women. *Journal of Substance Abuse Treatment, 14,* 1–11.

Nathensen, P., & Johnson, C. (1992). The psychiatric treatment plan. *Perspectives in Psychiatric Care, 28(3),* 32–35.

National Institute on Drug Abuse. (1994). *Mental health assessment and diagnosis of substance abuse.* Rockville, MD: U.S. Department of Health and Human Services.

Natterson, J. (1991). *Beyond countertransference: The therapist's subjectivity in the therapeutic process.* Northvale, NJ: Jason Aronson.

Nichols, M. P. (1987). *The self in the system: Expanding the limits of family therapy.* New York: Brunner/Mazel.

Nugent, F. A. (1994). *An introduction to the profession of counseling.* New York: Macmillan.

Nystul, M. S. (1993). *The art and science of counseling.* New York: Macmillan.

O'Conner, K. J. (1991). *The play therapy primer.* New York: Wiley Interscience.

Ogden, T. H. (1982). *Projective identification and psychotherapeutic technique.* New York: Jason Aronson.

Okun, B. F. (1997). *Effective helping: Interviewing and counseling techniques* (5th ed.). Pacific Grove, CA: Brooks/Cole.

Olson, K. R., Jackson, T. T., & Nelson, J. (1997). Attributional biases in clinical practice. *Journal of Psychological Practice, 3,* 27–33.

Orvaschel, H. (1990). Early onset psychiatric disorder in high risk children and increased family morbidity. *Journal of the American Academy of Child and Adolescent Psychiatry, 29,* 184–188.

Palmer, S., & McMahon, G. (1997). *Client assessment.* Thousand Oaks, CA: Sage.

Parham, T. A., & Helms, J. E. (1985). The relationship of racial identity attitudes to self-actualization of Black students and affective states. *Journal of Counseling Psychology, 32,* 431–440.

Parsons, P. J. (1986). Building better treatment plans. *Journal of Psychosocial Nursing, 24(4),* 9–14.

Pate, R. H. (1982). Termination: End or beginning. In W. H. Van Hoose & M. R. Worth (Eds.), *Counseling adults: A developmental approach.* Pacific Grove, CA: Brooks/Cole.

Patterson, L. E., & Welfel, E. R. (1993). *The counseling process.* Pacific Grove, CA: Brooks/Cole.

Paxton, S. J., & Sculthorpe, A. (1991). Disordered eating and sex role characteristics in young women: Implications for sociocultural theories of disturbed eating. *Sex Roles, 24,* 587–598.

Pearce, S. R. (1996). *Flash of insight: Metaphor and narrative in therapy.* Boston: Allyn and Bacon.

Pentz, M. A. (1994). Target populations and interventions in prevention research: What is high risk? In A. Cazares & L. A. Beatty (Eds.), *Scientific methods for prevention and intervention research.* Rockville, MD: National Institute on Drug Abuse.

Pipes, R. B., & Davenport, D. S. (1990). *Introduction to psychotherapy: Common clinical wisdom.* Englewood Cliffs, NJ: Prentice Hall.

Polster, E., & Polster, M. (1973). *Gestalt therapy integrated: Contours of theory and practice.* New York: Vintage.

Ponterotto, J. G., & Alexander, C. M. (1996). Assessing the multicultural competence of counselors and clinicians. In L. A. Suzuki, P. J. Meller, & J. G. Ponterotto (Eds.), *Handbook of multicultural assessment* (pp. 651–672). New York: Jossey-Bass.

Ponterotto, J. G., Casas, J. M., Suzuki, L. A., & Alexander, C. M. (1995). *Handbook of multicultural counseling.* Thousand Oaks, CA: Sage.

Ponterotto, J. G., & Wise, S. L. (1987). Construct validity study of the Racial Identity Attitude Scale. *Journal of Counseling Psychology, 34,* 218–223.

Pope, K. S. (1990a). Therapist–patient sexual involvement: A review of the research. *Clinical Psychology Review, 10,* 477–490.

Pope, K. S. (1990b), Therapist–patient sex as sex abuse: Six scientific, professional, and practical dilemmas in addressing victimization and rehabilitation. *Professional Psychology: Research and Practice, 21,* 227–239.

Pope, K. S. (1994). *Sexual involvement with therapists: Patient assessment, subsequent therapy, forensics.* Washington, DC: American Psychological Association.

Pope, K. S., & Brown, L. S. (1996). *Recovered memories of abuse: Assessment, therapy, forensics.* Washington, DC: American Psychological Association.

Pope, K. S., & Vetter, V. A. (1991). Prior therapist–patient sexual involvement among patients seen by psychologists. *Psychotherapy, 28,* 429–438.

Prather, H. (1970). *Notes to myself.* Moab, UT: Real People Press.

Regier, D. A., Farmer, M. E., Rae, D. S., Locke, B. Z., Keith, S. J., Judd, L. L., & Goodwin, F. K. (1990). Comorbidity of mental disorders with alcohol and other drug abuse: Results from the Epidemiological Catchment Area (ECA) study. *Journal of the American Medical Association, 264,* 2511–2518.

Reid, W. H. (1989). *The treatment of psychiatric disorders.* New York: Brunner/Mazel.

Rivera-Arzola, M., & Ramos-Grenier, J. (1997). Anger, *ataques de nervios,* and *la mujer puertorriquena:* Sociocultural considerations and treatment implications. In J. G. Garcia & M. C. Zea (Eds.), *Psychological interventions and research with Latino populations* (pp. 125–141). Boston: Allyn and Bacon.

Roberts, T. W. (1994). *A systems perspective of parenting: The individual, the family, and the social network.* Pacific Grove, CA: Brooks/Cole.

Robins, L. N., Helzer, J. E., Przybeck, T. R., & Regier, D. A. (1988). Alcohol disorders in the community: A report from the Epidemiological Catchment Area. In R. M. Rose & J. Barrett (Eds.), *Alcoholism: Origins and outcome* (pp. 15–29). New York: Raven Press.

Rogers, C. R. (1961). *On becoming a person.* Boston: Houghton Mifflin.

Rowe, C. E., & MacIsaac, D. S. (1989). *Empathic attunement: The technique of psychoanalytic self psychology.* Northvale, NJ: Jason Aronson.

Sanderson, C. (1996). *Counselling adult survivors of child sexual abuse* (2nd ed.). London: Jessica Kingsley.

Satir, V. (1967). *Conjoint family therapy: A guide to theory and technique.* Palo Alto, CA: Science and Behavior Books.

Scarff, M. (1987). *Intimate partners.* New York: Random House.

Schank, J. A., & Skovholt, T. M. (1997). Dual-relationship dilemmas of rural and small-community psychologists. *Professional Psychology: Research and Practice, 28,* 44–49.

Scissons, E. H. (1993). *Counseling for results: Principles and practices in helping.* Pacific Grove, CA: Brooks/Cole.

Seligman, L. (1993). Teaching treatment planning. *Counselor Education and Supervision, 32,* 287–297.

Seligman, L. (1996). *Diagnosis and treatment planning in counseling* (2nd ed.). New York: Plenum Press.

Selzer, L. F. (1986). *Paradoxical strategies in psychotherapy: A comprehensive overview and guidebook.* New York: Wiley.

Selzer, M. L. (1971). The Michigan Alcohol Screening Test: The quest for a new diagnostic instrument. *American Journal of Psychiatry, 127,* 1653–1658.

Sevy, S., Mendlewicz, J., & Mendelbaum, K. (1995). Genetic research in bipolar illness. In E. E. Beckham, & W. R. Leber (Eds.), *Handbook of depression.* New York: Guilford.

Sigelman, C. K., & Shaffer, D. R. (1995). *Life-span human development* (2nd ed.). Pacific Grove, CA: Brooks/Cole.

Silver, L. (1992). *Attention deficit hyperactivity disorder: A clinical guide to diagnosis and treatment.* Washington, DC: American Psychiatric Press.

Silverman, W. (1996). Cookbooks, manuals, and paint-by-numbers: Psychotherapy in the 90's. *Psychotherapy, 33,* 207–215.

Simmons, J. E. (1987). *Psychiatric examination of children* (4th ed.). Philadelphia: Lea and Febinger.

Skinner, H. A. (1990). Spectrum of drinkers and intervention opportunities. *Canadian Medical Association Journal, 143,* 1054–1059.

Skovholt, T. M., & Ronnestad, M. H. (1995). *The evolving professional self: Stages and themes in therapist and counselor development.* New York: Wiley.

Smart, D. M., & Smart, J. F. (1997). DSM-IV and culturally sensitive diagnosis: Some observations for counselors. *Journal of Counseling and Development, 75,* 392–398.

Sodowsky, G. R., Taffe, R. C., Gutkin, T., & Wise, C. L. (1994). Development of the Multicultural Counseling Inventory: A self-report measure of multicultural competencies. *Journal of Counseling Psychology, 41,* 137–148.

Sonne, J. L., & Pope, K. S. (1991). Treating victims of therapist–patient sexual involvement. *Psychotherapy, 28,* 174–187.

Spitzer, R. L., Gibbon, M., Skodol, A. E., Williams, J. B. W., & First, M. B. (1994). *DSM-IV case book.* Washington, DC: American Psychiatric Press.

Spitzer, R. L., & Williams, J. B. W. (1987). Revising DSM-III: The process and major issues. In G. Tischler (Ed.), *Diagnosis and classification in psychiatry: A critical appraisal of DSM-III* (pp. 425–433). New York: Cambridge University Press.

Stern, D. N. (1985). *The interpersonal world of the infant.* New York: Basic Books.

Strauss, J. S. (1996). Subjectivity. *Journal of Nervous and Mental Disease, 184,* 205–212.

Streissguth, A., Aase, J., Clarren, S., Randels, S., LaDue, R., & Smith, D. (1991). Fetal alcohol syndrome in adolescents and adults. *Journal of the American Medical Association, 265,* 1961–1967.

Streissguth, A., Barr, H. M., Olson, H. C., Sampson, P. D., Bookstein, F. L., & Burgess, D. M. (1994). Drinking during pregnancy decreases word attack and arithmetic scores on standardized tests: Adolescent data from a population-based prospective study. *Alcoholism: Clinical and Experimental Research, 18,* 248–254.

Strupp, H. H. (1992). The future of psychotherapy. *Psychotherapy, 29,* 21–27.

Strupp, H. H. (1996). Some salient lessons from research and practice. *Psychotherapy, 33,* 135–138.

Sullivan, A., & Brems, C. (1997). The psychological repercussions of the sociocultural oppression of Alaska Native peoples. *Genetic, Social, and General Psychology Monographs, 123,* 411–440.

Suzuki, L. A., Meller, P. J., & Ponterotto, J. G. (1996). *Handbook of multicultural assessment.* New York: Jossey-Bass.

Swenson, L. C. (1997). *Psychology and the law* (2nd ed.). Pacific Grove, CA: Brooks/Cole.

Szasz, T. S. (1973). *The second sin.* Garden City, NY: Anchor Press.

Teyber, E. (1997). *Interpersonal process in psychotherapy: A relational approach* (3rd ed.). Pacific Grove, CA: Brooks/Cole.

Thase, M. E., & Howland, R. H. (1995). Biological processes in depression: An updated review and integration. In E. E Beckham & W. R. Leber (Eds.), *Handbook of depression*. New York: Guilford.

Turkat, D., & Meyer, V. (1992). The behavior–analytic approach. In P. L. Wachtel (Ed.), *Resistance* (pp. 157–184). New York: Plenum Press.

Vandecreek, L., & Knapp, S. (1997). Record keeping. In J. R. Matthews & C. E. Walker (Eds.), *Basic skills and professional issues in clinical psychology*. Boston: Allyn and Bacon.

Warner, L. A., Kessler, R. C., Hughes, M., Anthony, J. C., & Nelson, C. B. (1995). Prevalence and correlates of drug use and dependence in the United States. *Archives of General Psychiatry, 52*, 219–229.

Watts, A. (1966). *The book: On the taboo against knowing who you are*. New York: Vintage.

Watts, F. N. (1996). Listening processes in psychotherapy and counseling. In *Hatherleigh guide to psychotherapy*. New York: Hatherleigh.

Weeks, G. R., & L'Abate, L. (1982). *Paradoxical psychotherapy: Theory and practice with individuals, couples, and families*. New York: Brunner/Mazel.

Weiss, J. (1993). *How psychotherapy works*. New York: Guilford.

Winnicott, D. W. (1958a). *Through pediatrics to psychoanalysis*. London: Hogart Press.

Winnicott, D. W. (1958b). *Collected papers*. London: Tavistock.

Winnicott, D. W. (1965). *The maturational process and the facilitating environment*. New York: International Universities.

Wirth, L. (1945). The problem of minority groups. In R. Linton (Ed.), *The science of man in the world crisis* (pp. 347–372). New York: Columbia University Press.

Wittchen, H. U., Zhao, S., Kessler, R. C., & Eaton, W. W. (1994). DSM-III-R generalized anxiety disorder in the national comorbidity survey. *Archives of General Psychiatry, 51*, 355–364.

Witztum, E., Greenberg, D., & Dasberg, H. (1990). Mental illness and religious change. *British Journal of Medical Psychology, 63*, 33–41.

Wolf, E. S. (1988). *Treating the self: Elements of clinical self psychology*. New York: Guilford.

Young, M. E., & Bemark, F. (1996). The role of emotional arousal and expression in mental health counseling. *Journal of Mental Health Counseling, 18*, 316–332.

Zeig, J. K. (1994). *Ericksonian methods: The essence of the story*. New York: Brunner/Mazel.

AUTHOR INDEX

SUBJECT INDEX